ORGANISATIONAL PSYCHOLOGY

Taken together, these studies inspire the next generation of researchers to ask the big questions and answer them in meaningful and creative ways. This book is a must read for students of psychology and business who want to do work that makes a difference in organizations and society.

Virginia E. Schein, Ph.D.
Professor Emerita of Management and Psychology
Gettysburg College

ORGANISATIONAL PSYCHOLOGY
REVISITING
THE CLASSIC STUDIES

EDITED BY:
NIKLAS K. STEFFENS
FLOOR RINK
MICHELLE K. RYAN

Los Angeles | London | New Delhi
Singapore | Washington DC | Melbourne

Los Angeles | London | New Delhi
Singapore | Washington DC | Melbourne

SAGE Publications Ltd
1 Oliver's Yard
55 City Road
London EC1Y 1SP

SAGE Publications Inc.
2455 Teller Road
Thousand Oaks, California 91320

SAGE Publications India Pvt Ltd
B 1/I 1 Mohan Cooperative Industrial Area
Mathura Road
New Delhi 110 044

SAGE Publications Asia-Pacific Pte Ltd
3 Church Street
#10-04 Samsung Hub
Singapore 049483

Editor: Amy Maher
Assistant Editor: Emma Yuan
Production Editor: Zoheb Khan
Copyeditor: Peter Williams
Indexer: KnowledgeWorks Global Ltd.
Marketing Manager: Ruslana Khatagova
Cover Design: Ginkhan Siam
Typeset by KnowledgeWorks Global Ltd.
Printed in the UK

Editorial arrangement, Niklas K. Steffens, Floor Rink, and Michelle K. Ryan 2023

Introduction © Niklas K. Steffens, Floor Rink, and Michelle K. Ryan
Chapter 1 © Giverny De Boeck and Sharon K. Parker
Chapter 2 © S. Alexander Haslam and Niklas K. Steffens
Chapter 3 © Jeffrey B. Vancouver, Timothy Ballard and Andrew Neal
Chapter 4 © Marylène Gagné
Chapter 5 © Naomi Ellemers and Dick de Gilder
Chapter 6 © Steven W. Whiting, Mark G. Ehrhart, and Philip M. Podsakoff
Chapter 7 © Sabine Sonnentag
Chapter 8 © Derek D. Rucker, Adam D. Galinsky, and Joe C. Magee
Chapter 9 © Peter D. Harms
Chapter 10 © Niels Van Quaquebeke and Catharina Vogt
Chapter 11 © Mary Uhl-Bien and Melissa Carsten
Chapter 12 © Russell S. Cropanzano, Nicole Strah, Deborah E. Rupp, and Jessie A. Cannon
Chapter 13 © Madeline Heilman and Francesca Manzi
Chapter 14 © C. Y. Edwina Wong, Floor Rink, and Michelle K. Ryan

Library of Congress Control Number: 2022937280

British Library Cataloguing in Publication data

A catalogue record for this book is available from the British Library

ISBN 978-1-5297-0666-6
ISBN 978-1-5297-0665-9 (pbk)

At SAGE we take sustainability seriously. Most of our products are printed in the UK using responsibly sourced papers and boards. When we print overseas we ensure sustainable papers are used as measured by the PREPS grading system. We undertake an annual audit to monitor our sustainability.

Contents

About the Editors

Niklas K. (Nik) Steffens is Associate Professor and Director of the Centre for Business and Organisational Psychology in the School of Psychology at the University of Queensland. His research focuses on leadership and followership, group processes and teamwork, and health and well-being in applied contexts – research he has conducted in collaboration with over 100 researchers across the globe. He collaborates with and consults to organisations, community groups and industry to use theory and evidence to solve applied problems and improve group and organisational functioning.

Floor Rink is full professor of Organisational Behaviour at the University of Groningen in the Netherlands. In her work, she explains organisational and economic phenomena through psychology theory. Her main lines of research centre around work situations that involve intra- and inter-group identity dynamics, such as responses to diversity, ethical decision-making and status differentiation.

Michelle K. Ryan is the inaugural Director of the Global Institute of Women's Leadership at the Australian National University where she is a Professor of Social and Organisational Psychology. She also holds a (part-time) position at the University of Groningen where she is a Professor of Diversity. She recently led a European Research Council Consolidator Grant examining the way in which context and identity shape and constrain women's career choices. With Alex Haslam, she uncovered the phenomenon of the glass cliff, whereby women are more likely than men to occupy leadership positions in times of crisis. The New York Times named the glass cliff as one of the Top 100 ideas that shaped 2008.

About the Contributors

Timothy Ballard is a Lecturer of Business and Organisational Psychology at the University of Queensland. His research focuses on understanding the dynamics of decision-making, motivation, fatigue and stress and how these processes affect our performance and mental health. He uses this knowledge to help design work environments that promote happier, healthier and more effective work. Practical applications of this work so far have included enhancing the capacity and safety of unmanned aerial systems operation, facilitating tactical decision-making in military contexts, providing tools to combat fatigue in submarine operations and improving climate change communication practices.

Giverny De Boeck is Assistant Professor at IESEG School of Management where she currently teaches courses on human resource management and change management. Her main research interests include, on the one hand, talent management and potential appraisal and, on the other hand, work design, work meaningfulness and work identity specifically in the context of change and technological innovation. She has presented her work at numerous international conferences and published her research in leading peer-reviewed journals including the *Journal of Management Studies* and *Journal of Organizational Behavior*.

Jessie Cannon is a doctoral student in the Industrial Organisational Psychology programme at George Mason University, studying under Dr Stephen Zaccaro and Dr Deborah Rupp. She previously received a Masters in I-O Psychology from Seattle Pacific University. At Mason, her research focuses on leadership, specifically in the areas of leader development and leader identity, as well as workplace discrimination, multi-team systems and well-being in the workplace.

Melissa Carsten is a Professor of Management at Winthrop University in Rock Hill, South Carolina. Dr Carsten's research focuses on the role that followers play in the leadership process and the beliefs that individuals hold about the follower role. She has published research on both leadership and followership in journals such as the *Leadership Quarterly, Journal of Organizational Behavior, Leadership, Organization Management Journal* and *Organizational Dynamics*. She currently sits on the editorial boards for *The Leadership Quarterly, Journal of Organizational Behavior*, and *Group and Organization Management*. She is also the series editor for the Leadership Horizons Book Series.

Russell S. Cropanzano is Professor of Organisational Behaviour at the Leeds School of Business. He is a past editor of the *Journal of Management* and a fellow in the Academy of Management, the Society for Industrial/Organisational Psychology, the Southern Management Association and the Association for Psychological Science. Dr Cropanzano publishes widely on organisational justice, workplace emotion and employee well-being. He has received the 2000 Outstanding Paper Award from *Consulting Psychology Journal*, the 2007 Best Paper Award from the *Academy of Management Perspectives*, the 2010 Best Paper Award from the *Journal of Management* and the 2018–19 Excellence in Research Award from the Boulder Faculty Assembly.

Mark G. Ehrhart is a Professor in the Industrial/Organizational Psychology Program at the University of Central Florida. He received his BS in Applied Psychology from the Georgia Institute of Technology and his MA and PhD in Industrial/Organizational Psychology from the University of Maryland, College Park. Dr Ehrhart's research interests include organisational citizenship behaviour, organisational climate and leadership, and the application of these topics across levels of analysis and in health and social service settings.

Naomi Ellemers is Distinguished University Professor at Utrecht University and a member of the supervisory board of PwC in the Netherlands. With a combination of experimental and applied research methods she examines the behaviour of people in groups and organisations. She applies her insights on organisational ethics, compliance and diversity in joint projects with regulators, policy-makers and organisational leaders.

Marylène Gagné is Professor at the Future of Work Institute at Curtin University, Perth, Australia. Her research examines how organisations, through their structures, cultures, rewards, tasks and management, affect people's motivational orientations towards their work, including volunteer work, and how quality of motivation influences performance and well-being in the workplace. She is a Fellow of the Society for Industrial and Organisational Psychology and past associate editor at the *European Journal of Work and Organisational Psychology*. Marylène has previously held appointments at the University at Albany (SUNY, New York State), Concordia University (Canada) and at the University of Western Australia.

Adam D. Galinsky is the Vice Dean of Diversity, Equity and Inclusion at Columbia Business School. His research focuses on leadership, negotiations, diversity and ethics. He has received numerous awards including the World's 50 Best B-School Professors (Poets & Quants, 2012), the Career Trajectory Award (Society of Experimental Social Psychology, 2016) and the Faculty Mentoring Award (Columbia University, 2022). He co-authored the best-selling book, *Friend & Foe* (2015) and his 2016 TED talk, *How to Speak Up for Yourself*, has had over 7.2 million views. He is a frequent legal expert and producer on two documentaries short-listed for Best Documentary (Academy Awards).

Dick de Gilder is Associate Professor of Organizational Sciences at the Vrije Universiteit Amsterdam. Previously he was consultant for applied research and innovation at TNO, and senior researcher/consultant at Labor Union CNV. He is an expert on error management in organisations, corporate philanthropy, teamwork and temporary work.

Peter D. Harms is the Morrissette Faculty Fellow in Leadership and Ethics in the Department of Management at the University of Alabama. His research focuses on the assessment and development of leadership, personality and psychological well-being. He has published over 170 articles, chapters, books and technical reports and has been featured in popular media outlets such as CNN, Scientific American, Forbes and the BBC. Dr Harms was selected as one of the '100 Knowledge Leaders of Tomorrow' by the St Gallen Symposium and is a fellow of both the Society of Industrial and Organisational Psychology and the Association for Psychological Science.

S. Alexander (Alex) Haslam is Professor of Social and Organisational Psychology and Australian Laureate Fellow at the University of Queensland. Together with over 400 colleagues around the world, he has written and edited 15 books and published over 300 peer-reviewed articles that explore the contribution of group and identity processes to social and organisational functioning. Alex has received a range of major awards from scientific bodies in Australia, the US, the UK and Europe including recognition for distinguished contributions to psychological science from both the British and Australian Psychological Societies.

Madeline Heilman is Professor of Psychology at New York University where she served as Coordinator of the Industrial/Organizational Psychology Program for over twenty years. She received her PhD from Columbia University and was a member of the faculty at Yale's School of Organization and Management. Professor Heilman currently serves on the board of the *Journal of Applied Psychology* and *Leadership Quarterly*. Her research has focused on gender bias in work settings and the dynamics of stereotyping.

Joe C. Magee is Professor of Management and Organizations at the Stern School of Business at New York University. Professor Magee and his colleagues have discovered a series of reliable changes in the psychology of power-holders that seem to be potentially damaging for relationships, organisations and society but which, under certain conditions, can contribute to interpersonal and organisational effectiveness. He has also studied other systems of inequality and the psychology of advantage and disadvantage within those systems.

Francesca Manzi is Assistant Professor of Management at the London School of Economics. She has a PhD in Social Psychology from New York University and a degree in Organisational Psychology from the Universidad Católica de Chile. In her research, she combines theories and methodological approaches from social, organisational and applied psychology to better understand the ways in which gender stereotypes manifest in modern society and organisations. Prior to obtaining her PhD, Dr Manzi worked as a researcher and consultant in Santiago, Chile.

Andrew Neal is Professor of Business and Organisational Psychology at the University of Queensland. His research examines human performance and motivation. The goals of his research programme are: (a) to improve scientific understanding of the basic cognitive and motivational processes that produce variability in performance over time and across different settings; and (b) to enhance the performance, safety and effectiveness of people at work. Industries in which work is carried out include defence, aviation and the emergency services.

Sharon K. Parker is an ARC Laureate Fellow and a John Curtin Distinguished Professor at Curtin University, Director of the Centre for Transformative Work Design at Curtin University and a Fellow of the Australian Academy of Social Science. In 2019, she was named among the world's most influential scientists and social scientists in the Web of Science Highly Cited Researchers list. She is a past Associate Editor for the *Academy of Management Annals* and the *Journal of Applied Psychology* and has published more than 200 articles in leading journals on topics including work design, proactive behaviour and job performance.

Philip M. Podsakoff is the Hyatt and Cici Brown Chair of Business in the Warrington College of Business at the University of Florida. His major research interests include the antecedents and consequences of organisational citizenship behaviours, transformational leadership and research methods. He is a Fellow of SIOP and the Academy of Management as well as the recipient of the Academy of Management's Research Methods Distinguished Career Award and APA's Samuel J. Messick Distinguished Scientific Contributions Award. Phil is a former associate editor of JAP and currently serves on the editorial boards of the *Journal of Management, Personnel Psychology* and *Leadership Quarterly*.

Niels Van Quaquebeke is Professor of Leadership and Organisational Behaviour at the Kühne Logistics University (KLU) in Germany and distinguished research professor at the University of Exeter in the UK. He is a psychologist by training and on a mission to improve workplace leadership through research evidence. As such, he is involved in the Research Institute on Leadership and Operations in Humanitarian Aid (RILOHA), which seeks to enhance the effectiveness of humanitarian aid operations via psychological insights, the Exeter Centre for Leadership, and the Erasmus Centre for Leadership Studies.

Derek D. Rucker holds the Sandy & Morton Goldman Professorship of Entrepreneurial Studies in Marketing. His research focuses broadly on social rank, social hierarchy compensatory consumption, persuasion and consumer behaviour. His work asks, and seeks answers to, what makes for effective advertising and what motives underlie consumer consumption. To answer these questions, Dr Rucker draws on his rich training in social psychology. His work has appeared in leading journals such as the *Journal of Personality and Social Psychology, Psychological Science* and the *Journal of Consumer Psychology*.

Deborah E. Rupp, PhD is Professor of Psychology at George Mason University. She was formerly Professor and Byham Chair in Industrial-Organisational Psychology at Purdue University and Associate Professor of Psychology, Labour/Employment Relations and Law at the University of Illinois. Her research focuses on EEO-related legal issues, organisational justice and CSR, as well behavioural assessment within organisations. Her research has been cited in US Supreme Court proceedings and she has consulted many organisations around the world. She has published six books and 100+ papers, sits on the editorial boards of five journals, and is the former editor of the *Journal of Management*.

Sabine Sonnentag holds a doctoral degree (Dr. rer. nat.) from the Technical University of Braunschweig, Germany and is currently a full professor of Work and Organisational Psychology at the University of Mannheim, Germany. Her research addresses the question of how individuals can stay healthy, energetic and productive on the job. She studies job stress and job-stress recovery, health behaviour (eating, physical exercise) and self-regulation. She served as an associate editor of the *Journal of Applied Psychology*, the *Journal of Organizational Behavior* and the *Journal of Business and Psychology*.

Nicole (Nikki) Strah is a Postdoctoral Research Fellow in Industrial-Organisational Psychology at George Mason University. Her research interests revolve around diversity and inclusion, organisational justice and the intersection between psychology and equal employment law/equal employment opportunities. She has published in outlets such as the *Journal of Applied Psychology*, *Industrial and Organizational Psychology: Perspectives in Science and Practice* and the *Journal of Vocational Behavior*.

Mary Uhl-Bien is the BNSF Railway Endowed Professor of Leadership in the Neeley School of Business at the Texas Christian University (TCU). Her research focuses on complexity leadership, relational leadership and followership. Mary was ranked the #6 Most Influential Leadership Scholar 1990–2017 and recognised by Poets and Quants as a Top 50 Undergraduate Business Professor. She is active in executive education nationally and internationally and has been a visiting scholar in the US, Canada, Australia and Europe, including Sweden, Denmark, Portugal and Spain. Mary also has been a regular commentator on CNBC and Squawk Box.

Jeffrey B. Vancouver is a Professor and Byham Chair for Industrial/Organisational Psychology at Ohio University. He received his degree in 1989 from Michigan State University (Department of Psychology). He studies the dynamics underlying human motivation in work contexts using a self-regulatory perspective, rigorous empirical protocols and computational models. He has published papers in a number of journals including the *Journal of Applied Psychology*, *Personnel Psychology*, *Journal of Management*, *Organizational Research Methods*, *Organizational Behavior and Human Decision Processes*, *Annual Review of Organizational Psychology* and *Psychological Bulletin*.

Catharina Vogt is part of the Hamburg-based think tank RespectResearchGroup and has worked as a researcher and consultant in the field of leadership, conflict management and service interactions since 2008. Trained as a psychologist, Dr Vogt coordinated the EU-funded projects COREPOL on intercultural conflict management in the police and IMPRODOVA on the interaction of frontline responders in cases of domestic violence at the German Police University (DHPol) in Münster.

Steven W. Whiting is an Associate Professor of Management in the College of Business at the University of Central Florida in Orlando. He earned his PhD in Organisational Behaviour and Human Resource Management from Indiana University. His research has appeared in leading peer-reviewed journals such as the *Journal of Applied Psychology*, the *Academy of Management Journal* and the *International Public Management Journal*. Dr Whiting is interested in understanding organisational citizenship behaviours (and other pro-social behaviours at work) and their impact on individuals, groups and organisations.

Chuk Yan (Edwina) Wong is a PhD researcher at the University of Groningen. Her research is based on researching and developing diversity interventions and organisational policies that are effective for different ethnic and racialised groups of women. She investigates how gender diversity initiatives can at times exclude racially marginalised women due to the prototypicality of Whiteness. In this way, in her research she hopes to find ways with which organisations can heed to the wants and needs of racially marginalised women and improve their experience at work.

An Introduction to Classic Studies in Organisational Psychology

Niklas K. Steffens, Floor Rink & Michelle K. Ryan

Industrial and organisational psychology emerged as an independent scientific discipline at the beginning of the 1900s as many countries saw an increasing number of people working in large organisations and factories. At the time, those developing the discipline – notably Hugo Münsterberg, James McKeen Catell and Walter Dill Scott – sought to apply psychological principles (as studied in experimental psychology advanced by Wilhelm Wundt in the preceding century) to build an independent discipline that focused on work and organisations. They were primarily occupied with questions of how to improve work practices and efficiency by enhancing productivity and improving worker morale. Since then, the discipline has matured substantially to explore an expanded repertoire of topics considered important to the behaviour, cognition and emotions of workers, such as those relating to leadership, organisational climate and culture, well-being and burnout, work–life balance and many others. Today, organisational psychology has become a core applied field in which many psychology graduates around the world practise, with the goal of understanding and improving how individuals, teams and organisations function.

Organisational psychology can be understood as an umbrella term referring to a field that has significant overlap with other related fields such as applied psychology, organisational behaviour, occupational psychology, business psychology and work psychology. Indeed, the *Journal of Applied Psychology*, commonly regarded as one of the most established journals in the field (see its 2017 centennial special issue that includes reviews on various key organisational phenomena; Kozlowski et al., 2017) and aims to publish theory and empirical work 'aimed at understanding of work, employment, and organizational phenomena' (p. 1) (Eby, 2021).

WHAT MAKES A STUDY IN ORGANISATIONAL PSYCHOLOGY CLASSIC?

In light of the rich history and breadth of inquiry within organisational psychology, a (if not the) question that we as editors spent much time discussing as we worked on this book is 'what is it that makes a study in organisational psychology classic?' In selecting the studies for this book from a wide range of possible studies, we consulted a number of sources: (a) studies that we as editors saw as foundational to the discipline; (b) studies that researchers discuss as pioneering and field-shaping in their articles; (c) studies suggested by colleagues via social media posts; (d) feedback from independent reviewers of the book proposal; and (e) feedback from the scholars who contributed to this volume.

There is of course no objectively correct answer to what defines a classic study in organisational psychology. Indeed, we are conscious that we could have made a case for many other impactful studies to be included in the volume, such as Herzberg (1968), Janis (1972), Münsterberg (1913) and Taylor (1911). In many ways, it is the idiosyncrasies of given studies and the endeavours of the researchers conducting them – as testified in the reviews of the studies in this volume – that make them a unique and special, and ultimately classic piece of work. However, we feel that there are several latent attributes of the studies revisited in this volume that, in our view, are foundational to their enduring influence. We identify four important characteristics germane to the classic studies in this volume: (a) their focus on big ideas; (b) their introduction of novel ways of looking at the world; (c) their use of rich, involving methods to address their questions; and (d) the researchers' commitment and passion and their curiosity about the intricacies of the subject.

First, a common feature of the studies in this volume is that they focused on ideas – and not any ideas, but big ideas and issues that mattered to society and had a profound impact on people's lives. The questions they tackled had importance far beyond the study itself – they were timely questions that were subject to much societal debate at the time and they had deeper, universal relevance to the functioning of individuals and the organisations of which they are a part. For instance, they sought answers to questions such as what is it about work that makes people sick (Chapter 7, Sonnentag) and are societies better off led democratically or autocratically (Chapter 9, Harms)?

A second common characteristic of the research included here is that in interrogating their questions, the researchers challenged the prevailing assumptions at the time (either implicit or explicit) and transformed how people viewed the world by allowing them to see it in a way they had never seen it before. Among other things, they challenged the idea that acting as a follower is the opposite of acting as leader by making us realise that leadership and followership go hand in hand (Chapter 11, Uhl-Bien & Carsten) and helped us realise that incentives can have opposing effects and backfire by undermining people's motivation (Chapter 4, Gagné). In their work, the researchers pioneered entirely new perspectives where there was little to work with or they broke the frame presented by existing perspectives at the time.

Third, this collection of studies is characterised by the use of diverse methods, many of which were innovative and highly involving. Many of the researchers relied on data collected in time-consuming ways using laborious procedures, which remains a rarity in contemporary science (e.g. use of observation, onerous experiments and field studies) – whether through the use of detailed time and motion studies examining the movements of individual workers to identify ways to maximise productivity and well-being (Chapter 1, De Boeck & Parker) or elaborate field experiments involving the introduction of a pay cut and assessing worker responses over a period of 30 weeks using survey assessments and behavioural data (Chapter 12, Cropanzano et al.).

At the same time, it is noteworthy that some of the studies did not require complex or sophisticated apparatus, scanners or other modern technological devices to make the study interesting (e.g. many used a combination of surveys and interviews to tap into people's experiences and observation to tap into work behaviours). Neither did they use overly complex research designs or statistical procedures to discover some profound aspects of individuals' psychology. Indeed, had the studies been conducted today, it is unlikely they would be published because they would not be seen as sufficiently 'sophisticated' in light of the growing emphasis on complex methodological and statistical procedures seen in contemporary science. Nevertheless, the studies used methods and statistics that allowed them to answer important conceptual questions and generate intriguing insights that paved the way for the subsequent development of entire bodies of research.

Fourth, and perhaps most important to the development of the discipline, the researchers did not go about their studies in mindless or dispassionate ways, following a predefined script of doing good research or ticking off a list of how to conduct a good study that people would deem worth publishing. They were intrigued about the motivations and well-being of humans and cared deeply about the general subject and the questions they asked. Indeed, it was commitment and curiosity that sparked their creativity and determination to get closer to the true drivers of people's behaviours and experiences. Indicative is the persistence of Locke and Latham in conducting their series of laboratory studies with the aim of uncovering how various aspects of goal difficulty and the task impact upon performance and underlying cognition (Chapter 3, Vancouver et al.). Similarly, the extraordinary efforts led by Smith in uncovering the behaviours of good organisational citizen that are overlooked in explicit performance measures despite dreadful energy-draining personal circumstances (facing terminal cancer) (Chapter 6, Whiting et al.). It is remarkable that the researchers not only approached their study with an open, inquisitive attitude but they were aware that their work was not 'finished' or perfect and in need of a community (a discipline) to get to grips with understanding the phenomenon at hand. These four qualities, together with many others, comprise what we believe is a wonderful compendium of classic works at the heart of a wide range of core organisational topics.

OVERVIEW OF THE CLASSIC STUDIES

The classic studies in this volume cover a breadth of topics in organisational psychology. The first three chapters speak to questions of organising work and include pioneering studies of fatigue by Lillian Gilbreth (Chapter 1, De Boeck & Parker) who also became known as 'the first lady of management' (Greenwood et al., 1978); Mayo's elaborate Hawthorne studies on the ways in which groups underpin how people engage with work (Chapter 2, Haslam & Steffens); and Locke and Latham's field-directing studies of goal-setting (Chapter 3, Vancouver et al.).

The four studies that follow deal with broader questions of motivation, cooperation and well-being, as interrogated by Deci's studies on the impact of rewards on intrinsic motivation (Chapter 4, Gagné); Mael and Ashforth's studies on organisational identification as the social glue that binds alumni to their alma mater (Chapter 5, Ellemers & De Gilder); Smith et al.'s study on the hard-to-capture behaviours of a good organisational citizen (Chapter 6, Whiting et al.); and Karasek's studies on how job demands combine with decision latitude to affect people's stress levels (Chapter 7, Sonnentag).

The next four studies reveal profound insights into questions of leadership and followership, covering French and Raven's studies on different sources of power in social hierarchies (Chapter 8, Rucker et al.); Lewin et al.'s studies exploring the profound consequences of democratic, autocratic and laissez-faire styles of leadership (Chapter 9, Harms); Fleishman and Harris's Ohio State studies expanding on how leaders are perceived by uncovering what leaders actually do and how they behave (Chapter 10, Van Quaquebeke & Vogt); and Hollander and Webb's study on the intriguing interrelationship between leadership and followership (Chapter 11, Uhl-Bien & Carsten).

The final three chapters shed light on studies that speak to issues of justice, equality and diversity, including Greenberg's study on the detrimental effects of pay inequity (Chapter 12, Cropanzano et al.); Schein's revealing study of gendered leadership stereotypes (Chapter 13, Heilman & Manzi), and Ancona & Caldwell's study of how demographic diversity impacts team functioning (Chapter 14, Wong et al.).

While the revisited studies are diverse with regard to the questions they address, they are less diverse in other regards. The overwhelming majority of the original studies were conducted by men in Northern America. Since then, the discipline has evolved to become somewhat more inclusive. We have tried to capture the diversity of excellent scholars in the field, such that more than half of the authors contributing to this volume are female, and that the authors represent a greater diversity of backgrounds and countries. We recognise, however, that more needs to be done before greater diversity and inclusion is achieved in the field.

These teams of scholars who conducted these reviews of the classic studies present wonderful in-depth analyses that bring the studies to life. They do this by shedding light on key aspects of the studies reinforced by the structure of the chapters: discussing the wider social context at the time and the motivations that drove the researchers, intriguing details of the studies and the ways they were conducted, the impact and significance of the findings, subsequent replications and generalisations of the findings of the studies, the ways in which contemporary science has moved beyond the studies, and implications for practitioners. The contributors each pose several discussion questions at the end of each chapter that anyone interested in engaging more deeply with these issues will find interesting to reflect on and discuss with others.

The collaborative efforts that went into this book have led to what we believe is a collection of insightful accounts of the enduring influence of classic studies of organisational psychology. By all accounts, the studies in this volume have been extraordinarily impactful – not only in terms of the radical ideas they shed light onto and the discoveries they made but perhaps even more so in terms of their generative power by providing a foundation for subsequent research that led to the state of the science as we know it today. We very much enjoyed and learnt a lot from working on this collective endeavour and thank everyone in this big team effort who contributed to the book – friends and colleagues, editors from Sage, as well as students with whom we have had many discussions in a course on the topic from classic studies to contemporary topics in organisational psychology. We hope that you will learn and discover new insights as much as we have from revisiting the classic studies in light of current understanding.

REFERENCES

Eby, L. T. (2021). Editorial. *Journal of Applied Psychology*, 106, 13.

Greenwood, R. G., Greenwood, R. A. & Severance, J. A. (1978). Lillian M. Gilbreth, First Lady of Management. In *Academy of Management Proceedings*. Academy of Management, pp. 2–6.

Herzberg, E. (1968/2003). One more time: How do you motivate employees? *Harvard Business Review*, 46, 53–62.

Janis, I. L. (1972). *Victims of Groupthink*. Boston: Houghton Mifflin.

Kozlowski, S. W., Chen, G. & Salas, E. (2017). One hundred years of the Journal of Applied Psychology: Background, evolution, and scientific trends. *Journal of Applied Psychology*, 102, 237–53.

Münsterberg, H. (1913). *Psychology and Industrial Efficiency*. Houghton Mifflin.

Taylor, F. (1911). *The Principles of Scientific Management*. Norton.

Part I | Organising the Workplace

1

Work Design: Revisiting Lillian Gilbreth's Fatigue Studies

Giverny De Boeck &
Sharon K. Parker

BACKGROUND

Historically, research on work design, or the content and organisation of one's work tasks, activities, relationships, and responsibilities (Parker, 2014), can be traced back to the rise of machine-operated work during the Industrial Revolution. Early in the twentieth century, the traditional practice of craftsmanship gradually started to be replaced by a new philosophy advocating that each person should only perform one single, specific function at work. This principle of functionalisation was central to Frederick Winslow Taylor's (1911) *Scientific Management*, a popular management theory that aimed to maximise efficiency in the workplace by breaking down work into basic operations and to redesign jobs to be highly simplified and standardised. Taylor's approach emphasised the importance of using time and motion studies to analyse existing jobs so as to scientifically determine the 'best' (most efficient) way for executing tasks (Sullivan, 1995).

First applied by Frederick Taylor in 1881 in the Midvale Steel Company in Philadelphia, the method of time study focused on timing the different procedures of a given work operation and identifying a standard time to perform the work. Later, Frank Gilbreth developed a complementary method called motion study. As the owner of a construction company, Frank sought to improve bricklayers' working methods (Krenn, 2011). Instead of just timing operations as did Taylor, Frank measured the movement patterns of bricklayers. Frank used motion study to identify a reduced set of fundamental and standard motions thereby minimising fatigue in bricklayers (Gilbreth, 1911). Various employers experimented with methods of time and motion study, the best-known being Henry Ford, who succeeded in reducing the assembly time for a Model T automobile from over 12 hours to 90 minutes.

The initial success of scientific management and its methods quickly resulted in the widespread adoption of job simplification as the preferred form of work design in manufacturing and other sectors (Davis, 1966). Despite its popularity, however, scientific management was also strongly criticised by opponents who argued that it was a dehumanising approach, transforming people into machines (Sullivan, 1995). The implementation of simplified work design often meant an increased degree of control over employee behaviour by managers who believed that workers lacked both the competency and motivation to oversee organisational activities (Hackman & Oldham, 1980). For instance, Frederick Taylor allegedly said that the ideal worker for shovelling pig iron should be 'as stupid as an ox' (Kelly & Kelly, 1990, p. 121). Unsurprisingly many workers suffered under Taylor's approach to work design, resulting in negative outcomes like job dissatisfaction, absenteeism, turnover and even formal legislation prohibiting the use of stopwatches to time workers' performance (Kelly & Kelly, 1990; Parker, 2014).

Against this background, we illuminate the work of Lillian Gilbreth who was a silent pioneer in research on work design and one of the earliest scholars to develop a humanistic view on scientific management. Specifically, we will focus on two of Lillian's core works in this chapter, *The Psychology of Management* and *Fatigue Study: The Elimination of Humanity's Greatest Unnecessary Waste*, to showcase her ground-breaking human-centred approach to work design.

DETAILED DESCRIPTION

GILBRETH'S FATIGUE STUDIES

Born on May 24 in 1878 in California as the oldest child of Ann and William Moller, Lillian Gilbreth grew up as a shy girl with a keen interest in music and literature, spending her high school days writing poetry for the school paper and making up lyrics for her self-composed songs. Although her father initially objected to the idea of her attending university in favour of staying home and learning to keep house, Lillian – encouraged by her favourite aunt Lillian Delger Powell – prepared herself for a professional career, assuming she was too plain for any man to marry her anyway. Her dream was to go to Columbia University to study with Brander Matthews, a world-renowned professor in English literature. However, with Brander refusing to teach women and Lillian falling ill soon after, she had to give up on that dream. She returned home to obtain her master's degree in English at the University of California – later she would also obtain her dissertation at this university (Kelly & Kelly, 1990; Miller & Lemmons, 1998; Yost, 1949).

The next summer on their way to Europe, Lillian's chaperone introduced Lillian to Frank Gilbreth during a stop in Boston. They got on so well that they later married on 19 October 1904. Frank convinced Lillian to shift the topic of her dissertation to psychology, foreseeing it would complement his own research on scientific management. For instance, their book *Motion Study: A Method for Increasing the Efficiency of the Workman* (Gilbreth, 1911) reflected Lillian's growing understanding of the psychology of workers. Afraid of damaging the book's credibility, however, the publisher did not want to include Lillian as a co-author, so Frank received all the credit as sole author (Kelly & Kelly, 1990; Krenn, 2011). Despite men dominating the management literature in the early twentieth century, Lillian did manage to publish her dissertation in 1914 as a book entitled *The Psychology of Management* using her initials, as publishers wished to keep her gender a secret (Kelly & Kelly, 1990; Koppes, 1997; Miller & Lemmons, 1998; Yost, 1949).

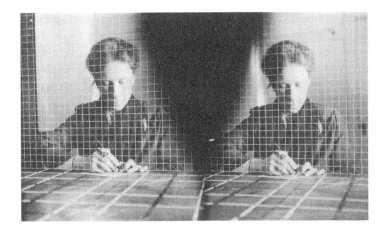

Figure 1.1   Stereograph of Lillian Gilbreth in motion study lab, undated.

Courtesy of Purdue University Libraries, Karnes Archives and Special Collections.

With *The Psychology of Management* (Gilbreth, 1914), Lillian contributed to the literature on work design in a ground-breaking way. She was one of the first to introduce a human-centred approach to work design, combining insights from psychology, management and engineering (Kelly & Kelly, 1990; Sullivan, 1995). Although Lillian saw great value in Frederick Taylor's principles to improve the efficiency of the production process, she felt that by focusing on the *managing* part of the organisation only, scientific management neglected another vital part almost entirely: the best interest of the *managed* (Gilbreth, 1914). Contrary to Taylor, Lillian Gilbreth was interested in the psychological dimension behind work efficiency or how workers experience work. She stated this explicitly in her dissertation:

> *The emphasis in successful management lies on the man, not on the work; that effi-ciency is best secured by placing the emphasis on the man, and modifying the equip-ment, materials and methods to make the most of the man.* (Gilbreth, 1914, p. 344)

Contrary to engineers and managers who focused dominantly on machines, prod-ucts, and profits, Lillian started from workers' psychological needs to develop work methods that could improve their happiness and health. Lillian argued that work design should allow individuals to express themselves and realise their potential, founded in the belief that worker well-being was a key asset for organisations (Sullivan, 1995).

FATIGUE STUDY

The complementary nature of Lillian's interest in the realisation of human potential and Frank's focus on improving work efficiency was most visible in their joint publication of the book *fatigue study* (Krenn, 2011). The goal of fatigue study was to eliminate all unnecessary waste of human energy caused by needless effort in industrial operations (Gilbreth & Gilbreth, 1916). Specifically, fatigue study aimed to help workers overcome fatigue and conserve their energy by developing optimal work methods and engaging in so-called *betterment work*, adapting working conditions to fit the needs of workers (e.g. using adjustable chairs, adaptable worktables and proper work clothing) (Kelly & Kelly, 1990). Betterment work included the creation of the best resting conditions for workers by for instance installing home reading boxes – a library of books and magazines that workers could take home to relax and educate themselves. Rather than limiting productivity, Lillian and Frank saw rest as a critical factor for organisational success, arguing that workers had a duty to rest to be able to think clearly (Gilbreth & Gilbreth, 1916). To achieve these goals, fatigue study relied not only on the measurement of workers' movements, methods and results, but also on the study of workers' fatigue – the rest interval needed to recover – as an indicator of their work efficiency: the smaller the rest interval that workers needed to recover, the higher their perceived work efficiency.

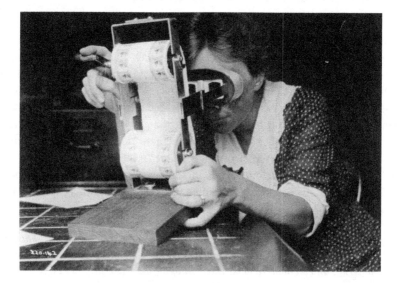

Figure 1.2   Lillian Gilbreth viewing movies demonstrating motion study, undated.

Courtesy of Purdue University Libraries, Karnes Archives and Special Collections.

    As explained in the introduction to this chapter, the key measurement methods the Gilbreths used to investigate fatigue were the time and motion study: timing the elements of the best method known and then dividing the work into its most fundamental motions which they called *therbligs* (Gilbreth, 1914). Specifically, Lillian and Frank used *micromotion* to record motions, tools, and surroundings aided by cinematography and special clocks. In addition, they used the *cyclograph method* to record and visualize the orbit or path of a (cycle of) motion(s) by attaching small electric lights to the hands or other body parts of the workers (Gilbreth & Gilbreth, 1916). Lillian and Frank analysed the data to develop procedures of least waste by getting rid of useless motions and recombining the remaining motions in an optimal manner. Besides synthesising a standard time to do a piece of work, they also standardised rest periods for workers to overcome fatigue. For instance, Lillian described significant changes made to the process of handkerchief folding based on the results of time and motion studies:

> *Each hour was divided into ten periods. The first four periods, that is, the first twenty-four minutes, the girl remained seated. She worked five minutes and rested one; again worked five minutes and rested one. That is to say, she had four minutes' rest out of the twenty-four, and spent this rest seated so that she might lose no time in getting back to the work. The next two periods, that is, for twelve minutes, the girl was standing.* (Gilbreth, 1914, p. 128)

Under the new standard conditions, the girls produced over three times the amount of their best work produced prior to the study, while showing more interest in their work than before and experiencing the same fatigue (Gilbreth, 1914). Besides determining a standard work method for workers, Lillian and Frank also standardised working conditions such as the colour, shape, size, weight, location, position and texture of walls, tools, furniture and clothing of workers. For example, when applying the fatigue study to the assembly of a braider – a machine for manufacturing braid – the Gilbreths optimised the positioning of assembly materials and the design of the worktable. They arranged parts of the used work sequence and placed tools on the table in standard positions so that the workers could grasp, transport, and release these in the least fatiguing way (Gilbreth, 1914). Lillian noted that the new method increased the output from 18 to 66 braiders per person per day with no added fatigue. Interestingly, Lillian and Frank also showed a remarkable eye for detail. They advised providing machinery with a dull black finish, for instance, because the shiny nickel polish that organisations typically used taxed workers' eyes and caused fatigue (Gilbreth & Gilbreth, 1916).

WELFARE

The main purpose of the standardisation of work resulting from Lillian and Frank's time and motion studies was the elimination of unnecessary fatigue to conserve workers' energy. In their fatigue study, they moved beyond the dominant focus on efficiency outcomes in terms of objective clock time and economic output by emphasising workers' subjective work experience – how workers felt at work. Lillian and Frank wrote that the fatigue study must increase *happiness minutes*, arguing that work was less fatiguing when workers enjoy what they are doing and are able to work with ease (Gilbreth & Gilbreth, 1916; Krenn, 2011). Therefore Lillian urged managers to ask themselves the following question:

> *Have you reason to believe that your workers are really happier because of the work that you have done on fatigue study? Do they look happier, and say they are happier? Then your fatigue eliminating work has been worthwhile in the highest sense of the term, no matter what the financial outcome.* (Gilbreth, 1914, p. 150)

According to Lillian, the fatigue study contributed to workers' general welfare allowing them to live a fuller life both inside and outside of work (Gilbreth, 1914). For instance, she described how some principles of the psychology of scientific management could stimulate the physical, mental, and moral development of workers, including:

- Individuality: workers should perform tasks that fit best with their abilities.

- Cooperation and empowerment: managers should actively involve workers in the process of work redesign.

- Squareness: the fatigue study should inform the work of all workers equally and workers should receive a fair compensation for improvements.

Contrary to Taylor, Lillian advocated the active involvement of workers in the process of work design as she felt they were best placed as specialists to provide the planning department with constructive criticism and suggestions for improving operations (Kelly & Kelly, 1990; Krenn, 2011). At the same time, Lillian also emphasised the importance of workers receiving a 'square deal' to prevent the fatigue study from becoming 'a new scheme for taking advantage of them' (Gilbreth, 1914, p. 157).

For Lillian, the fatigue study stimulated interest in workers for their work, appealed to workers' personal judgment, and developed their reasoning powers in constant efforts to improve existing work methods in cooperation with management (Gilbreth, 1914). She silenced objections of people who criticised scientific management for alienating workers from work and turning them into mindless robots, arguing that – when applied properly –scientific approaches to management can enrich workers' lives:

> *Far from making machines out of the men, standardization causes a mental state that leads to invention, for the reason that the worker's brain is in most intimate contact with the work, and yet has not been unnecessarily fatigued by the work itself. No more monotonous work could be cited than that of that boy whose sole duty was to operate by hand the valve to the engine, yet he invented the automatic control of the slide valve used throughout the world today.* (Gilbreth, 1914, p. 180)

IMPACT OF THE CLASSIC STUDY

By adopting a human-centred approach to scientific management and focusing on job enrichment instead of job simplification (Krenn, 2011), Lillian laid the foundation for the field of management and work design to move into a new direction. Unfortunately, being a female academic in the then male-dominated field of management studies, Lillian received little acknowledgment for her contributions and the revolution her work could have sparked at the time did not happen. The shift in focus of work design research only took place five decades later when a new generation of researchers (e.g. Emery and Trist, Herzberg, Vroom, Hackman and Oldham) started advocating the same ideas about how work design could support the satisfaction of human needs (Sullivan, 1995).

For example, Lillian's core idea to look at the interaction between people and machines when improving work design was present in Emery & Trist's (1969) sociotechnical systems theory. Instead of either designing people out of the system or micromanaging them as was common practice in Tayloristic systems, sociotechnical theory emphasised the importance of the joint optimisation of social and technical aspects of work (Clegg, 2000). This early theory of work design found its origin in Trist & Bamforth's (1951) now seminal study linking social and psychological problems in workers to the design of their work in the coal mines of Great Britain – 'the longwall method of coal getting'. They observed that, by changing from a 'hand-got' method in which miners dug out coal in small teams to a mechanical process in which miners operated in shifts spread out over long distances, social bonds weakened and problems with miners' morale appeared (Trist & Bamforth, 1951). These insights, in turn, inspired research on the power of self-managing teams – teams whose members have a range of skills and can autonomously complete an entire task (Cummings, 1978).

Lillian's ideas have featured prominently in later motivational theories of work design as well. For example, in his motivation hygiene theory Herzberg (1966) made a distinction between intrinsic work factors (e.g. achievement, recognition, responsibility) and extrinsic work factors (e.g. salary, relation with supervisor, job security) arguing that the former are stronger predictors of worker satisfaction while the latter better predict worker dissatisfaction. Here, Herzberg echoes Lillian who almost 50 years prior to the development of his two-factor theory distinguished between workers' natural instincts to work (e.g. ambition, pride) and external rewards and punishments (e.g. bonus, fine) as direct and indirect incentives, respectively (Gilbreth, 1914). Furthermore, Lillian acknowledged that people desire different rewards and managers should couple workers' performance to the rewards they desire (Gilbreth, 1914). This idea is central to Vroom's (1964) expectancy theory suggesting that workers are motivated when they expect that their efforts will have a positive impact on performance and good performance will lead to rewards that meet workers' specific needs.

Early motivational theories on work design stimulated the development of the now famous job characteristics model (JCM) (Hackman & Oldham, 1975, 1976), which aimed to identify the characteristics of jobs that foster a state of internal work motivation in workers (Oldham & Hackman, 2010). In the JCM, Hackman and Oldham highlighted five core job characteristics that determine the motivating potential (MP) of a job – the power of that job to tap into workers' intrinsic work motivation. These included:

- Skill variety: the degree to which a job involves the use of different skills in carrying out the work.

- Task identity: the degree to which a job requires the completion of a whole and identifiable piece of work.

- Task significance: the degree to which a job has a substantial impact on the lives or work of other people.

- Autonomy: the degree to which a job provides freedom to the individual in scheduling and choosing work methods.

- Job feedback: the degree to which a job provides direct and clear information about the effectiveness of workers' performance.

Although to our knowledge Hackman and Oldham did not reference Lillian Gilbreth, similar ideas about the importance of workers' subjective work experience and job enrichment evident in Lillian's work are at the heart of the JCM. At the same time, Hackman and Oldham extended Lillian's work as well as that of others by being the first to develop a testable and useful model of good work design for organisations. The five key job characteristics were argued to lead to positive work outcomes via three critical psychological states (perceived work meaningfulness, feelings of personal responsibility for work results, understanding of one's work performance) (Hackman & Oldham, 1975, 1976) which, in turn, were theorised to generate positive work outcomes. Early tests of the model using the job diagnostics survey (JDS), a measurement instrument to assess the presence of job characteristics, showed results that were particularly strong for affective reactions (e.g. satisfaction, motivation) (Hackman & Oldham, 1976).

A further important work design theory is Karasek's (1979) job demands-control model that introduced the importance of work demands and additionally focused on strain as an outcome (see Chapter 7 this volume). This model proposed that jobs combining high demands with high control were most motivating, whereas jobs that were highly demanding but gave no control to workers would increase their risk for psychological and physical strain. The importance of control for workers builds on Lillian's work on the need to empower and involve workers as a principle of the psychology of scientific management (Gilbreth, 1914). Karasek's (1979) insight that control helped workers cope with high demands, however, extends Lillian's work that focused mainly on decreasing demands by removing excessive motions and managing fatigue with rest periods.

In conclusion, even though Lillian Gilbreth was one of the first to propose that organisations should invest in making work more motivating for workers by designing it in a way that serves their needs instead of the other way around, the JCM and the demand-control model offered scholars more specific frameworks to study this broad proposition.

KEY REPLICATIONS AND GENERALISATIONS

After Hackman and Oldham's development of the JCM, studies on work design increased dramatically focusing on testing and extending the model (Oldham & Hackman, 2010; Parker et al., 2017). Over time, reviews and meta-analyses have provided convincing evidence for the positive impact of certain job characteristics on workers' attitudes and performance (Fried & Ferris, 1987; Humphrey et al., 2007; Morgeson & Humphrey, 2006). For example, Fried and Ferris (1987) showed that the relationship between job characteristics and work outcomes was generally stronger and more consistent for workers' attitudes (e.g. job satisfaction) compared to their behaviours (e.g. work performance). Thirty years later, Humphrey et al. (2007) reviewed 259 studies involving 219,625 participants and concluded that work design explained on average 43 per cent of the variance in workers' attitudinal and behavioural work outcomes. Interestingly, the impact of job characteristics was stronger for subjective than objective performance, with the latter predicted only by job autonomy (Humphrey et al., 2007).

In line with Lillian's early ideas on the importance of workers' subjective work experience, the meta-analytical studies partially supported the mediating role of workers' psychological states in the relationship between job characteristics and work outcomes (Fried & Ferris, 1987). Experienced work meaningfulness proved to be the key psychological state mediating the job characteristics–work outcomes relationship (De Boeck et al., 2019; Humphrey et al., 2007). Moreover, research confirmed Hackman and Oldham's proposition that individual differences influence workers' reactions to work design (Raja & Johns, 2010), although it failed to support concrete predictions about the moderating role of 'growth need strength' in the relationship between job characteristics and work outcomes (Johns et al., 1992; Tiegs et al., 1992). Overall, there is substantial support for Lillian's human-centric approach to work design as evidenced by the high scientific validity and practical usefulness of the JCM (Miner, 1984; Oldham & Hackman, 2005).

Unsurprisingly, although the JCM is still popular (Parker et al., 2017), it has not been free from criticism. One critique has been about the use of workers' subjective perceptions to measure job characteristics. Salancik & Pfeffer (1978) started questioning the results of the JCM from a social processing perspective, arguing that workers construct the characteristics of a job as a function of their social context and past experiences. This critique does not refute the validity of the JCM, however, as past research has found objective and subjective measures of job characteristics to be related (Fried & Ferris, 1987) and evidenced the validity of using perceptions to measure job characteristics (Parker, 2014).

The JCM has undergone considerable adaptations over time (Oldham & Hackman, 2005). First, researchers have expanded the JCM by broadening the initial set of job characteristics (Humphrey et al., 2007; Morgeson & Humphrey, 2006; Parker et al., 2001; Grant, 2007). Morgeson & Humphrey's (2006) work design questionnaire (WDQ) includes motivational, social, and contextual work characteristics. *Motivational characteristics* encompass both the classic JCM characteristics as well as knowledge characteristics, reflecting demands regarding workers' knowledge, skills, and abilities (e.g. job complexity). *Social characteristics* include interactional factors related to the relational architecture of jobs (e.g. social support) (Grant, 2007). Finally, *contextual characteristics* reflect the physical environment of work including physical demands, work conditions, and ergonomics (Morgeson & Humphrey, 2006). Besides being more comprehensive, the WDQ is also more sound methodologically with high scale reliability and consistent factor solutions making up for some psychometric issues of the JDS (Idaszak & Drasgow, 1987; Taber & Taylor, 1990).

A further adaptation is the refinement of the JCM over time with researchers systematically exploring alternative mediators, moderators and outcomes (Parker et al., 2001). For instance, due to the limited evidence for the mediating role of experienced responsibility and knowledge of results, studies investigated other motivational mechanisms such as the promotion of role breadth self-efficacy (Axtell & Parker, 2003; Parker, 1998), as well as non-motivational mechanisms such as willingness to respond quickly to changes. Researchers have also explored outcomes beyond those originally specified in the JCM including workers' physical and mental well-being as well as their learning related to cognitive and moral processes (Parker, 2014). For example, Demerouti et al.'s (2001) job-demands resources model suggests a dual-path with resources promoting well-being in workers via engagement and demands impairing workers' health via strain. This research goes back to Lillian's ideas about how work design could contribute to workers' happiness as well as their cognitive and moral development by cultivating personal responsibility and responsibility for others (Gilbreth, 1914; Gilbreth & Gilbreth, 1916).

BEYOND GILBRETH'S FATIGUE STUDIES: THEORETICAL DEVELOPMENTS

We started this chapter by discussing Lillian Gilbreth and her pioneering proposition that organisations should design jobs to be motivating for workers and less fatiguing, thereby shifting the focus from the work to the workers and their interests. We further described how the same fundamental belief in *job enrichment* later became the foundation of Hackman and Oldham's more tangible JCM that triggered an explosion of research testing and refining work design theory. In this section, we will focus on further theoretical developments that are currently happening in work design research. Specifically, we will address two emerging topics: the process of (bottom-up) work design and work design in a connected and digital world.

THE PROCESS OF (BOTTOM-UP) WORK DESIGN

An important topic emerging in the work design literature has to do with our limited understanding of the antecedents of work design (Parker, 2014). Researchers – including Lillian and others discussed in this chapter – have traditionally approached work design in a top-down manner assuming managers design jobs to meet specific goals and/or work design is the result of decisions made higher up in the organisation (Cohen, 2013; Parker, 2014). Yet, empirical studies on the process of how managers design work remain scarce (Parker et al., 2017). Exceptions include qualitative papers showing that work design is the product of a social and ongoing process (e.g. Barley, 1986; Cohen, 2013) and depends on individual factors such as the work designer's capacity and willingness to enrich jobs (Parker et al., 2019). For example, Cohen (2013) found that multiple organisational actors designed together the job of a DNA sequence operator in face of new technology.

The relative absence of knowledge about how managers design work contrasts with the exponential surge in research on job crafting or the 'bottom-up' process through which workers proactively design their own jobs to achieve a better person-job fit (Tims et al., 2012; Wrzesniewski & Dutton, 2001). The interest in this proactive, bottom-up approach to work design reflects a shift from studying the jobs of manual labourers in manufacturing organisations – as studied by Lillian Gilbreth – to enriching the jobs of managers, professionals and knowledge workers (Oldham & Hackman, 2005, 2010). Arguably, for individuals in higher and more autonomous positions, job crafting represents a useful strategy to shape work in function of their personal expertise and career aspirations, while providing them with a means to manage excessive demands (Parker, 2014). Recent reviews have shown that workers craft their own jobs – confirming Lillian's assumption that workers are motivated to improve their own work design – and that this is significantly related to outcomes such as engagement, burnout and work performance (Bruning & Campion, 2018; Lichtenthaler & Fischbach, 2016; Rudolph et al., 2017; Zhang & Parker, 2019).

WORK DESIGN IN A CONNECTED AND DIGITAL WORLD

A second set of topics emerging in the work design literature has to do with changes in the economic context as well as growing technological innovations in organisations. Today, knowledge and service work, rather than manufacturing, dominate developed economies. Thus researchers are increasingly focused on the work design of professionals and knowledge workers (Grant & Parker, 2009; Parker, 2014; Oldham & Hackman, 2010). For instance, one important work transformation that is currently taking place is the rise in collaboration between people both in- and outside of organisational boundaries (Grant & Parker, 2007), leading to a much stronger focus on the 'social systems of work' (Grant, 2007; Grant & Parker, 2009). Building on earlier interactional perspectives (Salancik & Pfeffer, 1978), Grant (2007) argued that jobs that provide workers with opportunities to interact with and have an impact on others (e.g. clients), will increase workers' effort and helping behaviours via processes of prosocial motivation – the desire to bring benefit to others (Parker, 2014). Similarly, scholars have emphasised the need to integrate insights from networks and teams in work design (Kilduff & Brass, 2010; Morgeson & Humphrey, 2008), and to focus on social characteristics such as social support and feedback (Morgeson & Humphrey, 2006; Humphrey et al., 2007).

Technological innovations in the form of digitalisation are also drastically changing the jobs of many contemporary workers (Frey & Osborne, 2017 not in refs). Although our understanding about the impact of digital technology on work design in these jobs is still limited, machine-learning enabled the ability of machines to be ever more autonomous, which has critical implications for the task and control structure of work, including for knowledge and professional jobs (Parker & Grote, 2020). To date, most research has been adopting a passive perspective focused on how workers need to adapt to technology, but Parker & Grote (2020) have called for researchers and practitioners to consider how organisations could design work proactively to minimise potential risks in terms of workers' safety, performance and well-being, while maximising the opportunities provided by new technologies. For example, designed by technologists with little attention to worker experiences, the contemporary practice of algorithmic management tends to increase management control over workers and intensify workers' workload (Parent-Rocheleau & Parker, 2021). An emphasis on the joint optimisation of social and technical aspects of work is consistent with past theory on sociotechnical systems (Trist & Emery, 1969, 2005), with research from this perspective showing that technological changes are more likely to fail when organisations merely adopt a techno-centric approach that neglects the human side of things (Clegg & Shepherd, 2007). The need for a sociotechnical perspective in today's digital world is a continuation of Lillian's call for an emphasis on workers' experiences, not just machines.

CONCLUSION

Over 100 years have passed since Lillian Gilbreth pioneered a human-centred approach to work design in her dissertation 'The Psychology of Management' and subsequent work. Contrary to her contemporaries who concentrated solely on managing, Lillian was among the first to highlight the importance of considering the interests and needs of those being managed. In doing so, Lillian advanced thinking on work design by introducing job enrichment and rightfully earned herself the title of 'first lady in management' (Koppes, 1997; Krenn, 2011). Her ideas feature prominently in later motivational theories of work design such as Hackman and Oldham's JCM. Although workers today face different challenges caused by the increasingly complex, interactive and digital nature of work, problems still occur because organisations prioritise profits and technology over human welfare. Therefore it seems timely to reinvigorate Lillian's work and call for a more human-centred approach to work design.

IMPLICATIONS FOR PRACTITIONERS

One might argue that poor work design is less of a problem in today's knowledge economies because work is more enriched than before. Research partially supports this thesis showing that on average jobs offer a greater level of skill variety to workers and provide them with more autonomy than in 1975 (Wegman et al., 2018). The gains in skill variety and autonomy are overshadowed, however, by recent losses in task identity and task significance due to ICT and automation (Wegman et al., 2018). Moreover, EU population statistics evidence that poor work design is still prevalent in modern societies with 20 per cent and 13 per cent of workers, respectively, holding poor-quality and overly demanding jobs (Sixth European Working Conditions Survey, 2016). Further, routine-biased technological change and offshoring are polarising job quality and thereby increasing the gap between low- and high-quality jobs (Goos et al., 2014). In a book on meaningless jobs, Graeber (2018) describes numerous examples including Clarence who was hired by a major global security firm as a guard for a museum and who testified: 'My job was to guard that empty room, ensuring no museum guests touched the ... well, *nothing* in the room, and ensure nobody set any fires. To keep my mind sharp and attention undivided, I was forbidden any form of mental stimulation, like books, phones, etc. Since nobody was ever there, in practice I sat still and twiddled my thumbs for seven and a half hours, waiting for the fire alarm to sound' (p. 95).

The result of societal and technological changes is that, on top of new pressing problems (e.g. burnout), problems of the past such as job dissatisfaction, absenteeism, poor performance and turnover still haunt contemporary organisations (Oldham & Hackman, 2010). A human-centred approach to work design provides organisations with an evidence-based way to improve the quality of work and make people love work more than hate it (Parker et al., 2017). Organisations can also indirectly support good work design by influencing the motivation, knowledge, skills, and abilities of, and opportunities for managers and other workers who are responsible – formally and/or informally – for designing work (Parker et al., 2017). Important to keep in mind is that work design both shapes and is shaped by the broader work context and therefore organisations should strive for alignment between both (Parker et al., 2017). For example, Campion et al. (2005) suggests to pair motivational work design such as highly autonomous jobs with commitment-based HR configurations (e.g. mentoring programmes) to achieve alignment.

Work design also offers practitioners a valuable perspective to understand the effects of technological changes on workers (Parker & Grote, 2020). As illustrated by Eriksson-Zetterquist et al. (2009), new technologies can disrupt good work design by reducing opportunities for workers to use their personal judgment and interact with others, which can diminish the perceived meaningfulness of the job. In this respect, it is important for organisations to design work in such a way that it allows workers to adapt to change by providing opportunities to explore and experiment with different professional identities, for instance. Finally, besides looking at how to adapt work roles to technology, organisations should also consider the proactive design of technological change in a human-centred way that maximises positive outcomes for workers (Parker & Grote, 2020).

DISCUSSION QUESTIONS

1. What parallels do you see when comparing Lillian Gilbreth's early ideas on scientific management with the motivational theories on work design that were developed afterwards?

2. Scientific management has been criticised for turning people into robots by standardising their work. Lillian did not agree with these criticisms but, on the contrary, saw some opportunities for workers arising from the standardisation of work. What positive worker attitudes and behaviours were likely to result from standardisation according to Lillian? What principles need to be met for these outcomes to occur?

3. To what extent is the job of Clarence, the museum guard, described in the section on Implications for Practitioners an example of poor work design? Which work characteristics do you see as problematic? Give an example of how Clarence could redesign his job in a bottom-up way?

FURTHER READINGS

Gilbreth, L. M. (1914). *The Psychology of Management*. Sturgis & Walton.

This is the main publication of Lillian Gilbreth's doctoral thesis, where she explains how psychology is imperative to make progress in the field of management. In the book, Lillian offers a comprehensive overview of the key principles of scientific management while integrating key insights from psychology.

Gilbreth, F. B. & Gilbreth, L. M. (1916). *Fatigue Study. The Elimination of Humanity's Greatest Unnecessary Waste*. Sturgis & Walton.

In this book, Frank and Lillian Gilbreth describe fatigue study, which combines time and motion studies to eliminate unnecessary fatigue and standardise working methods. It provides an interesting illustration of how both perspectives focusing on efficiency and on workers' experience were in fact complementary.

Hackman, J. R. & Oldham, G. R. (1976). Motivation through the design of work: Test of a theory. *Organizational Behavior and Human Performance*, 16(2), 250–79.

Hackman and Oldham describe the theory behind the Job Characteristic Model as well as the empirical evidence provided by a large-scale study that they conducted at the time.

Parker, S. K. (2014). Beyond motivation: Job and work design for development, health, ambidexterity, and more. *Annual Review of Psychology*, 65: 661–91.

Parker reviews the literature on motivational work design and discusses the importance of more recent theoretical developments.

Parker, S. & Grote, G. (2020). Automation, algorithms, and beyond: Why work design matters more than ever in a digital world. *Applied Psychology: An International Review*, Advance online publication. doi: https://doi.org/10.1111/apps.12241

Parker and Grote outline that work design plays a central role in understanding the effects of technology, including how work design and technology shape and are shaped by each other.

REFERENCES

Axtell, C. M. & Parker, S. K. (2003). Promoting role breadth self-efficacy through involvement, work redesign and training. *Human Relations*, 56(1), 113–31.

Barley, S. R. (1986). Technology as an occasion for structuring: Evidence from observations of CT scanners and the social order of radiology departments. *Administrative Science Quarterly*, 31(1), 78–108.

Bruning, P. F. & Campion, M. A. (2018). A role-resource approach-avoidance model of job crafting: A multimethod integration and extension of job crafting theory. *Academy of Management Journal*, 61(2), 499–522.

Campion, M. A., Mumford, T. V., Morgeson, F. P. & Nahrgang, J. D. (2005). Work redesign: Eight obstacles and opportunities. *Human Resource Management*, 44(4), 367–90.

Christensen, C. M. & van Bever, D. C. (2014). The capitalist's dilemma. *Harvard Business Review*. Retrieved 29 March 2021 from https://hbr.org/2014/06/the-capitalists-dilemma

Clegg, C. & Shepherd, C. (2007). The biggest computer program in the world … ever!': Time for a change in mindset? *Journal of Information Technology*, 22(3), 212–21.

Cohen, L. E. (2013). Assembling jobs: A model of how tasks are bundled into and across jobs. *Organization Science*, 24(2), 432–54.

Crawford, M. B. (2009). *Shop Class as Soulcraft: An Inquiry into the Value of Work*. Penguin.

Cummings, T. G. (1978). Self-regulating work groups: A socio-technical synthesis. *Academy of Management Review*, 3, 625–34.

Davis, G. F. (2010). Job design meets organizational sociology. *Journal of Organizational Behavior*, 31(2/3), 302–8.

Davis, L. E. (1966). The design of jobs. *Industrial Relations*, 6, 21–45. http://dx.doi.org/10.1111/j.1468-232X.1966.tb00833.x

De Boeck, G., Dries, N., & Tierens, H. (2019). The experience of untapped potential: Towards a subjective temporal understanding of work meaningfulness. Journal of Management Studies, 56(3), 529–557.

Demerouti, E., Bakker, A. B., Nachreiner, F. & Schaufeli, W. B. (2001). The job demands-resources model of burnout. *Journal of Applied Psychology*, 86(3), 499.

Elsbach, K. D. & Flynn, F. J. (2013). Creative collaboration and the self-concept: A study of toy designers. *Journal of Management Studies*, 50(4), 515–44.

Emery, F. E. & Trist, E. L. (1969). Socio-technical systems. In F. E. Emery (ed.), *Systems Thinking*. Penguin.

Eriksson-Zetterquist, U., Lindberg, K. & Styhre, A. (2009). When the good times are over: Professionals encountering new technology. *Human Relations*, 62(8), 1145–70.

Frey, C. B., & Osborne, M. A. (2017). The future of employment: How susceptible are jobs to computerisation?. Technological forecasting and social change, 114, 254–280.

Fried, Y. & Ferris, G. R. (1987). The validity of the job characteristics model: A review and meta-analysis. *Personnel Psychology*, 40(2), 287–322.

Gilbreth, F. B. (1911). *Motion Study: A Method for Increasing the Efficiency of the Workman*. Sturgis & Walton.

Gilbreth, F. B. & Gilbreth, L. M. (1916). *Fatigue Study. The Elimination of Humanity's Greatest Unnecessary Waste*. Sturgis & Walton.

Gilbreth, L. M. (1914). *The Psychology of Management*. Sturgis & Walton.

Goos, M., Manning, A. & Salomons, A. (2014). Explaining job polarization: Routine-biased technological change and offshoring. *American Economic Review*, 104(8), 2509–26.

Graeber, D. (2018). *Bullshit Jobs*. Simon & Schuster.

Grant, A. M. (2007). Relational job design and the motivation to make a prosocial difference. *Academy of Management Review*, 32(2), 393–417.

Grant, A. M. & Parker, S. K. (2009). 7 redesigning work design theories: The rise of relational and proactive perspectives. *Academy of Management Annals*, 3(1), 317–75.

Greenwood, B. N., Agarwal, R., Agarwal, R. & Gopal, A. (2019). The role of individual and organizational expertise in the adoption of new practices. *Organization Science*, 30(1), 191–213.

Hackman, J. R. & Oldham, G. R. (1975). Development of the job diagnostic survey. *Journal of Applied Psychology*, 60(2), 159–70.

Hackman, J. R. & Oldham, G. R. (1976). Motivation through the design of work: Test of a theory. *Organizational Behavior and Human Performance*, 16(2), 250–79.

Hackman, J. R. & Oldham, G. R. (1980). *Work Redesign*. Addison-Wesley.

Herzberg. F. (1966). *Work and the Nature of Man*. World.

Humphrey, S. E., Nahrgang, J. D. & Morgeson, F. P. (2007). Integrating motivational, social, and contextual work design features: A meta-analytic summary and theoretical extension of the work design literature. *Journal of Applied Psychology*, 92(5), 1332–56.

Idaszak, J. R. & Drasgow, F. (1987). A revision of the Job Diagnostic Survey: Elimination of a measurement artifact. *Journal of Applied Psychology*, 72(1), 69–74.

Johns, G., Jia, L. X. & Yongqing, F. (1992). Mediating and moderating effects in job design. *Journal of Management*, 18(4), 657–76.

Kalleberg, A. L. (2008). The mismatched worker: When people don't fit their jobs. *Academy of Management Perspectives*, 22(1), 24–40.

Karasek, R. A. Jr (1979). Job demands, job decision latitude, and mental strain: Implications for job redesign. *Administrative Science Quarterly*, 24, 285–308.

Kelly, R. M. & Kelly, V. P. (1990). Lillian Moller Gilbreth. In A. N. O'Connell & N. Felipe Russo (eds), *Women in Psychology: A Bio-Bibliographic Sourcebook*. New York: Greenwood Press, pp. 117–24.

Kilduff, M. & Brass, D. J. (2010). Job design: A social network perspective. *Journal of Organizational Behavior*, 31, 309–318. doi: 10.1002/job.609.

Koppes, L. L. (1997). American female pioneers of industrial and organizational psychology during the early years. *Journal of Applied Psychology*, 82(4), 500–15.

Krenn, M. (2011). From scientific management to homemaking: Lillian M. Gilbreth's contributions to the development of management thought. *Management & Organizational History*, 6(2), 145–61.

Leach, D. J., Wall, T. D. & Jackson, P. R. (2003). The effect of empowerment on job knowledge: An empirical test involving operators of complex technology. *Journal of Occupational and Organizational Psychology*, 76(1), 27–52.

Lichtenthaler, P. W. & Fischbach, A. (2016). A meta-analysis on promotion- and prevention-focused job crafting. *European Journal of Work and Organizational Psychology*, 28(1), 30–50.

Miller, T. R. & Lemons, M. A. (1998). Breaking the glass ceiling: Lessons from a management pioneer. SAM *Advanced Management Journal*, 63, 4–9.

Miner, J. B. (1984). The validity and usefulness of theories in an emerging organizational science. *Academy of Management Review*, 9(2), 296–306.

Morgeson, F. P. & Humphrey, S. E. (2006). The Work Design Questionnaire (WDQ): Developing and validating a comprehensive measure for assessing job design and the nature of work. *Journal of Applied Psychology*, 91(6), 1321.

Morgeson, F. P. & Humphrey, S. E. (2008). Job and team design: Toward a more integrative conceptualization of work design. *Research in Personnel and Human Resource Management*, 27, 39–91.

Morgeson, F. P., Dierdorff, E. C. & Hmurovic, J. L. (2010). Work design in situ: Understanding the role of occupational and organizational context. *Journal of Organizational Behavior*, 31(2/3), 351–60.

Oldham, G. R. & Hackman, J. R. (2005). Job characteristics theory: Richard Hackman, Edward Lawler, and Greg Oldham. In J. Miner (ed.), *Organizational Behavior 1: Essential Theories of Motivation and Leadership*. Routledge, pp. 75–93.

Oldham, G. R. & Hackman, J. R. (2010). Not what it was and not what it will be: The future of job design research. *Journal of Organizational Behavior*, 31(2–3), 463–79.

Parent-Rocheleau, X. & Parker, S. K. (2021). Algorithms as work designers: How algorithmic management influences the design of jobs. *Human Resource Management Review*, 100838.

Parker, S. K. (1998). Enhancing role breadth self-efficacy: The roles of job enrichment and other organizational interventions. *Journal of Applied Psychology*, 83(6), 835.

Parker, S. K. (2014). Beyond motivation: Job and work design for development, health, ambidexterity, and more. *Annual Review of Psychology*, 65, 661–91.

Parker, S. K. & Grote, G. (2020). Automation, algorithms, and beyond: Why work design matters more than ever in a digital world. *Applied Psychology: An International Review*. Advance online publication, 020, 0 (0), 1–45. doi: https://doi.org/10.1111/apps.12241

Parker, S. K., Andrei, D. M. & Van den Broeck, A. (2019). Poor work design begets poor work design: Capacity and willingness antecedents of individual work design behavior. *Journal of Applied Psychology*, 104(7), 907.

Parker, S. K., Morgeson, F. P. & Johns, G. (2017a). One hundred years of work design research: Looking back and looking forward. *Journal of Applied Psychology*, 102(3), 403–20.

Parker, S. K., Van den Broeck, A. & Holman, D. (2017b). Work design influences: A synthesis of multilevel factors that affect the design of jobs. *Academy of Management Annals*, 11(1), 267–308.

Parker, S. K., Wall, T. D. & Cordery, J. L. (2001). Future work design research and practice: Towards an elaborated model of work design. *Journal of Occupational and Organizational Psychology*, 74(4), 413–40.

Raja, U. & Johns, G. (2010). The joint effects of personality and job scope on in-role performance, citizenship behaviors, and creativity. *Human Relations*, 63(7), 981–1005.

Rudolph, C. W., Katz, I. M., Lavigne, K. N. & Zacher, H. (2017). Job crafting: A meta-analysis of relationships with individual differences, job characteristics, and work outcomes. *Journal of Vocational Behavior*, 102, 112–38.

Salancik, G. R. & Pfeffer, J. (1978). A social information processing approach to job attitudes and task design. *Administrative Science Quarterly*, 23, 224–53.

Sixth European Working Conditions Survey (2016). Retrieved from https://www.eurofound.europa.eu/publications/report/2016/working-conditions/sixth-european-working-conditions-survey-overview-report

Sullivan, S. E. (1995). Management's unsung theorist: An examination of the works of Lillian M. Gilbreth. *Biography*, 18(1), 31–41.

Taber, T. D. & Taylor, E. (1990). A review and evaluation of the psychometric properties of the Job Diagnostic Survey. *Personnel Psychology*, 43(3), 467–500.

Taylor, F. (1911). *Principles of Scientific Management*. Harper & Brothers.

Tiegs, R. B., Tetrick, L. E. & Fried, Y. (1992). Growth need strength and context satisfactions as moderators of the relations of the job characteristics model. *Journal of Management*, 18(3), 575–93.

Tims, M., Bakker, A. B. & Derks, D. (2012). Development and validation of the job crafting scale. *Journal of Vocational Behavior*, 80(1), 173–86.

Trist, E. & Emery, F. (2006). Socio-technical systems theory. In J. Miner (ed.), *Organizational Behavior 2: Essential Theories of Process and Structure*. Routledge, pp. 169–94.

Trist, E. L. & Bamforth, K. W. (1951). Some social and psychological consequences of the longwall method of coal-getting: An examination of the psychological situation and defences of a work group in relation to the social structure and technological content of the work system. *Human Relations*, 4(1), 3–38.

Vroom, V. H. (1964). *Work and Motivation*. Wiley.

Wegman, L. A., Hoffman, B. J., Carter, N. T., Twenge, J. M. & Guenole, N. (2018). Placing job characteristics in context: Cross-temporal meta-analysis of changes in job characteristics since 1975. *Journal of Management*, 44(1), 352–86.

Wrzesniewski, A. & Dutton, J. E. (2001). Crafting a job: Revisioning employees as active crafters of their work. *Academy of Management Review*, 26(2), 179–201.

Yost, E. (1949). *Frank and Lillian Gilbreth: Partners for Life*. Rutgers University Press.

Zhang, F. & Parker, S. K. (2019). Reorienting job crafting research: A hierarchical structure of job crafting concepts and integrative review. *Journal of Organizational Behavior*, 40(2), 126–46.

2

Engaging with Groups at Work: Revisiting Mayo's Hawthorne Experiments

S. Alexander Haslam &
Niklas K. Steffens

BACKGROUND

In August 1922 Elton Mayo, a 42-year-old Australian, left his position as a Professor of Philosophy and Psychology at the University of Queensland to continue his career in the United States – going on to become Professor of Industrial Psychology at Harvard Business School (Cullen, 1993; Smith, 1998). Mayo had trained as a psychotherapist and had a particular interest in the psychotherapeutic treatment of shell-shocked First World War veterans. However, partly as a result of his friendship with the social anthropologist Bronislaw Malinowski and his work as an activist for worker education, as his career progressed, he became increasingly interested in the psychology of organisations. When he left Australia he had no position to go to – just several letters of introduction and the proofs of five papers on industrial peace (Smith, 1998). However, after securing the support of some key donors for his research (notably the Rockefeller Foundation), in 1926 he was able to secure a position at Harvard where he continued to work until his retirement in 1947 (Bourke, 1982).

In large part, Mayo's interest in organisations was underpinned by his fascination with the psychology of *cooperation*. Reflecting on this at the time of his retirement, he observed:

> The inability of functional groups to cooperate and a consequent mutual hostility has been the great destroyer of civilizations ... A society must secure the effective participation and cooperation of everyone in addition to the contrivance of technical advance. Effective cooperation then, is the problem we face in the middle of the twentieth century. There is no 'ism' that will help us to a solution; we must be content to return to patient, pedestrian work at the wholly neglected problem of spontaneous participation ... In these matters our political leaders, or scientific leaders have failed us; we must try again. (Mayo, 1945, pp. xiii–xvi)

In the political realm, this sense of failure had been engendered by totalitarian regimes and the destructive power that had given rise to the horrors of the Holocaust and the atomic bomb. Yet Mayo was equally disturbed by the failure of organisational theorists and practitioners to come up with satisfactory analyses of – and solutions to – the challenges of achieving cooperation in the workplace. 'We have learned how to destroy scores of thousands of human beings in a moment of time', he wrote, yet 'we do not know how to set about the task of inducing various groups and nations to collaborate in the tasks of civilization' (Mayo, 1945, p. xvi).

Mayo's frustrations were rooted in his sense that the theories and approaches that were widely used to understand and tackle the key challenges of organisational life were peculiarly ill-suited to the task on both empirical and philosophical grounds (which we discuss further below). In particular, he was sceptical of the utility of both the economic approach espoused by Frederick Taylor (1911) in *Principles of Scientific Management* and the individual difference approach championed by Hugo Münsterberg (1913) in *Psychology and Industrial Efficiency*. Despite their enormous popularity and influence, both these approaches placed an emphasis on the individual *as individual* as both the proper unit of psychological enquiry and the key focus for efforts to achieve organisational efficiency and improvement. As with all other organisational problems, then, these approaches suggested that individual and ultimately collective outcomes were best achieved either by identifying the right person for a job (i.e. someone who was by nature able to do the task at hand) and/or by fashioning the organisational environment to suit an individual's circumstances and potential (i.e. through the application of principles of scientific management).

For Mayo, the key limitation of these approaches was that they were underpinned by an individualistic metatheory which failed to recognise the power of *social groups* – both in the workplace and beyond – to structure organisational behaviour and organisational life. These were sensibilities that he had developed through his clinical work with trauma sufferers (where groups proved central to rehabilitation) and anthropological deliberations with Malinowski which centred on the importance of ethnography and participant observation for scientific understanding (Bourke, 1982; Smith, 1998). Before leaving for America, he had thus concluded that 'the way in which each of us sees the world is determined in the main by the occupational group which claims us as a member' (Mayo, 1919, p. 37) and that 'in sport, in war, and in work it is [group] morale, the mental factor, which in the last resort determines every issue' (Mayo, 1922, p. 16).

Yet it was the research that he and his colleagues conducted at the Hawthorne Works of the Western Electric Company in Chicago (which later became absorbed by AT&T) between 1927 and 1932 that really brought home to Mayo the importance of studying and organising work in ways that do justice to the importance of group dynamics for organisational and societal functioning (see Figure 2.1). The research he oversaw there started off looking at just five workers but went on to involve about 20,000 and remains one of the most extensive and important pieces of research ever conducted in psychology and in the social sciences more generally.

Figure 2.1   a (left) The Hawthorne Works of the Western Electric Company in Chicago.

Note: The aerial view on the left gives a sense of the appearance of the Hawthorne factory complex in 1925; the image on the right (Figure 2.1b by Gary Eckstein) is all that remains of it today. The works were closed down in 1983 but at their peak employed around 45,000 people manufacturing a range of consumer goods (notably telephone equipment and domestic appliances).

DETAILED DESCRIPTION

THE HAWTHORNE EXPERIMENTS

PRELIMINARY STUDIES: AN ABUNDANCE OF CONFUSION

Mayo and his colleagues conducted their studies at the Hawthorne works on the back of two other significant pieces of research that had previously been carried out at the site. The first of these took place between November 1924 and October 1927 and involved attempts by the management to deal with problems of production and worker dissatisfaction. They had done this by calling in a team of researchers trained in the principles of scientific management (Snow, 1927; for discussions see Levitt & List, 2011; Roethlisberger & Dickson, 1939, pp.14–19). These research attempts had aimed to manipulate the working environment and identify the single set of conditions that, in line with Taylor's (1911) notion of 'the one best way', would maximise efficiency. However, they proved to be a spectacular failure.

In particular, experiments involving changes to the level of illumination in the areas where women worked assembling telephone components showed that lighting had no predictable or reliable impact on their work (Snow, 1927). When workers were divided into two groups and only one group was exposed to increasing levels of illumination, the performance of both groups increased (Experiments 1 and 2). Moreover, when one group's lighting was dramatically reduced both groups also maintained a high level of performance (Experiment 3). The workers also commented and reacted favourably when the experimenters pretended to change the light bulbs to give a higher level of illumination, but in fact did not change them at all. Improved performance was even sustained in a final study in which two women were exposed to a level of illumination 'approximately equal to that on an ordinary moonlight night' (Roethlisberger & Dickson, 1939, p. 17).

Totally at odds with the logic of Taylorism and its focus on creating the right structural work conditions for individual workers, the only conclusion to be drawn from what Mayo referred to as 'the illumination fiasco' was that 'somehow or other that complex of mutually dependent factors, the human organism, shifted its equilibrium and unintentionally defeated the purpose of the experiment' (Mayo, 1933, pp. 54, 62). Indeed, such was the importance of the pattern of results observed in these studies that the 'Hawthorne effect' has become a widely recognised phenomenon in psychological research. Nevertheless, researchers have been unclear about what exactly this effect relates to and how it should be defined and understood. For example, Adair (1984, p. 334) sees it as referring to the idea that 'measurements of behavior in a controlled study [are] altered by subjects' knowledge that they were in an experiment' (Adair, 1984, p. 334) while Chiesa & Hobbs (2008, p. 73) see the research as shedding light on 'the possibility that a variable of which the experimenter is unaware may be playing an active role' (see also Olson et al., 2004; Haslam & McGarty, 2018).[1]

In an interesting twist to this story, in recent years researchers have also argued that the findings of the initial Hawthorne experiments were rather less clear than Mayo and his colleagues suggested. In particular, Levitt & List (2011) uncovered the original data from these studies and, on the basis of forensic statistical analysis, concluded that 'existing descriptions of [these] supposedly remarkable data patterns prove to be entirely fictional' (p. 224). In large part, this was because the design of the studies was far from perfect and the procedure was imprecise. At the same time, though, Levitt & List (2011) note that, for all their imperfections, the studies still provide some reasonable (but not entirely satisfactory) evidence that workers 'respond positively to experimentation' (p. 237).

This new analysis is certainly problematic for traditional accounts of the Hawthorne effect (e.g. as found in methodology textbooks). Nevertheless, a systematic review of Hawthorne effects in another field (health) has observed that although research participation effects in interventions (e.g. randomised control trials) are small in magnitude and vary across studies, they are still reliably present (McCambridge et al., 2014).

---

[1]When researchers discuss the Hawthorne effect, they often indicate that this was first observed in the influential programme of research by Mayo and colleagues. In fact, though, as we can see here, Mayo's team were brought into the Hawthorne works to resolve the conundrum of the Hawthorne effect that earlier studies had (ostensibly) brought to light (Snow, 1927). With this in mind, it is important to distinguish between the earlier and later studies at the Hawthorne Plant at the Western Electric Company.

It is important to note too that Mayo's interest in the goings on at the Hawthorne works was more than just methodological. So rather than wanting to know how observations are influenced by 'research participation' effects, he was interested in broader questions about productivity. These were raised not just by these pre-liminary studies in the Hawthorne complex but also by research that he himself was conducting at around the same time in a textile mill in Philadelphia where a group of mule spinners was evincing very low productivity and extraordinarily high levels of turnover relative to workers in other departments at the mill (Mayo, 1924). Importantly, this was occurring despite the company having put in place a very attractive incentive system that rewarded workers for reaching particular productivity targets.

As a first intervention to address these problems, Mayo introduced a series of rest periods throughout the day in an attempt to understand how people deal with monotonous tasks and counteract fatigue. This was a strategy Taylor had recom-mended and previously perfected with pig iron handlers at the Bethlehem Steel Works. To look at the effects of this innovation, the spinners were divided into two groups. The smaller of these groups received the new breaks, while the larger (con-trol) group carried on as normal. The effect of the change was felt immediately. In particular, levels of satisfaction and production rose dramatically in the experi-mental group, to the point that its members now reached production targets and obtained bonuses for the first time ever, while turnover reduced from 250 per cent to 0 per cent. However, Mayo quickly realised that these effects could not simply be the result of a reduction in fatigue. This point was confirmed by the fact that a very similar pattern of improvement was apparent in the control group. This group had experienced no obvious change in their conditions, yet they too were now happier and more productive. What was going on?

Mayo realised that the seemingly objective economic analysis of the type put forward by Taylor was not up to the task of answering this question satisfactorily. He also suspected (though he later noted that this was not clear at the time) that a clue to the effects observed in the mule spinning department lay in some seemingly trivial features of the investigation. In particular, he noted that the only time pro-duction declined during the study was when a supervisor intervened to eliminate the rest breaks to cope with an influx of orders. Even when rest breaks were rein-troduced, the workers were still disenchanted and distrustful and they remained so until the president of the company intervened to take the side of the workers and fire the supervisor. By doing this, and in the process of talking and listening to the workers to discover their thoughts about the study, Mayo (1945) conjectured that the major contribution of the president lay in the fact that he had inadvert-ently 'transformed a horde of "solitaires" into a social group' (p. 67). This, then, was the insight that laid the foundation for the Hawthorne studies proper.

THE STUDIES PROPER: CLARITY FROM CONFUSION

The opportunity to examine this hypothesis in more detail came when Mayo and his colleagues – notably Fritz Roethlisberger from Harvard University and William

John Dickson from the Western Electric Company (who went on to author the definitive technical account of the research) (Roethlisberger & Dickson, 1939) – commenced a second series of studies at the Hawthorne works. The company's management encouraged the research because they were keen to know what psychological and environmental factors had been responsible for the marked improvements in performance observed in the initial illumination studies so that these principles could be used to inform changes in the plant as a whole.

As an initial focus for the research, the company isolated a group of five women (supervised by one operator) from the general workforce and placed them in a special room where they worked assembling 35-piece relays and could be observed more closely. The experimenters then set about systematically manipulating various features of the women's working conditions by introducing structured changes that lasted up to 31 weeks, including the number and duration of rest periods, the pay structure, the provision of refreshments and the length of working days and weeks. The researchers also fastidiously examined all aspects of the women's work and their reaction to it by monitoring the number of relays they assembled and their quality, as well as the women's health, details of their personal history, and any comments they made in relation to the study and its findings.

As discussed by Mayo (1945), the impact of the changes made during the first phase of research on the workers and their work was that 'slowly at first, but later with increasing certainty, the output record mounted' (p. 71). Later phases of the study that reproduced conditions in earlier periods also showed marked improvement. So, for example, each woman's average weekly output was fewer than 2,500 relays in the third period of investigation in mid-1927, but under exactly the same conditions in the twelfth period in late 1928 it was more than 2,900. Once workers had entered the test room, absences also fell from an average of 15.2 per person per year to just 3.5. Moreover, as the study continued the women in the room reported less fatigue, greater contentment and more convivial relations with their fellow workers both inside and outside the relay assembly room. The nature of these changes is summarised by Roethlisberger & Dickson (1939) in the observation that:

> No longer were the girls [sic] isolated individuals, working together only in the sense of an actual physical proximity. They had become participating members of a working group with all the psychological and social implications peculiar to such a group. In Period X a growing amount of social activity developed among the test room girls outside of the plant. The conversation in the test room became more socialized. In Period XIII the girls began to help one another out for the common good of the group. They became bound to one another by common sentiments and feelings of loyalty. (p. 86)

To account for these findings, the researchers tested and systematically eliminated a number of potential hypotheses (Roethlisberger & Dickson, 1939, pp. 90–160). Importantly, they were able to rule out the possibility that the results derived from factors that an economic approach would suggest were important – namely (a) an improvement to material conditions, (b) relief from fatigue or monotony or (c) economic incentive. Indeed, the only hypothesis that fitted with the data suggested that experimental interventions had some social impact in communicating information about a *changing state of relations* between the management and the workers. Moreover, it appeared not to be the *content* of change that mattered so much as the fact that the *process of change itself* redefined managers and workers so that they saw themselves as collaborative participants in a common venture. Where previously life in the factory had been characterised by a relationship of managers *over* workers, now those same managers were seen to be *with* workers. On the basis of these findings, as one of the company researchers concluded, it became apparent that 'we could more logically attribute the increase in efficiency to a betterment of morale than to any of the ... alterations made in the course of the experiment' (Putnam, 1929, cited in Mayo, 1933, p. 77).

To see whether this was the case, in a second phase of investigation, the researchers conducted an extensive series of open-ended interviews (described in Mayo, 1933). The content of these supported the researchers' hypotheses and pointed to a number of factors that appeared to have contributed to the earlier improvements. These included: (a) the introduction of a less formal and impersonal supervisory style; (b) an increased sense of control over work structures on the part of workers; (c) an increased feeling that the management was actually interested in, and had some concern for, their welfare; and (d) an emerging belief that management and workers were part of a team that was pulling together. The workers also commented favourably on the fact that, as a result of the experimental changes, they (e) took home more money and (f) worked shorter hours, but these factors appeared to have secondary importance. So, where previously workers had felt that managers were only concerned with their production, they now believed (mistakenly in some instances) that they were taking their feelings seriously and attending to their grievances. They felt that what they did mattered and, hence, were actively *self-involved* in their work.

Moreover, it was clear that the feeling of being in a team exerted a powerful influence on the workers' actual behaviour. In particular, this meant that where previously their contributions had been more or less idiosyncratic, they now became highly *uniform*. This uniformity was both internally and externally imposed, so that the workers both wanted to conform to the team's expectations and norms (e.g. to produce a certain number of relays – no more, no less) and also encouraged and exerted pressure on each other to do so (in ways that anticipated later work on the 'dark side' of organisational life, e.g. Roter, 2018). In a later phase of investigation carried out with male workers in a different area of the Hawthorne works (the Bank Wiring Observation Room) this was sometimes observed to take the form of subjecting those who over- or under-performed to sarcasm or ridicule, as the following exchange illustrates:

W4: (To W6) How many are you going to turn in?

W6: I've got to turn in 6,800.

W4: What's the matter – are you crazy? You work all week and turn in 6,800 for a full day, and now you're away an hour and a quarter and you turn in more than you do the other days.

W6: I don't care. I'm going to finish these sets tomorrow.

W4: You're screwy.

W6: All right, I'll turn in 6,400. (Roethlisberger & Dickson, 1939, p. 420)

Occasionally, though, workers also resorted to regulating output physically. This was something they typically did by hitting those they perceived to be out of line as hard as possible on the upper arm – a practice known as 'binging':

W8: (To W6) Why don't you quit work? Let's see, this is your thirty-fifth row today. What are you going to do with them all? ...

W6: Don't worry about that. I'll take care of it. You're getting paid by the sets I turn out. That's all you should worry about.

W8: If you don't quit work I'll bing you.

W8 struck W6 and finally chased him round the room. (Roethlisberger & Dickson, 1939, p. 422)

Mayo observed too that the groups with the best record of attendance were the ones where the foreman was concerned not only with the technical aspects of the job but also with handling human relationships. One concrete consequence of this was that workers in the company collectively arranged which day of the week they would each take off. Importantly, this meant that if a worker broke with this arrangement and thereby inconvenienced his colleagues, they would put pressure on him of a form that 'management would never dare to exercise' (Mayo, 1945, p. 90; see also Parker, 1993, p. 267). On this basis Mayo argued that it was not individual-based incentives but mechanisms that created *group solidarity and group norms* that were critical to bringing about sustained production.

The Hawthorne programme of research served to make two further points clear for Mayo. The first was that *work groups play a key role in shaping the behaviour of individuals.* As he noted:

The belief that the behaviour of an individual within the factory can be predicted before employment on the basis of a laborious and minute examination of his technical and other capacities is mainly, if not wholly, mistaken ... The usual situation is that after employment his relation to 'the team' will go far to determine the use he makes of such capacities as he has developed. (1945, p. 111)

This conclusion is clearly at odds with the logic of both the economic and individual difference paradigms that place an emphasis on careful analysis of the individual in isolation, and urge employment selection on that basis (e.g. after Münsterberg, 1913). For Mayo, then, it was the fact that organisational life was associated with a distinct way of engaging in and experiencing work such that *individual differences were transformed into group similarities* that was its defining feature. Moreover, he argued that it was this transformative feature that researchers and practitioners most needed to come to terms with.

Building on this insight, the second more general point that Mayo abstracted from his and his colleagues' research was that prevailing economic and organisational theory had contrived to completely misrepresent the nature of society. As he saw it, the dominant view (following Hobbes, Rousseau, and others) was built on three key assumptions – 'the rabble hypothesis' as he termed it (Mayo, 1945, p. 47). This suggests (a) that society is comprised of a horde of disorganised individuals, (b) that individuals act purely to further their own personal interests, and (c) that individuals act logically to service those interests. Mayo rejected this hypothesis and instead argued that *organised behaviour shaped by group membership and group interests was the rule, not the exception*. Rather than individuals tending naturally to act in terms of their personal self-interest, this, he argued, was something that they did only when social association failed them. As he stridently put it:

> The economists' presupposition of individual self-preservation ... is not characteristic of the industrial facts as ordinarily encountered. The desire to stand well with one's fellows, the so-called human instinct of association easily outweighs the merely individual interest and the logical reasoning upon which so many spurious principles of management are based. (Mayo, 1945, pp. 42–3)

BEYOND THE HAWTHORNE EXPERIMENTS: CONTROVERSY AND IMPACT

EMPIRICAL

At an empirical level, the key achievement of the Hawthorne studies was to challenge the hegemonic status that Taylor's scientific management approach had assumed in the organisational field in the early part of the twentieth century. Prior to this point Taylor's approach had had many detractors, but their criticisms had been largely theoretical and ideological, and lacked empirical teeth. For example, there was little empirical evidence to back up Farquhar (1924) when he mused:

> I wonder whether with our admirably proper insistence on considering each individual as an individual we have not obscured the possibility of making that individual and his fellows more productive and more contented through recognizing the psychological benefits to be gained through group dealings? (p. 48)

By providing evidence to substantiate such musings, and thereby turning the logic of scientific management on its head, the Hawthorne studies provided Taylor's critics with strong empirical ammunition. The fact that the studies had been conducted in a prestigious organisation and had the backing of both management and the august institution of Harvard gave their findings – and Mayo's analysis – yet further weight. Indeed, on the back of the studies, Mayo was much in demand as a public speaker, and by all accounts his lectures on the findings and messages of the studies were well received in all quarters (Smith, 1998).

At the same time, though, the popularity of Taylorism meant that the Hawthorne studies – and the researcher who led them – did not escape criticism. Early rumblings focused on the assertion that Mayo himself rarely visited the Hawthorne plant, and left most of the day-to-day running of his research to his trusted team of researchers (led by Roethlisberger & Dickson) (Smith, 1998). Others also questioned Mayo's partiality and found fault in the inherent paternalism of his perspective on the workforce, as well as in the cosy – even fawning – relationship he had with management (Baritz, 1960; Bell, 1956; Hassard, 2012) (for a review see Muldoon, 2017). Still others pointed to limitations in the design of the studies – notably the fact that (of necessity) neither the researchers nor the participants were blinded to the experimental treatment they received. And, as we have seen, these criticisms culminated in more thoroughgoing statistical critique of the conclusions drawn from the Hawthorne studies and, in particular, of the inferences drawn from the first phase of research in which the Hawthorne effect was first revealed (Levitt & List, 2011).

There is no doubt that much of this criticism is warranted. Certainly, by the scientific standards of today, the Hawthorne studies had manifold shortcomings. Nevertheless, in terms of their empirical depth and scale, the studies are unrivalled. Moreover, at a conceptual level, the core observations that Mayo and his team reported have proved to be very robust and they align well with a broad and growing contemporary literature that confirms his core insights about the importance of meaningful group memberships for organisational productivity and well-being (e.g. Lee et al., 2015; Steffens et al., 2017; for reviews see Ellemers et al., 2004; Haslam, 2004; van Dick, 2004).

THEORETICAL

So, although there are plenty of researchers today who bemoan the dry empiricism and lack of ethnographic texture in contemporary social and organisational psychological research (where one could be forgiven for forgetting that participants are real people; Bayer & Shotter, 1998; Billig, 2011), it is certainly the case that Mayo's methods look dated in the light of contemporary mores. Yet while he was of his time empirically, he was ahead of it (meta)theoretically. In particular, this was because, as well as anticipating disenchantment with individualism (e.g. of the form espoused by Taylor and Münsterberg), Mayo also anticipated a number of key developments in the field, two of which are particularly significant.

First, his work anticipated developments in the emerging human relations tradition. Recognising that the 'human' is routinely missing from dominant models of motivation and productivity, this placed an emphasis on people's experiences and their need for social connection in the workplace and beyond (e.g. McGregor, 1960). In particular, these were later to become major themes in a range of *needs theories* (e.g. *existence-relatedness-growth theory* (Aldferer, 1972); *self-determination theory* (Deci & Ryan, 1985)). In the process of challenging economic theories of organisational behaviour (after Taylor, 1911), all of these pick up on Mayo's observation that (a) connection to others provides a basis for people to find meaning and purpose in work; and (b) in being important for a person's sense of self, these connections are a major source of motivation, drive and well-being.

Relatedly, second, Mayo's work also anticipated later forms of *interaction-ism* which recognised the capacity for group life to (re)structure psychology and, through this, behaviour (Turner & Oakes, 1986). In particular, many of the quotes that we have culled from Mayo's writings are resonant of points subsequently made by social psychologists in the *social identity* tradition (after Tajfel & Turner, 1979; Turner et al., 1987). Recognising, like Mayo, that groups transform rather than merely aggregate individual dispositions, researchers in this tradition argue not simply that groups are important for organisational functioning, but also that meaningful group memberships are the basic building block of organisation life because they make organisation – and the cooperation that underpins it – *possible* (Haslam et al., 2003).

PROFESSIONAL

Although Mayo's core contributions to organisational psychology were primarily empirical and theoretical, it would be remiss not to note too that he had a trans-formative impact on the professions of organisational and management science. This was seen most clearly in the transformation that Harvard Business School underwent during his 21-year tenure there. As Smith (1998) notes, when Mayo arrived, the School was a fringe concern struggling to find favour either with busi-ness or with academia. However, Mayo's stewardship, and his passion for reaching out beyond his comfort zone to demonstrate the practical utility of organisational science, built a range of bridges that helped to establish the reputation that both the institution and the profession enjoy today.

This meant that when a range of luminaries from the School's past gathered in 1982 to celebrate its 75th anniversary, much was made of Mayo's 'mystique' and of the 'legend' of the Hawthorne studies – noting that they had played a foundational role in establishing an identity not just for Mayo, but also for his institution and his profession (Smith, 1998, p. 243). To be sure, these identities are a focus for a great deal of ongoing controversy, but down the years most commentators have conceded that organisational science is substantially richer and more mature as a result of Mayo's immense contribution to the field (e.g. Jung & Lee, 2015; Shepard, 1971; Sonnenfeld, 1985).

CONCLUSION

The Hawthorne studies, like the work of Elton Mayo more generally, did much to put the human at the heart of organisational psychology (O'Connor, 1999). In particular, it did this by challenging the idea that organisational life is largely the product of individuals acting in terms of their personal self-interests and instead championing the view that it is in their *group-based associations* that people dis-cover meaning, purpose and drive – both in the workplace and beyond.

This profoundly social view of human enterprise speaks to a wealth of empirical data of the form that the Hawthorne studies first highlighted. The human relations movement that it spawned also brought about a revolution in organisational science. Nevertheless, for a range of reasons – some of which have to do with a lack of empirical and theoretical sophistication, others which have to do with metatheoretical and ideological prejudices – Mayo's insights have tended to remain on the fringe of organisational thinking. Indeed, this is one of the reasons why many of the problems with which he was concerned – notably the subjugation of workers, industrial conflict and the proper functioning of democracy – have remained largely unaddressed and unresolved within the organisational sphere. Perhaps, then, as our interest in these problems is rekindled by world events, it is time to reacquaint ourselves with Mayo's work, and to explore its affordances with renewed enthusiasm. Certainly, as new theoretical frameworks have emerged to breathe fresh life into his insights (e.g. Deci & Ryan, 1985; Haslam, 2001; McGregor, 1960), the scientific and practical opportunities for doing this are more abundant than ever.

IMPLICATIONS FOR PRACTITIONERS

As discussed throughout this chapter, one important point for practice that emerges from Mayo's work concerns the importance of social relationships for work and organisational behaviour. Indeed, not only are a range of work experiences and behaviours (e.g. team morale, group performance) impacted directly by social factors but so too it is often the case that the impact of individual or personal factors is shaped in fundamental (sometimes hidden) ways by these same social factors (e.g. so that low team morale undermines personal self-efficacy). A further point that continues to be relevant to contemporary practice concerns the limitations of the idea that humans are rational actors who seek always to maximise their personal self-interest. Among other things, this explains why practices that are informed by this model (e.g. pertaining to pay structures or physical work conditions) often have mixed effects.

Mayo's work also has far-reaching implications for organisational change and intervention. In particular, it explains why change and intervention can backfire and exacerbate the problems they are meant to solve. A case in point are top-down approaches to change that fail to engage with, or give voice to, the experiences and concerns of those who are the focus of intervention. Moreover, Mayo's work shows that if one fails to take stock of the perceptions and experiences of individuals *as group members*, it can be very difficult (if not impossible) to understand why interventions produce the effects they do. This speaks more generally to the important role that group life and collective sense-making plays in determining people's reactions to physical and structural conditions. Among other things, this means that the very same events and conditions can have very different effects as a function of how people relate to groups in the workplace and how different groups relate to each other. It also suggests that leaders have an important role to play in shaping these social relations. More generally too, Mayo's work is an enduring reminder that in designing and evaluating useful practice and change, it is helpful to do this through the lens of (meta)theory and to spell out, and test, the key assumptions of this. Indeed, one of the ironies of Mayo's legacy is that while many people see this as centring on an effect (the Hawthorne effect), he himself was actually far more concerned with questions of social and psychological *process*. In this, he cautioned against the pitfalls of individualism and reductionism and invited researchers and practitioners alike to reflect on the importance of the social relationships that are the primary engines of organisations and society.

DISCUSSION QUESTIONS

1. Has Mayo been treated fairly or unfairly by historians of organisational science?

2. What is the legacy of Mayo's work and what is its relevance for contemporary organisational practice?

3. What would Mayo make of organisational science today?

FURTHER READINGS

Mayo, E. (1945). *The Social Problems of an Industrial Civilization*. Routledge & Kegan Paul (especially Chapters 2 to 5, pp. 31–100).

In this extremely engaging book Mayo provides a detailed account of the Hawthorne studies that explains the broad social and political context in which this work and his thinking developed. The book was a sequel to Mayo's earlier book *The Human Problems of an Industrial Civilization* (Mayo, 1933) and it was his intention to follow it up with a third title on political problems but he died in 1949 before its completion.

Roethlisberger, F. J. & Dickson, W. J. (1939). *Management and the Worker: An Account of a Research Program Conducted by the Western Electric Company, Hawthorne Works, Chicago*. Harvard University Press.

This is the definitive account of the main Hawthorne studies as provided by two of the senior researchers working on the project. In a poll of Fellows of the Academy of Management it was identified as one of the ten most influential management books of the twentieth century.

McGregor, D. (1960). *The Human Side of Enterprise*. McGraw-Hill.

This book gives a sense of how Mayo's work informed later work in the human relations tradition. In it, McGregor challenges the Taylorist view that workers are by nature indolent and therefore need to be coerced into working hard (what he termed a Theory X approach), and instead argues that, given appropriate encouragement and sufficiently enriching work, most people want to work hard (a Theory Y approach).

Haslam, S. A. (2004). *Psychology in Organizations: The Social Identity Approach*, 2nd edn. Sage.

This book contextualises Mayo's work by explaining both (a) how it related to, and challenged, other approaches to organisational psychology, and (b) how some of its key ideas were taken forward – particularly by social identity theorists. The description of the Hawthorne studies in the present chapter follows closely the account provided in this text.

REFERENCES

Adair, J. G. (1984). The Hawthorne effect: A reconsideration of the methodological artifact. *Journal of Applied Psychology*, 69, 334–45.

Alderfer, C. P. (1972). *Existence, Relatedness and Growth: Human Needs in Organizational Settings*. Free Press.

Baritz, L. (1960). *The Servants of Power: A History of the Use of Social Science in American Industry*. Wesleyan University Press.

Bayer, B. M. & Shotter, J. (eds). (1998). *Reconstructing the Psychological Subject: Bodies, Practices, and Technologies*. Sage.

Bell, D. (1956). *Work and Its Discontents*. Beacon Press.

Billig, M. (2011). Writing social psychology: Fictional things and unpopulated texts. *British Journal of Social Psychology*, 50, 4–20.

Bourke, H. (1982). Industrial unrest as social pathology: The Australian writings of Elton Mayo. *Australian Historical Studies*, 20, 217–33.

Chiesa, M. & Hobbs, S. (2008). Making sense of social research: How useful is the Hawthorne Effect? *European Journal of Social Psychology*, 38, 67–74.

Cullen, D. O. (1993). *A New Way of Statecraft: The Career of Elton Mayo and the Development of the Social Sciences in America, 1920–1940*. PhD dissertation. University of North Texas.

Deci, E. L. & Ryan, R. M. (1985). *Intrinsic Motivation and Self-Determination in Human Behavior*. Plenum.

Ellemers, N., De Gilder, D. & Haslam, S. A. (2004). Motivating individuals and groups at work: A social identity perspective on leadership and group performance. *Academy of Management Review*, 29, 459–78.

Farquhar, H.H. (1924). Positive contributions of scientific management. In E.E. Hunt (ed.), *Scientific Management Since Taylor: A Collection of Authoritative Papers*. McGraw-Hill.

Greenberg, J. (1990). Employee theft as a reaction to underpayment inequity: The hidden cost of pay cuts. *Journal of Applied Psychology*, 75, 561–8.

Haslam, S. A. (2004). *Psychology in Organizations: The Social Identity Approach*, 2nd edn. Sage.

Haslam, S. A. & McGarty, C. (2018). *Research Methods and Statistics in Psychology*, 3rd edn. Sage.

Haslam, S. A., Postmes, T. & Ellemers, N. (2003). More than a metaphor: Organizational identity makes organizational life possible. *British Journal of Management*, 14, 357–69.

Hassard, J. S. (2012). Rethinking the Hawthorne studies: The Western Electric research in its social, political and historical context. *Human Relations*, 65, 1431–61.

Jung, C. S. & Lee, S. Y. (2015). The Hawthorne studies revisited: Evidence from the US federal workforce. *Administration & Society*, 47, 507–31.

Lee, E. S., Park, T. Y. & Koo, B. (2015). Identifying organizational identification as a basis for attitudes and behaviors: A meta-analytic review. *Psychological Bulletin*, 141, 1049.

Levitt, S. D. & List, J. A. (2011). Was there really a Hawthorne effect at the Hawthorne Plant? An analysis of the original illumination experiments. *American Economic Journal: Applied Economics*, 3, 224–38.

Mayo, E. (1919). *Democracy and Freedom: An Essay in Social Logic*. Macmillan.

Mayo, E. (1922). *Civilisation and Morale*. Industrial Australian Mining Standard.

Mayo, E. (1924). Revery and industrial fatigue. *Personnel Journal*, 3, 273–81.

Mayo, E. (1933). *The Human Problems of an Industrial Civilization*. Macmillan.

Mayo, E. (1945). *The Social Problems of an Industrial Civilization*. Routledge & Kegan Paul.

McCambridge, J., Witton, J. & Elbourne, D. R. (2014). Systematic review of the Hawthorne effect: New concepts are needed to study research participation effects. *Journal of Clinical Epidemiology*, 67, 267–77.

McGregor, D. (1960). *The Human Side of Enterprise*. McGraw-Hill.

Muldoon, J. (2017). The Hawthorne studies: An analysis of critical perspectives, 1936–1958. *Journal of Management History*, 23, 74–94.

Münsterberg, H. (1913). *Psychology and Industrial Efficiency.* Houghton Mifflin.

O'Connor, E. (1999). Minding the workers: The meaning of 'human' and 'human relations' in Elton Mayo. *Organization*, 6, 223–46.

Olson, R., Verley, J., Santos, L. & Salas, C. (2004). What we teach students about the Hawthorne studies: A review of content within a sample of introductory IO and OB textbooks. *Industrial-Organizational Psychologist*, 41, 23–39.

Parker, M. (1993). Industrial relations myth and shop floor reality: The team concept in the auto industry. In N. Lichtenstein & J. H. Howell (eds), *Industrial Democracy in America*. Cambridge University Press, pp. 249–74.

Roethlisberger, F. J. & Dickson, W. J. (1939). *Management and the Worker: An Account of a Research Program Conducted by the Western Electric Company, Hawthorne Works*, Chicago. Harvard University Press.

Roter, A. B. (2018). *The Dark Side of the Workplace: Managing Incivility*. Routledge.

Shepard, J. M. (1971). On Alex Carey's radical criticism of the Hawthorne studies. *Academy of Management Journal*, 14, 23–32.

Smith, J. H. (1998). The enduring legacy of Elton Mayo. *Human Relations*, 51, 221–49.

Snow, C. E. (1927). A discussion of the relation of illumination intensity to productive efficiency. *Technical Engineering News* (November).

Sonnenfeld, J. A. (1985). Shedding light on the Hawthorne studies. *Journal of Organizational Behavior*, 6, 111–30.

Steffens, N. K., Haslam, S. A., Schuh, S. C., Jetten, J. & van Dick, R. (2017). A meta-analytic review of social identification and health in organizational contexts. *Personality and Social Psychology Review*, 21, 303–35.

Tajfel, H. & Turner, J. C. (1979). An integrative theory of intergroup conflict. In W. G. Austin & S. Worchel (eds), *The Social Psychology of Intergroup Relations*. Brooks/Cole, pp. 33–47.

Taylor, F. (1911). Principles of Scientific Management. Harper & Brothers.

Turner, J. C., Hogg, M. A., Oakes, P. J., Reicher, S. D. & Wetherell, M. S. (1987). *Rediscovering the Social Group: A Self-Categorization Theory.* Blackwell.

Turner, J. C. & Oakes, P. J. (1986). The significance of the social identity concept for social psychology with reference to individualism, interactionism and social influence. *British Journal of Social Psychology, 25,* 237-52.

van Dick, R. (2004). My job is my castle: Identification in organizational contexts. *International Review of Industrial and Organizational Psychology, 19,* 171–204.

3

Goal-Setting: Revisiting Locke and Latham's Goal-Setting Studies

Jeffrey B. Vancouver, Timothy Ballard & Andrew Neal

BACKGROUND

In 1968, Locke described the beginnings of a theory of motivation based on goals. The paper summarised the results of several empirical studies, many already published, as well as the logic underlying a theory of task performance. In 1974, Latham & Kinne published a paper describing a field study testing the implications of Locke's work. In 1979, Latham & Locke paired up to summarise the growing body of literature describing when goal-setting effects would most likely occur both in the field and the laboratory. By 1990, the body of research had grown so large that Locke and Latham needed a book to review the nearly 400 studies spanning 25 years of research and organise it into goal-setting theory (GST). More than two decades later they edited a book highlighting new research on GST and what might be avenues for future research and application (Locke & Latham, 2013). All this research and theoretical analysis has led to arguably one of the most successful theories in organisational psychology (Latham & Pinder, 2005). In this chapter, we describe the initial studies, the theory that derived from them and the unresolved issues and future directions for goal-setting theory. However, first we begin with a description of the state of psychology at the time the initial studies were done.

At the time Edwin Locke began his graduate degree in industrial psychology at Cornell in 1960, psychology was in the middle of the cognitive revolution. Behaviourism, with its focus on observable behaviour, was being replaced by a psychology that allowed theories to include possible roles for unobservable mental states and processes (i.e. cognitive psychology). While at Cornell, Locke was influenced by Thomas Ryan, who viewed intentions as an important mental state determining behaviour (Miner, 2002). Locke was also impressed by Kurt Lewin's (1951) work on levels of aspiration (i.e. goal levels) and the philosophical writings of Ayn Rand (1990), both of which emphasise goals and intentions in human behaviour.

Given the above influences, Locke developed a programme of research focused on goal-setting, beginning with his dissertation. Initially, the programme was intended to (1) examine the relevance of conscious goals and (2) provide an alternative to behaviourists' explanations of behaviour. Among the latter intent, Locke (1968) was particularly interested in testing whether goals mediated the effects of financial and other incentives on task performance. Using an approach many seek to emulate today and summarised below, Locke accomplished his intentions (i.e. goal) via a series of mostly experimental empirical studies collected into a compelling treatise of replication and explication. He navigated a space between the experimental and observational tradition of behaviourism – and science more generally – by seeking to manipulate and measure cognitive constructs to show their role in determining behaviour. That is, behaviourism used experimentation to great effect, but that approach tended to ignore the role of cognitive constructs like goals.

DETAILED DESCRIPTION

Sets of goal-setting studies: Locke's initial work

The first treatise on goal-setting was published in *Organizational Behavior and Human Performance*[1] in 1968. The paper consisted of several sections devoted to summarising the results of multiple studies illustrating the proximal role of intentions and goals. The first section described 12 lab studies on goals and goal-setting that established the relationship between goal difficulty, defined as the probability of success of reaching the goal, and quantifiable measures of task performance (e.g. number of generated uses in list-uses-of-object tasks). That is, the more difficult one's goal, the higher was one's performance. Overall, the correlation between goal difficulty and performance was a very impressive 0.78. In some of these studies, goal difficulty was manipulated by assigning different goal levels to individuals based on random assignment. In other studies, goal level was self-set and measured as a quantitative level of performance goal. When goals were assigned, interviews were used to confirm acceptance of the assigned goal, showing that the manipulation had 'taken' for each participant. Besides different operationalisations of goal difficulty, a variety of tasks, measures of performance and trial lengths were used across the studies, suggesting the generalisability of the findings.

The next section of Locke's 1968 paper described a set of eight laboratory studies that compared a difficult assigned goal to a condition where participants were ask to 'do their best'. The tasks included complex coordination tasks, perceptual speed tasks and addition tasks. For half the studies, the average performance of the individuals in the assigned goal condition significantly (i.e. $p < .05$) outperformed the average of the individuals in the do-your-best condition. Note, using Locke's

----

[1]Now titled *Organizational Behavior and Human Decision Processes*.

threshold of statistical inference of $p < .10$, two more studies showed significant effects. Regardless, beating an instruction to do one's best was an impressive and surprising finding at the time.

Next, three studies were presented where participants were to choose the difficulty of the words they were to unscramble. Difficulty was operationalised as the number of letters in the anagram (i.e. anagrams with more letters are more difficult to unscramble). The studies were designed to examine whether *intentions* predicted choice of difficulty, which they did. Among the studies, the most interesting used different instructions to motivate different intentions. That is, participants were asked to try to (1) succeed, (2) achieve a sense of personal achievement, or (3) overcome their greatest challenge. These instructions translated into participants tending to choose the easiest, middling and most difficult anagrams respectively.

The next set of studies described, none conducted by Locke, used a behaviourist conditioning paradigm where participants were rewarded with praise in different schedules (e.g. random variables) to reinforce certain responses (e.g. beginning sentences with 'I' or 'We' in a sentence construction task). The researchers also asked about the participants' intentions during the study. Across the five studies cited, they found that intentions were strongly related to behaviour within and between conditions. Note these studies were based on the behaviourist principle that the reward reinforced and motivated the desired behaviour. However, Locke suspected the reward taught the desired behaviour or its desired level of performance and thus acted like an assigned goal instruction. Indeed, Locke was trying to make the point that a cognitive concept (i.e. intention or goal) was responsible for the effect of the reward on behaviour. That is, the issue was not the motivating power of rewards but the mechanism by which rewards motivated.

Indeed, in the next several sections of the 1968 paper Locke sought to demonstrate that the concepts of knowledge of results, rewards, incentives or reinforcers might facilitate goal adoption and retention, but would not affect motivation directly. Motivation would be the job of the goal. To bring that point home, Locke (1968) described studies focused on knowledge of scores (KS) on previous performances. For example, one study manipulated KS by either allowing participants to calculate their performance at the end of each trial or not. They found no difference in performance between these groups. However, they found that a post-study qualitative assessment of goals was related to performance. Two subsequent studies included the KS factor, but added a goal difficulty assignment factor (i.e. assigned a hard goal, a do-your-best goal or an easy goal). The goal factor was shown to influence performance but the KS factor was not. Locke also described studies where KS might influence the difficulty of the goal one set for oneself without any independent effect. That is, the data was consistent with the hypothesis that goal level fully mediated the effect of KS on performance.

Like the KS studies, Locke also described a set of studies where incentive values were shown to be unrelated to performance once goal level was controlled for, either experimentally or statistically. Many of these studies involved the word-unscrambling task mentioned above. The results showed that when participants could choose the difficulty of the words to be unscrambled, they chose easier words when incentives were higher. For Locke, this illustrated the power of the cognitive construct in determining behaviour, but also showed that incentives could undermine motivation by incentivising choosing easier tasks. Locke was not trying to show that incentives were not motivating, but that goals were perhaps a more direct way of getting higher performances via a set of controlled laboratory studies.

IMPACT

Replication and generalisation: Latham's field work

In 1974, Gary Latham received his PhD from the University of Akron. That same year he published a paper with Sydney Kinne in the *Journal of Applied Psychology* on a field experiment focused on the goal-setting notions described by Locke (1968). Latham, who was also working in industry, saw the possible application of Locke's work and had the resources to conduct experimental and quasi-experimental field studies designed to test and assess the effects of assigning difficult goals to employees. In the Latham & Kinne (1974) study, they randomly assigned 26 pulpwood producers and their wood-sawing crews to a goal-setting training group or a control group. Groups were matched on several variables (e.g. crew size) and both groups were incentivised using a piece-rate system. The training group was provided a three-hour training on goal-setting where they were told the purpose of the research was to test the effectiveness of goal-setting on performance. The experimental group was also given production goals, which were described as a minimum standard level of acceptable performance with no penalties attached to failure to meet the goal and no special incentives attached to meeting the goal.

In contrast, the producers in the control group or their crews received no training and no specific goals. They were told that the study, which involved three months of data collection, was to examine the effects of injuries, absenteeism and turnover on production. Strengths of this design were the random assignment of matched pairs, ecological validity (i.e. a work context) and the time frame (i.e. 14 consecutive weeks of data collection). Besides the low *n* of only 20 crews in the final sample, a weakness was the supposed Hawthorne effect (see also Chapter 2) – the tendency for behaviour to change merely because one is being observed – due to the explanations given to the crews for the study, though an attempt to minimise these effects was made by keeping equal the visits to the crews across the data collection period (Latham & Locke, 1979).

To assess the effectiveness of the goal-setting intervention, Latham & Kinne (1974) compared cords (i.e. 3.5 cubic metres of wood) per crewperson-hour, cords cut per sawhand-hour, and crew injuries, turnover and absenteeism. Only the first and last outcomes differed significantly between the groups, with the experimental group cutting more cords per crewperson-hour and having less absenteeism. The cords cut per sawhand-hour were higher at a 'marginally significant' level (i.e. $p < .10$) for the experimental group as well.

Although the above findings were arguably modest, they were promising given the low cost of implementing the programme. Moreover, Latham continued to examine goal-setting effects in the field. For example, Latham & Baldes (1975) described a study involving logging trucks used to transport cut trees out of the forests. In this study, 36 logging trucks were tracked in terms of the percentage of the legal weight the trucks carried. Prior to any intervention, when a 'do your best' goal was typical, the trucks averaged 60 per cent of their capacities. This created an inefficiency that logging companies wanted to change. A goal of 94 per cent capacity was determined to be a 'difficult' but attainable goal for the truckers, who determined the load on their trucks. This goal level was presented to the truck drivers along with a claim of no retaliation if the goal was not attained, and no monetary rewards or other benefits would accrue if the goal was obtained.

In this study, the results were quite impressive. The percentage truck capacities rose to about 80 per cent the first few weeks after the goal was assigned. They then declined to about 70 per cent in what was assumed to be a test of the no retaliation claim. Following the decline, the capacities rose to 90 per cent and held steady for the remaining months of the study. No statistical analysis was conducted, but the within-person, repeated-measure, longitudinal design and the clear trendline made such analysis unnecessary. The effect found was undoubtedly impressive and, according to Locke & Latham (2002), saved the company $250,000 in nine months and lasted for years after the study ended. Indeed, a few years later Latham & Locke (1979) referenced nine more field studies showing positive effects of goal-setting on performance. The game was afoot.

BEYOND THE CLASSIC STUDY

GOAL-SETTING THEORY AND EVIDENCE OF ITS SUCCESS

The promising findings and the theoretical musings of Locke (1968) were further developed over the decades. Eventually, the level of research was enough for Locke & Latham (1990) to develop GST. Locke & Latham (2006) state GST's core notion in the following way: 'so long as a person is committed to the goal, has the requisite ability to attain it, and does not have conflicting goals, there is a positive, linear relationship between goal difficulty and task performance' (p. 265). The application of GST follows from the statement of the theory. That is, if one wants high task performance, one (i.e. self, supervisor or leader) should assign a goal with a specified level of performance that is difficult, but achievable, for the individual. Though not necessarily endorsed by Locke & Latham, the attributes of an effective goal, whether self or other assigned, are often captured in the acronym SMART (specific, measurable, attainable, relevant and time-bound). Moreover, these kinds of goals can be assigned to teams and organisations with similar effects expected. Finally, the context is not limited to work but can be useful in education, health (e.g. exercise) and other domains (see Locke & Latham, 2013, for a review).

Evidence of the success of GST theory begins with evidence of the size of the goal difficulty-task performance relationship. Locke & Latham (1990) reported meta-analyses showing moderate-to-large effect sizes (d) ranging from .41 to .82 and where the range of sizes corresponded with the moderators described above.

Indeed, nothing in the theory exists without strong empirical support for the role described for the variable (Locke & Latham, 1990, 2020). That is, no construct is part of the theory without an empirical basis for including the construct in the way demonstrated empirically (e.g. moderators must consistently be found to be related to effect sizes found between other constructs).

Probably owing to the empirical findings, coupled with the prolific writings of its protagonists, GST is very well known and very widely used. For example, searching 'SMART goals' on Google resulted in 677 billion hits! In the narrower domain of scientific writing (i.e. Google Scholar), a search on goal-setting theory garnered 4.48 million hits (at the time of writing). In comparison, expectancy theory (e.g. Vroom, 1964) yielded only .801 million hits, self-determination theory (e.g. Deci & Ryan, 2012) yielded 1.84 million hits, and the venerable social cognitive theory (e.g. Bandura, 1986) received 3.7 million hits. This evidence of success is unassailably impressive.

CONCLUSION

A PRACTICALLY USEFUL THEORY OF MOTIVATION

In 2002, Locke and Latham wrote an article for *American Psychologist* titled 'Building a practically useful theory of goal setting and task motivation: A 35-year odyssey'. By this time, the cognitive revolution had long morphed into the new normal. Goals especially were well-established as a mainstay of theories of cognition and motivation, thanks in part to Locke & Latham's work (Austin & Vancouver, 1996). Moreover, other cognitive constructs like self-efficacy, expectancy and anticipated satisfaction (i.e. valence) were important constructs in motivational theories in general and had been incorporated into explanations found within GST. Perhaps most impressive of all has been the nearly universal adoption of goal-setting within performance management systems and other motivational interventions (Locke & Latham, 2013).

Nonetheless, successful theories are likely to be challenged (e.g. Erez, 1977; Ordóñez et al., 2009; Vancouver et al., 2020). In some cases, GST has benefitted from the challenges. For example, Erez's (1977) challenge resulted in recognising that feedback is an important moderator of the goal-task performance effect, which was incorporated into the theory. In this case, feedback refers to information about progress on one's goal while striving for it as opposed to knowledge of the result once the goal-striving episode is complete (e.g. KS as described above). Meanwhile, Ordóñez et al.'s (2009) challenge cautioned practitioners that goal-setting may be so powerful that it leads to unintended consequences, such as unethical behaviour (e.g. cheating), inhibited learning and reduced intrinsic motivation. Indeed, a broader sense of the goals people might be pursuing raises questions of self-goals like the pursuit of happiness. The literature on goal-setting has been heavily focused on the relationship between goals and performance and has often neglected the impact that goals might have on well-being. It is true that goal achievement increases self-efficacy and feelings of satisfaction, particularly when the goal is challenging. However, difficult goals can often be highly demanding, place a person under considerable time pressure and have negative effects on self-efficacy and satisfaction when they're not achieved. All of this can increase the likelihood of stress, fatigue and burnout, which ultimately hinders performance in the longer term. It seems, therefore, that the effect of goal-setting on well-being is something of a double-edged sword. Finally, other challenges motivate continued advancement in terms of theory and practice. The recent Vancouver et al. (2020) paper presents such a challenge, elaborated on below.

IMPLICATIONS FOR PRACTITIONERS

GST has always been a very practically oriented theory. Locke was attempting to show the power of manipulating a key, proximal precursor to motivation, the goal level, via assignment of a specific, difficult goal. Latham showed that such a manipulation was likely to operate positively in work settings. To be sure, various factors might undermine successful goal-setting interventions, but the decades of research following those initial studies went a long way towards determining critical (e.g. presence of feedback) and trivial (e.g. most dimensions of the setting) contingencies.

Nonetheless, questions regarding the effectiveness of goal-setting interventions persist. The primary issues relate to how the process works, particularly in multiple goal and dynamic environments. These conditions are an issue for most organisational settings, whereas most of the studies examining goal-setting focus on single goal-settings in relatively narrow timeframes. One way to address this issue is using computational modelling. Computational models are computer programs representing a theory or process. Because they are computer programs, computational models can be simulated to test the ability of the theory to account for the phenomena the theory is presumed to explain (i.e. the internal consistency of the theory).

Vancouver et al. (2020) created such a model to evaluate the logic and internal consistency of GST. The computational model included the key elements of GST, including (a) the effects of assigned goals, incentives and self-efficacy on goal choice (i.e. personal goals); (b) the effects of goal choice and self-efficacy on effort and performance; (c) the effects of feedback, goal commitment and ability on the relationship between goal choice and performance; and (d) the effect of performance on subsequent self-efficacy. However, the process of creating the computational model revealed two main elements of the theory that were unclear, including the process by which a person sets their personal goal and the process by which performance affects self-efficacy.

To address the first issue, Vancouver et al. (2020) assumed that individuals set their personal goal based on the level of performance they think is achievable using their self-efficacy belief and the willingness to put resources toward the goal based on the value they place on achieving the goal. When confronted with an assigned goal, the model assumes that the assigned goal level replaces the personal goal if it is lower than the personal goal but not if it is higher. That is, if an assigned goal is more difficult than their personal goal, they will keep their personal goal, though an assigned difficult goal will also increase self-efficacy beliefs. To address the second ambiguous aspect of GST, Vancouver et al. (2020) developed three alternative specifications for how performance might affect self-efficacy: proportional increase depending on level of performance, increase or decrease as a function of change in performance over time, or increase or decrease as a function of the comparison between expected performance and performance achieved. Only this last specification showed reasonable behaviour by the model and was thus the one adopted.

Vancouver et al. (2020) conducted a series of simulations to evaluate whether the computational model could reproduce the empirical findings used to build and support the theory. For example, the simulations reproduced the positive effect between assigned or personal goal difficulty and performance. They also showed the moderating effects of the presence of feedback, goal commitment and ability. Furthermore, the model reproduced the performance trajectory reported by Latham & Baldes (1975) when a difficult goal was introduced to replace a 'do your best' goal. Together, these results suggest that the GST mechanisms operationalised by the model provide a coherent explanation for the observed change in performance.

However, the modelling process also brought to the fore substantial issues suggesting that GST might be wanting as a practically useful theory. For example, Locke & Latham (2020) claimed that assigning a difficult goal will positively impact task performance because the goal level will positively relate to performance. That is, a person will adopt a higher personal goal when assigned a difficult goal as opposed to an easy one. Although the simulations showed this, they also revealed that this effect was primarily because the easy goal undermined task performance; assigning a difficult goal barely had any positive effect. Locke (1997) was aware of this issue and found it in his own empirical work, but it means that the large effects found in the meta-analysis of goal-setting studies that compare difficult to easy goals emerge because the individual in the easy goal conditions did not work as hard as they would have had they been in a no goal condition. Meanwhile, assigning a difficult goal resulted in only a slight improvement in predicted performance over a 'do your best' or 'no goal' condition and sometimes even resulted in lower performance if the individuals had already retained a higher personal goal before being assigned with the difficult goal.

Another issue revealed by the simulations was that the effect that difficult goals had via self-efficacy went away with task experience. That finding is consistent with Earley & Lituchy's (1991) research showing that the cuing effect of assigning difficult goals on self-efficacy weakens the more experience one has on a task. That is, assigning difficult goals seems to imply competence to the individual assigned the goal. However, experience with the task provides feedback regarding one's competence that eventually eliminates the effect of goal difficulty on self-efficacy. This effect may be slow to materialise, such that it might not reveal itself even in longitudinal studies lasting months (Vancouver et al., 2020). Yet, this finding somewhat undermines the practicality of GST because it suggests that any beneficial effect of goal difficulty on self-efficacy is only temporary. Taken together, the results of the simulations suggest that assigning a difficult goal level might have a slight positive effect on performance that will go away with time, while undermining performance if the level of goal difficulty is below what one would strive to achieve without the goal.

Although the poor showing for goal-setting over the long run revealed by the simulations appears to be a problem for GST: there are possible empirical and theoretical responses. Using an empirical argument, Locke & Latham (2013) claim that longitudinal research shows long-term positive effects for goal-setting. This is true – some does. But other research shows null or negative effects (Brooks et al., 2020). Unfortunately, most of the research showing positive, long-term effects compares difficult to easy goal conditions. As noted above, this benefit likely occurs because easy goals are demotivating, not because difficult goals are motivating. Still, the empirical database of such studies is insufficient for making conclusions.

The second way to address the problems identified by the simulations is to develop a better understanding of goal processes. Vancouver et al. (2020) used this approach by examining a variation of their computational model of GST where assigning a goal changed the anticipated value associated with the goal. Simulating this revised model showed that the positive goal-difficulty effect held over time. However, to justify this revision, and to make it well-established, empirical work would be needed to examine it. Vancouver et al. (2020) also suggested, more speculatively, that a model explicitly representing multiple goal pursuit might reveal positive, lasting effects for goal-setting interventions. Indeed, Locke & Latham (2013) have wanted more attention paid to multiple goal pursuit so that GST could be expanded to include that empirical literature.

FUTURE DIRECTIONS

Despite decades of research and thought on goal-setting, issues related to both its theoretical accuracy and practical usefulness remain (e.g. Vancouver et al., 2020). However, the direction one might travel to resolve the issues is likely known. That is, it likely involves developing a greater understanding of the dynamics of multiple goal pursuit (Neal et al., 2017), particularly as those dynamics affect the anticipated value and expectations regarding reaching specific performances or conditions. To understand why this is the case, consider a common goal-setting situation: the New Year's resolution.

Every year many individuals contemplate and set goals for the coming year. These goals might relate to health (e.g. exercise, diet or weight goals), finances, work or relationships, among others. In recent years, the advice from self-help gurus has been to set SMART goals. As noted above, these specific, measurable, attainable, relevant, time-limited goals are more likely to be motivating and maintained. Nonetheless, most of these goals are abandoned within weeks or a couple of months of initiation. In other words, they do not last, suggesting some dynamic processes are at play that undermine them. Still, in other cases they do last, suggesting a possible different set of dynamics. Thus, a question is what are these dynamics? That is, what is happening that might undermine commitment to the goal and why might that process not always result in a loss of commitment, or maybe even an escalation of commitment?

One possible answer to the above question relates to the issue of rewards and their relationship to goals. That is, one might not only determine the goal and goal levels to pursue, but also set up (or not) reward or punishment contingencies around goal progress, goal attainment or goal failure. Indeed, the strong effects often associated with goals may really be more about the strong effects of incentives. For example, Ordóñez et al. (2009) claim that goal-setting is so powerful that a warning label ought to be provided with any intervention using it. They were particularly worried about the unethical behaviour individuals or organisations might engage in to achieve difficult goals. However, the observational examples used in that paper involve goals with high stakes. That is, the goal merely specifies the metrics used and contingencies (e.g. all or none for reaching or not reaching the goal level) for obtaining the reward. This raises an empirical question: if the stakes are removed leaving just the assigned, difficult goal, would the unethical behaviour still arise? Note that the early studies did not connect goals to rewards and Locke & Latham (2013) are clear that GST does not take a stand on how to connect rewards to goals.

Finally, when considering personal resolutions or work goals, a primary question to ask might be what other goals are relevant. Locke & Latham's (2002) statement of the theory noted that goal-setting works if there are no competing goals. However, they also suggest that the primary way goal-setting works is via determining the direction of behaviour. Part of the direction of behaviour issue might relate to adding a direction not previously on one's agenda, but mostly it is about winning the contest of where to allocate resources among the multiple goals one might allocate resources. This implies that to motivate pursuit of the important goals one might need to revisit and drop less important ones.

DISCUSSION QUESTIONS

1. What determines the likelihood you continue to strive for a goal over time?

2. What are the best ways to maintain key values (e.g. well-being and ethical behaviour) when pursuing difficult goals?

3. Under what conditions should one drop or postpone a goal?

FURTHER READINGS

Locke, E. A. & Latham, G. P. (1990). *A Theory of Goal Setting and Task Performance.* Prentice-Hall.

The definitive treatise on goal-setting theory.

Locke, E. A. & Latham, G. P. (2002). Building a practically useful theory of goal setting and task motivation: A 35-year odyssey. *American Psychologist*, 57, 705–17.

Very accessible summary of GST and the research supporting it.

Locke, E. & Latham, G. P. (eds) (2013). *New Developments in Goal Setting and Task Performance*. Routledge.

The edited book includes many chapters devoted to new developing directions for goal-setting theory.

Neal, A., Ballard, T. & Vancouver, J. B. (2017). Dynamic self-regulation and multiple-goal pursuit. *Annual Review of Organizational Psychology and Organizational Behavior*, 4, 401–23.

This article reviews research on the pursuit of single and multiple goals over time.

Vancouver, J. B., Wang, M. & Li, X. (2020). Translating informal theories into formal theories: The case of the dynamic computational model of the integrated model of work motivation. *Organizational Research Methods*, 23, 238–74.

The article describes the building of a static and dynamic computational model of the core of goal-setting theory.

REFERENCES

Austin, J. T. & Vancouver, J. B. (1996). Goal constructs in psychology: Structure, process, and content. *Psychological Bulletin*, 120(3), 338–75.

Bandura, A. (1986). The explanatory and predictive scope of self-efficacy theory. *Journal of Social and Clinical Psychology,* 4(3), 359–73.

Brooks, L. R., Vancouver, J. B. & Dhanani, L. Y. (2020, June). How long do goals last? A meta-analysis of the effects of assigned goals over time. In M. Keith (Chair), *Setting New Goals for Goal Research: Questioning Assumptions and New Directions*. Symposium conducted at the Annual Convention of the Society of Industrial and Organizational Psychology. Virtual conference.

Deci, E. L. & Ryan, R. M. (2012). Self-determination Theory. In P. A. M. Van Lange, A. W. Kruglanski & E. T. Higgins (eds), *Handbook of Theories of Social Psychology*. Sage, pp. 416–36.

Earley, P. C. & Lituchy, T. R. (1991). Delineating goal and efficacy effects: A test of three models. *Journal of Applied Psychology*, 76, 81–98.

Erez, M. (1977). Feedback: A necessary condition for the goal setting-performance relationship. *Journal of Applied Psychology*, 62(5), 624–27.

Latham, G. P. & Baldes, J. J. (1975). The 'practical significance' of Locke's theory of goal setting. *Journal of Applied Psychology*, 60, 122–24.

Latham, G. P. & Kinne, S. B. (1974). Improving job performance through training in goal setting. *Journal of Applied Psychology*, 59(2), 187–91.

Latham, G. P. & Locke, E. A. (1979). Goal setting – A motivational technique that works. *Organizational Dynamics*, 8(2), 68–80.

Latham, G. P. & Pinder, C. C. (2005). Work motivation theory and research at the dawn of the twenty-first century. *Annual Review of Psychology*, 56, 485–516.

Lewin, K. (1951). *Field Theory in Social Science: Selected Theoretical Papers*. Harper & Brothers.

Locke, E. A. (1968). Toward a theory of task motivation and incentives. *Organizational Behavior and Human Performance*, 3(2), 157–89.

Locke, E. (1997). The motivation to work: What we know. In M. Maehr & P. Pintrich (eds), *Advances in Motivation and Achievement*, Vol. 10. JAI Press, pp. 375–412.

Locke, E. A. & Latham, G. P. (1990). *A Theory of Goal Setting and Task Performance*. Prentice-Hall.

Locke, E. A. & Latham, G. P. (2002). Building a practically useful theory of goal setting and task motivation: A 35-year odyssey. *American Psychologist*, 57, 705–17.

Locke, E. A. & Latham, G. P. (2004). What should we do about motivation theory? Six recommendations for the twenty-first century. *Academy of Management Review*, 29, 388–403.

Locke, E. A. & Latham, G. P. (2006). New directions in goal-setting theory. *Current Directions in Psychological Science*, 15(5), 265–68.

Locke, E. A. & Latham, G. P. (eds) (2013). *New Developments in Goal Setting and Task Performance*. Routledge.

Locke, E. A. & Latham, G. P. (2020). Building a theory by induction: The example of goal setting theory. *Organizational Psychology Review*, 10(3–4), 223–39.

Miner, J. B. (2002). *Organizational Behavior: Foundations, Theories, and Analyses*. Oxford University Press.

Neal, A., Ballard, T. & Vancouver, J. B. (2017). Dynamic self-regulation and multiple-goal pursuit. *Annual Review of Organizational Psychology and Organizational Behavior*, 4, 401–23.

Ordóñez, L. D., Schweitzer, M. E., Galinsky, A. D. & Bazerman, M. H. (2009). Goals gone wild: The systematic side effects of overprescribing goal setting. *Academy of Management Perspectives*, 23(1), 6–16.

Rand, A. (1990). *Introduction to Objectivist Epistemology*. NAL Books.

Ryan, T. A. (1970). *Intentional Behaviour*. Ronald Press.

Vancouver, J. B., Wang, M. & Li, X. (2020). Translating informal theories into formal theories: The case of the dynamic computational model of the integrated model of work motivation. *Organizational Research Methods*, 23(2), 238–74.

Vroom, V. R. (1964). *Work and Motivation*. Wiley.

Part II | Motivation, Cooperation and Health

4

Motivation: Revisiting Deci's Rewards and Intrinsic Motivation Studies

Marylène Gagné

BACKGROUND

Fifty years ago, Edward L. Deci published an article in the *Journal of Personality and Social Psychology* on the effects of tangible rewards on intrinsic motivation (Deci, 1971). The series of experiments constituted his PhD dissertation, which he conducted in the social psychology programme at Carnegie Mellon University under the supervision of Victor H. Vroom, who was himself well-known for his work on expectancy theory (Vroom, 1964). Deci's PhD studies followed the completion of an MBA degree at the Wharton School of the University of Pennsylvania and a Bachelor's degree in mathematics at Hamilton College.

In his PhD experiments, he examined the effects of tangible and verbal rewards for engaging in an interesting task on the intrinsic motivation of participants for that task. Deci's interest in this research question stemmed from his curiosity around the phenomenon of intrinsic motivation. At the time he started his investigations, behaviourism was dominating the psychology field, so most psychologists did not believe in the existence of intrinsic motivation and strongly promoted the use of tangible contingent rewards (positive reinforcements) to shape and motivate behaviour. However, some behaviouristic assumptions were starting to be questioned at the time, which eventually led to a cognitive revolution in psychology (Ryan et al., 2018).

During the same period, agency theory (Jensen & Meckling, 1976) was being developed coincidentally at the University of Rochester Business School where Edward Deci was hired following the completion of his PhD. This theory, like behaviouristic theories, advocates for the use of performance-contingent rewards to motivate people, but with slightly different propositions, as explained later in this chapter. Agency theory has dominated the field of economics for decades and is used as a framework in management and human resources management, particularly for understanding and developing employee and executive compensation.

Given that Deci's experiments have also influenced some of the thinking behind the use of performance-contingent financial incentives to motivate workers, this chapter will focus on the experiments' broader influence on the fields of organisational psychology and management.

DETAILED DESCRIPTION

In his first published article on this topic, Deci (1971) presented two laboratory experiments and a quasi-experimental field study. Defining intrinsic motivation as performing an activity 'for no other apparent rewards except the activity itself' (p. 105), the studies were designed to ascertain whether the introduction of a reward for doing an activity that people would find generally interesting and enjoyable would increase, decrease or not change the degree of intrinsic motivation to engage with the activity.

In the first experiment, 24 male college students taking a psychology class participated in a study ostensibly on problem-solving. The study consisted of three individual sessions during which participants were asked to reproduce specific shapes using an engaging SOMA puzzle. Participants were evenly split into an experimental and a control group. In the first session, all participants worked on the puzzles for no reward. In the second session, participants in the experimental (but not in the control) group were paid $1 for each puzzle they solved, representing a performance-contingent reward (Deci et al., 1999). In the third session, none of the participants were rewarded. They had a maximum of 13 minutes to complete each puzzle, and if they could not solve a particular puzzle, they were shown how to succeed after 13 minutes to avoid them from wanting to bring closure to their efforts in the next phase of the session (Zeigarnik, 1927). At one point during each session, the experimenter left the room for eight minutes to analyse their performance on a 'teletype' computer to ostensibly determine the appropriate puzzle configurations to work on next. The experimenter told participants that while he was gone, they could do whatever they wanted (there was a stack of magazines on a table that participants could access). During this time, the experimenter observed participants through a one-way mirror to calculate how much time participants spent working on the puzzles. This was used as a behavioural measure of intrinsic motivation, assuming that people were free to do whatever they felt like and that what they chose reflected their interest/enjoyment of the activity. At the end of the session, participants were also asked if they found the puzzles interesting and enjoyable, taken as a self-report measure of intrinsic motivation.

Results for the behavioural measure of intrinsic motivation in the experimental group revealed that the introduction of rewards in the second session increased the amount of time spent on puzzles during the 'free-choice' period relative to the first session and relative to the control group. This is in line with behaviourist predictions, demonstrating that rewards increase engagement while they are present.

However, time spent on the puzzles during the third session's free choice period (after removal of the reward) decreased to an amount significantly inferior to that of the first session and to that of the control group. Results for the self-report measure of intrinsic motivation did not reveal any differences between the conditions and sessions. Deci interpreted the results as rewards working to increase performance while they are operational, but as causing 'damage' to intrinsic motivation which is detected when rewards are removed.

Deci followed up these findings with a second study conducted in the field. Eight college students were hired to voluntarily work for a real college newspaper in two teams of four scheduled on different days for a period of five months. Their work was to create headlines for articles, and their performance was measured in terms of how long it took them to create each headline, assuming that the quicker they worked, the more motivated they were (which participants were not aware of, and the time it took them was recorded by the supervisor who was also the experimenter). Absences were also recorded. Group 1 was the experimental group while group 2 was the control group. As in the first experiment, the period of work was split into three. During the first period, no one received any incentives. During the middle period, Group 1 received a payment of 50¢ per headline. They were told some extra funds allowed for this and were instructed not to tell other staff. During the third period, they were told the funds had run out. Deci also took a longer-term (period 4) measure of performance to observe the long-term effects of rewards on intrinsic motivation (five weeks after period 3, and for a period of two weeks).

Results revealed that the introduction of a reward in the experimental group did not change their speed across the four periods; however, the control group's speed kept increasing from periods 1 to 4. This was taken as showing the long-term negative effects of rewards on intrinsic motivation. Though absences increased in both groups during the second period, they exploded in the experimental group during the third period, after the rewards ceased (while they came back down slightly in the control group). This was taken as another indicator of a drop of intrinsic motivation.

To verify whether the effects of rewards on intrinsic motivation were limited to tangible rewards or generalised to non-tangible ones, Deci conducted a second lab experiment replacing monetary rewards with verbal rewards in the second experimental session. It was expected that contrary to monetary rewards, which make people reconsider why they are doing an activity (e.g. for the money), verbal rewards may not have such an effect. Participants in the experimental (but not in the control) condition were given positive feedback in the form of verbal reinforcement (e.g. 'That's very good'), comparative feedback (e.g. 'That's better than average'), or were told that it was a particularly difficult puzzle that very few people solve when they could not solve one. A second change in this experiment was the composition of participants due to the students who were enrolled in the psychology class, comprising more bachelor of engineering students than bachelor of arts students (the latter made up the majority in previous studies).

Unlike in the first experiment, results showed a steady decrease in intrinsic motivation (behavioural measure) over the three sessions in the control group, whereas it remained at the same level in the experimental condition. This was attributed to sampling differences, assuming that engineering students found the puzzles more boring because of having more developed spatial skills than the arts students. To support this, post-hoc analyses of data from Study 1 and Study 3 indicated that the behavioural measure among arts students remained more stable than among engineering students. Interestingly, although monetary rewards decreased all students' behavioural measure of motivation in the first experiment, in this second experiment, the verbal rewards seemed to enhance the motivation of arts students, while it decreased the motivation of engineering students. As in the first experiment, the self-report measure of intrinsic motivation did not differ across conditions and sessions.

Taken together, these studies were deemed to show that people cognitively reappraise the reasons for which they engage in an activity when they start getting monetarily rewarded for doing it. When monetary rewards for doing an engaging activity were introduced and then removed, participants spent less time on the activity, they stalled on improving their performance and they stopped showing up for volunteer work. When verbal rewards were introduced, they seemed to be helpful to the motivation of students who allegedly had something to learn from the activity, while they were detrimental to the motivation of students who allegedly had already mastered it. This was the beginning of cognitive evaluation theory (Deci & Ryan, 1980), which was further refined through a series of studies demonstrating that rewards can be perceived as controlling, decreasing one's sense of autonomy (Ryan et al., 1983), but can also be perceived as informational, increasing one's sense of competence (Deci, 1972). The interplay of these two perceptions determines the effect of a reward on intrinsic motivation, with tangible rewards tending to have a more controlling impact and verbal rewards tending to have a more informational impact.

Using today's research design standards, Deci's early experiments would be criticised on a few grounds. First, the sample sizes in each experiment were very small, and though some results were statistically significant, the risk of incorrect inferences is increased. Second, there was a ceiling effect in the two experiments as a sizable number of participants worked on the puzzles for the entire eight-minute free-choice period. These two concerns could have led to obtaining weaker effects than would have otherwise been obtained. Third, the experimenter was not blind to the conditions, which could have caused demand-characteristics (i.e. unconsciously treating participants in different conditions differently). Finally, there is the possibility that the removal of the reward could have caused an increase in negative affect that was not but could have been controlled for. Although the self-report enjoyment scale did not differ across conditions, negative affect caused by frustration of not being rewarded anymore could have been confounded with a drop in enjoyment. These last two concerns could have caused stronger effects than would have otherwise been the case.

IMPACT OF THE CLASSIC STUDIES

D eci's experiments did not go unnoticed. First, there were immediate reactions from scholars in the field, inquiring about the quality of certain aspects of the experiments (e.g. Calder & Staw, 1975). Second, soon after Deci completed his dissertation, he was hired by Bernard Bass on a joint appointment at the University of Rochester's Business School and Department of Psychology. Bass had been tasked by William Meckling, who was then the Dean of the Business School at Rochester and an economist who co-developed agency theory with Michael Jensen, to build an organisational behaviour programme. The assumptions and propositions advanced in agency theory happened to be somewhat oppositional to those about human motivation that Deci was developing at the time. We return to this later as it has important implications for use of financial incentives in the workplace. For now, it is important to note that there were animated discussions between members of the organisational behaviour group and the Dean around the research topics the group focused on. Deci was dismissed from the Business School as part of a total dismantlement of the organisational behaviour unit only three years after he had been hired, but he was taken in as a full-time faculty member by the Psychology Department at the University of Rochester where he spent the rest of his career (Deci, personal communication, 2020).

The experiments have also been criticised for not being generalisable to field settings, lacking external validity due to relying on artificial experiments with small rewards for non-meaningful short-term work (Fang & Gerhart, 2012). However, when revisiting these studies, we realise how history forgets some important details, such as the quasi-experimental field study in a real volunteer work setting that was included in this very first publication. Nonetheless, Deci (1975) agreed that experimental results should not be used in prescriptive ways in applied settings, but instead need to be tested out in different contexts.

REPLICATIONS AND META-ANALYSES

The experiments led to a boom of replications and extensions that informed the development of cognitive evaluation theory (CET) (Deci & Ryan, 1980) through working out some of the early criticisms of methods used in early experiments (e.g. Deci, 1975; Deci et al., 1975; Pinder, 1976; Ryan et al., 1983). More recently, neuropsychological studies have supported the idea that intrinsic and extrinsic motivation involve differential activation of areas of the brain that have been associated with processes involving reward and self-regulation, which can be affected by the administration of tangible rewards (Murayama et al., 2010).

Nonetheless, the debate continues to rage on the use of rewards for motivation and performance, particularly in the field of work motivation and management. A long list of published meta-analyses, each reaching different conclusions about the effects of rewards on intrinsic motivation (Cameron & Pierce, 1994; Deci et al., 1999; Eisenberger & Cameron, 1996; Rummel & Feinberg, 1988; Tang &

Hall, 1995; Wiersma, 1992), as well as the effects of rewards on performance (Cerasoli et al., 2014, 2016; Jenkins et al., 1998; Kim et al., 2022; Weibel et al., 2010), has contributed to the debate. What seemed to be driving the different results across these meta-analyses was the way each study was coded, particularly around the type of reward contingency and task characteristics (task interest and complexity), the way outliers were determined and excluded, and even how different experimental conditions within studies were at times collapsed or compared to different types of control groups (see Appendix A in Deci et al., 1999, for examples). Though the Deci et al. (1999) meta-analysis clarifies these issues in detail and provides support for CET, we still have things to learn about the effects of reward on motivation and performance through more experimental and field research that uses clear manipulations and operationalisations of rewards and their contingencies to performance, clear task characteristics and clear performance measures, and that takes into account the psychological processes (e.g. autonomy and competence) that are affected by rewards.

BEYOND THE CLASSIC STUDY: SELF-DETERMINATION THEORY

Deci continued to work on developing theory with his close colleague Richard Ryan, who together made it evolve into a comprehensive theory of human motivation, now known as self-determination theory (SDT) (Deci & Ryan, 1985; Ryan & Deci, 2017). CET is now considered one of six sub-theories of this overarching theory. SDT proposes a distinction between intrinsic and extrinsic motivation, but splits extrinsic motivation into different forms of motivational regulation that can be organised along a continuum of self-determination (Howard et al., 2017; Howard et al., 2018). Along this continuum, external regulation reflects activity engagement to obtain rewards or avoid punishment; introjected regulation reflects activity engagement to build or preserve one's self-esteem; identified regulation reflects activity engagement out of perceived importance and meaning; and integrated regulation reflects activity engagement out of the integration of personal goals and values. Research in the work domain has shown that more self-determined forms of motivation (i.e. identified to intrinsic motivation) yield better work outcomes than the less self-determined ones (i.e. external and introjected regulations) (see Van den Broeck et al., 2021, for a meta-analysis).

By proposing that not all work is inherently interesting, but can be perceived to be meaningful and important through the promotion of internalisation (i.e. coming to value and self-regulate an activity that was initially externally regulated; Ryan, 1995) made the theory more usable in the work domain. This concept of internalisation is also what made self-determination theory appealing to management. It connected with well-known management theories that proposed similar concepts, such as Kelman's (1958) development of the concepts of identification and internalisation, and the many theories of management that consider job autonomy and participation (Gagné & Bhave, 2011; Gagné & Deci, 2005).

The theory also proposes that all human beings have three fundamental psycho-logical needs, the needs for competence, autonomy and relatedness that, when sat-isfied, facilitate internalisation and intrinsic motivation, and promote well-being (see Van den Broeck et al., 2016, for meta-analyses in the work domain). This prop-osition has served as a guide to conduct research on factors that would influence work motivation, such as work design (Gagné et al., 1997; Van den Broeck et al., 2008), leadership (Gagné et al., 2020; Hetland et al., 2011; Slemp et al., 2018) and compensation (Gagné & Forest, 2008).

Workplace compensation is of particular relevance in the discussion of the impact of Deci's early experiments. Based on the idea that compensation systems may influence the satisfaction of psychological needs differently from rewards in laboratory-based settings, due to being larger and more important in the lives of the workers (Rynes et al., 2005), Gagné & Forest (2008) proposed a model based on SDT to understand the effects of compensation on work motivation and work-related outcomes (i.e. performance and well-being). While compensation typically includes many components that are often broken down into base pay, incentive pay and benefits, the model instead argues for breaking down monetary compen-sation into psychologically meaningful characteristics, including the total amount of money received (meeting basic life needs and value-signalling), the ratio of fixed to variable compensation components (i.e. determining reinforcement con-tingency and stakes), the perceived equity of pay as well as the subjective nature of the appraisal of performance (i.e. influencing procedural justice), and whether variable compensation determination is based on individual or collective perfor-mance (i.e. reflecting a reward's instrumentality). Each of these characteristics of compensation is proposed to influence the needs for competence, autonomy and relatedness to co-workers, which in turn should influence intrinsic and extrinsic motivation.

There is good initial support for this model. Base pay has been shown to be more strongly related to intrinsic and identified motivation, while variable pay has been more strongly related to externally regulated motivation (Kuvaas, 2006; Kuvaas et al., 2016). The strength of the contingency between an incentive and performance has been shown to influence need satisfaction, and how intrinsic motivation influences performance quality and quantity (Cerasoli et al., 2014; Cer-asoli et al., 2016), while the introduction of bonus systems has been shown to lead to increases in both turnover intentions (Kuvaas et al., 2016) and the use of pre-scribed psychotropic medication (Dahl & Pierce, 2020). In addition, the negative effects of variable pay on intrinsic motivation are explained through perceptions of being controlled by the reward, or lower autonomy (Kuvaas et al., 2020a).

Contrary to the predictions of equity theory, distributive justice has not been found to be related to need satisfaction or intrinsic motivation, while procedural justice has been (Olafsen et al., 2015). This means that the perceptions that rewards are equitably distributed according to performance matters less than perceptions of the methods used to determine rewards, such as the consistent use of appropri-ate and objective performance measures. Finally and contrary to predictions from expectancy theory (Vroom, 1964), perceptions of instrumentality (i.e. the degree of certainty that if one performs at the desired level, the reward will follow) between performance and rewards have been shown to play a non-significant role in the determination of future performance, while feedback and perceptions of autonomy play a significant role through enhancing need satisfaction (Nordgren-Selar et al., 2020). Some of these relationships depend on other boundary conditions. The attractiveness and complexity of work tasks and the type of performance measures both influence the direction and strength of incentive effects on motivation and performance. Generally, performance-contingent rewards tend to have positive effects on the performance of simple tasks, and negative effects on the performance of interesting and complex tasks (Bailey & Fessler, 2011; Weibel et al., 2010; though for different findings, see Kim et al., 2022). Performance-contingent rewards also tend to have positive effects on performance quantity but not on quality or creativity (Byron & Khazanchi, 2012; Cerasoli et al., 2014; Jenkins et al., 1998).

Meanwhile, behaviouristic and agency theory assumptions continue to dominate other business and economics fields. For a long time now, the compensation principles taught in business schools centre around the importance of sharing the success of the organisation with employees to get them to commit to organisational goals, and the importance of paying fairly by giving larger rewards to better, rather than poorer, performers (Lawler, 2000). Three oft-used psychological theories in compensation research underlie these compensation principles. Behaviourism is used to argue for the use of contingent rewards (i.e. reinforcements), while expectancy theory (Vroom, 1964) breaks this down into more cognitive components including an expectancy that efforts lead to the adequate performance of a behaviour (i.e. akin to perceptions of competence in SDT), and the expectation that adequate performance is contingently linked to a desired reward (i.e. instrumentality). Equity theory (Adams, 1965) adds that rewards, in addition to being desirable based on how attractive they are to a person, are also judged to be desirable on the basis of comparison with what other people get for similar performances.

Agency theory has also had significant influence on compensation research and practice. Contrasting its assumptions about human nature with those of SDT illustrates well how assumptions drive the types of variables and measures scholars use to test their hypotheses (Merchant et al., 2003). The major assumption in agency theory is that humans are rational and self-interested, hence everything is about the utility functions of effort expenditure (i.e. risk). The only way for employers (i.e. principals) to reap the benefits of employing people (i.e. agents) is by using control mechanisms (i.e. monitoring, rules and incentives) to align the interests of the agents to those of the principals. However, these are costly to principals (i.e. involve agency costs) because their goal is to maximise their welfare (which agency theory narrowly defines as capital gains). This view resulted in promoting the use of incentives to motivate employees to expand efforts towards the attainment of the principals' goals (i.e. capital gains through enhancing stock value), and the best way to pay agents is through stock ownership (this way they share the principals' goals by becoming a principal themselves). The same principles have also been used to argue for other forms of incentives, such as commissions and bonus systems based on individual or group performance.

SDT's assumptions about human nature are completely different to those of agency theory. SDT borrows biology's organismic model, which describes organisms in terms of both differentiation and integration (Deci & Ryan, 1985). Psychological differentiation is manifested in the exploration drive and in SDT illustrated through the concept of intrinsic motivation. Integration is manifested in human tendencies to internalise the value of acting in a particular way (so the behaviour is internally motivated instead of being reinforced by external agents (Grusec & Goodnow, 1994), and captured through self-reports of identified/integrated motivation. If the environment provides satisfaction for the needs for competence, autonomy and relatedness, people internalise behaviours and are more intrinsically motivated (Deci & Ryan, 1985; Ryan & Deci, 2017). As Deci (1995) describes, the nutrients provided by the environment to satisfy these needs allow humans to do what they would do naturally: they would be energised into both goal-directed and exploratory action. If the needs are not satisfied, extrinsic forms of motivation take over (leading to suboptimal performance and stress), or motivation can even completely disappear (leading to disengagement, despair and depression). Fundamentally, SDT recognises the importance of human agency but conceptualises this in very different ways – not just around 'rational' economic self-interest but around the fulfilment of basic psychological needs.

CONCLUSION

HOW DECI'S EXPERIMENTS HAVE INFLUENCED THINKING AND RESEARCH ABOUT COMPENSATION

The influence of CET and SDT in the design and use of financial rewards in organisations is experiencing a revival caused by many factors. The evidence for this lies before our eyes when looking at who has been publishing research on the effects of compensation on motivation and performance in the past few decades. It used to be dominated by scholars from the fields of accounting and finance, but we now see a switch to scholars from the fields of human resource management, organisational behaviour and organisational psychology in more recent years. This is in part due to scholars becoming more aware of SDT from its 'introduction' to the field of organisational behaviour over 15 years ago (Gagné & Deci, 2005).

The second alleged reason is that agency theory is increasingly being criticised on various grounds through research unsupportive of its predictions (Christen et al., 2006; Kosnik & Bettenhausen, 1992). Attempts to adjust agency theory to accommodate results that do not conform to its classical predictions abound (Bosse & Phillips, 2016; Pepper & Gore, 2015). Behavioural agency theory, for example, argues for taking into account several findings from psychology to modify certain assumptions, including bounded rationality, time effects on decision-making, equity concerns and the goal-setting method as a contracting model (Pepper & Gore, 2015). More importantly, it borrows from economists Frey & Jegen's (1997) crowding-out hypothesis (informed by CET), proposing that incentives can have adverse effects on the intrinsic motivation of agents.

Another attempt at countering agency theory is stewardship theory (Davis et al., 1997), which uses several management theories in line with the humanistic management movement to challenge rational utilitarian assumptions in agency theory and replaces them with self-actualising motives, social exchange relationship rules and trust as control mechanisms. Its main argument is that managerial assumptions determine whether hired executives and employees will become agents versus stewards for the organisation. Managers with Theory X assumptions (i.e. the belief that employees or agents are inherently unmotivated and effort-averse: McGregor, 1960) will tend to use control and incentives, whereas managers with Theory Y assumptions (i.e. the belief that employees or stewards are motivated and responsible) will trust and give autonomy (Kopelman et al., 2010). These assumptions turn to self-fulfilling prophecies whereby employees react to these managerial methods by acting as managers expect (Lawter et al., 2015; Prottas & Nummelin, 2018). Compensation components can similarly influence the sort of assumptions employees think their employer has: while base pay seems to foster the development of social exchange relationships based on trust, variable pay seems to foster the development of economic exchange relationships based on distrust (Kuvaas et al., 2020b).

What is missing from these theories is a full account of how organisational practices lead to the psychological transformation of its employees. SDT offers a complex conceptualisation of internalisation (with introjection, identification and integration representing degrees of internalisation) and a well-developed account of factors that predict the degree to which a particular goal would be internalised (support for the three psychological needs) (Gagné, 2018). Taking into account the three psychological needs also puts into question the motivational effects of other control mechanisms proposed in agency theory (and not dismissed in subsequent theorising), such as monitoring and performance evaluation, particularly as they are likely to affect the need for autonomy (Deci, 1972).

What we need is for future research to more thoroughly test predictions emanating from SDT to more fully understand the effects of incentive systems on the needs for competence, autonomy and relatedness, and subsequently on the different types of motivation (along the continuum of self-determination). The type of work and performance requirements/measures need to be taken into consideration as potential moderators of the effectiveness of different types of pay systems. Finally, beyond considering performance (individual and organisational) as the ultimate outcome, other outcomes should be considered such as interpersonal conflict, cheating, knowledge-sharing and well-being.

IMPLICATIONS FOR THE DESIGN OF COMPENSATION SYSTEMS

The earlier discussion on the consequences of adopting different assumptions about human motivation have significant consequences for organisations, management and organisational behaviour. Focusing particularly on compensation systems and the use of financial incentives, Deci's experiments lead to drastically different recommendations to those offered by agency theory. Whereas CET and SDT would warn against the liberal use of financial incentives that are performance-based and pressured, agency would highly recommend them. Though recent recommendations from behavioural agency theory and stewardship theory would also recommend using financial incentives with care, agency theory, in conjunction with expectancy and equity theories, still dominate the field of compensation and performance management, which is a problem given the questionable assumptions about human motivation that underlie agency theory (Evans & Tourish, 2017).

Agency theory is blamed for creating a balance in executive pay that shifted from salaries to stock options (Jensen & Murphy, 1990), which has not only led to significant increases in income inequality, but has led executives to solely focus on short-term capital gains to the detriment of other goals, such as corporate social responsibility (Fourcade & Khurana, 2017). To compound the issue, scholars are still debating about whether executive incentives (in the form of stocks) lead to company performance (see Gerhart et al., 2009, for a review). The same agency theory logic is often applied to bonus and commission-based pay systems, which, together with CEO pay schemes, have been credited for causing many financial scandals and unethical behaviours (Dalton et al., 2007; Dobbin & Jung, 2010; Harris & Bromiley, 2007). Thus the very things that the control mechanisms proposed by agency theory aim to avoid (i.e. self-serving behaviours) seem to create them! Evidence for this is emerging: accounting and auditing cases of misconduct in S&P 1500 firms reported by the Securities Exchange Committee between 1999 and 2012 were positively associated with the proportion of shares owned by shareholders who actively monitor executive behaviour (i.e. the influence power of shareholders), lower executive takeover protections (i.e. lower risk pressure) and pressures through financial analysts' forecasts on stock prices (Shi et al., 2017). The authors argue these results support CET more than agency theory (Shi et al., 2017).

The lesson to learn from the application of agency theory is that the assumptions we hold about human motivation have implications for the practices we put in place to influence it. Stewardship theorists focus on this aspect using Argyris's (1973) arguments (as well as Theory X/Y arguments from McGregor, 1960) that when you design organisations based on economic assumptions, it creates a self-fulfilling prophecy whereby employees behave consistently with these assumptions. Interestingly, SDT-informed research has demonstrated that teachers who perceive their students to be extrinsically motivated tend to act in a more controlling manner towards them (Pelletier et al., 2002; Taylor et al., 2008). This has been demonstrated in laboratory studies as well where 'teachers' are given bogus information about their students' motivation (Pelletier & Vallerand, 1996; Sarrazin et al., 2006). In turn, when people work under an authoritarian leader, they display less initiative, fearing it would be negatively evaluated (Haddad, 1982). This leads to an ever-reinforcing cycle of control now perceived to be necessary to get employees to work. Deci himself has eloquently discussed this issue saying that 'if you control people enough, they may begin to act as if they want to be controlled. As a self-protective strategy, they become focused outward – looking for clues about what the people in one-up positions expect of them, looking for what will keep them out of trouble' (1995, p. 148).

In conclusion, Deci's experiments sparked research that has uncovered some of the complexities of incentive systems as well as the complexity of human motivation, hopefully leading to more research that unpacks this complexity to gain a better understanding of the effects of financial rewards on employee motivation, performance and well-being (Gerhart & Fang, 2015). This will help us design more efficient compensation systems and, ultimately, more fulfilling work and better functioning organisations.

DISCUSSION QUESTIONS

1. To what extent is it possible to design incentive programmes that promote intrinsic motivation and internalisation, while at the same time be perceived as equitable?

2. What could be used instead of monetary rewards to create instrumentality between performance and outcomes that workers care about?

3. How could organisations guide and steer employee behaviour toward accomplishing organisational goals without linking pay to performance?

FURTHER READINGS

Deci, E. L., Koestner, R. & Ryan, R. M. (1999). A meta-analytic review of experiments examining the effects of extrinsic rewards on intrinsic motivation. *Psychological Bulletin*, 125, 627–68.

Provides a thorough account of the multiple meta-analyses on the effects of rewards on intrinsic motivation with a very well documented re-analysis.

Fourcade, M. & Khurana, R. (2017). The social trajectory of a finance professor and the common sense of capital. *History of Political Economy*, 49(2), 347–81.

Provides a very interesting historical account of influences in the development of agency theory.

Gagné, M. & Deci, E. L. (2005). Self-determination theory and work motivation. *Journal of Organizational Behavior*, 26(4), 331–62.

Introduces self-determination theory as a theory of work motivation.

Gerhart, B. & Fang, M. (2015). Pay, intrinsic motivation, extrinsic motivation, performance, and creativity in the workplace: Revisiting long-held beliefs. *Annual Review of Organizational Psychology and Organizational Behavior*, 2, 489–521.

Reviews the literature on extrinsic rewards from a motivational point of view and argues self-determination theory should be considered more to study the effects of financial rewards.

Kuvaas, B., Shore, L. M., Buch, R. & Dysvik, A. (2020). Social and economic exchange relationships and performance contingency: Differential effects of variable pay and base pay. *International Journal of Human Resource Management*, 31(3), 408–31.

Demonstrates how pay contingency influences the types of relationships employees form with their employer.

REFERENCES

Adams, J. S. (1965). Inequity in social exchange. In L. Berkowitz (ed.), *Advances in Experimental Social Psychology*, Vol. 2. Academic Press, pp. 267–79.

Argyris, C. (1973). Organization man: Rational and self-actualizing. *Public Administration Review*, 33, 354–57.

Bailey, C. D. & Fessler, N. J. (2011). The moderating effects of task complexity and task attractiveness on the impact of monetary incentives in repeated tasks. *Journal of Management Accounting Research*, 23, 189–210.

Bosse, D. A. & Phillips, R. A. (2016). Agency theory and bounded self-interest. *Academy of Management Review*, 41(2), 276–97.

Cameron, J. & Pierce, W. D. (1994). Reinforcement, reward, and intrinsic motivation: A meta-analysis. *Review of Educational Research*, 64, 363–423.

Cerasoli, C. P., Nicklin, J. M. & Ford, M. T. (2014). Intrinsic motivation and extrinsic incentives jointly predict performance: A 40-year meta-analysis. *Psychological Bulletin*, 140(4), 980–1008.

Cerasoli, C. P., Nicklin, J. M. & Nassrelgrgawi, A. S. (2016). Performance, incentives, and needs for autonomy, competence, and relatedness: A meta-analysis. *Motivation and Emotion*, 40, 781–813.

Christen, M., Iyer, G. & Soberman, D. (2006). Job satisfaction, job performance, and effort: A reexamination using agency theory. *Journal of Marketing*, 70(1), 137–50.

Dahl, M. S. & Pierce, L. (2020). Pay-for-performance and employee mental health: Large sample evidence using employee prescription drug usage. *Academy of Management Discoveries*, 6(1), 12–38. https://doi.org/10.5465/amd.2018.0007

Dalton, D. R., Hitt, M. A., Certo, S. T. & Dalton, C. M. (eds) (2007). *The Fundamental Agency Problem and Its Mitigation*, Vol. 1. Erlbaum.

Davis, J. H., Schoorman, F. D. & Donaldson, L. (1997). Toward a stewardship theory of management. *Academy of Management Review*, 22(1), 20–47.

Deci, E. L. (1971). Effects of externally mediated rewards on intrinsic motivation. *Journal of Personality and Social Psychology*, 18, 105–15.

Deci, E. L. (1972). The effects of contingent and noncontingent rewards and controls on intrinsic motivation. *Organizational Behavior and Human Performance*, 8, 217–29.

Deci, E. L. (1975). Notes on the theory and metatheory of intrinsic motivation. *Organizational Behavior and Human Performance*, 15, 130–45.

Deci, E. L. (1995). *Why We Do What We Do: The Dynamics of Personal Autonomy*. Penguin Books.

Deci, E. L. & Ryan, R. M. (1980). The empirical exploration of intrinsic motivational processes. In L. Berkowitz (ed.), *Advances in Experimental Social Psychology*, Vol. 13. Academic Press, pp. 39–80.

Deci, E. L. & Ryan, R. M. (1985). *Intrinsic Motivation and Self-determination in Human Behavior*. Plenum.

Deci, E. L., Cascio, W. F. & Krusell, J. (1975). Cognitive evaluation theory and some comments on the Calder and Staw critique. *Journal of Personality and Social Psychology*, 31, 81–5.

Deci, E. L., Koestner, R. & Ryan, R. M. (1999). A meta-analytic review of experiments examining the effects of extrinsic rewards on intrinsic motivation. *Psychological Bulletin*, 125, 627–68.

Dobbin, F. & Jung, J. (2010). The misapplication of Mr. Michael Jensen: How agency theory brought down the economy and why it might again. *Research in the Sociology of Organizations*, 30(1), 29–64.

Eisenberger, R. & Cameron, J. (1996). Detrimental effects of reward: Reality or myth? *American Psychologist*, 51(11), 1153–66.

Evans, S. & Tourish, D. (2017). Agency theory and performance appraisal: How bad theory damages learning and contributes to bad management practices. *Management Learning*, 48(3), 271–91.

Fang, M. & Gerhart, B. (2012). Does pay for performance diminish intrinsic interest? *International Journal of Human Resource Management*, 23(6), 1176–96.

Fourcade, M. & Khurana, R. (2017). The social trajectory of a finance professor and the common sense of capital. *History of Political Economy*, 49(2), 347–81. https://doi.org/10.1215/00182702-3876505

Frey, B. S. & Jegen, R. (1997). Motivation crowding theory. *Journal of Economic Surveys*, 15(5), 589–611.

Gagné, M. (2018). From strategy to action: Transforming organizational goals into organizational behavior. *International Journal of Management Review*, 20. https://doi.org/10.1111/ijmr.12159

Gagné, M. & Bhave, D. (2011). *Autonomy in the Workplace: An Essential Ingredient to Employee Engagement and Well-Being in Every Culture*, Vol. 1. https://doi.org/10.1007/978-90-481-9667-8_8

Gagné, M. & Deci, E. L. (2005). Self-determination theory and work motivation. *Journal of Organizational Behavior*, 26(4), 331–62. https://doi.org/10.1002/job.322

Gagné, M. & Forest, J. (2008). The study of compensation systems through the lens of self-determination theory: Reconciling 35 years of debate. *Canadian Psychology – Psychologie Canadienne*, 49(3), 225–32. https://doi.org/10.1037/a0012757

Gagné, M., Sénécal, C. & Koestner, R. (1997). Proximal job characteristics, feelings of empowerment, and intrinsic motivation: A multidimensional model. *Journal of Applied Social Psychology*, 27, 1222–40.

Gagné, M., Morin, A. J. S., Schabram, K., Wang, Z. N., Chemolli, E. & Briand, M. (2020). Uncovering relations between leadership perceptions and motivation under different organizational contexts: A multilevel cross-lagged analysis, 35, 713–32. *Journal of Business and Psychology*. https://doi.org/10.1007/s10869-019-09649-4

Gerhart, B. & Fang, M. (2015). Pay, intrinsic motivation, extrinsic motivation, performance, and creativity in the workplace: Revisiting long-held beliefs. *Annual Review of Organizational Psychology and Organizational Behavior*, 2, 489–521. https://doi.org/10.1146/annurev-orgpsych-032414-111418

Gerhart, B., Rynes, S. L. & Fulmer, I. S. (2009). Pay and performance: Individuals, groups, and executives. *Academy of Management Annals*, 3. https://doi.org/10.1080/19416520903047269

Grusec, J. E. & Goodnow, J. J. (1994). Impact of parental discipline methods on the child's internalization of values: A reconceptualization of current points of view. *Developmental Psychology*, 30, 4–19.

Haddad, Y. S. (1982). *'The Effect of Informational versus Controlling Verbal Feedback on Self-determination and Preference for Challenge'*. Unpublished dissertation, University of Rochester.

Harris, J. & Bromiley, P. (2007). Incentives to cheat: The influence of executive compensation. *Organization Science*, 18, 350–67.

Hetland, H., Hetland, J., Andreassen, C. S., Pallesen, S. & Notelaers, G. (2011). Leadership and fulfillment of the three basic psychological needs at work. *Career Development International*, 16. https://doi.org/10.1108/13620431111168903

Howard, J., Gagné, M. & Bureau, J. S. (2017). Testing a continuum structure of self-determined motivation: A meta-analysis. *Psychological Bulletin*, 143, 1346–77.

Howard, J., Gagné, M., Morin, A. J. S. & Forest, J. (2018). Using bifactor-exploratory structural equation modeling to test for a continuum structure of motivation. *Journal of Management*, 44, 2638–64.

Jensen, M. C. & Meckling, W. H. (1976). Theory of the firm: Managerial behavior, agency costs, and ownership structure. *Journal of Financial Economics*, 3, 305–60.

Jensen, M. C. & Murphy, K. J. (1990). CEO incentives – It's not how much you pay, but how. *Journal of Applied Corporate Finance*, 3, 138–53.

Kelman, H. (1958). Compliance, identification, and internalization: Three processes of attitude change. *Conflict Resolution*, 2, 51–60.

Kim, J. H., Gerhart, B. & Fang, M. (2022). Do financial incentives help or harm performance in interesting tasks? *Journal of Applied Psychology*, 107(1), 153–67. doi: http://dx.doi.org/10.1037/apl0000851

Kosnik, R. D. & Bettenhausen, K. L. (1992). Agency theory and the motivational effect of management compensation: An experimental contingency study. *Group and Organization Management*, 17(3), 309–30.

Kuvaas, B. (2006). Work performance, affective commitment, and work motivation: The roles of pay administration and pay level. *Journal of Organizational Behavior*, 27, 365–85.

Kuvaas, B., Buch, R., Gagné, M., Dysvik, A. & Forest, J. (2016). Do you get what you pay for? Sales incentives and implications for motivation and changes in turnover intention and work effort. *Motivation and Emotion*, 40(5), 667–80. https://doi.org/10.1007/s11031-016-9574-6

Kuvaas, B., Buch, R. & Dysvik, A. (2020a). Individual variable pay for performance, controlling effects, and intrinsic motivation. *Motivation and Emotion*. https://doi.org/10.1007/s11031-020-09828-4

Kuvaas, B., Shore, L. M., Buch, R. & Dysvik, A. (2020b). Social and economic exchange relationships and performance contingency: Differential effects of variable pay and base pay. *International Journal of Human Resource Management*, 31(3), 408–31. https://doi.org/10.1080/09585192.2017.1350734

Lawler, E. E. I. (2000). *Rewarding Excellence: Pay Strategies for the New Economy*. Jossey-Bass.

McGregor, D. (1960). *The Human Side of the Enterprise*. McGraw-Hill.

Merchant, K. A., Van der Stede, W. A. & Zheng, L. (2003). Disciplinary constraints on the advancement of knowledge: The case of organizational incentive systems. *Accounting, Organizations, and Society*, 28, 251–86.

Nordgren-Selar, A., Sverke, M., Falkenberg, H. & Gagné, M. (2020). *It's [not] all 'bout the Money: The Relative Importance of Performance-based Pay and Support for Psychological Needs for Job Performance*. Stockholm University.

Olafsen, A. H., Halvari, H., Forest, J. & Deci, E. L. (2015). Show them the money? The role of pay, managerial need support, and justice in a self-determination theory model of intrinsic work motivation. *Scandinavian Journal of Psychology*, 56(4), 447–57. https://doi.org/10.1111/sjop.12211

Pelletier, L. G. & Vallerand, R. J. (1996). Supervisors' beliefs and subordinates' intrinsic motivation: A behavioral confirmation analysis. *Journal of Personality and Social Psychology*, 71, 331–40. https://doi.org/10.1037/0022-3514.71.2.331

Pelletier, L. G., Séguin-Lévesque, C. & Legault, L. (2002). Pressure from above and pressure from below as determinants of teachers' motivation and teaching behaviors. *Journal of Educational Psychology*, 94(1), 186–96. https://doi.org/10.1037/0022-0663.94.1.186

Pepper, A. & Gore, J. (2015). Behavioral agency theory: New foundations for theorizing about executive compensation. *Journal of Management*, 41(4), 1045–68.

Pinder, C. C. (1976). Additivity versus nonadditivity of intrinsic and extrinsic incentives: Implications for work motivation, performance, and attitudes. *Journal of Applied Psychology*, 61(6), 693–700.

Rummel, A. & Feinberg, R. (1988). Cognitive evaluation theory: A meta-analytic review of the literature. *Social Behavior and Personality*, 16, 147–64.

Ryan, R. M. (1995). Psychological needs and the facilitation of intrinsic motivation, social development and well being. *American Psychologist*, 63, 397–427.

Ryan, R. M. & Deci, E. L. (2017). *Self-determination Theory: Basic Psychological Needs in Motivation, Development, and Wellness*. Guilford Press.

Ryan, R. M., Mims, V. & Koestner, R. (1983). Relation of reward contingency and interpersonal context to intrinsic motivation: Review and test using cognitive evaluation theory. *Journal of Personality and Social Psychology*, 45, 736–50.

Ryan, R. M., Ryan, W. S. & Di Domenico, S. I. (2018). Beyond reinforcement – intrinsic and extrinsic motivation: Building on Deci (1971). In P. Corr (ed.), *Personality and Individual Differences: Revisiting the Classic Studies*. Sage.

Rynes, S. L., Gerhart, B. & Parks, L. (2005). Personnel psychology: Performance evaluation and pay for performance. *Annual Review of Psychology*, 56, 571–600.

Sarrazin, P. G., Tessier, D. P., Pelletier, L. G., Trouilloud, D. O. & Chanal, J. P. (2006). The effects of teachers' expectations about students' motivation on teachers' autonomy-supportive and controlling behaviors. *International Journal of Sport and Exercise Psychology*, 4(3), 283–301. https://doi.org/10.1080/1612197X.2006.9671799

Shi, W., Connelly, B. L. & Hoskisson, R. E. (2017). External corporate governance and financial fraud: Cognitive evaluation theory insights on agency theory prescriptions. *Strategic Management Journal*, 38, 1268–86.

Slemp, G. R., Kern, M. L., Patrick, K. J. & Ryan, R. M. (2018). Leader autonomy support in the workplace: A meta-analytic review. *Motivation and Emotion*, 42, 706–24. https://doi.org/10.1007/s11031-018-9698-y

Tang, S.-H. & Hall, V. C. (1995). The overjustification effect: A meta-analysis. *Applied Cognitive Psychology*, 9, 365–404.

Taylor, I. M., Ntoumanis, N. & Standage, M. (2008). A self-determination theory approach to understanding the antecedents of teachers' motivational strategies in physical education [empirical study, quantitative study]. *Journal of Sport & Exercise Psychology*, 30(1), 75–94.

Van den Broeck, A., Ferris, D. L., Chang, C.-H. & Rosen, C. C. (2016). A review of self-determination theory's basic psychological needs at work. *Journal of Management*, 42(5), 1195–229.

Van den Broeck, A., Vansteenkiste, M., De Witte, H. & Lens, W. (2008). Explaining the relationships between job characteristics, burnout, and engagement: The role of basic psychological need satisfaction [empirical study, quantitative study]. *Work & Stress*, 22(3), 277–94. https://doi.org/http://dx.doi.org/10.1080/02678370802393672

Vroom, V. (1964). *Work and Motivation*. Wiley.

Weibel, A., Rost, K. & Osterloh, M. (2010). Pay for performance in the public sector – benefits and (hidden) costs. *Journal of Public Administration Research and Theory*, 20(2), 387–412.

Wiersma, U. J. (1992). The effects of extrinsic rewards in intrinsic motivation: A meta-analysis. *Journal of Occupational and Organizational Psychology*, 65, 101–14.

Zeigarnik, B. (1927). Das behalten erledigter und unerledigter handlungen. *Psychologische Forschung*, 9, 1–85.

5

Organisational Identification: Revisiting Mael & Ashforth's 'Alumni and their Alma Mater' Study

Naomi Ellemers & Dick de Gilder

The classic study revisited in this chapter was based on the doctoral disserta-tion of first author Fred Mael, which was supervised by second author Blake Ashforth. They developed a scale to assess organisational identification, and exam-ined how this correlates with rated features of the organisation and self-reported willingness to support the organisation. They tested their predictions in a sample of 297 alumni of an all-male religious college located in the northeast of the United States (Mael & Ashforth, 1992). The materials developed for this study specifically catered to the school context and inquired about displays of support typical for alumni of educational institutions in the US. Nevertheless, the relations first dem-onstrated by Mael and Ashforth inspired researchers to adopt a similar approach to the examination of organisational identification as a key psychological variable that is relevant to many other organisational problems in a broad range of sam-ples and contexts. This broad and lasting influence of the seminal work of Mael & Ashforth on other researchers in the field is what made the study a classic in organ-isational psychology.

Organisational identification broadly refers to the experience individuals may have that they belong, want to belong and feel they belong to a specific organisa-tion. People can experience the successes and failures of an organisation as their own, for instance claiming 'We developed a new medicine for cancer'. Sometimes they do this regardless of how central or peripheral their job would seem to the organisation's performance and key products or services delivered (e.g. in the can-teen, in office maintenance, or in the research team). This sense of self-involve-ment might even guide the feelings and behaviours of individuals who technically do not really belong to the organisation, such as customers, fans – or in the case of the classic study we will be discussing here – alumni who have left the organisation many years ago.

The phenomenon that individuals can consider a place of employment – or organisation they are associated with in another way (as students, clients or patients) – as defining their sense of who they are, also implies that they can come to think of convictions, practices and achievements of the organisation as their own. Understanding how organisations might be able to instill such a powerful impact on the thoughts, feelings and behaviours of individuals who feel somehow connected to them, is of interest to organisational leaders who seek to guide, control, improve or change the behaviour of individuals. Hence, organisational identification has become an important topic in the social and management sciences: a Web of Science search yielded over 10,000 hits when we prepared this text.

BACKGROUND

The manuscript of the classic study was first submitted to the *Journal of Organizational Behavior* in 1989. It is no coincidence that this was also the year in which the same two authors published a theory paper on 'social identity theory and the organisation', in the *Academy of Management Review* (Ashforth & Mael, 1989), which became a seminal publication, with over 4,000 citations in Web of Science (14,000 on Google Scholar) at the time of writing.

This theoretical paper, and the classic study which provided its first empirical test, are best considered a joint effort to introduce a new way of thinking about these issues in the management literature. Both were based on the analysis of basic cognitive mechanisms offered by social identity theory (SIT) (Tajfel & Turner, 1979, 1985) with later extensions referred to as self-categorisation theory (SCT) (Turner, 1985). To date, these are well-known and highly influential theories in social and organisational psychology, specifying when, how and why people think of themselves in terms of their membership in social groups – instead of as separate and unique individuals.

This way of thinking had originally been developed to understand cooperative versus competitive relations between members of different groups in society. By the late 1980s researchers in social psychology had begun to apply this approach to the behaviour of individuals at work, for instance at a paper factory (Brown et al., 1986), or among hospital nurses (Oaker & Brown, 1986). So in a way, the ideas put forth by Mael and Ashforth were already known and tested by other researchers. However, these were scholars working in another intellectual tradition. Social identity theory was developed in Europe based on evidence from 'minimal group' studies. These highly controlled experimental procedures provided 'proof of principle' that even arbitrary group boundaries can acquire symbolic and psychological meaning and have far-reaching behavioural implications. Management theories at the time were mostly inspired by the reality of US companies, and analyses relying on economic approaches that emphasised selfish motives, interdependency and exchange relations as key drivers of human behaviour.

At the time, such disciplinary and geographical divides were even more difficult to overcome than today (see also Ellemers, 2021; Ellemers et al., 2020). Each group of scholars had their own theoretical and methodological approaches, which they considered as being of superior quality and value. Management scholars characterised the experimental procedures and laboratory simulations used by social psychologists to test specific hypotheses as 'reductionist' and lacking external validity. By the same token, social psychologists criticised organisational researchers for being unable to specify causal mechanisms – with their favoured method of regressing available information that might capture variables of interest on a multitude of potential predictors.

It is essential to note that the classic study was conducted in this context, but also in an era before scholars across the world were connected through the World Wide Web. The exchange of ideas with other scholars was mainly facilitated by the activities of disciplinary associations. Researchers would not often be aware of or attend conferences organised by associations representing other disciplines or located in another continent. The books and journals further disseminating these ideas were only published in hard copy, to be distributed among members of the association and a limited number of library subscribers. One had to be particularly open-minded, motivated and persistent to overcome these known barriers to interdisciplinary knowledge-sharing.

This was the challenge faced by Mael & Ashforth: how to introduce the ideas developed by European experimental social psychologists to an audience consisting of US-based organisational scholars with their own research traditions? What was their strategy? This is the perspective we take in revisiting their classic study. Here, we highlight two important features of their work that helped convince US-based management scholars of the added value of the European approach to social identity.

First, we note that the theoretical analysis offered by Mael and Ashforth tapped into the emerging awareness that 'identity' might be a relevant construct for organisational scholars – while pointing to shortcomings in prior conceptualisation and measurement of this construct. The authors do this by citing different sources of data attesting to the general relevance of identity in organisations, which is captured, for instance, by the use of symbols (Albert & Whetten, 1985). At the same time, they lament the lack of theory and inconsistency of definitions and measures in prior studies. They then refer to their theory paper, and its aim to resolve this conceptual confusion, when they define organisational identification as: '... *the perception of oneness with or belongingness to an organization, where the individual* defines *him or herself in terms of the organization(s) in which he or she is a member*' (Mael & Ashforth, 1992, p. 104).

Accordingly, the stated goal of the classic study was: '*to operationalize this conceptualization ... and provide a partial test of the associated model of antecedents and consequences*' (p. 104). Drawing on their theoretical paper (Ashforth & Mael, 1989), Mael and Ashforth introduced four aspects of the conceptualisation of organisational identification:

(a) The nature of identification as a perceptual/cognitive construct is abstract and generic and does not depend on specific behaviours or affective states.

(b) Identity has no meaning in itself, but acquires meaning by comparison to other individuals and their relationships to other groups.

(c) People identify with groups partly because these can enhance their self-esteem – even if this can also harm them in case of group failure.

(d) Although individuals may be classified into discrete categories (e.g. male vs. female; white collar vs. blue collar worker), this does not necessarily mean individuals adopt such categorisations, nor identify strongly with – or have strong feelings about – their group membership.

Second, Mael and Ashforth designed their study according to research traditions that were known and accepted by management scholars. They did this, for instance, by including a number of individual level predictors that are not specified in their model, and by adding existing measures to differentiate organisational identification from related constructs. In their conceptualisation, the authors emphasise the perceptual/cognitive aspects of organisational identification – indicating the *psychological* connection with the group. This helped them to explain the added value of this construct beyond and above other existing measures that mainly capture people's feelings (satisfaction, loyalty) or behaviours (citizenship displays, effort) relating to the group.

Specifically, Mael & Ashforth (1992) distinguish organisational identification from organisational commitment. The authors note that the organisational identification measure they used in this study correlates relatively highly ($r = 0.69$) with the organisational commitment questionnaire (OCQ) (cf. Mowday et al., 1979). Yet the authors characterise the latter as a broader construct, encompassing acceptance of the organisation's goals and values, willingness to exert effort and desire to maintain membership of the organisation (Mowday et al., 1979). This refers to behaviour, as well as affect, and internalisation (what I believe), which the authors consider as separate from organisational identification (who I am).

Likewise, the authors discuss the distinction between organisational identification and professional/occupational identification. They specify the latter as referring to a particular type of profession or work people can do (e.g. being a journalist, or a doctor), instead of indicating the inclination to define themselves in terms of the *organisation* to which they belong.

In retrospect, it seems that these two distinctive aspects of their approach were instrumental in bridging the gap between the two traditions of scholarship. These allowed Mael and Ashforth to empirically demonstrate the distinction and added value of their theoretical approach in a way that was understood by their management audience. We think this is an important reason why the publication of the classic study (Mael & Ashforth, 1992) following up on their seminal theory paper (Ashforth & Mael, 1989) marked a turning point for the adoption of ideas from social identity theory in organisational scholarship. Their study became a classic because it introduced a different audience to an existing theoretical perspective. It allowed management scholars and practitioners to embrace the relevance of these insights for organisations, and to adopt an empirical measure of organisational identification as a key variable in the examination of many research questions (see Haslam, 2004, for an overview of social identity research in organisations).

DETAILED DESCRIPTION

The main goal of the classic study is to examine the added value of organisational identification – in the specific conceptualisation provided by the authors. This separates organisational identification from other related constructs, and emphasises the 'meaning making' aspects of the organisation for the individual and their sense of self.

The model to be tested relies on social identity reasoning offered by Ashforth & Mael's (1989) theoretical analysis, and treats the variables included in the study as (individual and organisational level) antecedents versus consequences of organisational identification, assuming these are related in a causal model (see Figure 5.1).

Yet the actual study consists of a single self-report survey, yielding correlational data in a cross-sectional design. While this limits the possibility of making firm causal inferences, it represents the empirical approach that was common at the time and well-known by management scholars. It seems that the authors were well aware of these limitations, as is communicated in the subtitle in which they describe their classic study as 'a partial test of the reformulated model of organisational identification'.

First, the study specifies *organisational antecedents*, which are derived from social identity theory. These include scales to assess:

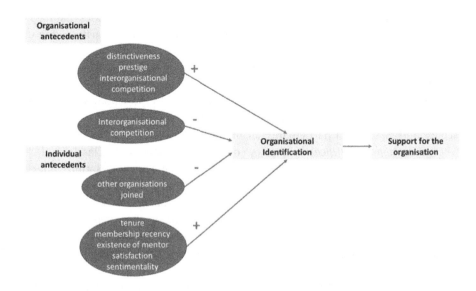

Figure 5.1   The theoretical model tested in the classic study.

(a) The *distinctiveness* of the organisation's values and practices that differentiate the group from other groups, and define the unique identity of its members (15 items, newly developed).

(b) The perceived *prestige* of the organisation (e.g. whether others think highly of the organisation) that is relevant for self-esteem (8 items).

(c) The perceived competition *between* this organisation and others, which is seen as a trigger for the accentuation of differences between organisational members as 'us' and others outside the organisation as 'them' (8 items).

(d) The perceived competition *within* the organisation, as a factor that might enhance a focus on sub-units and reduces cohesion and feelings of one-ness at the organisational level (8 items).

Second, the study specifies *individual antecedents*. Again, the authors acknowledge these are not included in their theory paper (Ashforth & Mael, 1989). Nevertheless, these measures resemble individual-level background or control variables that are commonly used in management studies as additional predictors and to correct for individual differences in regression analyses. The individual antecedents are assessed with single items and factual questions that are relevant to the school context, including the amount of time actively involved with the school, the length of time since leaving, the number of different schools attended and the frequency of contact with a mentor-like faculty member. Additionally, 15 items assessed satisfaction with the contribution of the school to personal, social and career development and 'sentimentality' with seven items such as 'I like to reminisce about my youth'. At the same time, the authors observe that the study did not include measures assessing other interpersonal and group-level characteristics that might impact on identification, such as interpersonal interaction, similarity, liking or internalisation of shared values.

Organisational consequences are considered the main outcome variable of interest. Willingness to donate money is indicated by asking respondents to state the priority they assign to offering financial contributions to the school. Further, single items ask about their willingness to advise their son and others to attend the school, and assess their participation in alumni events and functions offered.

Organisational identification, the key construct examined in the classic study, is assessed with six items ('When someone criticises (name of organisation), it feels like a personal insult'; 'I am very interested in what others think about (name of organisation)'; 'When I talk about this organisation, I usually say "we" rather than "they"'; 'This organisation's successes are my successes', 'When someone praises this organisation, it feels like a personal compliment', 'If a story in the media criticised the organisation, I would feel embarrassed'), which have an internal reliability of 0.87.

The results showed that 35 per cent of the variance in organisational identification is explained by the different predictors when these are included in a regression analysis. At the organisational level, significant predictors were: organisational distinctiveness ($\beta = 0.13$), prestige ($\beta = 0.26$) and intraorganisational competition ($\beta = -0.12$). Significant predictors at the individual level were individual tenure ($\beta = 0.12$), satisfaction ($\beta = 0.33$) and sentimentality ($\beta = 0.15$). When turning to the 'outcomes' of organisational identification, significant relationships emerged for the stated priority of donating to the college ($\beta = 0.30$), the willingness to advise one's son ($\beta = 0.22$) or others ($\beta = 0.23$) to attend, and listening to tapes ($\beta = 0.29$) and lectures ($\beta = 0.33$) offered to alumni from the college.

The statistical analysis also is in line with common procedures at the time and reflects the aim of the study to demonstrate the added value of organisational identification. First, all predictors are included in the regression analysis to examine their unique predictive value. Then, the role of organisational identification as the key factor that connects antecedents with outcomes is examined by testing mediation for each of the separate outcome indicators, using the stepwise procedure in regression analysis.

These analyses reveal that half of the outcome indicators are still significantly related to the antecedents after inclusion of organisational identification as an additional predictor. The authors interpret this as indicating partial mediation, to convey that identification does not fully mediate the effects of antecedents on outcomes. While the intent is to demonstrate the added value of organisational identification as a cognitive/perceptual construct that is different from esteem or motivation, these results also show that relevant outcome indicators are primarily predicted by variables indicating the *esteem* (prestige and satisfaction) derived from the group – as these reveal the highest β-weights. Revisiting this study after so many years also reveals how statistical approaches have developed over time. Nowadays reviewers would likely request the use of more sophisticated methods, such as confirmatory factor analysis or structural equation modelling, comparing the fit of the hypothesised model to alternative models – probably with a larger and more highly powered sample.

At several points in the text, Mael & Ashforth draw attention to the special nature of their respondents. These are 297 alumni of an all-male college for religious education, where they stayed for 6.1 years on average. This implies that the school focuses on a specific and relatively homogeneous (all male) professional group which makes it more likely that its attendants are aware of the distinct (religious) values they share and determine 'who they are'. Unfortunately, no further information is provided about the items used to assess this type of distinctiveness or how the attitudes, values and practices endorsed by the organisation are specific for this type of college or the religious community it serves. Another relevant observation is that the college seems to be an institution with relatively low status. That is, the extent to which research participants report interorganisational competition, this indicates more negative ratings of organisational prestige and individual satisfaction.

These specific features of the research context and sample used do not invalidate the classic study or its conclusions. Yet, they might imply that the support obtained for the hypotheses tested would not necessarily generalise to other types of organisation (e.g. where individuals are tied by interdependence instead of shared values), other samples (e.g. capturing day-to-day experiences of current employees of the organisation instead of capturing recollections of early professional training) and other organisational outcomes (e.g. displaying work-related efforts instead of showing an interest in networking and educational events). This fits with our analysis that the contribution of this study to scholarship in management is not contained in the specific results obtained but in demonstrating the feasibility of applying this theoretical approach to the examination of organisational problems.

Yet, the broad adoption of these ideas was probably facilitated not only by the research approach adopted by the authors but also by the generalisations they provided when discussing the implications of the classic study. The authors highlight how the data from this unique sample and context might point to implications for mergers, the loyalty of employees to their place of work and competition between organisations. This is consistent with their stated goal to test the applicability of their general theoretical approach – and treating this study primarily as proof of principle. Is also exhibits another feature that editors nowadays might no longer appreciate: building on empirical observations to 'go beyond the data' in further theory development – rather than only considering whether the findings obtained with this sample and measures support specific a priori predictions.

IMPACT OF THE CLASSIC STUDY

As a first indicator of its impact, we consider the number and nature of subsequent publications referencing this and other social identity sources in the Web of Science. When preparing this chapter we found 1,672 publications referring to the classic study accumulating in almost three decades. The rate of citations has clearly grown over the years, with an exponential increase to about 200 citations per year in the last five years considered (see Figure 5.2). The classic study is included in 80 systematic, meta-analytic or narrative reviews on the topic. Most of these citations emerge in journals in the field of management, followed by psychology journals and journals catering for other social sciences such as communication and specific topics such as environmental behaviour or education. Not all these publications citing the classic study are 'about' organisational identification, however. Only in one-third (543 of 1,672) of the publications we found is organisational identification mentioned as a key construct in the abstract. We consider these publications in more detail below.

One way in which the Mael and Ashforth study has been influential, is by prompting researchers to consider organisational identification as a construct to explain variations in the attitudes and behaviours of individuals employed within a given organisation. An analysis of the keywords used most frequently by such researchers to characterise their publications gives an indication of the types of issues commonly examined. Resonating with the goal of the classic study, these tend to address the relationship between organisational identification and similar

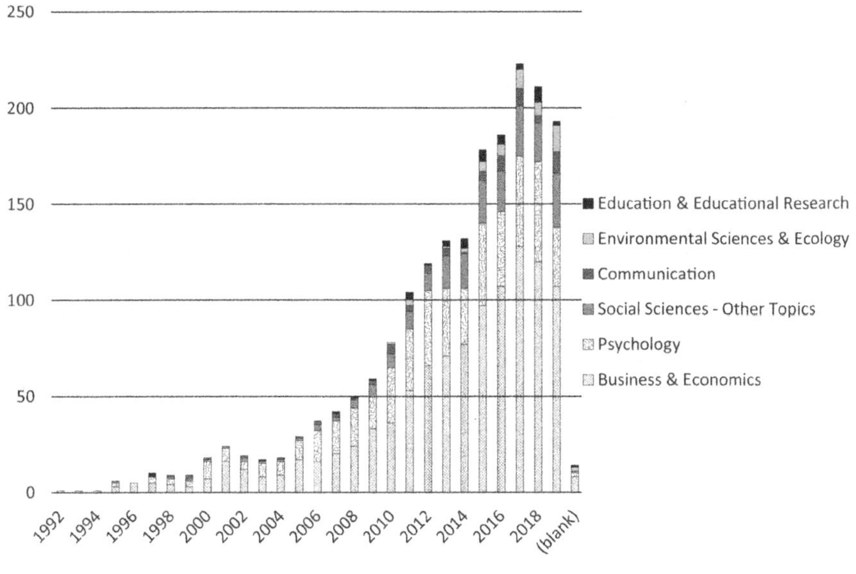

Figure 5.2 Number of references per year and per discipline to the classic study.

constructs, such as organisational commitment. Further, these publications extend the classic study by exploring different organisational-level antecedents that might encourage or discourage organisational identification. These include perceived characteristics of the organisation, such as its reputation and prestige and corporate social responsibility activities.

Additionally, to explain the extent to which employees identify with the organisation researchers have examined aspects of the organisational climate and the day-to-day treatment of employees by the organisation. In this context, studies have examined the role of organisational justice, quality of leadership and general organisational support. Extending the results of Mael and Ashforth, researchers have also explored the range of outcomes that might be predicted by the extent to which employees identify with the organisation. On the one hand, these include work-related attitudes and intentions of individual employees toward the organisation, such as their satisfaction, trust, loyalty and motivation. On the other, these refer to more concrete (positive and negative) outcomes that might affect the organisation, such as overall turnover and performance of employees, or more specific indicators of their innovation, service quality and citizenship behaviour.

The classic study has also inspired researchers to examine variations in the behaviour of individual employees. By focusing on organisational identification as a key explanatory construct, they explicitly consider the *psychological* and the subjective ties individuals might experience with their organisation as inherently related to the self. This goes beyond more economic and rational approaches that conceptualise this relation in terms of the organisation's ability to implement sanctions and rewards, or the existence of formal rights and contractual obligations. These approaches are commonly used in management studies to explain relations

between organisations and their stakeholders in terms of individual need fulfilment (e.g. Bauman & Skitka, 2012).

This strand of research has yielded new insights on factors that facilitate or
impede the emergence of organisational identification – beyond rational exchanges
or selfish concerns. Of particular interest in this context are factors that can be
influenced by management, such as the diversity climate in organisations with
racial (dis-)similarity between employees (Cole et al., 2016), or the extent to which
the organisation offers support to employees and reciprocates employees' efforts
to invest in the relation (He et al., 2014; Sluss et al., 2012). Thus employees should
be more willing to consider the organisation's goals as if these were their own,
when the organisation makes an effort to manage diversity and inclusion well or
when it goes out of its way to offer support to individual employees, for instance
facilitating work–life balance.

Further, Mael and Ashforth's study introduced some interesting organisational
outcomes that were context-specific, and not directly performance-related, such
as making donations to the organisation and attending alumni activities. Other
studies that built on the classic study did likewise, as these include the influence
employees have on each other (Kraus et al., 2012) and the relations employees
have with their customers (Anaza, 2015) or – in a number of cases – their leaders
(Chen et al., 2017; Moriano et al., 2014; Wieseke et al., 2009).

Finally, the research questions offered in the classic study have also inspired
researchers to consider additional implications of the psychological relation
between the individual and the organisation – that is captured by assessing their
organisational identification. This has helped them tackle a range of thorny issues
that cannot be fully anticipated by formal guidelines, such as the occurrence of
unethical behaviour (Ploeger & Bisel, 2013), or the choice of a representative for
work negotiations (Demoulin et al., 2016).

KEY REPLICATIONS AND GENERALISATIONS

Notwithstanding the impact of the classic study as characterised above, we
have found no examples of direct replications. This fits the goal of the authors
to introduce the construct of organisational identification to researchers in management, rather than to develop scholarship on the organisational ties of school
alumni. A few studies since have addressed support offered by alumni to the
organisation where they were trained, without being modelled on the classic study
or making use of the specific operationalisation or measure proposed by Mael &
Ashforth (1992). For instance, McDearmon (2013) examines the relation between
identification with the organisation and support from alumni by assessing how
others consider this relation, from a symbolic interactionist perspective. Thus,
instead of considering how important the university is for people's self-views and
behavioural intentions, this study focuses on other people's awareness of one's
identity as an alumnus, and relates this to social expectations about the duty of
alumni to support their university (McDearmon, 2013). This study can be seen

as a conceptual replication of the classic study, in that it observes a relationship between the meaning alumni assign to the relationship with their alma mater and their willingness to participate in alumni events and offer charitable donations to the institution. However, this study does not conceive of organisational identification as defined in the classic study (Mael & Ashforth, 1992) or the theory paper (Mael & Ashforth, 1989). Nor does it use the measure proposed in the classic study. Both these features were cited by the authors as central goals of the classic study. In this sense, the examination of alumni responses by McDearmon (2013) cannot be considered as a replication or as following from the new theoretical approach to these issues started by the classic study.

Other studies refer too loosely to organisations and the ties individuals have with them to qualify as replications or extensions of the classic study. For instance, one study examined whether the degree to which alumni of an accountancy firm identified with their former employer related to their willingness to send business to the firm (Iyer et al., 1997). Another study related alumni's ownership of university insignia goods to monetary donations made to their alma mater, however, without explicitly assessing the degree to which they identified with the organisation (Tom & Elmer, 1994). Likewise a study showed that after infractions in college sports came to light, alumni increased donations, while non-alumni decreased financial support. The authors explained this by arguing that the support offered by alumni attested to solidarity resulting from their higher identification with the organisation, but this was not explicitly measured (Zavyalova et al., 2016).

When considering publications citing the classic study, the vast majority do not address alumni or how they continue to support the college where they were trained. Instead, most research inspired by the classic study focuses on the work motivation and performance of individuals employed at different jobs in a range of (mostly for profit) organisations. Indeed, one of the key goals of the classic study – to test a specific conceptualisation and measure of organisational identification – seems to have been overlooked by many researchers that followed. For instance, of the 543 articles 'about' organisational identification citing the classic study, only 28 also address social identity theory as a relevant perspective. Of these 28 articles, only ten actually use the conceptualisation and scale that were introduced – while this constitutes a central feature and goal of the classic study.

Again, this state of affairs fits our conclusion that the significance of the classic study mainly consisted of introducing organisational identification as a relevant construct in research on organisations. Indeed, the classic study inspired a number of generalisations. Following up on the classic study, other researchers have examined organisational identification in other types of samples and in relation to other types of research questions, albeit conceptualised and measured in different ways. These efforts have revealed that organisational identification can benefit a range of employee attitudes and behaviours, including employee turnover (Conroy et al., 2016), job satisfaction (Van Dick et al., 2004) and extra-role performance (Liu et al., 2011). This reflects one of the future directions already mentioned in the classic study. That is, Mael & Ashforth (1992) envisioned that considering the organisation as an extension of the self might be adaptive and healthy, as this indicates individual connectedness and empowerment. This view also resonates with the emerging body of evidence on the beneficial relationship between social identification and a range of health outcomes (Jetten et al., 2011).

However, in line with the original conceptualisation, further studies also revealed that organisational identification only speaks to the *strength* of the relationship between the individual and the organisation – which can have beneficial as well as adverse effects on the behaviour that is desired. This downside of organisational identification is extensively documented in research (for an overview, see Conroy et al., 2016). It has also been argued that identification with the organisation allows employees to be socialised into corrupt practices and to accept collective rationalisations of unethical acts (Anand et al., 2004).

For instance, those who 'overidentify' with the organisation (Dukerich et al., 1998) find it difficult to curb organisational demands and are at risk of being defensive about the organisation's shortcomings. Studies have associated high levels of organisational identification, for instance, with unethical behaviour (Umphress et al., 2010) and work–family conflict (Li et al., 2015). Further, those who identify strongly with the organisation in its current form tend to resist change in the organisation's identity – for instance in the case of organisational mergers (Van Leeuwen et al., 2003; see also Van Dick et al., 2004). This work documenting the 'dark side' of organisational identification was also envisioned by the authors of the classic study, who predicted that high levels of organisational commitment might indicate resistance to change, ethnocentrism and overdependence of individuals on the organisation.

Finally, a substantial strand of research inspired by the classic study is the work showing that groups or work teams can also be the focus of feelings of oneness and identification (Riketta & Van Dick, 2005; Van Knippenberg & Van Schie, 2000). Some have even argued that the more proximal day-to-day experiences in work teams constitute a more important and powerful reason for individuals to feel involved with the workplace and exert themselves towards shared goals (Ellemers et al., 2004). Another key insight is that individual's feelings of identification with their work team or the organisation is a crucial outcome of successful leadership (Haslam et al., 2010; Hogg & Terry, 2000).

BEYOND THE CLASSIC STUDY: THEORETICAL DEVELOPMENTS

After publishing their classic study, together with others, the authors have continued to address conceptual and measurement issues to further develop and refine their reasoning about organisational identification (Ashforth, 2016). They were not satisfied with having others embrace the general notion that organisational identification is a relevant construct. Instead, in subsequent publications they continued to emphasise their specific conceptualisation, focusing on the perception that the self shares particular experiences or characteristics with the organisation. The authors see this as essential to the process of meaning making, enacting and accounting for one's identity as a member of the organisation (Ashforth et al., 2008). They argue this is also what makes it different from related constructs with which it may converge, such as relational identification with organisational leaders (Sluss & Ashforth, 2008) or occupational identification (Ashforth et al., 2013).

Further efforts aimed at clarifying this conceptualisation, that had already been made in the classic study, but were not always picked up by others. In this context, researchers have addressed the distinction between organisational *identification* and organisational *commitment* in particular (Mael & Tetrick, 1992; Van Knippenberg & Sleebos, 2006). On the one hand, empirical studies seem to support this position. For instance, a meta-analysis summarising results from 96 statistical analyses concluded that organisational identification better predicts employees' work behaviour than organisational commitment (Riketta, 2005). On the other hand, caution is warranted in drawing this conclusion because the studies included in this summary used different scales to assess these constructs, yielding different results. The lack of consensus in the literature about the conceptualisation and measurement of organisational identification and how this relates to organisational commitment implies that different studies have addressed different issues. This makes it difficult to draw clear conclusions from reviews of this literature (Edwards, 2005).

Some have proposed to resolve this by simply broadening the construct of organisational identification beyond its original cognitive/conceptual meaning indicated in the classic study, also taking into account affective aspects (Bergami & Bagozzi, 2000). This is in line with theories on commitment that refer to organisational identification as affective commitment to the organisation (Meyer et al., 1991). It also resonates with the original conception of social identity that goes beyond cognitive self-categorisation and includes the evaluative and emotional significance of the group for the individual (Tajfel, 1978; see also Ellemers et al., 1999). Indeed, empirical examinations of people's behaviour in work teams and organisations resulted in the conclusion that their emotional involvement is the key to motivation and group-serving behaviour (Ellemers et al., 2003; Ouwerkerk et al., 1999). It could even be argued that the identification scale by Mael & Ashforth (1992) actually is already operationalised more broadly than their definition of identification suggests. That is, taking a closer look at the identification items in the classic article, it appears that the scale that was used not only refers to perception or cognition aspects. In the original scale, 3 of the 6 items refer to feelings, including affective components in the measurement of organisational identification. Yet, the scale has a high reliability, suggesting that together these cognitive and affective components contribute to a single homogeneous construct. In retrospect, this operationalisation also clarifies why the identification scale correlates relatively strongly with the organisational commitment scale (Mowday et al., 1979; see also Van Knippenberg & Sleebos, 2006).

Regardless of how exactly it is conceptualised and measured, the ongoing interest in organisational identification attests to the broad significance of connecting one's definition of the self to key features and values of the organisation. This is particularly relevant in view of ongoing developments in labour relations, and with organisations that are increasingly dynamic and complex. This has resulted in a decrease in long-term employment prospects and is characterised by ongoing developments in the types of contracts and tasks, expecting increasingly diverse individuals to work together at different locations across the world. An important consequence of these developments is that organisations, and people's ties to them, mainly take shape in their 'hearts and minds' rather than being rooted in specific structures, relations or locations (Ellemers & Van Nunspeet, 2013). In this context, the ability of individuals to identify with the organisation is more important than ever in affording meaning to their association with the organisation, to feed their motivation and to provide direction to their efforts (Albert et al., 2000; Ellemers et al., 2004).

Thus, in a more general sense, the classic study – together with the theory paper preceding it – prompted theories on organisational behaviour and scholarship on management to take into account the convergence between organisational attributes and people's self-constructs (Dutton et al., 1994). The key insight is that factors that cause individuals to see themselves as part of the organisation – at a psychological level – may be more important predictors of their responses than narrowly selfish and calculating concerns that are so often the focus of managerial practices.

Further, because identification is about subjectively meaningful social entities rather than objective dependence relations, people can choose and shift the focus of their identification in the organisation to their work team (the sales department), their occupational group (IT specialists) or their demographic group at work (female partners in the firm) (see Ashforth & Johnson, 1999; Ellemers et al., 1998; Ellemers & Rink, 2005). Indeed, a sense of psychological engagement with the organisation not only stems from the extent to which the organisation benefits the individual and is a source of pride (Tyler & Blader, 2003). People essentially want to be respected and valued by others within the organisation to be able to feel they belong (Rogers & Ashforth, 2014). The desire for a positive identity is so strong that even when such respect is lacking, people may still 'cope' with such situations by reframing their identity (Petriglieri, 2011). People can derive a strong sense of identity from organisations and occupations even those that tend to be seen as shameful or 'dirty', such as garbage collectors or sex workers (Ashforth & Kreiner, 2013).

In general, then, the self-defining aspects of organisational identification relate to the attraction, selection and attrition of individuals in organisations (Pratt, 1998). This is also the conclusion that emerges from a meta-analysis statistically comparing 149 correlations observed in 114 different studies (Lee et al., 2015). Notwithstanding the downsides of 'overcommitment' summarised above, organisational identification generally relates to positive attitudes towards the organisation, such as job involvement, job satisfaction and organisational commitment. Individuals who display extra-role performance, indicating behaviour that supports the organisation, also are the ones who identify with the organisation.

CONCLUSION

The theory paper and the classic study (Ashforth & Mael, 1989; Mael & Ashforth, 1992) have successfully raised interest in organisational identification, in some ways making this approach 'too successful' (Ashforth, 2016). Management scholars have embraced the general notion that individuals can identify with an organisation and generally acknowledge the beneficial effects this can have. However, many have not explicitly considered whether, and how, individuals actually experience unity between the self and the organisation – even if this was the main focus of the classic study. Further, they often conceive of organisational identification as something that should be desired, without taking into account that there also might be a dark side to this.

Since the classic study was published, organisational identification has become a standard outcome to be monitored by organisations. It is used to indicate the impact of changes in the nature and content of the organisation's goals and practices on the continuity of its relation with different types of stakeholders. It is also used to monitor the continued ability of different groups of employees to see the organisation as connected to the self – despite increasing diversity. In this sense, the classic study has successfully implemented the notion that in trying to optimise the financial and business success of the organisation, strategic decision-making should make sure that individuals can continue to see the organisation as part of who they are and where they belong.

IMPLICATIONS FOR PRACTITIONERS

People are an important asset for organisations. They can be of great value, even if they are not directly included or formally related to the organisation – as is the case for the alumni investigated in the classic study. Alumni are known to make donations to their alma mater, which can constitute quite substantial sources of funding for primary activities. Likewise, existing and former employees can contribute to an organisation beyond the labour they put in. They do this, for instance, by deploying their network connections to find suitable interns or candidates for vacancies or recommending the organisation to customers through word of mouth, for instance on social media. Mael & Ashforth's classic study provides evidence that attempts to strengthen the psychological ties between the self and the organisation, can induce this supportive behaviour by enhancing the level of the identification with the organisation.

The outcomes studied in the classic study are specific and context-dependent. Yet, in the decades since, a wealth of empirical contributions, using different operationalisations, have broadened the scope of outcomes that relate to identification with the organisation, department, profession and work teams, which are in themselves consequences of aspects of the social situation that contribute to the emergence and enhancement of social identities. As management involves the creation of situations to make a thriving organisation possible, such a situational approach yields suggestions about opportunities to change the situation in such a way that positive outcomes become more likely. As indicated above, many of such outcomes of high identification are positive for organisations and their employees. People become more motivated, are more inclined to help colleagues and to enhance the organisation's reputation, and so on.

One of the interesting aspects of social identity theory, however, is that it also theorises about situations that may lead to negative outcomes for the organisation or society as a whole: research on 'the dark side of identification', sometimes alluded to as over-identification, explains that people may in some situations engage in unlawful behaviour, bullying or a failure to disclose errors or dangerous situations to protect their group or organisation from scrutiny and reputational damage. Thus attempts to fortify the psychological ties between the individual and the organisation are not necessarily beneficial but also carry the risk of inducing misplaced loyalty.

DISCUSSION QUESTIONS

1. Imagine this study were to be conducted among alumni of your university in the present time. Do you expect the results would be replicated, given the country in which your university is located, the characteristics of the students in your university (or your faculty), the present time and the distinctiveness, prestige and inter- and intra-group competition that characterises your university. Why or why not?

2. Would it invalidate the results of the Mael & Ashforth study, making it a less 'classic study' if their results would not be replicated in another type of context or sample? Why or why not?

3. A university is an organisation, but it differs in several respects from companies and not-for-profit organisations. Describe why the theoretical ideas and the results of the study could be worthwhile to consider in other types of organisations. Also try to describe some findings in the study that would be hard to apply in other types of organisations.

4. No study is perfect. Can you think of improvements that could be made in the design of the study, the operationalisations, the choice of variables, that might lead to the next 'classical study'? Don't get stuck in generalities; describe your suggestions in some detail.

5. One of the interesting characteristics of the study is that the proposed antecedents – distinctiveness, prestige, inter- and intra-group competition – were measured after the respondents had left the college, even after many years. Hence, the antecedents were measured post hoc, whereas the outcomes measured in the study, such as attending college activities, necessarily have taken place more recently. Do you think this may have influenced the results of the study and, if so, in what way?

FURTHER READINGS

Ashforth, B. E. & Mael, F. A. (1989). Social identity theory and the organisation. *Academy of Management Review*, 14, 20–39.

The theoretical basis of the classic study that is the subject of this chapter is discussed in this earlier work by the same authors and is an excellent background to the classic study.

Conroy, S., Henle, C. A., Shore, L. & Stelman, S. (2016). Where there is light, there is dark: A review of the detrimental outcomes of high organisational identification. *Journal of Organizational Behavior*, 38, 184–203. https://doi.org/10.1002/job.2164

Although the focus in the management literature and organisational psychology is on the positive outcomes of identification, there is now a substantial research on its possible negative consequences as well. As these consequences may be harmful to organisations as well as society as a whole, this research is extremely relevant.

Ellemers, N., De Gilder, T. C. & Haslam, S. A. (2004). Motivating individuals and groups at work: A social identity perspective on leadership and group performance. *Academy of Management Review*, 29, 459–78. https://doi.org/10.2307/20159054

A relatively short introduction on the relevance of social identity theory to motivation and leadership, two key topics in management literature and organisational psychology.

Haslam, S. A. (2004) *Psychology in Organizations*. Sage.

This monograph offers a thorough overview of social identity theory and social categorisation theory and its relevance for organisations.

Riketta, M. (2005). Organizational identification: A meta-analysis. *Journal of Vocational Behavior*, 66(2), 358–84. https://doi.org/10.1016/j.jvb.2004.05.005

As always, a meta-analysis gives a good insight into the most robust findings on a topic, in this case on the antecedents and consequences of organisational identification.

REFERENCES

Albert, S. & Whetten, D. A. (1985). Organizational identity. *Research in Organizational Behavior*, 7, 263–95.

Albert, S., Ashforth, B. E. & Dutton, J. E. (2000). Organizational identity and identification: Charting new waters and building new bridges. *Academy of Management Review*, 25, 13–17. https://doi.org/10.5465/amr.2000.2791600

Anand, V., Ashforth, B. E. & Joshi, M. (2004). Business as usual: The acceptance and perpetuation of corruption in organizations. *Academy of Management Perspectives*, 18, 39–53. https://doi.org/10.5465/ame.2005.19417904

Anaza, N. A. (2015). Relations of fit and organizational identification to employee-customer identification. *Journal of Managerial Psychology*, 30, 925–39. https://doi.org/10.1108/JMP-12-2012-0389

Ashforth, B. E. (2016). Distinguished scholar invited essay: Exploring identity and identification in organizations: Time for some course corrections. *Journal of Leadership & Organizational Studies*, 23, 361–73. https://doi.org/10.1177/1548051816667897

Ashforth, B. E. & Johnson, S. A. (1999). Which hat to wear? The relative salience of multiple identities in organizational contexts. In M. A. Hogg & D. J. Terry (eds), *Social Identity Processes in Organizational Contexts*. Psychology Press, pp. 31–48.

Ashforth, B. E. & Kreiner, G. E. (2013). Profane or profound? Finding meaning in dirty work. In B. J. Dik, Z. S. Byrne & M. F. Steger (eds), *Purpose and Meaning in the Workplace*. American Psychological Association, pp. 127–50.

Ashforth, B. E. & Mael, F. A. (1989). Social identity theory and the organization. *Academy of Management Review*, 14, 20–39.

Ashforth, B. E. & Mael, F. A. (1998). The power of resistance: Sustaining valued identities. In R. M. Kramer & M. A. Neale (eds), *Power and Influence in Organizations*. Sage, pp. 89–119.

Ashforth, B. E., Harrison, S. H. & Corley, K. G. (2008). Identification in organizations: An examination of four fundamental questions. *Journal of Management*, 34, 325–74. https://doi.org/10.1177/0149206308316059

Ashforth, B. E., Joshi, M., Anand, V. & O'Leary-Kelly, A. M. (2013). Extending the expanded model of organizational identification to occupations. *Journal of Applied Social Psychology*, 43, 2426–448. https://doi.org/10.1111/jasp.12190

Bauman, C. W. & Skitka, L. J. (2012). Corporate social responsibility as a source of employee satisfaction. *Research in Organizational Behavior*, 32, 63–86. https://doi.org/10.1016/j.riob.2012.11.002

Bergami, M. & Bagozzi, R. P. (2000). Self-categorization, affective commitment and group self-esteem as distinct aspects of social identity in the organization. *British Journal of Social Psychology*, 39, 555–77. https://doi.org/10.1348/014466600164633

Brown, R., Condor, S., Mathews, A., Wade, G. & Williams, J. (1986). Explaining intergroup differentiation in an industrial organization. *Journal of Occupational Psychology*, 59, 273–86. https://doi.org/10.1111/j.2044-8325.1986.tb00230.x

Chen, Q., Wen, Z., Kong, Y., Niu, J. & Hau, K. T. (2017). Influence of leaders' psychological capital on their followers: Multilevel mediation effect of organizational identification. *Frontiers in Psychology*, 8, 1776. https://doi.org/10.3389/fpsyg.2017.01776

Cole, B., Jones, R. J. & Russell, L. M. (2016). Racial dissimilarity and diversity climate effect organizational identification. *Equality, Diversity and Inclusion: An International Journal*, 35, 314–27. https://doi.org/10.1108/EDI-09-2015-0072

Conroy, S., Becker, W. & Menges, J. (2016). The meaning of my feelings depends on who I am: Work-related identifications shape emotion effects in organizations. *Academy of Management Journal*, 60, 1071–93. https://doi.org/10.5465/amj.2014.1040

Conroy, S., Henle, C. A., Shore, L. & Stelman, S. (2016). Where there is light, there is dark: A review of the detrimental outcomes of high organizational identification. *Journal of Organizational Behavior*, 38, 184–203. https://doi.org/10.1002/job.2164

Demoulin, S., Teixeira, C. P., Gillis, C., Goldoni, E. & Stinglhamber, F. (2016). Choosing a group representative: The impact of perceived organizational support on the preferences for deviant representatives in work negotiations. *Negotiation and Conflict Management Research*, 9, 120–40. https://doi.org/10.1111/ncmr.12070

Dukerich, J. M., Kramer, R. M. & Parks, J. M. (1998). The dark side of organizational identification. In D. Whetten & P. Godfrey (eds), *Identity in Organizations: Developing Theory Through Conversations*. Sage, pp. 245–56.

Dutton, J. E., Dukerich, J. M. & Harquail, C. V. (1994). Organizational images and member identification. *Administrative Science Quarterly*, 39, 239–63. https://doi.org/10.2307/2393235

Edwards, A. (2005). Relational agency: Learning to be a resourceful practitioner. *International Journal of Educational Research*, 43, 168–82. http://dx.doi.org/10.1016/j.ijer.2006.06.010

Ellemers, N. (2021). Science as collaborative knowledge generation. *British Journal of Social Psychology*, 60, 1–28. doi:10.1111/bjso.12430

Ellemers, N. & Rink, F. (2005). Identity in work groups: The beneficial and detrimental consequences of multiple identities and group norms for collaboration and group performance. In S. Thye & E. Lawler (eds), *Social Identification in Groups: Advances in Group Processes*, Vol. 22. Elsevier Press, pp. 1–41. https://doi.org/(...)0882-6145(05)22001-5

Ellemers, N. & Van Nunspeet, F. (2013). Moral accountability and prejudice control: Evidence from cardiovascular and EEG responses. In B. Derks, D. Scheepers & N. Ellemers (eds), *The Neuropsychology of Prejudice and Intergroup Relations*. Psychology Press, pp. 209–26.

Ellemers, N., De Gilder, D. & van den Heuvel, H. (1998). Career-oriented versus team-oriented commitment and behavior at work. *Journal of Applied Psychology*, 83, 717–30. https://doi.org/10.1037/0021-9010.83.5.717

Ellemers, N., De Gilder, T. C. & Haslam, S. A. (2004). Motivating individuals and groups at work: A social identity perspective on leadership and group performance. *Academy of Management Review*, 29, 459–78. https://doi.org/10.2307/20159054

Ellemers, N., Kortekaas, P. & Ouwerkerk, J. W. (1999). Self-categorisation, commitment to the group and group self-esteem as related but distinct aspects of social identity. *European Journal of Social Psychology*, 29, 371–89. https://doi.org/10.1002/(SICI)1099-0992(199903/05)29:2/3<371::AID- EJSP932>3.0.CO;2-U

Ellemers, N., Haslam, S. A., Platow, M. J. & van Knippenberg, D. (2003). Social identity at work: Developments, debates, directions. In S. A. Haslam, D. van Knippenberg, M. J. Platow & N. Ellemers (eds), *Social Identity at Work: Developing Theory for Organizational Practice*. Psychology Press, pp. 3–26.

Ellemers, N., Fiske, S., Abele, A. E., Koch, A. & Yzerbyt, V. (2020). Adversarial alignment enables competing models to engage in cooperative theory-building, toward cumulative science. *Proceedings of the National Academies of Sciences*, 117, 7561–7. https://doi.org/10.1073/pnas.1906720117

Haslam, S. A. (2004) *Psychology in Organizations*. Sage.

Haslam, S. A., Reicher, S. D. & Platow, M. J. (2010). *The New Psychology of Leadership: Identity, Influence and Power*. Psychology Press.

He, H., Pham, H. Q., Baruch, Y. & Zhu, W. (2014). Perceived organizational support and organizational identification: Joint moderating effects of employee exchange ideology and employee investment. *International Journal of Human Resource Management*, 25, 2772–95. https://doi.org/10.1080/09585192.2014.908315

Hogg, M. A. & Terry, D. J. (2000). The dynamic, diverse, and variable faces of organizational identity. *Academy of Management Review*, 25, 150–152.

Iyer, V. M., Bamber, E. M. & Barefield, R. M. (1997). Identification of accounting firm alumni with their former firm: Antecedents and outcomes. *Accounting, Organizations and Society*, 22, 315–336.

Jetten, J., Haslam, C. & Haslam, S. A. (2011). *The Social Cure: Identity, Health and Well- Being.* Psychology Press.

Kraus, F., Ahearne, M., Lam, S. K. & Wieseke, J. (2012). Toward a contingency framework of interpersonal influence in organizational identification diffusion.

Organizational Behavior and Human Decision Processes, 118, 162–78. https://doi.org/10.1016/j.obhdp.2012.03.010

Lee, E. S., Park, T. Y. & Koo, B. (2015). Identifying organizational identification as a basis for attitudes and behaviors: A meta-analytic review. *Psychological Bulletin*, 141, 1049. https://doi.org/10.1037/bul0000012

Li, Y., Fan, J. & Zhao, S. (2015). Organizational identification as a double-edged sword: Dual effects on job satisfaction and life satisfaction. *Journal of Personnel Psychology*, 14, 182–91. https://doi.org/10.1027/1866-5888/a000133

Liu, Y., Loi, R. & Lam, L. W. (2011). Linking organizational identification and employee performance in teams: The moderating role of team-member exchange. *International Journal of Human Resource Management*, 22, 3187–201. https://doi.org/10.1080/09585192.2011.560875

Mael, F. A. & Ashforth, B. E. (1992). Alumni and their alma mater: A partial test of the reformulated model of organizational identification. *Journal of Organizational Behavior*, 13, 103–23.

Mael, F. A. & Tetrick, L. E. (1992). Identifying organizational identification. *Educational and Psychological Measurement*, 52, 813–24. https://doi.org/10.1177/0013164492052004002

McDearmon, J. T. (2013). Hail to thee, our alma mater: Alumni role identity and the relationship to institutional support behaviors. *Research in Higher Education*, *54*, 283–302.

Meyer, J. P., Bobocel, D. R. & Allen, N. J. (1991). Development of organizational commitment during the first year of employment: A longitudinal study of pre-and post-entry influences. *Journal of Management*, 17, 717–33.

Moriano, J. A., Molero, F., Topa, G. & Mangin, J. P. L. (2014). The influence of transformational leadership and organizational identification on intrapreneurship. *International Entrepreneurship and Management Journal*, 10, 103–19.

Mowday, R. T., Steers, R. M. & Porter, L. W. (1979). The measurement of organizational commitment. *Journal of Vocational Behavior*, 14, 224–47. https://doi.org/10.1016/0001-8791(79)90072-1

Oaker, G. & Brown, R. (1986). Intergroup relations in a hospital setting: A further test of social identity theory. *Human Relations*, 39, 767–78. https://doi.org/10.1177/001872678603900804

Ouwerkerk, J. W., Ellemers, N. & de Gilder, D. (1999). Group commitment and individual effort in experimental and organizational contexts. In N. Ellemers, R. Spears & B. Doosje (eds), *Social Identity: Context, Commitment, Content*. Blackwell Science, pp. 189–204.

Ploeger, N. A. & Bisel, R. S. (2013). The role of identification in giving sense to unethical organizational behavior: Defending the organization. *Management Communication Quarterly*, 27, 155–83. https://doi.org/10.1177/0893318912469770

Pratt, D. D. (1998). *Five Perspectives on Teaching in Adult and Higher Education*. Krieger.

Riketta, M. (2005). Organizational identification: A meta-analysis. *Journal of Vocational Behavior*, 66, 358–84. https://doi.org/10.1016/j.jvb.2004.05.005

Riketta, M. & Van Dick, R. (2005). Foci of attachment in organizations: A meta-analytic comparison of the strength and correlates of workgroup versus organizational identification and commitment. *Journal of Vocational Behavior*, 67, 490–510. https://doi.org/10.1016/j.jvb.2004.06.001

Rogers, K. M. & Ashforth, B. E. (2014). Respect in organizations: Feeling valued as 'we' and 'me'. *Journal of Management*, 43, 1578–608. https://doi.org/10.1177/0149206314557159

Sluss, D. M. & Ashforth, B. E. (2008). How relational and organizational identification converge: Processes and conditions. *Organization Science*, 19, 807–23. https://doi.org/10.1287/orsc.1070.0349

Sluss, D. M., Ployhart, R. E., Cobb, M. G. & Ashforth, B. E. (2012). Generalizing newcomers' relational and organizational identifications: Processes and prototypicality. *Academy of Management Journal*, 55, 949–75.

Tajfel, H. (1978). *Differentiation between Social Groups: Studies in the Social Psychology of Intergroup Relations*. Academic Press.

Tajfel, H. & Turner, J. C. (1979). An integrative theory of intergroup conflict. In W. G. Austin & S. Worchel (eds), *Social Psychology of Intergroup Relations*. Brooks/Cole, pp. 33–47.

Tajfel, H. & Turner, J. C. (1985). The social identity theory of intergroup behaviour. In S. Worchel & W. G. Austin (eds), *Psychology of Intergroup Relations*. Nelson Hall, pp. 7–24.

Terry, D. J., Hogg, M. A. & White, K. M. (2000). Attitude–behavior relations: Social identity and group membership. In D. J. Terry & M. A. Hogg (eds), *Applied Social Research. Attitudes, Behavior, and Social Context: The Role of Norms and Group Membership*. Lawrence Erlbaum, pp. 67–93.

Tom, G. & Elmer, L. (1994). Alumni willingness to give and contribution behavior. *Journal of Services Marketing*, 8, 57–62. http://dx.doi.org/10.1108/08876049410058442

Turner, J. C. (1985). Social categorization and the self-concept: A social-cognitive theory of group behavior. In E. J. Lawler (eds), *Advances in Group Processes: Theory and Research*. JAI Press, pp. 77–122.

Tyler, T. R. & Blader, S. L. (2003). The group engagement model: Procedural justice, social identity, and cooperative behavior. *Personality and Social Psychology Review*, 7, 349–61. https://doi.org/10.1207/S15327957PSPR0704_07

Umphress, E. E., Bingham, J. B. & Mitchell, M. S. (2010). Unethical behavior in the name of the company: The moderating effect of organizational identification and positive reciprocity beliefs on unethical pro-organizational behavior. *Journal of Applied Psychology*, 95, 769. https://doi.org/10.1037/a0019214

Van Dick, R., Christ, O., Stellmacher, J., Wagner, U., Ahlswede, O., Grubba, C. [...] & Tissington, P. A. (2004). Should I stay or should I go? Explaining turnover intentions with organizational identification and job satisfaction. *British Journal of Management*, 15, 351–60. https://doi.org/10.1111/j.1467-8551.2004.00424.x

Van Knippenberg, D. & Van Schie, E. C. (2000). Foci and correlates of organizational identification. *Journal of Occupational and Organizational Psychology*, 73, 137–47.

Van Knippenberg, D. & Sleebos, E. (2006). Organizational identification versus organizational commitment: Self-definition, social exchange, and job attitudes. *Journal of Organizational Behavior*, 27, 571–84. https://doi.org/10.1002/job.359

Van Leeuwen, E., van Knippenberg, D. & Ellemers, N. (2003). Continuing and changing group identities: The effects of merging on social identification and ingroup bias. *Personality and Social Psychology Bulletin*, 29, 679–90. https://doi.org/10.1177/0146167203029006001

Wieseke, J., Ahearne, M., Lam, S. K. & Van Dick, R. (2009). The role of leaders in internal marketing. *Journal of Marketing*, 73, 123–45. https://doi.org/10.1509/jmkg.73.2.123

Zavyalova, A., Pfarrer, M. D., Reger, R. K. & Hubbard, T. D. (2016). Reputation as a benefit and a burden? How stakeholders' organizational identification affects the role of reputation following a negative event. *Academy of Management Journal*, 59, 253–76. https://doi.org/10.5465/amj.2013.0611

6 | Organisational Citizenship Behaviour: Revisiting Smith, Organ & Near and Lessons Learned in Persistence, Determination and Citizenship

Steven W. Whiting, Mark G.
Ehrhart & Philip M. Podsakoff

BACKGROUND

The completion and publication of any original academic study involves considerable time, effort and perseverance on the part of the authors. Naturally, this is the case with studies that have such a profound influence on their field that they later warrant the designation of being a 'classic'. However, when it comes to the classic article 'Organisational Citizenship Behavior: Its Nature and Antecedents' published by Smith, Organ & Near in 1983, the story of its creation and publication is a truly remarkable one. The conduct of the research and publication of this article required extraordinary scholarly curiosity and insight, a sophisticated design and methodology that was well ahead of its time, and an astonishing level of perseverance in the face of incredible hardship.

It is impossible to imagine the field of Organisational Behaviour today without the existence of the organisational citizenship behaviour (OCB) construct. Its influence since being introduced in Smith et al.'s (1983) article has been profound, and yet without the persistence of its authors it might never have been. In the course of this chapter, we will discuss the work of Smith and colleagues and address what the authors of the article did, how they did it, why it was important and what has happened since. However, in our view, perhaps the greatest lesson we as scholars and students can learn from this classic study is the importance of determination and perseverance. Its authors were remarkable examples of these traits and their story is an inspiring one.

In 1977 Organ published an article in the *Academy of Management Review* that he would later characterise as 'meant only as an exercise in devil's advocacy' (Organ et al., 2006, p. 15). In that article, he suggested that organisational researchers should take the 'satisfaction causes performance' hypothesis more seriously. Put quite simply, this hypothesis proposes that happy workers are more likely to be productive workers. This notion seems almost too simple to warrant investigation, yet Organ began his article by reviewing the decades of research suggesting that the notion was 'intellectually bankrupt' (1977, p. 46). For this reason, the idea had been widely abandoned by scholars and viewed as a somewhat naive notion of the uninformed.

However, Organ could not let go of the idea. He suggested that the 'widespread belief' in the hypothesis itself was worthy of consideration. Indeed, why would so many managers and workers report a belief that happy workers are more productive workers if there were not some truth to it? In the course of the article, Organ (1977) reviewed a number of reasons why empirical research to date might have failed to find support for the popular hypothesis and speculated on the causal direction of the relationship (perhaps performance causes satisfaction). However, most insightfully, in our view, Organ observed that the problem might be in the measurement of job performance.

Studies investigating the satisfaction causes performance link to that point had used fairly narrow definitions and measures of job performance, most typically limiting performance to the types of outcomes that can be easily tallied, counted or weighed. Organ (1977) observed that such outcomes, which would subsequently be termed task performance, might not always be in the volitional control of employees. Certain minimum levels of output are required to maintain employment, and thus the dissatisfied do not necessarily have the ability to lower their performance beyond an acceptable minimum. Additionally, increasing productivity beyond given levels can be a physical impossibility and thus the satisfied have a limited space in which to express their satisfaction. Perhaps, Organ speculated, employee satisfaction could be expressed in some other forms of performance that don't get measured as frequently or easily. In summarising this idea Organ stated, 'whoever first voiced agreement with the proposition that satisfaction affects performance might not have been limiting the concept of performance to a narrow definition of the sort usually measured by industrial psychologists' (1977, p. 50).

In this first article, and the thinking that led to it, Organ demonstrated a level of intellectual humility and persistence that were crucial. In terms of humility, Organ recognised the importance of listening to managers and workers and taking them seriously, rather than treating their views as those of naive, unsophisticated observers of human behaviour not capable of understanding the scholarly literature that refuted their simple hypothesis. In terms of persistence, Organ understood that something terribly important could be hiding under the surface of this failure of the academic literature to confirm a hypothesis so simple and intuitive.

In the years that followed, Organ began to work more seriously on these ideas together with doctoral student C. Ann Smith, whose dissertation would form the basis for the 1983 Smith et al. paper. The resulting article bears a rather unusual postscript: 'The data reported in this article are drawn from a doctoral dissertation project conducted by the first author, who died on April 27, 1982. She was posthumously awarded the degree of Doctorate in Business Administration in August, 1982' (Smith et al., 1983, p. 653). While collecting data and transporting the boxes of paper questionnaires from bank branch to bank branch throughout Indiana in order to generate the ultimate sample of 422 employees in 58 departments, Smith began to experience significant pain in her arms. This pain would soon be diagnosed as a recurrence of an aggressive form of bone cancer and doctors estimated she had only six months to live.

One of Smith's most important goals for the remaining months of her life was to complete her dissertation. With the help of her dissertation committee members and subsequent co-authors Dennis Organ and Janet Near, she conducted statistical analyses (converting questionnaires into punch-cards and conducting analyses on the university's mainframe computer capable of running regressions) and wrote the chapters for her dissertation from home while receiving chemotherapy. With her remaining strength and the help of family members, she typed the manuscript (in an age before the availability of word processing programs) and completed her dissertation shortly before her death.[1] In our view, for Smith to complete her dissertation under the circumstances represents a truly heroic example of persistence and determination, and for Organ and Near to subsequently publish this work, a marvellous example of the very citizenship behaviour being studied. The fact that the article itself was so innovative, important and ahead of its time is perhaps equally remarkable.

DETAILED DESCRIPTION

Smith and colleagues made a number of important conceptual and methodological contributions that we will discuss in the section 'Key insights'. However, before doing so, we want to provide a brief outline of the nature of the research that was conducted as a reminder to the reader. To begin with, Smith et al. outlined the construct of organisational citizenship behaviour and developed a measure of the construct. Measurement items were generated via semi-structured interviews with managers (who did not provide data for the primary study) who were essentially asked to provide examples of behaviours that were not required or a formal part of an employee's job, but that were beneficial to the organisation.

This interview process generated a pool of items that were then provided to 67 managers (also not in the primary sample) who rated one of their employees on each of the items. An exploratory factor analysis was conducted on the data (the substantive results of which were replicated in the primary sample), that resulted in a two-factor solution. The authors labelled these dimensions 'altruism' and 'generalised compliance'. The altruism items largely focused on helping behaviours, including helping both co-workers and the supervisor, but also included volunteering for unrequired activities and making innovative suggestions. The generalised compliance items were more varied, capturing issues related to being on time, attendance, taking breaks, giving notice for absence, taking time off unnecessarily,

---

[1]Personal correspondence with J. P. Near, 4 February 2020.

spending time on personal phone conversations and spending time in idle conversation. These two dimensions were positively correlated at .45.

The primary study reported in Smith et al. focused on a variety of predictors of OCB. Although the study is perhaps best known for investigating the relationship between job satisfaction and OCB, the research also included the antecedents of leader supportiveness, interdependence, personality (extraversion and neuroticism), belief in a just world and the demographic variables of birth position, educational level and geography.

The final sample for the primary study included 422 employees from two banks in the Midwestern United States. These employees represented 58 departments and only departments of four or more employees were included in the final analysis. The sample was split into a subject group and a descriptor group, such that each department had at least two employees in each side of the split. The subject group was used for the data on satisfaction, personality/beliefs and demographics, and the descriptor group was used for the data on leader supportiveness and task interdependence. The OCB data came from supervisor ratings. A lie scale from Eysenck's (1958) personality measure and the company the participants worked for were included as controls.

The primary analysis utilised was path analysis. Initially all variables were included as predictors of each OCB dimension (i.e. separate analyses were conducted for altruism and generalised compliance), and then those that were not statistically significant were dropped and added in a second analysis as having indirect effects through those predictors that had direct effects on the relevant OCB dimension. For altruism, this resulted in three direct predictors: job satisfaction, education and geography (with positive relationships for the first two and individuals from rural/smaller cities reporting higher altruism than those from large cities). In addition, leader supportiveness and neuroticism had indirect effects on altruism through job satisfaction, with positive and negative relationships, respectively. For generalised compliance, direct effects were found for leader supportiveness, the lie scale, and geography (positive relationships for the first two and a similar relationship for geography as was found for altruism). Effects for company and company tenure were mediated by leader supportiveness (with higher tenure being associated with lower leader supportiveness). Additional analyses controlling for department did not have an effect on job satisfaction's relationship with altruism, but leader supportiveness did become non-significant. In addition, the authors highlighted that job satisfaction had the strongest zero-order correlation with generalised compliance despite the fact that it did not predict generalised compliance in the path analyses.

KEY INSIGHTS

DEFINING OCB AND ITS DISTINCTION FROM TASK PERFORMANCE

The Smith et al. study was instrumental in defining the OCB construct and distinguishing it from task performance. Although some of the defining properties and exemplars of OCB were discussed in Organ (1977) and Bateman & Organ (1983), in our view the work of Smith et al. did the most comprehensive job, up to that point in time, of providing a strong conceptual case for the OCB construct. Indeed, in a single page of the Smith et al. article a number of critical conceptual arguments about OCB relative to task performance are made that both link OCB to work that came before it, and set the stage for much of the research on OCB that would follow.

For example, the authors argued that to achieve the task-focused and operational accomplishments of the organisation, human interaction is needed, and task performance alone is inadequate to account for how individuals can effectively and interdependently work together to accomplish their task-related goals. Here Smith et al. first proposed that OCBs are important 'because they lubricate the social machinery of the organization' (p. 654). The authors further argued that no formal role or job description can possibly capture a comprehensive listing of tasks that might need to be accomplished for every variety of situation, and thus workers must perform OCB to take the necessary steps to adjust to circumstance. In so doing, OCBs 'provide the flexibility needed to work through many unforeseen contingencies' (p. 654).

Another key feature of OCB in comparison to task performance the authors argued for was that the behaviours result from different motivational bases. Employees are motivated to perform OCB by sources outside of their formal contract with the organisation. In other words, OCB cannot 'be accounted for by the same motivational bases as those that induce people to join, stay, and perform within contractual, enforceable role prescriptions' (p. 654). OCB, the authors maintained, is difficult to formally recognise and incentivise. It is 'not easily governed by individual incentive schemes, because it is often subtle, difficult to measure, and may contribute more to others' performance than one's own, and may even have the effect of sacrificing some portion of one's immediate individual output' (p. 654). In this way, OCB shifts the focus from the individual and an economic exchange to the good of the group and the group's overall effectiveness.

Additionally, the authors made the case that because of the sometimes infrequent and arbitrary nature of appraisal systems combined with the ad hoc nature of OCBs, it is difficult to imagine that 'variance in "good citizen" behaviour is explained by the calculated anticipation that they will pay off in largesse for the person' (p. 654). In other words, motives to perform OCB were not likely to be economic or the result of a self-interested cost-benefit calculation, but must have a different basis, thereby distinguishing the behaviour from task performance.

Along similar lines, the authors claimed, OCB should be difficult to induce via threat or punishment (i.e. failure to perform OCB). Because citizenship behaviours are not part of an employee's formal organisational role, but instead are discretionary, they cannot be induced by threats but are driven by other antecedents (e.g. social exchange). Here the authors stated that OCB 'is not easily enforced by the threat of sanctions' (p. 654).

Thus, even though Smith et al. acknowledged from the beginning that OCB and in-role behaviour could overlap and that there could be some influence of formal structures and systems on OCB, they provided compelling arguments that for the most part, OCB occurs outside the formal system and, as such, should have unique predictors.

Foundation in Previous Literature in the Field

Although the contributions of Smith et al. have been highly influential, the authors were careful to note that they did not 'invent' the concept, but that it evolved from the theoretical work of others, most notably Katz (1964) and Roethlisberger & Dickson (1939, 1964; see also Chapter 2 of this volume), as well as the social psychological literature on altruism. For instance, Smith et al. highlighted that Katz (1964) had discussed three types of necessary behaviours in organisations related to attraction and retention, performance of role-prescribed behaviours, and innovative and spontaneous behaviours beyond what is prescribed in the role, and included the following quote: 'An organization which depends solely upon its blueprints of prescribed behavior is a very fragile social system' (Katz, 1964, p. 132).

With regard to Roethlisberger and Dickson (1964) and the 'Human Relations' school, Smith et al. highlighted the distinction made by those authors between cooperation, which was a product of the informal organisation, and productivity, which was founded on the organisation's formal structure. They highlighted Roethlisberger & Dickson's conceptualisation of cooperation as including 'the day-to-day spontaneous prosocial gestures of individual accommodation to the work needs of others (e.g., co-workers, supervisor, clients in other departments)' (Smith et al., 1983, p. 653). This historical link to the Human Relations school is important, because although this school focused its attention on the importance of relationships and informal teams in organisations (or what are often called 'maintenance' functions), the concrete behaviours related to these concepts had not been clearly articulated. Smith et al. moved this literature forward by identifying the behaviours that individuals within teams perform that enhance the team's (not to mention the organisation's) overall effectiveness.

In our view, these linkages to previous work are illustrative of the humility of the authors, and more importantly were a critical part of making the article so interesting and ultimately influential. By more formally specifying the behaviours that might be indicative of maintenance functions, or innovative and spontaneous behaviours, Smith et al. put 'meat on the bones' of Katz (1964) and Roethlisberger & Dickson (1964), thereby facilitating the investigation of these behaviours, and their antecedents and consequences for subsequent generations of organisational researchers.

Dimensions of OCB

The two OCB dimensions identified in the Smith et al. study (altruism and generalised compliance) are included in some meaningful way in virtually all the current conceptualisations of the OCB domain (e.g. George & Brief, 1992; Organ, 1988, 1990; P. M. Podsakoff et al., 1990; P. M. Podsakoff et al., 2000; Van Dyne & LePine, 1998; Van Scotter & Motowidlo, 1996; Williams & Anderson, 1991). Indeed, the two dimensions captured what has perhaps been the most influential distinction in categories of OCB between OCB directed towards other individuals (or OCB-I, as represented by altruism), and OCB directed toward the organisation as a whole (or OCB-O, as represented by generalised compliance).

The items in the measure foreshadowed a number of the dimensions that would be proposed in later work. For instance, the altruism item 'volunteers for things that are not required' aligns with the later dimension of civic virtue. Similarly, the item 'makes innovative suggestions to improve the department' could be seen as a precursor to constructs such as individual initiative and voice behaviour. On the generalised compliance side, the item 'gives advance notice if unable to come to work' overlaps with what would later become the courtesy dimension. Thus the original scale from Smith et al. was an important first step to understanding the dimensions of OCB and developing measures of OCB which would be built on in later work by Organ (1988) and Podsakoff et al. (1990).

ANTECEDENTS OF OCB

In addition to defining a construct and distinguishing it from other, related constructs, it is important to specify the construct's nomological network, and to provide theoretical rationales to explain how the variables included in this network relate to the focal construct. One of the lasting contributions of the Smith et al. article is that it identified a set of important theoretical frameworks to explain why the antecedents that they included in their study were expected to be related to altruism and generalised compliance.

Several of these frameworks have remained important to this day in the literature. Perhaps most notably, Smith et al. emphasised the role of social exchange, which has formed the foundation of much of the literature on OCB. Smith et al. highlighted that OCB may be driven by reciprocity for support from the organisation and its leaders, and that reciprocity through OCB would be more likely than through increased productivity 'because variation in the latter is more constrained by ability, work scheduling, or task design' (p. 655). In terms of specific categories of predictors, Smith et al. included job attitudes (i.e. satisfaction), personality (i.e. extraversion and neuroticism), leadership (i.e. leader supportiveness), task characteristics (i.e. interdependence) and even impression management motives (i.e. the lie scale) as antecedents of OCB. Notably, all of these general categories of predictors continue to be viewed as important drivers of OCB in the contemporary OCB literature, and have received considerable research attention.

MULTI-LEVEL THINKING

Although it has not been a widely acknowledged contribution of the Smith et al. study, a review of the original article uncovers numerous references to thinking about OCB beyond the individual level, to include both higher levels of analysis (e.g. groups and organisations) and lower levels of analysis (e.g. within-person effects). Perhaps most importantly, Smith et al. drew from Roethlisberger & Dickson (1964) to highlight that OCB would impact the performance of the organisation 'at the aggregate level of analysis (e.g., the firm) and over the long run' (Smith et al., 1983, p. 653). This idea was emphasised later in Organ's (1988) book and has been foundational in how research has been conducted to show the benefits of OCB (N. P. Podsakoff et al., 2009).

Smith et al. also highlighted how leaders create norms throughout their groups, noting how leaders role model and 'provide cues for what behavior is appropriate and make salient the situational needs for prosocial gestures' (p. 655), in addition to creating norms for compliance that are created based on the leader being 'highly supportive of the whole group' (p. 662). These ideas align closely with later theoretical work by Ehrhart and Naumann (2004) about OCB norms and how they are created. Methodologically and analytically, the Smith et al. study also demonstrated a keen insight by the authors about multi-level issues that were uncommon at that time. For instance, responses from individuals in the descriptor group were averaged because they were theorised to be consistent within those units. Smith et al. then emphasised the need for between-unit variance and ran aggregation statistics (i.e. eta-squared) to justify their aggregation. Although such analyses are the norm today, they were far ahead of their time in 1983.

In addition to the effects of OCB at higher levels of analysis, Smith et al. highlighted within-person effects that have become increasingly common in contemporary OCB research. For instance, when discussing the causes of altruistic behaviour, they noted that 'the eliciting stimuli appear to be situational, that is, someone has a problem, needs assistance, or requests a service' (p. 661). In other words, helping behaviour tends to happen as individual episodes or events, and the specific nature of those episodes will vary. Smith et al. also highlighted within-person effects when discussing job satisfaction as a predictor of OCB. In short, they highlighted that affect includes both trait and state components, and that job satisfaction captures an 'enduring positive mood state' (p. 654) that should predict OCB. This distinction emphasises that OCB can vary within persons (e.g. because of mood) and between persons (e.g. because of traits); researchers are just now beginning to fully disentangle the antecedents of OCB at these different levels.

ADDITIONAL INSIGHTS AND CONTRIBUTIONS

Although we have highlighted the most notable insights of the Smith et al. article above, there are a number of additional, perhaps subtler contributions to the article that bear some discussion as well. First, in addition to the compelling conceptual and theoretical basis provided for the OCB construct in general, Smith et al. were prescient in noting several areas of interest that would turn into major foci of study in the OCB literature. For example, the authors discussed at length the benefits of OCB for workers and the organisation, but they were not so naive as to think that it could not have negative impacts as well. By noting that OCB 'may even have the effect of sacrificing some portion of one's immediate individual output' (p. 654) for the good of the group and organisation's long-term effectiveness, they foreshadowed contemporary work on how and when OCB can be costly for employees. Work related to the downsides of OCB, particularly for the individual employee (e.g. Bergeron, 2007; Bolino & Turnley, 2005), can trace its roots to Smith et al. Another example of this foreshadowing was the inclusion of the lie scale. Although it was not even a hypothesised predictor in their paper, the lie scale (included only as a control) was found to predict generalised compliance. This laid the groundwork for future work on motives as predictors of OCB, specifically impression management motives (Bolino, 1999). In their discussion, Smith et al. noted how the results for the lie scale likely reflect a need for social approval and that individuals high in the lie scale are more likely to follow norms and behave in a socially desirable manner.

Second, the studies described in the article were well ahead of their time in terms of methodology. To begin with, the studies used a mixed methods approach, combining qualitative interviews with quantitative survey methods. Although the use of mixed method research designs has increased in the past decade, such an approach remains relatively uncommon. The interviews with managers allowed the authors to get a handle on the specific behaviours that practitioners felt were exemplars of OCB. Notably, the interviews conducted by Smith with managers provided rich information that became an important source of insight for Organ as he went on to further explicate the OCB construct in subsequent work (Organ, 1988, 1990). This highlights the value and importance of the mixed methods approach.

The studies were well ahead of their time in terms of design and statistical analysis. In the case of study design, Smith et al. utilised three sources of data by splitting participants from different departments and then using supervisor ratings of OCB. Such a design is noteworthy for its sophistication and awareness of avoiding possible same-source effects. Importantly, the problem of same-source effects has plagued the OCB literature for some time, with multiple authors outlining the problems in this domain of obtaining ratings of OCB and its antecedents or consequences from the same source. It is remarkable that in this first investigation of OCB, and well before the publication of highly cited works on same-source effects (P. M. Podsakoff et al., 2003; P. M. Podsakoff & Organ, 1986) the authors were prescient enough to understand this challenge and to design around it. Notably, such designs have only become the norm in recent years, with a great deal of literature published regarding OCB suffering from problems of same-source effects.

In terms of statistical analysis, the paper was also well ahead of its time. Although path analysis has become common in the field today, that was not the case in the early 1980s, and thus the incorporation of these methods is noteworthy. Given the limited computing capacity available at the time, the analyses represent quite an accomplishment by the authors. Moreover, Smith et al. ran multiple models assessing the nature of the mediated effects several years before Baron & Kenny's (1986) influential work on the topic was even published. Although we take these kinds of analyses for granted now, there were not many examples of them in the early 1980s. Their implementation here in Smith et al. is certainly an important part of the article's influence and staying power.

Finally, it is important to note that we believe a critical part of the continued influence of the Smith et al. article was its practical relevance to managers and employees. Although anecdotal, the experiences of the three authors of this chapter are very consistent on this front. Whether teaching executive education, working on consulting engagements or gathering data within organisations, the OCB construct always seems to resonate with practitioners. They can understand it immediately, readily think of examples of the behaviour in their setting, and tend to understand the importance of those behaviours to the success of their particular unit or organisation. Additionally, we find that they are immediately interested as managers and leaders to understand how better to elicit these behaviours from employees to create a workplace where OCB is a part of the norms and culture. Thus Smith et al. did ground-breaking work with a topic that was not of mere academic or scholarly interest, but that has profound implications for practitioners.

This discussion of 'Additional Insights' demonstrates that, even beyond providing the foundational explication of the OCB construct, the article provided a number of other contributions that have resulted in its immense influence over the years. In our view, there is no question that it is worthy of the title 'classic'.

IMPACT OF THE CLASSIC STUDY

As we mentioned at the beginning of this chapter, it is difficult to imagine the contemporary field of organisational behaviour without the construct of OCB. Along with task performance and workplace deviance behaviour, it has come to be viewed as a critical component of the job performance domain (Rotundo & Sackett, 2002), and after all, job performance is the ultimate outcome variable of the field. At the writing of this chapter, the Smith et al. article has been cited 1,610 times according to the Web of Science and 6,498 times according to Google Scholar. Interestingly, eight fairly recent articles that the Web of Science designates as 'Highly Cited in the Field Articles' cite Smith et al. and relate to topics as diverse as OCB itself, leadership, talent management and the provision of health services.

Of course, the influence of the construct of OCB is even broader than this. A topic search for the term organisational citizenship behaviour in the Web of Science returned 7,456 publications, and a similar search in Google Scholar returned over 100,000 results! Notably, these searches only used the term OCB and did not include keywords to later emerging and related constructs such as extra-role behaviour, employee voice behaviour or prosocial organisational behaviour. OCB was arguably a critical precursor to the development of several of these related constructs, as well as constructs on the opposite side of the performance continuum investigating employee workplace deviance behaviours (e.g. Bennett & Robinson, 2000). This vast literature was made possible in large part by Smith et al. Research into OCB also led to Organ's 1988 book on the topic, Organ et al.'s 2006 book reviewing the construct, and the recent *Oxford Handbook of Organizational Citizenship Behavior* (P. M. Podsakoff et al., 2018), which included contributions from dozens of scholars at some of the world's finest academic institutions.

Indeed, the field of OCB has grown to be so large that scholars can be considered experts of particular subfields of study within OCB: helping, voice, OCB in groups, the downsides of OCB, etc. The influence of OCB has spread well beyond the organisational sciences as well to be used most prominently in the fields of political science and health care. Finally, the construct has been studied and shown to have important organisational implications in multiple parts of the world. Put simply, the impact of Smith et al. has been felt over multiple fields of academic inquiry across the globe.

IMPLICATIONS FOR PRACTITIONERS

Given that Organ's journey into OCB started with taking practitioners seriously and wondering why the 'satisfaction causes performance' hypothesis persisted among them, it seems only appropriate to address the implications of Smith et al. for and subsequent OCB research on those who practise management. To begin with, Smith et al. and subsequent work on OCB confirmed the 'satisfaction causes performance' hypothesis at least when it comes to behaviours that are largely in the control of employees such as OCB. A considerable amount of empirical evidence has accumulated demonstrating that job satisfaction and similar job attitudes are important predictors of OCB (Organ et al., 2006). As such, the persistence of the hypothesis among practitioners was certainly rational.

Second, as presaged by Smith et al. in their investigation of leader supportiveness, leader behaviours have been demonstrated to be critical determinants of OCB. A variety of leadership behaviours and models have been linked to OCB, including leader member exchange (LMX), transformational leadership and servant leadership among others. Indeed, leader behaviours have been perhaps the most consistent and substantial predictors of OCB suggesting that the manner in which managers and leaders behave in the workplace plays a critical role in eliciting OCBs.

Finally, it seems critically important to practitioners to note that OCB at the unit level has been shown to substantially influence both top- and bottom-line results in organisations. Unit OCB has been shown to be a significant predictor of the quantity and quality of production, unit costs and customer satisfaction (N.P. Podsakoff et al., 2009). As such, we now know that perhaps the best way to elicit OCBs is for managers and leaders to treat employees well, and that OCBs are strong predictors of unit success including bottom line financial success. Indeed, this confirms one of the most important predictions of the human relations movement, that treating employees well will pay dividends.

CONCLUSION

In this chapter we have addressed the theoretical, conceptual and methodological reasons to consider Smith et al. (1983) a 'classic' of organisational studies. However, we wish to conclude by emphasising again the human side of this article. It came to fruition from a remarkable brew of intellectual curiosity and humility combined with human drive and persistence in the face of daunting odds. Smith herself demonstrated tremendous courage and tenacity to complete her dissertation while facing terminal cancer. Her co-authors Organ and Near demonstrated the best of what we should hope for from scholars and mentors as they worked to help Smith achieve her goal and ultimately publish her work posthumously. It is sometimes said that the cobbler's children go barefoot. Gladly, Organ in particular was the antithesis of this well-known phrase. In preparing this chapter we corresponded with several scholars who have most frequently cited Smith et al. in their own work. A surprising number of the responses we received included personal anecdotes about the manner in which Organ practised OCB himself – helping young scholars in the field, providing valuable feedback without seeking credit, making way and providing space for others to succeed in publishing in the OCB space. As one author put it, Organ exemplified OCB. These anecdotes match our own experiences. As friends, colleagues and students of Organ, we continue to marvel that he studied and understood OCB so thoroughly, but also practised it so well.

DISCUSSION QUESTIONS

1. How should researchers in the organisational sciences balance the drive to conduct work with practical implications for managers and leaders of organisations, that also contributes to the scholarly literature on the topic?

2. What have been your own experiences with organisational citizenship behaviour in the workplace that illustrates its important contribution to organisational effectiveness?

3. What are the implications of thinking about and studying OCB at the within-person (e.g. variability in behaviour by individuals across situations), between-person (e.g. differences between one person and another in OCB) and between-unit (e.g. differences in groups, departments or organisations in normative OCB) levels? What might be some unique predictors and outcomes at each of these levels?

FURTHER READINGS

Organ, D. W. (1977). A reappraisal and reinterpretation of the satisfaction-causes-performance hypothesis. *Academy of Management Review*, 2, 46–53.

This short article is a conceptual, 'thought' piece in which Organ briefly reviews decades of research that failed to find support for the satisfaction-causes-performance hypothesis and speculates as to why the hypothesis continues to resonate with managers. In so doing, Organ focuses on what exactly job performance means, and begins to speculate that some other form of performance (that would subsequently be named OCB) could explain the hypothesis.

Bateman, T. S. & Organ, D. W. (1983). Job satisfaction and the good soldier: The relationship between affect and employee 'citizenship'. *Academy of Management Journal*, 26, 587–95.

This article can be viewed as a companion piece to Smith et al. (1983), representing a collaboration between Organ and another doctoral student Bateman. They specifically investigated the relationship between job satisfaction and job performance in the form of citizenship behaviour, and found that the two were correlated much more strongly than in past research on the relationship between job satisfaction and task performance.

Organ, D. W., Podsakoff, P. M. & MacKenzie, S. B. (2006). *Organizational Citizenship Behavior: Its Nature, Antecedents, and Consequences*. Sage.

In this book Organ and colleagues review the state of the OCB literature after more than two decades of research. Topics reviewed include the conceptual and theoretical roots of OCB, research results related to multiple categories of predictors of OCB as well as outcomes of OCB, and the implications of OCB for practitioners. A comprehensive review to that date of various survey measures of OCB is also provided.

Podsakoff, N. P., Whiting, S. W., Podsakoff, P. M. & Blume, B. (2009). Individual- and organizational-level consequences of organizational citizenship behaviors: A meta-analysis. *Journal of Applied Psychology*, 94, 122–41.

In this article research related to the outcomes of OCB for both individuals, groups and units is reviewed and statistically combined in a series of meta-analyses. These analyses provide estimates of the size of the correlations between OCB and various outcomes (e.g. performance appraisals, reward decisions, unit effectiveness, etc.) using data from multiple prior empirical studies. By and large, results indicate substantial correlations between OCB and a host of outcomes of interest to employees and managers alike.

Podsakoff, P. M., MacKenzie, S. B. & Podsakoff, N. P. (eds) (2018). *The Oxford Handbook of Organizational Citizenship Behavior*. Oxford University Press.

In this edited handbook, over 70 authors provide contributions to 31 chapters reviewing the state of the art in OCB research and related constructs. A wide variety of topics are addressed by some of the best OCB scholars in the field in this comprehensive volume.

REFERENCES

Baron, R. M. & Kenny, D. A. (1986). The moderator-mediator variable distinction in social psychological research: Conceptual, strategic, and statistical considerations. *Journal of Personality and Social Psychology*, 51, 1173–82.

Bateman, T. S. & Organ, D. W. (1983). Job satisfaction and the good soldier: The relationship between affect and employee 'citizenship'. *Academy of Management Journal*, 26, 587–95.

Bennett, R. J. & Robinson, S. L. (2000). Development of a measure of workplace deviance. *Journal of Applied Psychology*, 85, 349–60.

Bergeron, D. M. (2007). The potential paradox of organizational citizenship behavior: Good citizens at what cost? *Academy of Management Review*, 32, 1078–95.

Bolino, M. C. (1999). Citizenship and impression management: Good soldiers or good actors? *Academy of Management Review*, 24, 82–98.

Bolino, M. C. & Turnley, W. H. (2005). The personal costs of citizenship behavior: The relationship between individual initiative and role overload, job stress, and work-family conflict. *Journal of Applied Psychology*, 90, 740–48.

Ehrhart, M. G. & Naumann, S. E. (2004). Organizational citizenship behavior in work groups: A group norms approach. *Journal of Applied Psychology*, 89, 960–74.

Eysenck, H. U. (1958). A short questionnaire for the measurement of two dimensions of personality. *Journal of Applied Psychology*, 42, 14–17.

George, J. M. & Brief, A. P. (1992). Feeling good doing good: A conceptual analysis of the mood at work – organizational spontaneity relationship. *Psychological Bulletin*, 112, 310–29.

Katz, D. (1964). The motivational basis of organizational behavior. *Behavioral Science*, 9, 131–3.

Organ, D. W. (1977). A reappraisal and reinterpretation of the satisfaction-causes-performance hypothesis. *Academy of Management Review*, 2, 46–53.

Organ, D. W. (1988). *Organizational Citizenship Behavior: The Good Soldier Syndrome*. Lexington Books.

Organ, D. W. (1990). The motivational basis of organizational citizenship behavior. *Research in Organizational Behavior*, 12, 43–72.

Organ, D. W., Podsakoff, P. M. & MacKenzie, S. B. (2006). *Organizational Citizenship Behavior: Its Nature, Antecedents, and Consequences*. Sage.

Podsakoff, N. P., Whiting, S. W., Podsakoff, P. M. & Blume, B. (2009). Individual- and organizational-level consequences of organizational citizenship behaviors: A meta-analysis. *Journal of Applied Psychology*, 94, 122–41.

Podsakoff, P. M. & Organ, D. W. (1986). Self-reports in organizational research: Problems and prospects. *Journal of Management*, 12, 531–44.

Podsakoff, P. M., MacKenzie, S. B., Lee, J. Y. & Podsakoff, N. P. (2003). Common method biases in behavioral research: A critical review of the literature and recommended remedies. *Journal of Applied Psychology*, 88, 879–903.

Podsakoff, P. M., MacKenzie, S. B., Moorman, R. H. & Fetter, R. (1990). Transformational leader behaviors and their effects on followers' trust in leader, satisfaction, and organizational citizenship behaviors. *Leadership Quarterly*, 1, 107–42.

Podsakoff, P. M., MacKenzie, S. B., Paine, J. B. & Bachrach, D. G. (2000). Organizational citizenship behaviors: A critical review of the theoretical and empirical literature and suggestions for future research. *Journal of Management*, 26, 513–63.

Podsakoff, P. M., MacKenzie, S. B. & Podsakoff, N. P. (eds). (2018). *The Oxford Handbook of Organizational Citizenship Behavior*. Oxford University Press.

Roethlisberger, F. J. & Dickson, W. J. (1939). *Management and the Worker*. Harvard University Press.

Roethlisberger, F. J. & Dickson, W. J. (1964). *Management and the Worker*, 13th edn. Wiley Sciences Editions.

Rotundo, M. & Sackett, P. R. (2002). The relative importance of task, citizenship, and counterproductive performance to global ratings of job performance: A policy-capturing approach. *Journal of Applied Psychology*, 87, 66–80.

Smith, C. A., Organ, D. W. & Near, J. P. (1983). Organizational citizenship behavior: Its nature and antecedents. *Journal of Applied Psychology*, 68, 653–63.

Van Dyne, L. & LePine, J. A. (1998). Helping and voice extra-role behaviors: Evidence of construct and predictive validity. *Academy of Management Journal*, 41, 108–19.

Van Scotter, J. R. & Motowidlo, S. J. (1996). Interpersonal facilitation and job dedication as separate facets of contextual performance. *Journal of Applied Psychology*, 81, 525–31.

Williams, L. J. & Anderson, S. E. (1991). Job satisfaction and organizational commitment as predictors of organizational citizenship and in-role behaviors. *Journal of Management*, 17, 601–17.

7 | Job Stress: Revisiting Karasek's Job Demand–Job Control Studies

Sabine Sonnentag

BACKGROUND

Robert A. Karasek (1979) developed one of the most influential models of employee health and well-being. Karasek was trained as an architect and later moved to work in sociology following his award of a PhD (in Sociology and Labor Relations) from MIT with a thesis on 'The Impact of the Work Environment on Life outside the Job' (1976).

The 1960s and 1970s were a time when researchers became increasingly interested in workers' health and when companies searched for ways to improve working conditions to protect worker health and well-being (Gibson, 1973; Kornhauser, 1965). These developments happened against the background of broader discussions and initiatives targeting the quality of working life (Hespe & Wall, 1976; Walton, 1973). Karasek's work was influenced by contemporary approaches that relied on case studies and survey research.

When Karasek started his research in the 1970s, research on job stress and on job design coexisted rather independently. One line of research mainly focused on job demands and their detrimental effects on worker health (Caplan et al., 1975) and another line concentrated on job design principles, particularly job autonomy (Hackman & Oldham, 1976). Karasek succeeded in bringing these two lines of research together by suggesting that the combination of job demands and job decision latitude is crucial for understanding strain as well as learning and individual growth at work. During the time of his research, other research programmes addressing the interplay between stressful conditions and individual control also advocated the idea that job demands and job decision latitude need to be seen in conjunction (e.g. Frankenhaeuser & Gardell, 1976), but it was Karasek's studies that had the most pronounced and lasting impact on the field.

DETAILED DESCRIPTION

KARASEK'S JOB DEMAND–JOB CONTROL STUDIES

In his seminal article, Karasek (1979) introduced his job-strain model (often also referred to as the job-demand-control model, the job-demand-job-control model, or the job-demands-job decision latitude model) as a 'stress-management model of strain' (p. 287) which describes environmental factors as the main sources of stress at work. The core proposition of this model is that the interaction between job demands and job decision latitude predicts mental strain. Job demands refer to job stressors in the work environment (e.g. a high workload). Job decision latitude refers to control or discretion in one's job (e.g. about ways to structure one's workday and to complete tasks, cf. p. 290). According to Karasek, job demands and job decision latitude combine into 'job strain' as an input or 'independent variable' (p. 287) that in turn is related to 'mental strain' as an output or 'dependent variable' (ibid.). Karasek presented a 2 × 2 model of different types of job as a function of high versus low levels of job demands and high versus low levels of job decision latitude.

Karasek (1979) suggested that a person's strain increases when job demands increase while job decision latitude decreases, and that a person's activity level increases when job demands increase while job decision latitude increases as well. In other words, he proposed that whether or not high job demands are a source of stress depends on people's job decision latitude. Karasek introduced job demands and job decision latitude as 'instigators' of and 'constraints' on actions, respectively. More specifically, he argued that job demands 'place the individual in a motivated or energized state of "stress"' (p. 287). Job decision latitude should enable the 'release or transformation of "stress" (potential energy) into the energy of action' (ibid.). In the case of low decision latitude, energy cannot be released and will result in 'mental strain'. Karasek did not provide an in-depth elaboration on how job decision latitude should help to transform stress as 'potential energy' into 'energy of action'. Later, Frese (1989) summarised several mechanisms why job control (i.e. decision latitude) should be beneficial when dealing with high job demands. For instance, workers with a high degree of job control are often more able to influence the actual demands, to adjust their working procedures to the stressful environment (e.g. with respect to timing of task completion and choice of work methods) and to be more persistent in their coping efforts.

Karasek cited empirical studies that demonstrated that usually correlations between job demands and job decision latitude are low. For instance, both assembly-line workers and high-level managers are facing a high degree of job demands, with assembly-line workers traditionally experiencing low decision latitude and high-level managers enjoying high decision latitude.

Referring to his 2 × 2 model of job demands and decision latitude, Karasek described (i) jobs characterised by high demands and low decision latitude as 'high strain' jobs, (ii) jobs characterised by high demands and high decision latitude as 'active' jobs, (iii) jobs characterised by low demands and high decision latitude as 'low strain' jobs and (iv) jobs characterised by low demands and low decision latitude as 'passive' jobs. Karasek further suggested that (a) compared to low-strain jobs, high-strain jobs would be associated with mental strain and that (b) active jobs should be associated with an increased activity level compared to passive jobs. In the theoretical part of his article the concept of mental strain remains vague and Karasek did not provide an explicit definition. In his empirical studies, he used measures of exhaustion and depression (depressivity) as indicators of mental strain.

Karasek used two data sets to test the strain hypothesis of his model. The first data set comprised two-wave data from a random sample of the Swedish adult population (N = 1,896; data collection took place in 1968 and again in 1974). The second data set comprised cross-sectional data from a US sample (N = 911), collected in 1972 from a national stratified sample of housing units. In both studies, Karasek limited his analysis on male workers only.

Across the data sets, job-demand measures captured high quantitative demands (e.g. 'Does your job require you to work very fast, hard, or to accomplish large amounts of work?' (p. 291)). Job decision latitude included aspects of both intellectual discretion and decision authority, concepts that are similar to some of the job characteristics discussed by other scholars during the 1960s and 1970s (i.e. variety in skill use and autonomy). Specifically, in the Swedish sample, he used two self-report items assessing intellectual discretion ('skill level required' and 'repetitious or monotonous work') and an expert rating of required skill level to determine decision latitude. In the US sample, he measured skill discretion and decision authority with four self-report items each (e.g. 'high skill level required' for assessing skill discretion and 'allows a lot of decisions' for assessing decision latitude). As mentioned above, he assessed mental strain using measures of exhaustion and depression. As additional indicators of strain, in the Swedish data set, he also included information about pill consumption and sick days, and in the US data set he included information about job satisfaction and life satisfaction.

Analyses in which Karasek (1979) used demands and decision latitude as additive predictors of strain showed that employees in both countries had the highest levels of exhaustion and depression when they worked in jobs characterised by a high level of demands and a low level of decision latitude. Thus workers in jobs that combine high demands with low decision latitude were most exhausted and depressed, and in some of the analyses workers were worst off when demands exceeded decision latitude, as became obvious in significant discrepancy scores. Importantly, Karasek did not include a typical multiplicative interaction term between the predictors (i.e. the mathematical product of job demands × job decision latitude) – usually used to test interaction effects (Cohen, 1968) – into his analytical model as he argued that these would require 'more precise theory and data' (p. 293). The inclusion of the typical multiplicative interaction term, however, would be needed in order to conclude that job decision latitude attenuates the detrimental effect of high job demands. Although omitting a multiplicative interaction term from the analyses, Karasek concluded that there was 'moderate evidence for an interaction effect' (p. 293), based on his observation of a 'relative excess model'

(Southwood, 1978) in which the level of one predictor variable (here: job demands) exceeded the level of the other predictor variable (here: decision latitude). Analyses of job and life dissatisfaction (in the US sample) and pill consumption and sick days (in the Swedish sample) as additional outcomes partly confirmed the findings observed for exhaustion and depression, again with the most unfavourable outcomes (at least in terms of job dissatisfaction and pill consumption) for workers in jobs with high demands combined with low discretion.

The data set from Sweden provided the opportunity to examine change in exhaustion and depression over the six-year period from 1968 to 1974. For exhaustion as an outcome variable, Karasek reported that exhaustion levels increased when job strain increased over time (i.e. when high demands increased while decision latitude decreased). For depression as an outcome variable, he found an increase in depression along with increased job strain only for employees who did not experience depression at the first measurement point in 1968.

To sum up, Karasek presented a rather simple model that brought together two core job aspects present in a broad range of workplaces (job demands and job decision latitude). Findings from two empirical studies in different countries showed that high demands together with low decision latitude are risk factors for poor mental health. These results led Karasek to conclude 'that the opportunity for a worker to use his skills and to make decisions about his work activity is associated with reduced symptoms at every level of job demands. We do not find, therefore, support for the belief that individuals 'overburdened' with decisions face the most strain ... in an industrialized economy. Literature lamenting the stressful burden of executive decision making misses the mark ... Constraints on decision making, not decision making per se, are the major problem, and this problem affects not only executives but workers in low status jobs with little freedom for decision' (p. 303).

IMPACT OF THE CLASSIC STUDIES

After the publication of Karasek's (1979) studies, researchers were inspired by the core idea that job demands and job control (i.e. decision latitude) 'interact' in the prediction of poor well-being and negative health outcomes. Typically, subsequent studies examined further (1) the relationship between job demands and (negative) health outcomes, (2) the relationship between job control and outcomes, and (3) the interaction between job demands and job control as predictor of outcomes.

In 1991, Ganster & Schaubroeck expected that 'the job-demands-job decision latitude model, despite its lack of clear empirical support, will likely continue to exert a major influence on the field of occupational stress' (p. 244). And the number of citations accumulated over the decades supported this prediction. The Karasek model inspired theoretical developments that aimed at a broader coverage of resources in organisational life (Demerouti et al., 2001) and that sketched a more differentiated picture of the interplay between job demands and job resources (de Jonge & Dormann, 2003). I will describe these models in greater detail below.

KEY REPLICATIONS AND GENERALISATIONS

Following the publication of Karasek's study, a controversial debate about what 'interaction' means and how the interaction term should be computed unfolded (e.g. Payne & Fletcher, 1983). In essence, researchers debated whether the inclusion of a multiplicative interaction term should be an essential part of the model, with Karasek (1989) emphasising that the test of the strain hypothesis does not require a multiplicative interaction term, whereas Ganster (1989) viewed the inclusion of a multiplicative interaction term as essential for an appropriate test of the model.

Van der Doef & Maes (1999) provided a first extensive review ($k = 63$ samples) of this research and explicitly distinguished between the strain hypothesis (employees working in a job with high demands and low control should experience the lowest level of well-being) and the buffer hypothesis (job control attenuates the association between high demands and low well-being), which requires the inclusion of a multiplicative interaction term in the empirical analysis. Van der Doef & Maes reported some support – albeit not unequivocal – for the strain hypothesis, but only limited support for the buffer hypothesis. Häusser and colleagues (2010) presented an update and extension of Van der Doef & Maes' (1999) analysis, now including a total of 83 empirical studies, with 23 per cent of them implementing a longitudinal design. Again, there was some support for the strain hypothesis referring to additive effects of high demands and low job control. More specifically, with respect to general psychological well-being, Häusser et al. (2010) reported at least partial support (i.e. support for some but not all occupational groups or all gender groups) for the additive model in 60 per cent of the relevant 47 studies (full support for all hypotheses tested: 36 per cent). With respect to job satisfaction and emotional exhaustion at least partial support was observed in 69 per cent of the 48 studies (full support: 54 per cent) and 57 per cent of the 35 studies (full support: 46 per cent), respectively.

However, evidence for the multiplicative effect corresponding to the buffer hypothesis was much weaker. With respect to general psychological well-being, 39 per cent of 28 studies provided at least partial support (full support: 14 per cent) for the buffer hypothesis. With respect to job satisfaction and emotional exhaustion, at least partial support was reported in 31 per cent of 36 studies (full support: 6 per cent) and 26 per cent of 27 studies (full support: 15 per cent), respectively.

In another qualitative review article, De Lange and colleagues (2003) focused on longitudinal studies testing the original job-demands-control model as well as an extension of this model that included social support as an additional predictor and moderator variable. These researchers located a total of 45 studies, of which they classified 19 as high-quality studies. However, they did not fully disentangle the additive and multiplicative effects in their summary. Again, support for the job-demands-control model (in its original and extended version) was modest. Out of the high-quality studies, 42 per cent showed that combinations of job demands, job control, and social support predicted poor health and well-being, 'usually in the form of additive effects' (p. 300).

The conclusions of these review articles that high demands and low control are associated with poor health and well-being received support from quantitative meta-analyses. For instance, Podsakoff et al. (2007) reported an uncorrected meta-analytical correlation between high job demands (i.e. 'challenge stressors') and strain of $r = .33$ (based on $k = 25$ studies comprising $N = 7,440$ participants) and Alcaron (2011) reported an uncorrected correlation between workload and emotional exhaustion of $r = .40$ ($k = 86$, $N = 51,529$). Furthermore, Humphrey and colleagues (2007) reported an uncorrected correlation between high job control (i.e. 'autonomy') and exhaustion of $r = -.25$ ($k = 14$, $N = 14,825$). In addition, a meta-analysis focusing on longitudinal studies only (Lesener et al., 2019) found that high job demands predicted an increase in burnout above and beyond the protective effects of job resources (including job control). A recent meta-analysis provided estimates not only for additive main effects of job demands and job control – as did previous meta-analyses – but also estimates of the multiplicative interaction effect of job demands and job control (Gonzalez-Mulé et al., 2021). Results for the additive effects tended to be in line with earlier meta-analytical findings with job demands showing an uncorrected correlation of $r = .26$ ($k = 65$, $N = 71,792$) with psychological strain symptoms, and job control showing an uncorrected correlation of $r = -.18$ ($k = 52$, $N = 63,027$) with psychological strain symptoms (correlations of job demands and job control with physical and behavioural strain symptoms were substantially lower). Support for the multiplicative effect of job demands and job control was weak: In regression models with estimates corrected for measurement error, the multiple correlation between the predictors and overall strain symptoms (psychological, physical, behavioural) was $R = .24$ for the additive model and $R = .25$ for the multiplicative model ($\Delta R = .01$; for psychological strain symptoms only, multiple correlations were $R = .42$ and $R = .43$ respectively, $\Delta R = .01$). This finding implies that the improvement of the multiplicative model of the additive model was minimal. Another recent meta-analysis, relying on longitudinal studies only, also did not find a moderator effect of job control on the relationship between job demands and strain (Guthier et al., 2020).

Taken together, there is evidence from cross-sectional and longitudinal field studies that high job demands and low job control predict poor health and well-being, and the combination of high demands and low job control is the most detrimental configuration. However, the buffer hypothesis that high job control attenuates the negative effects of high job demands has not received convincing empirical support. This finding means that in order to avoid negative consequences to workers' health and well-being, it is important to address both job demands and job control. The negative impact of high job demands cannot be buffered by increasing job control: although job control in itself is a beneficial factor for workers' health and well-being, job demands remain negatively related to workers' health and well-being, also at workplaces where job control is high.

Interestingly, the activity hypothesis inherent in Karasek's (1979) original model was neglected over many years, possibly because it remained relatively vague what activity really means and because it could be interpreted in various ways (Taris & Kompier, 2005). However, empirical studies that did examine learning-related variables as outcomes of job demands and job decision latitude reported evidence that particularly high job control is associated with learning, with high job demands showing mixed effects and multiplicative interaction being rarely tested (for reviews, Parker, 2017; Taris & Kompier, 2005).

BEYOND KARASEK'S JOB DEMAND–JOB CONTROL STUDIES: THEORETICAL DEVELOPMENTS

Over the years, Karasek's (1979) initial job-demand-control model motivated not only empirical research but theoretical extensions and refinements as well. An early extension was the inclusion of co-worker social support into the job-demand-control model (Johnson & Hall, 1988). The resulting job-demand-control-support model proposed that social support plays an important role for the relationship between job demands and job control on the one hand and diseases (particularly cardiovascular diseases) on the other. More specifically, this extended model differentiates between isolated and socially supportive work conditions and describes that the combination of high job demands and low job control is most aversive under conditions of low social support. Building on this research, Johnson et al. (1989) combined high job demands, low job control and low social support into one multiplicative term (coined 'iso-strain') and showed that employees in jobs with high iso-strain had higher risks of cardiovascular disease morbidity and mortality, compared to employees in jobs with low iso-strain.

One of the most influential extensions of Karasek's (1979) model is the job-demands-resources model introduced by Demerouti and her co-workers (2001). These researchers argued that job demands and job resources are two broad categories of workplace features that contribute to the development of burnout. Similar to Karasek and the broader job-stress literature, Demerouti et al. described job demands as 'those physical, social, or organisational aspects of the job that require sustained physical or mental effort and are therefore associated with certain physiological and psychological costs' (p. 501). These include factors such as time pressure, physical workload or taxing customer interactions. Demerouti et al. characterised job resources as 'physical, psychological, social, or organisational aspects of the job' (p. 501) that help to achieve work goals, that reduce job demands and that facilitate personal growth and development such as job control, social support, feedback, reward and participation. Thus, by incorporating job control as an important job resource, Demerouti et al.'s model overlaps with that of Karasek. But by conceptualising job resources more broadly, it goes beyond it at the same time. In essence, the job-demands-resources model is a dual pathway model with high job demands argued to contribute to exhaustion via an energy-depletion path and with lack of job resources feeding into a de-motivating path resulting in low work engagement (Bakker & Demerouti, 2007; Bakker et al., 2014).

Later, personal resources were added to the model. Xanthopoulou et al. (2007) started this line of research by analysing optimism, self-efficacy and organisation-based self-esteem as individual factors that play a protective role against exhaustion. Subsequently, researchers examined other factors such as sense of coherence (i.e. individual perceptions of one's life as comprehensible, manageable and meaningful) (Vogt et al., 2016)) and work ability (i.e. 'an individual's ability to continue working in their job', for instance with increasing age or during/after an illness (Brady et al., 2020, p. 639)) as personal resources, primarily focusing on main effects of these personal resources, instead of testing interaction effects with job demands. This inclusion of personal resources into research on job demands and job resources is interesting because Karasek (1979) himself was critical about a strong reliance on individual-difference factors as drivers of strain experiences at work.

Over the past 20 years, the job-demands-resources model received substantial research attention. Importantly, the basic premise that job demands are associated with exhaustion symptoms and that job resources are related to work engagement has largely been supported by meta-analytical evidence (Crawford et al., 2010; Lesener et al., 2019). The extension of Karasek's relatively narrow focus on job decision latitude as a rather formal aspect of a job to the broad conceptualisation of job resources in the job-demands-resources model is noteworthy. It may reflect the more general shift in research attention to factors that keep people healthy at work (Demerouti et al., 2001) and the perspective that in different situations, different kinds of job resources are important (Bakker & Demerouti, 2007). This wider coverage of resources is reflected in other theoretical accounts as well (Halbesleben et al., 2014; ten Brummelhuis & Bakker, 2012), with social resources being particularly important (Halbesleben et al., 2006).

The DISC-model (demand-induced strain compensation model) (de Jonge & Dormann, 2003) has been suggested as a further extension of the job-demands-control model (Karasek, 1979) and the job-demands-resources model (Demerouti et al., 2001). This DISC-model is based on the triple match principle (de Jonge & Dormann, 2006). The developers of this model argue that resources are not generally effective but must match the specific demands and be relevant for the specific outcome in question. For instance, physical resources (e.g. good technical equipment) are functional in alleviating physical demands (e.g. heavy work) but not emotional demands. Emotional resources (e.g. emotional social support), however, are functional in alleviating emotional demands (e.g. angry customers), particularly with respect to emotional outcomes (e.g. emotional exhaustion). This model has received some empirical support (Chrisopoulos et al., 2010; Stiglbauer, 2017), suggesting that the match between demands, resources and outcomes plays a role. However, it seems that the findings do not give a sufficiently conclusive answer as to the precise interactive pattern between job demands and job resources in the prediction of poor employee well-being.

CONCLUSION

Karasek's article from 1979 has been highly successful in terms of citation. As of August 2021, it has been cited more than 16,000 times (Google Scholar).

This high citation count shows that Karasek's model has been highly influential: it inspired many empirical studies and fruitful theoretical developments such as the job-demands-resources model (Demerouti et al., 2001) and the DISC model (de Jonge & Dormann, 2003). Empirical studies testing the model demonstrated that it is important to look at both job demands and job control in order to understand the strain and learning potential of people's jobs. Nevertheless, the empirical support for the model's core proposition, namely that the interaction of job demands and job control is crucial for employees' health and well-being is modest – at best.

Despite the weak empirical evidence for a multiplicative interaction effect between job demands and job control, Karasek's model attracted a lot of attention during past decades. Scholars discussed conceptual problems of the model, shortcomings with respect to the operationalisation of core variables (mainly decision latitude), the ecological fallacy when generalising from correlational patterns at the occupational level to patterns at the individual level, and questions of cross-cultural generalisability (de Jonge & Kompier, 1997; Ganster & Schaubroeck, 1991; Schaubroeck et al., 2000; Wall et al., 1996). The general ideas of the model persist to shape thinking about stress and health (regardless of the state of the evidence) such that Taris (2006) even described Karasek's model as an example of 'zombie theories' in occupational health psychology: 'In practice, some theories do not seem to need empirical support to persist ... [the] ideas keep coming back to haunt us, in spite of the fact that the evidence that supports them is apparently very thin' (p. 99).

Why was (and still is) Karasek's model so popular? One reason for the continued popularity of the model could be that some of its propositions (i.e. the main effects of job demands and low job control) have been supported, obscuring the weak results with respect to the interaction (i.e. buffer) effects. Thus, by highlighting the important main effects of job demands and low job control, the proposed interaction moved into the background.

Second, the model is rather simple and applies to a broad range of jobs. Thus it could be easily picked up not only in psychological research, but also in large epidemiological studies (e.g. Theorell et al., 1998). Typically, these studies did not test the multiplicative interaction effect but used a dummy-coding procedure to contrast what researchers classified as 'high-strain jobs' with other types of jobs.

Third, it could be that the core idea of increasing job control to attenuate the detrimental effects of high job demands appears to be particularly attractive in today's highly demanding work environments so that researchers and practitioners cling to this idea. If there was this buffer effect of high job control, efforts to reduce job demands would be less urgent. It would be important to increase job control, but the implication would be that one could neglect interventions that address high demands. Thus it may be the case that researchers and practitioners wanted to 'save' the core theoretical idea by discounting the lack of empirical support.

Fourth, it might even be that the popularity of Karasek's model did not develop *despite* the weak empirical support for the interaction effect, but *because* of the weak empirical support that led to lively discussions about the model. Specifically, weak empirical support stimulated debates around the model where, for example, some authors like to defend the core ideas of the model by arguing that the empirical tests failed because of methodological shortcomings such as poor operationalisations, omission of additional moderator variables or lack of power.

In addition to its scholarly impact, Karasek's research also influenced the thinking about job stress among policy-makers and change agents within organisations. For instance, questions about job demands and job control became essential in large-scale European surveys (Andries et al., 1996) and findings were illustrated by explicitly referring to the Karasek model (Eurofound, 2005). Moreover, an increase in workers' decision latitude was documented in practical interventions such as job-redesign initiatives (Rydstedt et al., 1998) and health circles (Aust & Ducki, 2014).

Facing the fact that the multiplicative interaction effect of job demands and job control is not well supported, discussions around Karasek's studies highlight the ongoing need to develop and refine models to develop a deeper understanding of how work affects individual health and well-being. For example, it continues to be the case that rather little is known about the precise temporal processes underlying the detrimental impact of high demands and low job control (Sonnentag et al., 2014). Here questions such as the following are important. How long does it take until high job demands and low job control result in strain symptoms? Are the temporal patterns the same for job demands and for job control? If strain symptoms resulting from high demands and low control are reversible, how long does it take to reverse them? Is there an 'expiring duration' after which strain symptoms are not reversible any longer? How do daily strain experiences translate into more longer-term strain symptoms? Recent work by Guthier et al. (2020) illustrates how some of these questions could be addressed. It is imperative that future studies pay more attention to the processes that account for the effects of an unfavourable work situation on individual health and well-being over shorter and longer-term periods of time.

IMPLICATIONS FOR PRACTITIONERS

In terms of practical implications of his research, Karasek underlined the necessity to increase job decision latitude, particularly in occupational groups that traditionally suffer from a low level of decision latitude. Addressing job demands in workplace interventions was not in his focus: 'Possibly the most important implication of this study is that it may be possible to improve job-related mental health without sacrificing productivity. It would appear that job strain can be ameliorated by increasing decision latitude, independently of changes in workload demands. If, as would be expected, workload is related to organisational output levels, these levels could be kept constant if mental health "externalities" were improved' (pp. 303–304).

Based on later studies and meta-analyses that resulted in a more critical evaluation of the assumed interaction effect between job demands and job decision latitude, a slightly different perspective on the practical implications of Karasek's model is needed. Without doubt, increasing job control should be one core principle of job design (Parker & Grote, 2020). However, based on the more recent evidence (Gonzalez-Mulé et al., 2021), organisational policies and interventions should not focus alone on increasing job control but need to address job demands as well. This is because the degree to which high job control attenuates the potential negative impact of high demands is minimal and because the positive relationship between high job demands and impaired mental health is stronger than the relationship between job control and positive aspects of mental health. Therefore, it is crucial to address job demands when aiming at building healthy workplaces.

In striving to decrease job demands, it is also important to prioritise the reduction of hindrance demands (i.e. demands that constrain task accomplishment such as hassles caused by technological or organisational constraints, role ambiguity or role conflict) (LePine et al., 2005) over the reduction of challenge demands (i.e. high workload, time pressure) because hindrance demands – as opposed to challenge demands – show higher correlations with strain symptoms (Crawford et al., 2010; Gonzalez-Mulé et al., 2021). Here, investments not only in better technology but also in clarification of procedures and an improvement in communication skills are needed.

DISCUSSION QUESTIONS

1. Why do you think the empirical evidence for a multiplicative interaction effect between job demands and job control is so weak?

2. What can organisations, supervisors and individual employees do to reduce job demands and increase job control?

3. What other factors might attenuate the negative impact of high job demands on well-being and mental health? Are there factors that might strengthen or weaken the positive impact of job control on well-being and mental health?

FURTHER READINGS

Karasek, R. (1979). Job demands, job decision latitude, and mental strain: Implications for job redesign. *Administrative Science Quarterly*, 24, 285–306. doi:10.2307/2392498

This is Karasek's original article that describes the model and presents two empirical studies. It provides a good overview of the model's key assumptions and Karasek's line of reasoning.

de Jonge, J. & Kompier, M. A. J. (1997). A critical examination of the demand-control-support model from a work psychological perspective. *International Journal of Stress Management*, 4, 235–58. doi:10.1023/B:IJSM.0000008152.85798.90

This article discusses Karasek's model. It elaborates on nine aspects that are crucial in the elaboration of the model, including the conceptualisation and operationalisation of the model's core components, curvilinear relationships and the role of personality.

Gonzalez-Mulé, E., Kim, M. M. & Ryu, J. W. (2021). A meta-analytic test of multiplicative and additive models of job demands, resources, and stress. *Journal of Applied Psychology*, 106(9), 1391–411. doi:10.1037/apl0000840

This is a recent meta-analysis that tests core assumptions of Karasek's model. The authors characterise the model and its extension (including social support) as 'the dominant lens through which to study stress in a variety of fields for the last 40 years' (p. 1).

Parker, S. K., Morgeson, F. P. & Johns, G. (2017). One hundred years of work design research: Looking back and looking forward. *Journal of Applied Psychology*, 102, 403–20. doi:10.1037/apl0000106

This article discusses Karasek's model within the broader work-design literature, covering approaches from sociotechnical systems and autonomous work groups to integrative and contemporary perspectives.

Demerouti, E., Bakker, A. B., Nachreiner, F. & Schaufeli, W. B. (2001). Job demands-resources model of burnout. *Journal of Applied Psychology*, 86, 499–512. doi:10.1037//0021-9010.86.3.499

Demerouti and her co-workers present the job-demands-resources model as an extension of Karasek's model. This new model emphasises the broader range of useful job resources.

REFERENCES

Alcaron, G. M. (2011). A meta-analysis of burnout with job demands, resources, and attitudes. *Journal of Vocational Behavior*, 79, 549–62. doi:10.1016/j.jvb.2011.03.007

Andries, F., Kompier, M. A. J. & Smulders, P. G. W. (1996). Do you think that your health or safety are at risk because of your work? A large European study on psychological and physical work demands. *Work & Stress*, 10(2), 104–18. doi:10.1080/02678379608256790

Aust, B. & Ducki, A. (2004). Comprehensive health promotion interventions at the workplace: Experiences with health circles in Germany. *Journal of Occupational Health Psychology*, 9(3), 258–70. doi:10.1037/1076-8998.9.3.258

Bakker, A. B. & Demerouti, E. (2007). The job demands-resources model: State of the art. *Journal of Managerial Psychology*, 22, 309–28. doi:10.1108/02683940710733115

Bakker, A. B., Demerouti, E. & Sanz-Vergel, A. I. (2014). Burnout and work engagement: The JD-R approach. *Annual Review of Organizational Psychology and Organizational Behavior*, 1, 389–411. doi:10.1146/annurev-orgpsych-031413-091235

Brady, G. M., Truxillo, D. M., Cadiz, D. M., Rineer, J. R., Caughlin, D. E. & Bodner, T. (2020). Opening the black box: Examining the nomological network of work ability and its role in organizational research. *Journal of Applied Psychology*, 105(6), 637–70. doi:10.1037/apl0000454

Caplan, R. D., Cobb, S., French, J. R. P., Jr, Harrison, R. V. & Pinneau, S. R. (1975). *Job Demands and Worker Health*. NIOSH.

Chrisopoulos, S., Dollard, M. F., Winefield, A. H. & Dormann, C. (2010). Increasing the probability of finding an interaction in work stress research: A two-wave longitudinal test of the triple-match principle. *Journal of Occupational and Organizational Psychology*, 83, 17–37. doi:10.1348/096317909X474173

Cohen, J. (1968). Multiple regression as a general data-analytic system. *Psychological Bulletin*, 70, 426–43. doi:10.1037/h0026714

Crawford, E. R., LePine, J. A. & Rich, B. L. (2010). Linking job demands and resources to employee engagement and burnout: A theoretical extension and meta-analytic test. *Journal of Applied Psychology*, 95, 834–48. doi:10.1037/a0019364

de Jonge, J. & Dormann, C. (2003). The DISC model: Demand-induced strain compensation mechanisms in job stress. In M. F. Dollard, A. H. Winefield & H. R. Winefield (eds), *Occupational Stress in the Service Professions*. Taylor & Francis, pp. 43–74.

de Jonge, J. & Dormann, C. (2006). Stressors, resources, and strain at work: A longitudianal test of the triple-match principle. *Journal of Applied Psychology*, 91, 1359–74. doi:10.1037/0021-9010.91.5.1359

de Jonge, J. & Kompier, M. A. J. (1997). A critical examination of the demand-control-support model from a work psychological perspective. *International Journal of Stress Management*, 4, 235–58. doi:10.1023/B:IJSM.0000008152.85798.90

De Lange, A. H., Taris, T. W., Kompier, M. A. J., Houtman, I. L. D. & Bongers, P. M. (2003). 'The very best of the millenium': Longitudinal research and the demand-control-(support) model. *Journal of Occupational Health Psychology*, 8, 282–305.

Demerouti, E., Bakker, A. B., Nachreiner, F. & Schaufeli, W. B. (2001). Job demands-resources model of burnout. *Journal of Applied Psychology*, 86, 499–512. doi:10.1037//0021-9010.86.3.499

Eurofound. (2005). *Work-Related Stress*. European Foundation for the Improvement of Living and Working Conditions.

Frankenhaeuser, M. & Gardell, B. (1976). Underload and overload in working life: Outline of a multidisciplinary approach. *Journal of Human Stress*, 2, 35–46. doi:10.10 80/0097840X.1976.9936068

Frese, M. (1989). Theoretical models of control and health. In S. L. Sauter, J. J. H. Jr & C. L. Cooper (eds), *Job Control and Worker Health*. Wiley, pp. 107–28.

Ganster, D. C. (1989). Worker control and well-being: A review of research in the workplace. In S. L. Sauter, J. J. H. Jr Hurrell & C. L. Cooper (eds), *Job Control and Worker Health*. Wiley, pp. 375–411.

Ganster, D. C. & Schaubroeck, J. (1991). Work stress and employee health. *Journal of Management*, 17, 235–71. doi:10.1177/014920639101700202

Gibson, C. H. (1973). Volvo increases productivity through job enrichment. *California Management Review*, 15(4), 64–8. doi:10.2307/41164460

Gonzalez-Mulé, E., Kim, M. M. & Ryu, J. W. (2021). A meta-analytic test of multiplicative and additive models of job demands, resources, and stress. *Journal of Applied Psychology*, 106(9), 1391–411. doi:10.1037/apl0000840

Guthier, C., Dormann, C. & Voelkle, M. C. (2020). Reciprocal effects between job stressors and burnout: A continuous time meta-analysis of longitudinal studies. *Psychological Bulletin*, 146(12), 1146–73. doi:10.1037/bul0000304

Hackman, J. R. & Oldham, G. R. (1976). Motivation through the design of work: Test of a theory. *Organizational Behavior and Human Performance*, 16(2), 250–79. doi:10.1016/0030-5073(76)90016-7

Halbesleben, J. R. B. (2006). Sources of social support and burnout: A meta-analytic test of the conservation of resources model. *Journal of Applied Psychology*, 91(5), 1134–45. doi:10.1037/0021-9010.91.5.1134

Halbesleben, J. R. R., Neveu, J.-P., Paustian-Underdahl, S. C. & Westman, M. (2014). Getting to the 'COR': Understanding the role of resources in conservation of resources theory. *Journal of Management*, 40(5), 1334–64. doi:10.1177/0149206314527130

Häusser, J. A., Mojzisch, A., Niesel, M. & Schulz-Hardt, S. (2010). Ten years on: A review of recent research on the job demand-control(-support) model and psychological well-being. *Work & Stress*, 24(1), 1–35. doi:10.1080/02678371003683747

Hespe, G. & Wall, T. (1976). The demand for participation among employees. *Human Relations*, 29, 411–28. doi:10.1177/001872677602900503

Humphrey, S. E., Nahrgang, J. D. & Morgeson, F. P. (2007). Integrating motivational, social, and contextual work design features: A meta-analytic summary and theoretical extension of the work design literature. *Journal of Applied Psychology*, 92, 1332–56. doi:10.1037/0021-9010.92.5.1332

Johnson, J. V. & Hall, E. M. (1988). Job strain, work place social support, and cardiovascular disease: A cross-sectional study of a random sample of the Swedish working population. *American Journal of Public Health*, 78, 1336–42. doi:10.2105/AJPH.78.10.1336

Karasek, R. A. (1976). *The Impact of the Work Environment on Life outside the Job.* Doctoral dissertation, Massachusetts Institute of Technology, Cambridge MA.

Karasek, R. A. (1979). Job demands, job decision latitude, and mental strain: Implications for job redesign. *Administrative Science Quarterly*, 24, 285–306. doi:10.2307/2392498

Karasek, R. A. (1989). Control in the workplace and its health-related aspects. In S. L. Sauter, J. J. H. Jr Hurrell & C. L. Cooper (eds), *Job Control and Worker Health*. Wiley, pp. 129–60.

Kornhauser, A. (1965). *Mental Health of the Industrial Worker: A Detroit Study*. Wiley.

LePine, J. A., Podsakoff, N. P. & LePine, M. A. (2005). A meta-analytic test of the challenge stressor-hindrance stressor framework: An explanation for inconsistent relationships among stressors and performance. *Academy of Management Journal*, 48(5), 764–75. doi:10.5465/amj.2005.18803921

Lesener, T., Gusy, B. & Wolter, C. (2019). The job demands-resources model: A meta-analytic review of longitudinal studies. *Work & Stress*, 33(1), 76–103. doi:10.1080/02678373.2018.1529065

Parker, S. K. (2017). Work design growth model: How work characteristics promote learning and development. In R. A. Noe & J. E. Ellingson (eds), *Autonomous Learning in the Workplace*, SIOP Frontiers Book Series. New York: Taylor & Francis, pp. 137–61.

Parker, S. K. & Grote, G. (2020). Automation, algorithms, and beyond: Why work design matters more than ever in a digital world. *Applied Psychology*. doi:10.1111/apps.12241

Payne, R. & Fletcher, B. C. (1983). Job demands, supports, and constraints as predictors of psychological strain among schoolteachers. *Journal of Vocational Behavior*, 22(2), 136–47. doi:10.1016/0001-8791(83)90023-4

Podsakoff, N. P., LePine, J. A. & LePine, M. A. (2007). Differential challenge stressor-hindrance stressor relationships with job attitudes, turnover intention, turnover, and withdrawal behavior: A meta-analysis. *Journal of Applied Psychology*, 92(2), 438–54. doi:10.1037/0021-9010.92.2.438

Rydstedt, L. W., Johansson, G. & Evans, G. W. (1998). The human side of the road: Improving the working conditions of urban bus drivers. *Journal of Occupational Health Psychology*, 3(2), 161–71. doi:10.1037/1076-8998.3.2.161

Schaubroeck, J., Lam, S. & Xie, J. L. (2000). Collective efficacy versus self-efficacy in coping responses to stressors and control: A cross cultural study. *Journal of Applied Psychology*, 85, 512–25. doi:10.1037//0021-9010.85.4.512

Sonnentag, S., Pundt, A. & Albrecht, A.-G. (2014). Temporal perspectives on job stress. In A. J. Shipp & Y. Fried (eds), *Time and Work. Vol. 1: How Time Impacts Individuals*. Psychology Press, pp. 111–40.

Southwood, K. E. (1978). Substantive theory and statistical interaction: Five models. *American Journal of Sociology*, 83, 1154–203. doi:10.1086/226678

Stiglbauer, B. (2017). Under what conditions does job control moderate the relationship between time pressure and employee well-being? Investigating the role of match and personal control beliefs. *Journal of Organizational Behavior*, 38, 730–48. doi:10.1002/job

Taris, T. W. (2006). Bricks without clay: On urban myths in occupational health psychology. *Work & Stress*, 20, 99–104. doi:10.1080/02678370600893410

Taris, T. W. & Kompier, M. A. J. (2005). Job demands, job control, strain and learning behavior: Review and research agenda. In A.-S. Antoniou & C. L. Cooper (eds), *Research Companion to Organizational Health Psychology*, Edward Elgar, pp. 132–50.

ten Brummelhuis, L. L. & Bakker, A. B. (2012). A resource perspective on the work-home interface: The work-home resources model. *American Psychologist*, 67(7), 545–56. doi:10.1037/a0027974

Theorell, T., Tsutsumi, A., Hallquist, J., Reuterwall, C., Hogstedt, C., Fredlund, P., … Johnson, J. V. (1998). Decision latitude, job strain, and myocardial infarction: A study of working men in Stockholm. The SHEEP Study Group. Stockholm Heart Epidemiology Program. *American Journal of Public Health*, 88, 382–8. doi:10.2105/AJPH.88.3.382

Van der Doef, M. & Maes, S. (1999). The job demand-control (-support) model and psychological well-being: A review of 20 years of empirical research. *Work & Stress*, 13, 87–114. doi:10.1080/026783799296084

Vogt, K., Hakanen, J. J., Jenny, G. J. & Bauer, G. F. (2016). Sense of coherence and the motivational process of the job-demands-resources model. *Journal of Occupational Health Psychology*, 21(2), 194–207. doi:10.1037/a0039899

Wall, T. D., Jackson, P. R., Mullarkey, S. & Parker, S. K. (1996). The demands-control model of job strain: A more specific test. *Journal of Occupational and Organizational Psychology*, 69, 153–66. doi:10.1111/j.2044-8325.1996.tb00607.x

Walton, R. E. (1973). Quality of working life: What is it? *Sloan Management Review*, 15, 11–21.

Xanthopoulou, D., Bakker, A. B., Demerouti, E. & Schaufeli, W. B. (2007). The role of personal resources in the job-demands-resources model. *International Journal of Stress Management*, 14, 121–41. doi:10.1037/1072-5245.14.2.121

Part III | Leadership and Followership

8

The Bases of Social Hierarchy: Revisiting French & Raven's Bases of Power (and Status)

Derek D. Rucker, Adam D. Galinsky & Joe C. Magee

BACKGROUND

In 1959, John French and his former graduate student Bertram Raven co-authored a landmark chapter in the edited volume *Studies in Social Power* (Cartwright, 1959). In that chapter, French and Raven introduced the reader both to the construct of social power and to the common characteristics of social structures and social relationships that give rise to power. They offered a formal theoretical analysis of the psychology of dependence, rooted in the principles of social influence as they were understood at the time. However, what their piece has been most remembered for is their typology of five bases of power.

On the one hand, the origins of French & Raven (1959) appear humble; it was one of many chapters tucked inside an edited volume. On the other hand, the work is nothing short of a juggernaut when it comes to impact. It continues to guide academic thought on the topic, decades after its inception, and is required reading in seminars on social power, social hierarchy, social influence and related topics. Moreover, the work still makes frequent appearances in articles devoted to the study of social power. According to Google Scholar, French & Raven (1959) has been cited over 16,000 times – which includes over 3,000 times since 2018 – across a wide variety of disciplines, including psychology, sociology, political science, management and marketing.

In this review, we reflect on the ambition and aims of French and Raven's original research, paying homage to their prescient insights into the bases of social power. We then discuss how the study of social power has evolved over the course of half a century in ways that reinforce, augment and challenge their original ideas. Two of the main advances during the past two decades have been to (a) more precisely define social power and (b) broaden the focus from bases of social power to bases of social hierarchy by differentiating power and status. We issue an updated typology of the bases of social hierarchy which we hope provides fertile ground for future research.

DETAILED DESCRIPTION

French & Raven sought to understand the idea of social power by identifying, in their own words, 'the major types of power'. Their idea was that, by distinguishing between different types of power, they could account for different effects found in studies of social influence. In fact, central to French and Raven's thesis was that social power was inherently tethered to social influence; they wrote, 'we shall define power in terms of influence and influence in terms of psychological change' (p. 150). The idea that power should be equated with influence had appeared elsewhere (see Cartwright, 1965), but, as we shall review, more contemporary theoretical explorations of power have sought to conceptually separate power from influence (Fiske & Berdahl, 2007; Magee & Galinsky, 2008).

With their definition in place, French and Raven introduced and delineated five distinct bases of power: *reward power*, *coercive power*, *legitimate power*, *referent power* and *expert power*. One of the authors later added a sixth base – information power (Raven, 1965, 1993) – to the original set. Even with this addition, the authors never claimed this taxonomy to be exhaustive. Rather, in their original work, French & Raven delineated five bases because they believed each base was easily identifiable and important for understanding the influence of a social 'agent' (e.g. an individual, group, role or norm) on a target person. We dive into the original definitions and common understandings of French and Raven's bases because they are integral to appreciating the extent to which they were supported or challenged in subsequent research.

Reward power was used to describe actual or perceived differences in an agent's ability to distribute rewards.[1] French and Raven observed that the more control over rewards an individual possessed, the more that individual could influence a person that valued those rewards. They conceptualised reward power as involving both the ability to administer stimuli of positive valence (e.g. offering a worker a raise or overtime pay) or to remove or reduce stimuli of negative valence (e.g. changing an undesirable work schedule). Indeed, as we will discuss, the ability to control resources, such as rewards, remains central to contemporary definitions of power.

French and Raven defined *coercive power* around negative outcomes, specifically an individual's ability to punish another person. They recognised that coercive power is intimately tied to reward power because both involve the ability of one person to directly determine the outcomes of another. Whereas reward power reflected the ability of one person to improve another individual's situation (either through adding an outcome of positive valence or removing an outcome of negative valence), coercive power captured a person's ability to make another individual's situation worse, either by adding an outcome of negative valence or removing an

---

[1] An agent, according to French & Raven (1959), could be a person, group, role or norm. For the sake of brevity, we will refer exclusively to agents as people in our illustrative examples.

outcome of positive valence. In their original work, French & Raven acknowledged that the conceptual distinction between reward power and coercive power was difficult. They suggested the primary difference may ultimately be a psychological one, whether an individual perceived an action as improving (i.e. through rewards) or worsening (i.e. through punishment) their current state.

Legitimate power was used to describe whether one actor perceived another person as having the authority or right to dictate the actor's behaviour. The idea of legitimate power was grounded in the notion that social norms govern what behaviour is acceptable or unacceptable. Social norms vary across cultures and contexts, as well as across organisations and groups within the same culture. In some organisations or contexts people might welcome some degree of disagreement and dissent (e.g. in a classroom), whereas in other situations, disagreement and dissent might not be tolerated at all (e.g. in the military). French & Raven further noted that legitimate power ultimately had to be accepted by the low-power actor – that is, the actor had to internalise that the ability of another to exert influence was legitimate. For example, individuals are more inclined to view the influence attempts from those with power as valid if they perceived the social structure as legitimate, as opposed to illegitimate.

Referent power was used to describe influence that a source had over another indivdual because that individual identified with the source. By identify, French & Raven referred to two related but independent ideas. First, that one actor likes and respects another person. Second, that one actor desires to be similar to another person. As a consequence of identification, an individual might change his or her behaviour in a manner that fosters similarity to the person they wanted to identify with. For example, if an individual respects her boss, she might take similar positions on issues within the organisation. And the more a person seeks to identify with a particular actor, the more influence, and thus power, that actor will have. Again, the notion of referent power is closely tied to French & Raven's conceptualisation of power as influence.

Finally, *expert power* was used to refer to an individual's control over some specialised knowledge or expertise. For example, French & Raven gave the example of a lawyer that might be viewed as having expertise on legal matters and thus would be afforded power by those without such knowledge. For expert power to exist, an individual must be viewed as both an expert and trustworthy. That is, individuals must believe that the actor not only possesses expertise, but that they are motivated to use their knowledge in an accurate and unbiased manner. In this regard, expert power was analogous to aspects of source credibility in the literature on persuasion (e.g. see Dholakia & Sternthal, 1977).

One strength of French & Raven's taxonomy of the bases of power was its face validity. Readers could, and still can, easily generate examples of politicians, supervisors at work and people in their lives whose power rests on a base put forth by French & Raven. This conceptual strength was accompanied by empirical evidence supporting some of the distinctions. Namely, an experiment by Raven & French (1958) explored the distinction between legitimate and coercive power. They created two conditions involving group work. In one condition, the supervisor was represented as having legitimate power because they were elected. In the other condition, the supervisor took the job without group support (i.e. coercive power). The authors found that whether the supervisor's position was viewed as rooted in legitimate or coercive power affected how participants responded. Participants that had a supervisor with legitimate power privately accepted the supervisor's influence more than those that had a supervisor with coercive power. However, there was no difference between groups in their public conformity. This experiment illustrates that the distinction between legitimate and coercive power can lead both to differences (private acceptance) and to similarities (public conformity).

BEYOND THE CLASSIC STUDY: THEORETICAL AND EMPIRICAL ADVANCES SINCE FRENCH & RAVEN

As noted at the outset of this chapter, French and Raven's work has had tremendous impact. Beyond using their taxonomy to organise their thinking, a number of scholars have offered significant theoretical and empirical advances. Indeed, these theoretical and empirical advances may help explain the growing interest in power in the last decade (see Galinsky et al., 2015). Here, we cover four advances made by researchers over the last two decades. First, scholars have refined the definition of social power. Second, they have broadened the higher-order concept to be social hierarchy, where power is one base and status is a second distinct base of social hierarchy. Third, following the second advance, researchers have made strides toward empirically distinguishing these two distinct bases of social hierarchy. Fourth, they have explored power as a psychological state.

ADVANCE 1: DEFINITIONS

Magee & Galinsky (2008) provided a contemporary review of power that both complemented and challenged the views of French & Raven. Similar to the original conceptualisation by French & Raven, Magee & Galinsky recognised that social power reflected a relationship between two or more individuals. However, Magee & Galinsky challenged the definition of power as influence (see also Cartwright, 1959). They suggested that defining power as influence conflated the concept of power with either its antecedents or downstream consequences (see also Fiske & Berdahl, 2007; Keltner et al., 2003).

Rather than conflating power with influence, Magee & Galinsky (2008) contended that social power was better defined as 'asymmetric control over valued resources in social relations' (p. 361). For differences in power to arise between parties, at least one individual must possess, and another individual must desire, a specific resource. They further noted that these resources could vary across situations and might comprise (among others) physical resources, decision rights or privileged information. Overall, Magee & Galinsky recognised that power as control over resources was tightly related to three of the original power bases specified by French & Raven (reward, coercive and expert power) as well as the addition suggested by Raven (information).

Magee and Galinsky's (2008) definition of social power separated the possession of power from its antecedents or downstream consequences. Thus they saw influence, both the attempts to alter the behaviour of others and their successes and failures, as antecedents or consequences of power. From their perspective, one might have power without actually using that power to exert influence. They argued that equating power to influence essentially equated the independent variable with the dependent variable and created a tautology (see also Simon, 1953). Moreover, they observed that the possession of power could lead to failed influence attempts, which suggests that the possession of power is not tantamount to influence. Indeed, if one considers French & Raven's original proposition that influence was tied to psychological change, the intimate connection between power and influence seems difficult to reconcile with observations where no psychological change is observed despite clear differences in power. This separation of power and influence has led to other novel insights. For example, Lammers et al. (2016) found that people primarily seek power not to *have* influence over others but to be free *from* the influence of others. That is, the desire for power often reflects a need for autonomy more than a need for influence.

ADVANCE 2: THE BASES OF SOCIAL HIERARCHY

A second advance involves expanding the scope of analysis from power to social hierarchy. By social hierarchy, we refer to 'an implicit or explicit rank order of individuals or groups with respect to a valued social dimension' (Magee & Galinsky, 2008, p. 354). This social dimension of value might be power, but it need not be. Indeed, the move to this broader conceptualisation began when researchers questioned the bases of power specified by French & Raven. First, scholars wondered whether other prominent bases of power exist. Second, researchers challenged some of French & Raven's original bases.

Raven (1965) himself offered one of the first major revisions to the original bases of power. Although he supported the five power bases outlined in his work with French, he suggested the existence of an important sixth base: informational power. According to Raven, informational power consisted of the ability to exert influence because of the logic or evidence contained in a message. That is, power is contained in the persuasiveness of one's message, which is why Raven (1993) eventually equated informational power with persuasion. Although Raven also recognised that informational power is similar to expert power, he differentiated the two by noting that expert power might lead to influence based on a source's expertise, even if one did not understand the information in the message (see also Petty & Cacioppo, 1986). In contrast, informational power, according to Raven, involved being persuaded by the message arguments (i.e. the content of the information). Raven (1965) further argued that how information is presented, rather than the content of the information itself, could also affect persuasion. Because the words one uses and how one uses them is a particular skill that others can covet, we view these skills as a specific form of expertise.

As we have discussed, Magee & Galinsky (2008) echoed several of French & Raven's original bases of power. They noted that central to their own definition of social power was a difference in valued resources and, in this respect, their definition contained French and Raven's reward, coercive and expert bases because they are each different types of resources that parties might value. Because coercive power is linked to control over punishments, we use the label *punishment power*. The term coercive power was more appropriate when power was defined in terms of influence as the mere threat of using force or punishment on another could influence another person's behaviour. Given the contemporary definition of power around asymmetric control of resources in a social relationship, control over this negative resource is its key feature, hence the term punishment power.

Expert power was particularly interesting for Magee & Galinsky (2008) because expertise could upend a traditional social hierarchy. For example, a professor typically has reward, coercive and expert power over a doctoral student; however, a doctoral student may have knowledge of methodological advances that the professor seeks to understand or at least use, giving the doctoral student some expert power in their relationship. With respect to information power, Magee and Galinsky highlighted one way in which information constitutes a meaningful difference in resources (see also Galinsky et al., 2017). Specifically, a person may have inside information that another person desires. This access to privileged information has nothing to do with its persuasiveness or logic but is a resource that one person controls and another person desires.

In sharp contrast to French & Raven, Magee & Galinsky (2008) challenged the ideas that legitimate power and referent power should be construed as bases of power. For legitimate power, Magee & Galinsky (2008) suggested that, at least as represented by French and Raven, it did not reflect a base of power. Rather, they identified legitimacy as a moderator of other forms of power as well as other bases of social hierarchy. That is, legitimacy is not a base of power in and of itself, but it affects how people respond to other bases of power. For example, the possession or use of rewards or punishment could be viewed as legitimate or illegitimate. Importantly, how power is construed in terms of legitimacy will affect how one reacts to having or lacking power (Lammers et al., 2008, 2012; Willis et al., 2010). However, in the absence of one of the other power bases, the idea of legitimacy or illegitimacy holds little meaning within a social hierarchy and thus does not constitute a fundamentally unique base of power.

For referent power, Magee & Galinsky (2008) invoked the concept of social status. Specifically, they equated referent power with social status, which they identified as a distinct base of social hierarchy along with power. They defined social status, or simply status, as 'the extent to which an individual or group is respected or admired by others' (p. 359). Because status must be conferred by others, it does not represent a resource under the direct control of an actor and thus cannot be equated to power. Again, part of the difference in classifications between French & Raven (1959) and Magee & Galinsky (2008) arises from differences in how they define social power. Having conflated power with influence, French & Raven view status as a base of power since it allows one to exert influence. In contrast, Magee and Galinsky separate power from influence, and the fact that status is not a resource controlled by an actor but is bestowed by observers led them to conclude that it constitutes a separate construct. Indeed, Anderson et al. (2015) have also argued that status is separate from power.

We propose that power and status are separate bases of social hierarchy. Further, we propose that reward, punishment, expertise and information are bases of power and of status, i.e. each can increase one's power, one's status, or both. When expertise is viewed as a valuable resource that others desire, it is a form of power. However, when expertise is primarily an aspect of a person that is respected by others, it is a form of status. Similarly, an individual has power when they possess inside information or control over rewards that others value and desire, but they have status when they are respected for having that information or for being able to allocate a set of rewards. As such, in some cases, it is possible that the same base can give rise to both status and power; for example, a legislator might have private information that gives them power (i.e. other legislators want that information) and gains them respect (i.e. other legislators admire the possession of such information).

It should be pointed out that while Magee & Galinsky (2008) separated power from status – because an individual can have one without the other – we recognise that it is possible that in some cases the ability to confer respect could be viewed as a resource. For example, if an actor craves being respected by a specific individual, the ability to confer or withhold respect is a valuable resource that aligns with Magee and Galinsky's definition of power. In contrast, if an actor does not care about being respected by a given person, the person's ability to confer or withhold respect does not give them power.

In summary, our analysis suggests that both power and status serve as distinct bases of social hierarchy and that rewards, punishments, expertise and information can serve as independent bases of both power and status (see Table 8.1). Despite refining what constitutes a base of power, French and Raven's original five bases of power remain important constructs. That is, what the authors termed legitimate and referent power, as we have reviewed, remain important in understanding the inner workings of social hierarchy even though they do not, based on our reasoning, reflect bases of power.

ADVANCE 3: EMPIRICALLY DISTINGUISHING DIFFERENT BASES OF SOCIAL HIERARCHY

Central to French & Raven's thesis was the idea that their five bases of power are distinct constructs. Indeed, subsequent research demonstrated it was possible to measure and empirically separate out these constructs. For example, Frost & Stahelski (1988) provided a 23-item questionnaire that showed these constructs were orthogonal and some research has provided empirical evidence for the conceptual distinctions raised by French & Raven (Podsakoff & Schriescheim, 1985).

Table 8.1 Power and status are bases of social hierarchy. Rewards, punishment, expertise and information are bases of power and status. Each can be a source of power, a source of status, or both, depending on the context.

Base	Definition
Reward Power	A person's asymmetric control over the granting of positive resources or removal of negative resources
Punishment Power	A person's asymmetric control over the administration of negative resources or removal of positive resources
Expert Power	A person's asymmetric control over knowledge or skills
Information Power	A person's asymmetric control over privileged or inside information
Base	**Definition**
Reward Status	Respect a person is given for having discretion over positive resources
Punishment Status	Respect a person is given for having discretion over negative resources
Expert Status	Respect a person is given for having knowledge or skills
Information Status	Respect a person is given for having privileged or inside information

Building on these distinctions, a third advance has been to understand how the bases of social hierarchy produce distinct consequences as well as how the different bases interact with each other.

One line of research has explored how power and status produce different effects. For example, Blader et al. (2016) found that high-power individuals were less likely to engage in perspective-taking and empathy compared to low-power individuals, replicating earlier work by Galinsky and colleagues (2006). However, they found that high-status individuals were more likely to engage in perspective-taking and empathy compared to low-status individuals. This research suggests that different bases of social hierarchy can be associated with distinct outcomes.

Another line of research has demonstrated that the bases of social hierarchy can interact with each other to influence behaviour. Researchers have found evidence for a 'little tyrant effect', the toxic cocktail that emerges when high power is combined with low status (Fast et al., 2012; Anicich et al., 2016). When individuals have high power and low status (Fragale, Overbeck & Neale, 2011), they tend to be more demeaning to others than any other combination of power and status because power allows one to act on one's disgruntled feelings produced by low status. The demeaning behaviour precipitated by power without status has two consequences. First, people have low regard for roles defined by high power and low status (e.g. bouncer at a club, airport security official, reimbursement clerk; Fragale et al., 2011). Second, the demeaning treatment by these little tyrants triggers a vicious cycle of interpersonal conflict (Anicich et al., 2016).

As we mentioned previously, contemporary scholars see legitimacy not as a separate base of social hierarchy but as a moderator or qualifier of the other bases. Legitimacy reflects both how a base of social hierarchy is acquired – that is, whether it is deserved or not – and how it is exercised. Lammers and colleagues (2008) demonstrated that the legitimacy of one's position of power moderates the effects of power. When power was viewed as legitimate, individuals with power exhibited more assertiveness and risk-taking than individuals without power. However, when power was illegitimate, those without power exhibited more assertiveness and risk-taking than those with power (see also Lammers et al., 2012; Willis et al., 2010). Similarly, Hays & Blader (2017) found that status increased generosity when the status hierarchy was seen as illegitimate because people felt the need to demonstrate that they deserved status through their beneficence. Each of these studies shows that legitimacy transforms the meaning, psychological experience and expectations for a base of social hierarchy.

In this section, we have highlighted how scholars have successfully distinguished power from status as bases of social hierarchy. However, little research has distinguished the individual bases of power and status that we have identified: rewards, punishment, expertise and information. For example, how might reward power versus punishment power lead to different behaviour by the powerholder? Or, how might someone with expertise act differently than someone with inside information? When does being an expert lead to more or less status than having access to rewards? Is there a higher legitimacy threshold for punishment power than reward power? These are all questions that the next generation of social hierarchy scholars might tackle.

ADVANCE 4: POWER AS A PSYCHOLOGICAL STATE

A final advance has been understanding the psychological experience of power. Social power is a structural variable (Blau, 1964; Ng, 1980) that arises or exists in social relationships (Emerson, 1962). However, social psychologists have recognised that the possession of power produces a psychological experience that influences people's emotions, thoughts and behaviour (Keltner et al., 2003). As a result, studying the psychological state of power can ultimately inform how people might behave as a function of differences in structural power. As such, researchers have begun studying the psychological state produced by power, what is often identified as an individual's *sense of power* (Anderson et al., 2012; Galinsky et al., 2003; Galinsky et al., 2015).

This advance is important because it reveals that an individual can experience a sense of having or lacking power which then can affect their subsequent behaviour. As such, one does not need to study power by assigning people to different roles with different degrees of power. In fact, starting with Galinsky et al. (2003), hundreds of studies have manipulated a sense of power by simply having people recall an experience where they were in a high- or low-power position. This perspective has provided methodological advances in how to study power and suggests that a number of the effects of social power ultimately occur because of the psychological experience that power produces (Galinsky et al., 2015).

Social hierarchy research is only now starting to tackle the psychological state of status (see Hays et al., 2022). Historically scholars have tackled status by understanding how people with status are treated (e.g. status characteristics theory) (Ridgeway, 1991; Ridgeway et al., 1985). This makes sense given that status is a property of other people's perception whereas power is a property of the self with regard to the resources one controls. We hope future research will seek to understand the psychological state of status at the same level of specificity and nuance as research has for power.

CONCLUSION

French & Raven (1959) is a seminal and foundational article for researchers interested in power, social hierarchy, influence and related constructs. Their chapter was ambitious in its original scope; it challenged researchers to move from studying power in a vague and all-inclusive fashion to delineating the distinct bases of power. The work was a significant contribution at the time of its publication and, despite its age, has persisted as an influential piece in the area. As a sign of its enduring impact, their paper has led scholars to both refine and rethink the construct of power and to include it in an overarching understanding of social hierarchy.

Although many advances have been made since the original publication, we highlighted four as particularly important. First, the literature on social power has evolved with regard to its definition to represent asymmetric control over valued resources in social relations. As a result, scholars have suggested that influence is better situated as a cause or a consequence of social power as opposed to its defining feature. Second, researchers have challenged whether French & Raven's five bases were all encompassing or too inclusive. In terms of challenging whether it is all encompassing, scholars (including one of the original authors) have recognised additional potential bases (Galinsky et al., 2017; Raven, 1965, 1993). In terms of being too inclusive, others have suggested, especially given the updated definition of power, that not all of the original bases are truly bases of power or even bases of social hierarchy (Magee & Galinsky, 2008). Here, we have argued that power and status are the two fundamental bases of social hierarchy and rewards, punishment, expertise and information represent four specific bases of power and status. Third, researchers have begun to focus empirically on how the different bases of social hierarchy lead to different outcomes and/or interact. However, more research is needed to distinguish between the effects of the different bases of power and status (e.g. whether control over or the respect that comes from controlling rewards, punishments, expertise or information produces different effects). Finally, contemporary research has made a conceptual and methodological case for studying power as a psychological experience.

Together, these advances are important amendments to French & Raven's (1959) analysis of social power. We expect that as the study of social power evolves, the impact of this original treatise will continue to ripple through the field of social hierarchy.

IMPLICATIONS FOR PRACTITIONERS

The study of social power has a number of potential implications for practitioners. Here, we consider two implications that result from both the original research paper by French & Raven and the work that has followed.

First, the bases of social power offered by French & Raven provide a blueprint for practitioners to analyse how social hierarchy is arranged in their own organisation and operations. Specifically, practitioners can use this structure to explore and understand the types of power held in their organisation and the types of status that are most prevalent. Do managers operate through the use of reward or punishment power? What are the norms that formally define the legitimacy of power or status, and is the current power or status hierarchy one that is perceived as legitimate (see Magee & Frasier, 2014)? What individuals possess power versus status in the organisation? In short, having an appreciation for the constructs laid out by French & Raven produces a structured means to think about and understand one's environment.

Second, more recent work that has focused on the psychological experience of power and status highlights a central question for practitioners to ask of their organisations. Do employees feel powerful or respected in their environment? Differences in such psychological states – irrespective of actual power or status levels – may have important implications for whether employees share their views, take decisive action and ultimately succeed in the workplace. For example, individuals that feel less power are less likely to take action (Galinsky et al., 2003) and to speak up in conversations (Anderson & Berdahl, 2002). As such, organisational leaders may put extra effort into both understanding their employees' sense of power and finding means to empower them.

DISCUSSION QUESTIONS

1. Consider the five bases of social power put forth by French & Raven. These authors themselves noted their bases were not exhaustive. Indeed, Raven (1965) suggested informational power to be a sixth base, which we reconceive as rhetorical skill and Galinsky et al. (2017) identified control over inside information as a source of power. Can you generate a novel base of power or status? More generally, how would you conceptualise, separate and empirically test whether a variable constitutes a novel base of power or status?

2. Magee & Galinsky (2008) suggest that neither legitimate power nor referent power are distinct bases of power. Instead, referent power is a separate base of social hierarchy (status) and legitimacy qualifies the effects of both power and status. Do you agree?

3. The study of power has broadened to understand how the psychological experience of power can guide and direct behaviour independent of the actual power one possesses. As such, it is also possible for people

to perceive they have more (or less power) than they actually have in a situation. What are the potential implications of a misalignment between how powerful people feel (i.e. their sense of power) and the actual power they possess?

FURTHER READINGS

Blader, S. L. & Chen, Y. R. (2012). Differentiating the effects of status and power: A justice perspective. *Journal of Personality and Social Psychology*, 102(5), 994.

This paper empirically distinguishes power from status. Specifically, it demonstrates that power and status can have divergent consequences when it comes to the fairness of people's behaviour.

Galinsky, A. D., Rucker, D. D. & Magee, J. C. (2015). Power: Past findings, present considerations, and future directions. In *APA Handbook of Personality and Social Psychology, Vol. 3: Interpersonal Relations.* American Psychological Association, pp. 421–60.

This paper provides a contemporary review of the power literature. In particular, it focuses on how power transforms the psychology of the individual, and the consequences of the psychological experience of power for thought and behaviour.

Keltner, D., Gruenfeld, D. H. & Anderson, C. (2003). Power, approach, and inhibition. *Psychological Review*, 110(2), 265–84.

The authors offer a new theory of how power affects thought and behaviour. The theory links the psychological effects of power to the neuropsychological systems of approach and inhibition. They suggest that power is associated with approach and powerlessness with inhibition. The paper ignited the study of power and inspired hundreds of studies testing the theory.

Magee, J. C. & Galinsky, A. D. (2008). Social hierarchy: The self-reinforcing nature of power and status. *Academy of Management Annals*, 2(1), 351–98.

This work provides an alternative conceptualisation of power and reviews and synthesises prior research. In addition, it suggests some of the original bases of power – legitimate and referent power – might be better construed as moderators of power as opposed to fundamentally distinct bases.

Raven, B. H. (1993). The bases of power: Origins and recent developments. *Journal of Social Issues*, 49(4), 227–51.

Provides an updated perspective on French & Raven (1959) from the vantage point of one of the original authors. Notably, this paper suggests a sixth base of power defined as *informational power* or *persuasion.*

REFERENCES

Anderson, C. & Berdahl, J. L. (2002). The experience of power: Examining the effects of power on approach and inhibition tendencies. *Journal of Personality and Social Psychology*, 83(6), 1362.

Anderson, C., Hildreth, J. A. D. & Howland, L. (2015). Is the desire for status a fundamental human motive? A review of the empirical literature. *Psychological Bulletin*, 141(3), 574.

Anderson, C., John, O. P. & Keltner, D. (2012). The personal sense of power. *Journal of Personality*, 80(2), 313–44.

Anicich, E. M., Fast, N. J., Halevy, N. & Galinsky, A. D. (2016). When the bases of social hierarchy collide: Power without status drives interpersonal conflict. *Organization Science*, 27(1), 123–40.

Blader, S. L. & Chen, Y. (2012). Differentiating the effects of status and power: A justice perspective. *Journal of Personality & Social Psychology*, 102, 994–1014.

Blader, S. L., Shirako, A. & Chen, Y. (2016). Looking out from the top: Differential effects of status and power on perspective taking. *Personality and Social Psychology Bulletin*, 42, 723–37.

Blau, P. M. (1964). *Exchange and Power in Social Life*. Wiley.

Cartwright, D. P. (ed.) (1959). *Studies in Social Power*. Institute for Social Research, University of Michigan.

Cartwright, D. (1965). Influence, leadership, control. In J. G. March (ed.), *Handbook of Organizations*. Rand McNally, pp. 1–47.

Dholakia, R. & Sternthal, B. (1977). Highly credible sources: Persuasive facilitators or persuasive liabilities? *Journal of Consumer Research*, 3, 223–32.

Emerson, R. M. (1962). Power-dependence relations. *American Sociological Review*, 31–41.

Fast, N. J., Halevy, N. & Galinsky, A. D. (2012). The destructive nature of power without status. *Journal of Experimental Social Psychology*, 48(1), 391–94.

Fiske, S. T. & Berdahl, J. (2007). Social power. In A. W. Kruglanski & E. T. Higgins (eds), *Social Psychology: Handbook of Basic Principles*. Guilford, pp. 678–92.

Fragale, A. R., Overbeck, J. R. & Neale, M. A. (2011). Resources versus respect: Social judgments based on targets' power and status positions. *Journal of Experimental Social Psychology*, 47(4), 767–75.

French, J. R. & Raven, B. (1959). The bases of social power. In D. P. Cartwright (ed.), *Studies in Social Power*. Institute for Social Research, University of Michigan, pp. 150–67.

Frost, D. E. & Stahelski, A. J. (1988). The systematic measurement of French and Raven's bases of social power in workgroups. *Journal of Applied Social Psychology*, 18(5), 375–89.

Galinsky, A. D., Gruenfeld, D. H. & Magee, J. C. (2003). From power to action. *Journal of Personality and Social Psychology*, 85(3), 453.

Galinsky, A. D., Rucker, D. D. & Magee, J. C. (2015). Power: Past findings, present considerations, and future directions. In *APA Handbook of Personality and Social Psychology, Vol. 3: Interpersonal Relations*. American Psychological Association, pp. 421–60.

Galinsky, A. D., Schaerer, M. & Magee, J. C. (2017). The four horsemen of power at the bargaining table. *Journal of Business & Industrial Marketing*, 32(4), 606–11.

Hays, N. A. & Blader, S. L. (2017). To give or not to give? Interactive effects of status and legitimacy on generosity. *Journal of Personality and Social Psychology*, 112(1), 17.

Hays, N. A., Lee, A. J., Blader, S. L. & Galinsky, A. D (2022). *The Interdependence-Efficacy Theory of Social Hierarchy: Understanding the Psychological Effects of Status and Power*. Unpublished manuscript.

Keltner, D., Gruenfeld, D. H. & Anderson, C. (2003). Power, approach, and inhibition. *Psychological Review*, 110(2), 265.

Lammers, J., Galinsky, A. D., Gordijn, E. H. & Otten, S. (2008). Illegitimacy moderates the effects of power on approach. *Psychological Science*, 19(6), 558–64.

Lammers, J., Galinsky, A. D., Gordijn, E. H. & Otten, S. (2012). Power increases social distance. *Social Psychological and Personality Science*, 3(3), 282–90.

Lammers, J., Stoker, J. I., Rink, F. & Galinsky, A. D. (2016). To have control over or to be free from others? The desire for power reflects a need for autonomy. *Personality and Social Psychology Bulletin*, 42(4), 498–512.

Magee, J. C. & Frasier, C. W. (2014). Status and power: The principal inputs to influence for public managers. *Public Administration Review*, 74(3), 307–17.

Magee, J. C. & Galinsky, A. D. (2008). Social hierarchy: The self-reinforcing nature of power and status. *Academy of Management Annals*, 2(1), 351–98.

Ng, S. H. (1980). *The Social Psychology of Power.* Academic Press.

Overbeck, J. R. & Kim, Y. K. (2013). Power, status, and influence in negotiation. In *Handbook of Research on Negotiation*. Edward Elgar.

Petty, R. E. & Cacioppo, J. T. (1986). The elaboration likelihood model of persuasion. In *Communication and Persuasion*. Springer, pp. 1–24.

Podsakoff, P. M. & Schriescheim, C. A. (1985). Field studies of French and Raven's bases of power: Critique, reanalysis, and suggestions for future research. *Psychological Bulletin*, 97, 387–411.

Raven, B. H. (1965). Social influence and power. In I. D. Steiner & M. Fishbein (eds), *Current Studies in Social Psychology*. Holt, Rinehart & Winston, pp. 371–81.

Raven, B. H. (1993). The bases of power: Origins and recent developments. *Journal of Social Issues*, 49(4), 227–51.

Raven, B. & French, J. R. P. (1958). Legitimate power, coercive power, and observability in social influence. *Sociometry*, 21, 83–97.

Ridgeway, C. L. (1991). The social construction of status value: Gender and other nominal characteristics. *Social Forces*, 70, 367–86.

Ridgeway, C. L., Berger, J. & Smith, L. (1985). Nonverbal cues and status: An expectation states approach. *American Journal of Sociology*, 90, 955–78.

Rucker, D. D. & Galinsky, A. D. (2017). Social power and social class: Conceptualization, consequences, and current challenges. *Current Opinion in Psychology*, 18, 26–30.

Simon, H. (1953). Notes on the observation and measurement of political power. *Journal of Politics*, 15, 500–16.

Willis, G. B., Guinote, A. & Rodríguez-Bailón, R. (2010). Illegitimacy improves goal pursuit in powerless individuals. *Journal of Experimental Social Psychology*, 46(2), 416–19.

9 | Leadership Styles: Revisiting Lewin, Lippitt and White's Leadership in Boys Club Studies

Peter D. Harms

BACKGROUND

The geography of the plains in the American heartland means that an observer can see storms coming long before they arrive. But in the 1930s the storm that was spotted by a team of researchers at the University of Iowa had a very different, and more sinister, quality than that of a funnel cloud. Across the Atlantic Ocean in Europe, powerful forces were rising to challenge the very foundations of western democracy.

In both Germany and Italy, the citizenry had willingly turned control over to fascist parties promising to restore their nations to greatness. In just a few years, these parties had transformed countries whose economies, populations and infrastructure had been devastated by the First World War and then by the Great Depression. Now with powerful armies and booming economies, they confidently asserted their national interests on the world stage. Adolf Hitler's Germany dominated the Olympic Games held in Berlin and used the event as a propaganda opportunity to showcase their successes. Italy's dictator Benito Mussolini was seen so positively that he was mentioned in Cole Porter's song 'You're the top' alongside Fred Astaire, the Mona Lisa, Mickey Mouse and Mahatma Gandhi. As the world looked on with both fear and amazement, Kurt Lewin felt compelled to act. What followed would perhaps be the most famous study in what would become a storied career studying the nature of group dynamics and the determinants of social and organisational behaviour. Lewin's contributions in these areas of research would earn him recognition as the 'founder of social psychology' and one of the most important figures in all of psychology.

A German-born Jew, Lewin grew up in a small rural community in what is now Poland experiencing widespread anti-Semitism and discrimination (Lewin, 1992). When he was a teenager, his family moved to Berlin so that he and his brothers could receive a good education. Lewin began university with the goal of becoming a doctor, but quickly discovered a distaste for dissection and anatomy. Instead, he began to explore topics in philosophy as well as the nascent discipline of psychology. He became so enamoured with the scientific endeavour that he decided to enrol in a doctoral programme with the goal of becoming a professor, even though attaining such a position was near-impossible for a Jew in Germany at that time. When the First World War broke out in 1914, Lewin was enlisted even though he was only a month away from graduating and in spite of his own distaste for militarism. Lewin attempted to continue his research during the war, even after he was wounded in 1918, and went on to publish a paper on the psychological experience of soldiers at the front. After the war, Lewin completed his training and began to study the topic of organisational behaviour. Always the outsider, Lewin tended to break with social conventions, welcoming women and students from Japan and the Soviet Union into his research group. Even in his research, Lewin defied convention, rejecting the prevailing attitudes of the time by arguing that the goal of organisational research should be more than just increasing productivity. Rather, that psychologists could and should try to facilitate enjoyment or satisfaction in one's work for all workers. 'The worker wants his work to be rich and ... not crippling and narrow. Work should not limit personal potential but develop it. Work can involve love, beauty, and the soaring joy of creating' (Kurt Lewin, as translated by Papanek, 1973). Just as Lewin's career was beginning to flourish, he was forced to flee to the US in 1933 by the rise of fascism and Hitler coming to power in Germany.

Lewin's experiences as a child, a soldier and later as an adult with anti-Semitism and the rigidly hierarchical culture pervasive in Germany at the time left him all too aware of threats facing not just his family and friends, but the world. His concern was not only the terrors that might be unleashed by the fascist regimes in Europe, but also what he saw as a more insidious threat, the rising sympathies for fascist ideologies in the US and the existential threat it presented to American democracy. Lewin himself was a fierce believer in the virtues of democracy: 'Democracy – people are fighting for it, people are dying for it. It is the most precious possession we have' (Kurt Lewin, p. viii; White & Lippitt, 1960).

At the same time, Lewin believed that many people didn't appreciate the importance of democracy. 'Maybe it is only because these young people are growing up in a comparatively democratic setting and do not have a chance for comparison, that democracy does not become real to them' (Lewin, p. ix; White & Lippitt, 1960). Lewin contrasted these individuals with refugees from fascist countries. Even though these refugees had grown up being told that democracies were decadent, soft, unable to act and chaotic, they sincerely wanted to believe that Western democracies would reflect and enable their hopes and dreams, even as they may have harboured secret fears that their dreams might be based on hollow promises. Further, for Lewin and his co-authors, the young seemed particularly prone to being attracted to ideologies like national socialism or communism that promised to put the needs of the group above those of other individuals and to bring about a more authentic form of 'rule of the people' than democracy ever could.

With this in mind, and the threat of war looming, Kurt Lewin and his colleagues Ronald Lippitt and Ralph White set out to conduct a series of experiments at the

Iowa Child Welfare Research Station designed to test the question as to which form of governance is superior: democracy or autocracy?

DETAILED DESCRIPTION

LEWIN AND COLLEAGUES' LEADERSHIP IN BOYS CLUB STUDIES

The first study to address the consequences of democracy and autocracy was conducted by Ronald Lippitt with two groups of five children. The children themselves were middle-class, Midwestern, 11-year-old boys and girls. These groups met twice a week at after-school clubs and worked to create theatre masks. Although there was a team of five observers who discretely took notes on the behaviour of the groups, the experimental team suggested that this seemed to have little impact on the children's behaviour since they attended a university-affiliated school and having outside observers in their classroom was not uncommon. Lippitt himself acted as the leader for both groups, taking on a different pattern of behaviour for each group, one autocratic and one democratic.

For the autocratic group, as leader, Lippitt determined and dictated which tasks would be done and what roles each member would take. Each step of the activity was provided only upon the completion of the previous task so as to keep the children unsure of what they would be doing next. As the autocratic leader, Lippitt also maintained a more formal, aloof social relationship with the group, standing upright and rigid while frequently pointing to direct action to tasks and individuals. Praise and criticism were given, but without providing reasons.

For the democratic group, in contrast, as leader, Lippitt prompted group discussions, solicited and provided feedback, and allowed children to decide their own division of labour. As a democratic leader, Lippitt also engaged the children in a more informal manner, frequently sitting or bending down so as to position himself as if he was a fellow member of the group, albeit one who didn't actually work on the projects. He also criticised or praised members or projects, but always provided reasoning for doing so (see Figure 9.1).

The results of this initial study showed that quarrelling and hostility were more common in the autocratic group. For example, the group members would argue over who was responsible for specific job roles on tasks, insulting one another, threatening violence and even instances of destroying the products they were creating once they had been completed. At the same time, acts of friendliness and group spirit such as offers to help one another or praising the work of other group members were more common in the democratic group. The results were interesting enough for the research team to decide that they needed to replicate this initial study and improve on it in several ways. Specifically, they aimed to increase the sample size to make it unlikely that the effects they found could be the product of non-random assignment and the individual differences and personalities of the children in each group. They also intended to shift group climates between autocracy and democracy by rotating in different leaders over time. This meant that the

Figure 9.1a.   (on the left) a screenshot taken from the original study showing an autocratic leader and Figure 9.1b. (on the right) screenshot taken from the original study showing a democratic leader, from Lewin et al. (1938). Experimental studies in social climates of groups. [Iowa City, IA], [State University of Iowa].

experiment itself would play out over a much longer period of time so that they could observe short- and long-term effects of shifts in institutional climates.

This second study, detailed in the now famous paper by Lewin et al. (1939; see also White & Lippitt, 1960), aimed to provide deeper scientific answers to key questions of group life including:

> 'What underlies such differing patterns of group behavior as rebellion against authority, persecution of a scapegoat, apathetic submissiveness to authoritarian domination, or attack upon an outgroup? How many differences in subgroup structure, group stratification, and potency of ego-centered and group-centered goals be utilized as criteria for predicting the social resultants of different group atmospheres? Is not democratic group life more pleasant, but authoritarianism more efficient?' (Lewin et al., 1939, p. 271)

Once again they examined school children from a university-affiliated school. However, this time there were four groups consisting of five 11-year-old boys, each of which met weekly. The boys were recruited from two classrooms and so the group members already had extensive familiarity with one another. The experimenters pre-screened the boys by asking them to rate the other boys in their classes for how much they liked one another and then tried to balance the groups in terms of their popularity and the degree to which the members had stated an interest in being in a group with particular others. Unpopular children were not selected so as to ensure that the groups would not have pre-existing hostilities present between group members. Although efforts were made to balance the groups in terms of temperament, subsequent ratings of personality by their teachers indicated that one group was populated by children who tended to be more quarrelsome while another group was characterised by children who were rated as being more conscientious. The goal of these selection procedures was to try to isolate the effects of social climates by controlling other potential confounding factors that might impact social behaviours such as age, sex, prior relationships and temperament.

The clubs were themed around fictional police detectives (e.g. Dick Tracy), but the activities involved carpentry, carving, model construction, painting signs and other craft projects that would keep the boys engaged. The groups met in an attic room surrounded by burlap sheets that could be decorated but also allowed individuals to move in and out of the workspace freely. Once again, there were multiple observers present, of whom the boys were aware, but who were discreetly hidden behind a screen and recorded aspects of behavioural interactions and transcribed verbal exchanges.

As noted above, one of the key features of the second study was that every six weeks, the groups rotated leaders, each of whom enacted behaviours consistent with different forms of governing. Over the course of 18 weeks, each group experienced three different leaders (see Table 9.1). Although the original plan was to only rotate between the democratic and the autocratic leaders, in the first wave of the study one of the leaders (who happened to be Ralph White) failed to properly enact the role of the democratic leader. Rather than engaging actively with the children, White instead was passive and permissive with them, simultaneously being aloof, but providing no direction. In other words, his mistake was to act in ways that equated 'democratic' with the absence of leadership. This group ended up being unruly, dysfunctional and not at all productive. The research team, seizing on the opportunity this mistake had provided, opted to embrace this pattern of leadership as a third style which they labelled 'laissez-faire' leadership and added it as an option in the subsequent sessions (see Figure 9.2). The laissez-faire leader did not participate in group decisions, answered questions only when asked, and provided no feedback on the quality or progress of the work. The inclusion of this third style of leadership meant that the experiment was no longer perfectly counterbalanced, but it did provide a powerful contrast for the other two styles.

Because a key focus of the experiment were the conditions under which aggression might arise, the experimenters also built in scenarios that would instigate or provide an opportunity for problems to emerge. One of these involved having the leader leave the room for a period of time. This happened on several occasions within each time period and was designed to assess what effects the presence of the leader had on the boys' behaviour. Another planned situation involved a stranger, typically dressed as an electrician or janitor, who entered the room while the leader was away and initiated a conversation with the boys, asking them about the nature of their club and what they thought of their leader. Later in the conversation, he would criticise their work, some members of the group or the club itself. These episodes were intended to see how the boys reacted to an external threat.

Table 9.1 Overview of the experimental design displaying experimental groups and their progression through different periods (of six week duration each).

Experimental Group	Period 1	Period 2	Period 3
Dick Tracy Club	Autocracy	Democracy	Autocracy
Sherlock Holmes Club	Autocracy	Laissez-faire	Democracy
Secret Agents Club	Democracy	Autocracy	Democracy
Charlie Chan Club	Laissez-faire	Autocracy	Democracy

Figure 9.2   Screenshot taken from the original study showing a laissez-faire leader from Lewin, K., Lippitt, R. & White, R. (1938). Experimental studies in social climates of groups. [Iowa City, IA], [State University of Iowa].

Because the nature of the leader was contrived, the differences in their behaviours were often quite stark. For example, 45 per cent of the verbal statements made by the autocratic leaders were orders (as opposed to 3 per cent of those for the democratic leaders and 4 per cent for the laissez-faire leaders). In addition, 11 per cent of the autocrat's commands were disruptive in nature. That is, they were intended to stop the boys from doing something that they wanted to do and to make them do something else. This happened in only 1 per cent of the communications by the democratic and laissez-faire leaders. For the democratic leaders, 24 per cent of the communications were guiding suggestions (versus 6 per cent for the autocrats and 14 per cent for the laissez-faire leaders) and 16 per cent were stimulating self-direction (versus 1 per cent for the autocrats and 13 per cent for the laissez-faire leaders) by informing the boys that it was their job to make a decision or take a vote.

Ultimately then, what did this study end up showing? To Lewin and colleagues, there were six key findings that they believed to be important for understanding group life and human society.

1. *Democracies can be efficient.* One of the prime motivators of the study was the concern that autocracies were simply more efficient in the way in which they reached decisions and delegated tasks. But across sessions and across tasks, democratically led groups achieved their work goals with similar degrees of efficiency as those of the autocratically led groups. However, the democratically led groups also achieved social goals (having fun with one another). It was also noted that the quality and creativity of the work was somewhat higher in these groups.

   Perhaps even more notable was the reaction of the boys to the 'leader out' situations. In the democratic groups, where the boys had selected their own tasks and roles, the groups maintained almost the same levels of productivity when the leader was absent as when they were present, falling from 50 per cent to 46 per cent of the time being spent on work tasks. However, in the autocratic groups, the fall-off in productivity when the leader was absent was profound, falling from 52 per cent to 16 per cent.

2. *Laissez-faire is not the same as democracy.* The laissez-faire groups were less organised, less productive and less satisfying to work in than the democratic groups. The work projects were typically of poor quality and there were more complaints. A closer analysis of why the laissez-faire groups were disliked by their members suggested a number of crucial factors. Laissez-faire groups provided a lower sense of social structure, one's place in it and the purpose of the organisation. There was a lack of a clear understanding of when things were expected to be done and the lower levels of productivity and work quality meant that there was little sense of accomplishment in the work.

   There was a lack of clear limits in terms of what behaviours were acceptable. When the boys misbehaved, they waited for the adult to act and the uncertainty as to if and when they might promote anxiety. This problem became acute when the boys tried to reinforce moral behaviours towards one another, but the leader failed to support them. Overall, there was a feeling among the boys that the adult in charge was not fulfilling the role obligations of a responsible adult who would be in charge of a club.

3. *Being in an autocracy can create hostility and aggression, including aggression against scapegoats.* Though their earlier study had suggested that there was a tendency for autocratic groups to be characterised by hostility (open hostility between autocratic group members was almost 30 times more likely), the second study showed a much more nuanced pattern. In the autocratic groups, there was markedly less overt aggression than in the other two groups, even democracy. That said, there was a tendency for these groups to scapegoat within their ranks. The targeting of particular individuals became so problematic that it led to some boys quitting the groups. Moreover, aggressive displays towards outgroups (such as visitors or the other clubs) were far more common in autocratic groups.

4. *Autocracy can create discontent that does not appear on the surface.* Only one of the autocratic groups ever displayed open disagreement with their leader. However, attrition from the clubs only occurred in the groups in autocratic periods (four boys quit) and only in the ones where overt rebellion did not occur. Moreover, the children were more likely to complain to one another in the autocratic group about the club and its activities than they did when they were in the democratic group condition.

   One telling behaviour occurred when the groups shifted from an autocratic culture to the democratic one. There seemed to be a 'release' behaviour where the boys would get particularly aggressive with one

Figure 9.3 Screenshot taken from the original study showing a scuffle breaking out from Lewin, K., Lippitt, R. & White, R. (1938). Experimental studies in social climates of groups. [Iowa City, IA], [State University of Iowa].

another just after the transition, although this dissipated quickly as democratic norms took hold.

Consequently, the authors concluded that autocracies may appear, on the surface, to be better behaved. But these findings, combined with other findings concerning a tendency to scapegoat their fellow members and to quit the groups, demonstrated that autocratic groups seem to be characterised by discontent and the possibility of explosive aggression when the forces suppressing their ability to express themselves was removed.

5. *There was more dependence and less individuality in autocracy.* Overall, conversations between group members and the leader tended to follow a more submissive pattern in the autocratic groups. The boys mostly limited themselves to asking for permission to take specific actions. Moreover, the topics covered were far more limited in scope and were almost entirely limited to the work tasks. There were also fewer conversations overall in the autocratic condition than in the democratic one. That the boys' individuality had been suppressed and their behaviour and conversations limited to work tasks was noted by the observers, some of whom reported that it made it more difficult to remember which boy said or did a particular thing.

6. *There was more group-mindedness and more friendliness in democracy.* In contrast to the autocratic groups, communication in the democratic groups was more open and the boys were more likely to display friendly or playful behaviours with one another. In terms of the language they used, the boys were less inclined to use the pronoun 'I' and more likely to refer to themselves as a member of the group, 'we'. Mutual praise was more common among team members and the boys were also more likely to confide in the leader.

Overall, the study by Lewin and his colleagues provided powerful evidence of the superiority of democratic groups over autocratic ones. Democratic groups could be just as effective as autocratic ones, but they were also far more cohesive and less likely to destroy themselves. The opinions of the boys themselves seemed to reflect this. When interviewed late in the experiment to compare leaders, 19 of the 20 boys expressed a preference for the democratic leader over the autocratic leader.[1] Lewin himself was so taken by the unfolding results of the study that he had parts of it filmed, a radical innovation at the time, to demonstrate the powerful differences that the study revealed.[2]

IMPACT OF THE CLASSIC STUDY

In many ways, it is hard to overstate the importance of Lewin's study. It certainly didn't prevent the rise of autocratic regimes or 'win' wars against them, but it provided much needed optimism that the war against fascism could be won, that autocratic systems were inherently unstable and inefficient, demanding the constant monitoring and oppression of their own people, and that in the long-term, democracies could and would prevail. Beyond its immediate impact, Lewin's study became foundational for theorising and research in organisational culture and climate (Schnieder & Reichers, 1983; Schnieder et al., 2013), organisational change (Schein, 1996) and the study of social influence mechanisms (Raven, 1993). But perhaps there is no discipline that has benefitted from Lewin's study as much as the field of leadership. In a review of all the various leadership models and types, Bernard Bass, a pre-eminent leadership scholar and founder of *The Leadership Quarterly*, noted 'it is possible to encapsulate many of these types into the dichotomy of autocratic versus democratic' (2008, p. 44).

One of the earliest major models of leadership behaviours suggested that there were two important dimensions: initiating structure and showing consideration, which seem to broadly reflect the autocratic and democratic styles in the original Lewin studies (Fleishman, 1953; Stogdill, 1974; see Chapter 10, this volume). Initiating structure reflected behaviours that directed and organised followers in completing tasks. Showing consideration reflected behaviours related to displaying respect and concern for followers and their welfare and acting in a supportive manner. Reviews of the research literature that developed around these two styles have demonstrated that both behaviours are associated with leader success, with both styles being similarly related to group performance, but showing consideration being much more highly associated with follower job satisfaction (Judge et al., 2004). Indeed, dozens of studies on thousands of adults have largely reached the

_____

[1]The twentieth boy was the son of a military officer whom the boy greatly admired. He indicated that he appreciated the discipline shown by the autocratic leader.

[2]The silent movie 'Experimental Studies in Group Climates' is available at https://archive. org/details/social_climates_of_groups

same core conclusions about autocratic and democratic leadership as did Lewin and his colleagues decades earlier using children in an attic in Iowa. That said, a key difference between the studies by Lewin and colleagues and those by subsequent leadership scholars is that the Lewin experiments had leaders enact only behaviours consistent with their assigned style. That is, they treated the styles as distinct types. Later leadership research either treated leadership styles as a continuum or as two distinct dimensions where excellent leaders were those who were able to enact both directive and relational aspects of leadership. Moreover, it should be noted that simply being focused on task and performance does not necessarily mean that a leader is autocratic nor that building relationships with one's followers necessarily means that a leader is democratic. Rather, an autocratic or democratic style is dependent on *how* decisions are made, not what the leader's priorities are. Nonetheless, as Bass (2008) noted, these behaviours are often linked and become conflated in the eyes of subordinates.

As scholarship in the study of leaders advanced over the subsequent decades, many new models of leadership were developed which continued to utilise very similar dimensions of leadership behaviour, but with a somewhat different aim. Instead of trying to determine *which* leadership style was superior, researchers instead focused on *when* a particular leadership style was more effective. Key among these were the contingency model of leadership (Fiedler, 1964, 1971), the path-goal theory of leadership (House, 1996), the Vroom-Yetton normative decision-model (Vroom & Yetton, 1973) and situational leadership theory (Hershey & Blanchard, 1969).

The essence of these models is that either a leader could be chosen for specific situations or a leader could shift their own behaviours to reflect either an autocratic or democratic style depending on the requirements of the situation. For example, Fiedler suggested that an autocratic style would be most effective when the nature of the group task was either very poorly defined or extremely well-defined, but that in most other conditions, a democratic style would be preferred. Vroom & Yetton (1973) refined this idea by suggesting that autocratic leadership would only be more effective when tasks had a clear structure and the group consisted of committed, supportive followers. Hershey and Blanchard (1969) added in another contingent factor, arguing that the ability of the followers also mattered in addition to their motivation. In their model, an autocratic style would be more appropriate if followers were unskilled and unmotivated, but that a shift towards more participative and hands-off leadership would be more effective when followers were skilled and motivated. All of these models have found some support for their contention that autocratic-type styles might be more effective than democratic styles under some circumstances, but not always under the particular conditions they predicted (Schriesheim et al., 1994; Thompson & Vecchio, 2009; Wofford & Leska, 1993; see also Harms et al., 2018).

More recent models of leadership have reflected this idea that leadership is not an either/or choice, but that effective leaders should be flexible in their styles and willing to enact behaviours appropriate to situations that are defined by both their followers and the task at hand. For example, the full-range model of leadership

(Bass, 2000) argues that directive behaviours typical of the autocratic style are essential for organising group efforts, but that the supportive, relational behaviours more typical of the democratic style are needed to increase motivation and build a sense of team unity (see also Judge & Piccolo, 2004). Interestingly, the full-range model is the only leadership model that fully integrated the three styles showcased in the Lewin studies. Under the full-range model, the least effective leadership style is, in fact, the laissez-faire style, which is described as leaders who avoid making decisions and are absent when needed.

One final cluster of leadership theories that really embraces the idea of democratic systems for leadership in that group functioning is best when the members themselves take on leadership roles. For example, empowering leadership (Cheong et al., 2019) refers to a style of leadership where the leader delegates power and decision-making authority to their subordinates. The shared leadership perspective (Pearce & Sims, 2002) treats leadership as an emergent property of groups where there is no formally designated leader and so the group members organise themselves. Followership research (Uhl-Bien et al., 2014; see Chapter 11, this volume) reverses the typical lens of leadership processes by examining when and how subordinates can actively influence and guide the actions of leaders. These approaches are typically framed in positive terms[3] and research has shown that groups adhering to these styles can be successful. However, reviews have also noted that there is a very thin line between empowering workers and laissez-faire leadership (Wong & Giessner, 2018) and that excessive delegation of responsibilities may ultimately lead to inefficiencies and negative outcomes.

But perhaps the most telling aspect of the legacy of the Lewin studies was how quickly and widely embraced their ideas were and for how long they went without being seriously challenged or called into question. Our modern political lexicon readily embraces the distinction between democratic and autocratic leaders and regimes. And the idea that autocratic regimes are typically corrupt, violent and unpleasant to live in is often taken for granted, particularly by those who have never lived under such regimes. It is notable that the negative reputation of autocratic regimes is so widely held across the globe that even the most rigidly autocratic regimes will formally declare themselves to be democratic (e.g. the country which many people call North Korea is formally known as the Democratic People's Republic of Korea), frequently run sham elections, and often have rubber-stamp legislative bodies in an effort to conceal their true nature. It would be a gross overstatement to attribute such behaviours to the Lewin studies specifically, but these studies were part and parcel of a paradigm shift that occurred in the aftermath of the Second World War that fundamentally changed perceptions of the moral standing of democracies and autocracies. That said, these shifts are not necessarily permanent, and scholars have noted that a number of societies are beginning,

[3]A less charitable take on these approaches is that leaders are often a hygiene factor in organisations (Hogan, 2008). That is when employees are motivated and competent, a leader is not necessary and that any actions they take will necessarily interfere with productive actions by the group.

once again, to embrace the idea that autocrats can bring with them efficiencies and structure that democracies cannot (Harms et al., 2018; Jones, 2020).

KEY REPLICATIONS AND GENERALISATIONS

As noted above, the preponderance of the literature has generally supported the core findings of the Lewin studies. Moreover, there have been two meta-analytic reviews comparing the effects of autocratic and democratic groups that have concluded that overall there is little difference in the productivity or efficiency of the two forms of leadership, but that workers tend to be more satisfied when working under democratic leaders or systems (Foels et al., 2000; Gastil, 1994).

There have, however, been some notable studies motivated by the original work by Lewin and his colleagues that are worth mentioning. One very early effort to replicate Lewin's work was done to evaluate whether the results would hold in other cultures, particularly one that was, at the time, characterised as very autocratic, namely Japan (Misumi et al., 1958). The results broadly reflected those of the Lewin studies, but with a few notable differences. Overall, the children were far less aggressive than the American children had been. Moreover, the laissez-faire groups once again showed the poorest results, but the nature of the task seemed to be critical for determining the performance levels of the other groups. For interesting tasks, the democratic groups performed at a higher level, but in the less interesting tasks, the autocratic groups outperformed. However, consistent with the studies by Lewin and his colleagues, the democratic groups maintained the highest morale and motivation (see also Misumi, 1959).

A more recent replication of this work examined the issue of attrition from autocratic groups. As noted above, multiple children left the study before it completed, but only when led autocratically. To explore this phenomenon in more detail, Van Vugt and colleagues (2004) simulated remote work groups through computers and used pre-programmed communications from the unseen leader to reflect autocratic, democratic and laissez-faire styles. The participants were led to believe that they were completing a group task that required a subset of the groups' members to contribute their own resources in order to win a bonus for the group as a whole. Consequently, the best outcomes for the individual were to contribute as little as possible, but to share the bonus. The experimenters manipulated not only the communication style of the leader, but also the extent to which the leader required the participant to contribute their resources. Afterwards, participants were asked if they wanted to remain with their group or to move to another. Their results showed not only that members of autocratic groups were more inclined to quit, but that they were more likely to do so even if they had received more favourable treatment from the leader by not being asked to contribute their own resources as often as other group members. Because of this, the authors concluded that people tended to leave autocratic groups because the processes were objectionable, not because of unfavourable results.

One other recent replication by Harms (2008) attempted to explore the role of individual differences as a moderator of how the Lewin leadership styles were enacted. Specifically, rather than instructing an experimenter or participant to behave in a particular manner, small groups of university students were instead given a construction task, but with one of either two sets of instructions, randomly assigned beforehand, that either stated that the leader would have sole authority to determine the order of work and the resulting pay allocations (autocratic condition) or that the group would vote to determine the order of the work and the pay allocations and that the leader was simply there to facilitate discussion (democratic condition). Thus in the autocratic condition the choice of whether to be a benevolent dictator (i.e. soliciting feedback, explaining their reasoning and trying to be equitable and fair in their payouts) or a selfish tyrant was left up to the participants. Moreover, although the groups were told that the individual who was appointed the leader had been chosen on the basis of a personality test they had taken beforehand, they were determined randomly as well so as to ensure that a wide range of different individuals, and not just the most dominant individuals, served as leaders. Results showed an interesting interaction between personality and leadership condition. Autocratic leaders with high power motivation tended to be less likely to discuss decisions and were less liked by their subordinates. However, democratic leaders with high power motivation tended to have more discussions and were more liked by their subordinates. Individuals with lower levels of power motivation tended to fall in between. This suggested that for individuals who are highly motivated to take on a leadership role, it is not necessarily power itself that can have corruptive influences. Rather, individuals take cues from their culture and their experiences as to how a leader should behave and then enact those styles accordingly (see also Tett & Burnett, 2003).

BEYOND LEWIN AND COLLEAGUES' LEADERSHIP STUDY: THEORETICAL DEVELOPMENTS

Lewin himself concluded that leadership and culture were not fixed but rather dynamic in nature. Just as a leader could create a culture, so too a culture could create a leader (Lewin, 1947; see also Kozlowski & Doherty, 1989). In subsequent follow-up studies, he demonstrated that individuals who were particularly dominant and aggressive in autocratic environments would fall into a much more prosocial set of behaviours when switched into democratic social groups (Lewin, 1947). Moreover, the original research team suggested that organisational norms and procedures could have long-lasting effects on the personalities of their members (White & Lippitt, 1960). Specifically, that by persistently reinforcing ideas, the examples of leaders and practices of the social group could shape the normative expectancies of individuals and that these perceptual tendencies would influence how individuals understood and responded to the situations they encountered. For example, if a worker (or child) makes a mistake and is regularly met with abusive behaviours by their leader (parent), they are likely to become more timid, more paranoid and less willing to divulge when accidents happen. Moreover, the expectations they develop based on their experiences for these situations may carry over to other individuals or settings. The idea that individuals tended to change in response to their work environments would later be explored and expanded in the personality change literature in a number of studies demonstrating that early job experiences could shape later personality in systematic ways (Harms, 2017; Jackson et al., 2012; see also Wood & Denissen, 2015). For example, Roberts and colleagues (2001) showed that when individuals are allocated leadership roles, they tend to become more dominant over time. They argued that this can be explained by role enactment leading to behaviour regularities that, in turn, become internalised as part of the self-concept. In other words, if being a leader requires individuals to engage in public speaking and to tell others what to do, individuals gain more comfort with these behaviours over time, and gradually come to see themselves as a more dominant individual because of their competency and confidence in this domain.

One other early life experience that seems to shape behaviour is the relationship that one has with one's parent. Although not discussed in the original article, Lewin and colleagues believed that there was an untold story concerning the importance of parenting (White & Lippitt, 1960). Even though the research team had done as much as they could to balance the groups in terms of demographics and popularity, there were still notable exceptions to the overall trends in the data. In particular, there were two boys who had trouble adjusting to the democratic group norms. They reported that these children had been raised by arbitrary and abusive parents and tended to perceive adults as enemies rather than potential allies. On the other hand, one of the boys who was most successful in the democratic condition was actually the one child who reported preferring the rules of the autocratic leader, the son of a military officer. This child had been raised in a strict home, but it was also a loving home, and one where responsible leadership was both taught and displayed. In fact, when briefly made 'dictator' over his group, this child acted with complete restraint, never abusing his power and acting only in the service of others. To the team, this illustrated a powerful implication not initially intended to be a subject of the study, that of the role of parents in shaping the character of the leaders of the future. Even today, most organisational researchers consider what happens in childhood to be outside their scope of interest, but there is increasing evidence that childhood experiences, and particularly those surrounding one's parents, can and do shape adult work behaviours and perceptions of leadership (Harms, 2011; Roberts et al., 2007).

CONCLUSION

It may seem strange to us now, but the studies by Lewin and colleagues (1939) with boys in an attic making crafts and pretending to fight crime, were intended to not just test, but also to showcase the enduring power of democracy over autocracy.[4] Lewin and his colleagues believed that it did just that. But the Lewin studies ended up being so much more. They provided a framework for the study of group and organisational climates and how they can shape the experiences of those within them. They showed us that group and organisational change can be difficult, even chaotic. And they provided an intellectual legacy that has shaped leadership research to this day.

Lewin and colleagues demonstrated not only the power of a comprehensive, well-designed and carefully executed experiment, but also that the most important insights are not always gained through sophisticated statistical analyses. Rather, really coming to understand the individuals in our studies and the reasons for why they behave the way they do, can be facilitated by getting to know them on a personal level, watching them as they interact across different situations, and understanding their backgrounds. Most importantly of all, the Lewin studies showed the value of being passionate about research and of seeking to address questions that really mattered.

Thousands of years ago, the Greek historian Thucydides chronicled the events of the Peloponnesian War between autocratic Sparta and democratic Athens, and in particular the stresses and strains of free societies being pushed to their limits and being forced to question their values. Thucydides labelled his work 'a possession for all of time' (*ktema es aei*), hoping that it would serve as a guide for future generations facing the same challenges. When considering the legacy and the contribution of Lewin's studies, one cannot help but recognise that it too is a possession for all of time.

IMPLICATIONS FOR PRACTITIONERS

Lewin and colleagues' work is suggestive of the superiority of democratic leadership and climates, but this message does not reflect the full nature of what Lewin and colleagues believed. For them, democracy was defined not only by rule by the people, but it was also characterised by a shared sense of responsibility for one another among its members as well as placing a priority on the welfare, dignity and freedom of the individual. It was not just about voting, but involved soliciting opinions, attempting to persuade others to adopt shared goals

---

[4]It should be acknowledged that many features of Lewin et al. (1939) would be looked upon very critically by modern researchers. For example, the sample sizes were extremely small, the samples in the main study were unrepresentative in that they consisted entirely of Caucasian males, the involvement of the experimenters as leaders could have led them to prompt behaviours to confirm their hypotheses, the procedures and tasks of the group seemed largely ad hoc, the length of the study was potentially too short to examine long-term effects of these systems, and it is not at all clear that the political and social understanding of children is representative of how mature adults would react to similar conditions. That said, for all these potential issues, the fundamental findings of these studies have been replicated many times over and have stood the test of time.

and procedures, and establishing warm, trusting relationships. In other words, it required investing in others as individuals and developing institutions and norms based on mutual respect. Importantly, their view of leadership contrasted with models of leadership based on traits. In the eyes of Lewin and colleagues, leadership was a role that could be enacted by anyone. Leaders were not limited to one particular style.

More broadly, Lewin and colleagues believed that even in a democracy, leaders should not simply acquiesce to the wishes of the majority. Rather, that in a democracy it was important for the leader to show support for, engage with and understand the needs and desires of the minority. Democracies, particularly in small groups, can often come to be dominated by a few loud, persistent individuals, and all too often by those who suppress dissent by insisting that everyone else endorses their opinions. It is the responsibility of the leader to make sure that even the quiet voices in the group are heard as well.

Far from advocating that democratic norms be utilised at all times, Lewin and his colleagues emphasised that there were times when leaders needed to set limits. However, they were clear that the responsible use of power involved (a) making sure penalties and sanctions are not excessive, (b) giving explanations for why limitations on freedoms are necessary, and (c) seeking group acceptance of goals and processes, particularly when the leader may be required to serve as an enforcer. In other words, that leaders needed to display self-control and humility, be transparent, and get buy-in from the other members of their group.

DISCUSSION QUESTIONS

1. Are you convinced that democratic systems are necessarily superior to autocratic and laissez-faire systems? Under what circumstances can you think of may other systems be more effective?

2. Lewin's study centred mostly on the actions of boys in an experimental setting. To what degree are these results generalisable to other settings? Do you believe that the results would have been different if the groups had consisted of girls or mixed-gender groups? How?

3. One of the features of the Lewin studies was the transition between autocracy, democracy and laissez-faire systems. The results suggested that such transitions tended to be chaotic and frequently violent. Consider real-world transitions that have occurred when nations have shifted from autocracy to democracy or some democracy to autocracy. To what extent were these transitions characterised by violence or chaos?

4. Although democracies seem to be generally preferred to autocracies by the people who live in them, sometimes groups or nations voluntarily give up their freedoms. Under what conditions might a people decide that having less freedom may be preferable or legitimate?

FURTHER READINGS

White, R. & Lippitt, R. (1960). *Autocracy and Democracy: An Experimental Inquiry.* Harper Brothers.

White and Lippitt wrote this book as an extended treatment of their original paper with Lewin. In it, they add further details about the study, the participants and what they felt were the major implications of their work.

Harms, P. D., Wood, D., Landay, K., Lester, P. & Vogelgesang-Lester, G. (2018). Autocratic leaders and authoritarian followers revisited: A review and agenda for the future. *Leadership Quarterly*, 29, 105–22.

Harms and colleagues review not only the literature on autocratic leadership but also authoritarianism. The paper covers both theory and measurement and provides an extensive review of the conditions under which autocratic leadership can be successful and situations where populations may come to see autocratic leaders as preferable.

Hanson, V. D. (2001). *Carnage and Culture.* Anchor Books.

Hanson's book echoes the Lewin, Lippitt and White studies by asserting that cultural values and norms are not only essential for understanding geo-politics and warfare, but that they can play a determining role in the success or failure of nations on both on and off the battlefield.

Van Vugt, M., Hogan, R. & Kaiser, R. (2008). Leadership, followership, and evolution: Some lessons from the past. *American Psychologist*, 63, 182–96.

Van Vugt and colleagues discuss theorising concerning why we have leaders, what makes leaders effective and the frequent disconnect between the leaders we want and the leaders we get.

Jones, G. (2020). *10% Less Democracy: Why You Should Trust Elites More and the Masses a Little Less*. Stanford University Press.

Based on evidence from economics, political science, finance and his own personal experience, Jones makes the argument for refining western democracies to make them less accountable to the voting public and instead more accountable to trusted well-educated technocrats to act in their best interests.

REFERENCES

Bass, B. (2000). The future of leadership in learning organizations. *Journal of Leadership Studies*, 7, 18–40. https://doi.org/10.1177/107179190000700302

Bass, B. (2008). *The Bass Handbook of Leadership: Theory, Research, and Managerial Implications*, 4th edn. Free Press.

Cheong, M., Yammarino, F., Dionne, S., Spain, S. & Tsai, C.-Y. (2019). A review of the effectiveness of empowering leadership. *Leadership Quarterly*, 30, 34–58. https://doi.org/10.1016/j.leaqua.2018.08.005

Fielder, F. E. (1964). A contingency model of leadership effectiveness. In L. Berkowitz (ed.), *Advances in Experimental and Social Psychology*, Vol. 1. Academic Press, pp. 149–90.

Fiedler, F. E. (1971). Evaluation and extension of the contingency model of leadership effectiveness: A review of empirical findings. *Psychological Bulletin*, 76, 128–48. https://doi.org/10.1037/h0031454

Fleishman, E. A. (1953). The description of supervisory behavior. *Journal of Applied Psychology*, 37, 1–6. https://doi.org/10.1037/h0056314

Foels, R., Driskell, J., Mullen, B. & Salas, E. (2000). The effects of democratic leadership on group member satisfaction: An integration. *Small Group Research*, 31, 676–701. https://doi.org/10.1177/104649640003100603

Gastil, J. (1994). A meta-analytic review of the productivity and satisfaction of democratic and autocratic leadership. *Small Group Research*, 25, 384–410. https://doi.org/10.1177/1046496494253003

Haney, C., Banks, C. & Zimbardo, P. (1973). Interpersonal dynamics in a simulated prison. *International Journal of Criminology and Penology*, 1, 69–97.

Harms, P. D. (2008). *One or Many? An Experimental Study of Power and Personality in Autocratic and Democratic Groups*. University of Illinois.

Harms, P. D. (2011). Adult attachment styles in the workplace. *Human Resource Management Review*, 21, 285–96. https://doi.org/10.1016/j.hrmr.2010.10.006

Harms, P. D. (2017). The place makes the people. *Talent Quarterly*, 16, 14–16.

Harms, P. D., Wood, D., Landay, K., Lester, P. & Vogelgesang-Lester, G. (2018). Autocratic leaders and authoritarian followers revisited: A review and agenda for the future. *Leadership Quarterly*, 29, 105–22. https://doi.org/10.1016/j.leaqua.2017.12.007

Hershey, P. & Blanchard, K. (1969). Life cycle theory of leadership. *Training and Development Journal*, 23, 26–34.

Hogan, R. (2008). *Leadership Is a Hygiene Factor*. Paper presented at the 23rd annual conference of the Society for Industrial-Organizational Psychology.

House, R. J. (1996). Path-goal theory of leadership: Lessons, legacy, and reformulated theory. *Leadership Quarterly*, 7, 323–52. https://doi.org/10.1016/S1048-9843(96)90024-7

Jackson, J., Thoemmes, F., Jonkmann, K., Ludtke, O. & Trautwein, U. (2012). Military training and personality trait development: Does the military make the man, or does the man make the military? *Psychological Science*, 23, 270–77. https://doi.org/10.1177/0956797611423545

Jones, G. (2020). *10% Less Democracy: Why You Should Trust Elites More and the Masses a Little Less*. Stanford University Press.

Judge, T. & Piccolo, R. (2004). Transformational and transactional leadership: A meta-analytic test of their relative validity. *Journal of Applied Psychology*, 89, 755–68. https://doi.org/10.1037/0021-9010.89.5.755

Judge, T., Piccolo, R. & Ilies, R. (2004). The forgotten ones? The validity of consideration and initiating structure in leadership research. *Journal of Applied Psychology*, 89, 36–51. https://doi.org/10.1037/0021-9010.89.1.36

Kozlowski, S. & Doherty, M. (1989). Integration of climate and leadership: Examination of a neglected issue. *Journal of Applied Psychology*, 74, 546–53. https://doi.org/10.1037/0021-9010.74.4.546

Lewin, K. (1947). Frontiers in group dynamics. *Human Relations*, 1, 5–41.

Lewin, K., Lippitt, R. & White, R. (1939). Patterns of aggressive behavior in experimentally created 'social climates'. *Journal of Social Psychology*, 10, 271–99. https://doi.org/10.1080/00224545.1939.9713366

Lewin, M. (1992). The impact of Kurt Lewin's life on the place of social issues in his work. *Journal of Social Issues*, 48, 15–29. https://doi.org/10.1111/j.1540-4560.1992.tb00880.x

Misumi, J. (1959). Experimental studies on 'group dynamics' in Japan. *Psychologia*, 4, 229–35.

Misumi, J., Nakano, S. & Ueno, Y. (1958). A study of group dynamics concerning class atmosphere (20): A cross-cultural study concerning effects of autocratic and laissez-faire leadership types. *Research Bulletin of Kyushu University Education Faculty*, 5, 41–57.

Papanek, M. L. (1973). Kurt Lewin and his contributions to modern management theory. *Academy of Management Proceedings, August*, 317–22. https://doi.org/10.5465/ambpp.1973.4981410

Pearce, C. & Sims, H. (2002). Vertical versus shared leadership as predictors of the effectiveness of change management teams: An examination of aversive, directive, transactional, transformational, and empowering leader behaviors. *Group Dynamics: Theory, Research, and Practice*, 6, 172–97. https://doi.org/10.1037/1089-2699.6.2.172

Raven, B. (1993). The bases of power: Origins and recent developments. *Journal of Social Issues*, 49, 227–51. https://doi.org/10.1111/j.1540-4560.1993.tb01191.x

Roberts, B. W., Caspi, A. & Moffitt, T. E. (2001). The kids are alright: Growth and stability in personality development from adolescence to adulthood. *Journal of Personality and Social Psychology*, 81, 670–83. https://doi.org/10.1037/0022-3514.81.4.670

Roberts, B. W., Harms, P. D., Caspi, A. & Moffitt, T. (2007). Predicting the counterproductive employee? Evidence from a 23-year longitudinal study. *Journal of Applied Psychology*, 92, 1427–36. https://doi.org/10.1037/0021-9010.92.5.1427

Schein, E. (1996). Culture: The missing concept in organization studies. *Administrative Science Quarterly*, 41, 229–40. https://doi.org/10.2307/2393715

Schnieder, B. & Reichers, A. (1983). On the etiology of climates. *Personnel Psychology*, 36, 19–39. https://doi.org/10.1111/j.1744-6570.1983.tb00500.x

Schnieder, B., Ehrhart, M. & Macey, W. (2013). Organizational climate and culture. *Annual Review of Psychology*, 64, 361–88. https://doi.org/10.1146/annurev-psych-113011-143809

Schriesheim, C. A., Tepper, B. J. & Tatrault, L.A. (1994). Least preferred co-worker score, situational control, and leadership effectiveness: A meta-analysis of contingency model performance predictions. *Journal of Applied Psychology*, 79, 561–73. https://doi.org/10.1037/0021-9010.79.4.561

Stogdill, R. M. (1974). *Handbook of Leadership: A Survey of Theory and Practice*. New York: Free Press.

Tett, R. & Burnett, D. (2003). A personality trait-based interactionist model of job performance. *Journal of Applied Psychology*, 88, 500–17. https://doi.org/10.1037/0021-9010.88.3.500

Thompson, G. & Vecchio, R. (2009). Situational leadership theory: A test of three versions. *Leadership Quarterly*, 20, 837–48. https://doi.org/10.1016/j.leaqua.2009.06.014

Uhl-Bien, M., Riggio, R., Lowe, K. & Carsten, M. (2014). Followership theory: A review and research agenda. *Leadership Quarterly*, 25, 83–104. https://doi.org/10.1016/j.leaqua.2013.11.007

Van Vugt, M., Jepson, S., Hart, C. & De Cremer, D. (2004). Autocratic leadership in social dilemmas: A threat to group stability. *Journal of Experimental Social Psychology*, 40, 1–13. https://doi.org/10.1016/S0022-1031(03)00061-1

Vroom, V. H. & Yetton, P. W. (1973). *Leadership and Decision-making.* University of Pittsburgh Press.

White, R. & Lippitt, R. (1960). *Autocracy and Democracy: An Experimental Inquiry.* Harper Brothers.

Wofford, J. C. & Leska, L. Z. (1993). Path-goal theories of leadership: A meta-analysis. *Journal of Management*, 19, 857–76. https://doi.org/10.1016/0149-2063(93)90031-H

Wong, S. & Giessner, S. R. (2018). The thin line between empowering and laissez-faire leadership: An expectancy-match perspective. *Journal of Management*, 44, 757–83. https://doi.org/10.1177/0149206315574597

Wood, D. & Denissen, J. J. (2015). A functional perspective on personality trait development. In K. Reynolds & N. R. Bramscombe (eds), *Psychology of Change: Life Contexts, Experiences, and Identities*, pp. 97–115.

10 | Leadership Behaviour: Revisiting the Ohio State Studies

Niels Van Quaquebeke[*] &
Catharina Vogt[*]

BACKGROUND

For centuries, people generally believed that leadership was a question of inheritance, status and, to some extent, personality. This view started to change in the early 1940s, when researchers at Ohio State University began using questionnaires to investigate leadership from a behavioural point of view. Starting at the end of the Second World War, the studies were part of an interdisciplinary research programme 'Leadership in a Democracy', which enabled large-scale research aimed at classifying relevant leadership aspects (Schriesheim & Bird, 1979). The motivation to structurally research leadership was fuelled by the fear of atom bombs born out of the uranium isotope U238 (Hemphill, 1949, p. 3):

> When U238 became known to the modern world, both scientists and laymen, after the initial shock, began to seek some security in a science of 'human relations' – a science that might save us all from the unleashed forces of physical nature. A large segment of this interest in human relations has been focussed on leadership. Both laymen and scientists agree that if we can understand the selection and training of leaders, we can begin to take adaptive steps toward controlling our own social fate. But when we compare the concepts of 'U238' or 'nucelar fission' with the concept 'leadership', the immediately apparent differences in the precision and power of the terms gives us little hope that social science can compete successfully, if it comes to that, with the physical sciences.

To respond to this lack of research, the university president appointed a multidisciplinary committee of deans, department heads, bureau directors and interested professors to engage in the Personnel Research Board in 1945. The research team from the Ohio State University Personnel Research Board was led by the psychologists Hemphill, Shartle and Stogdill. John K. Hemphill studied

---

* Equal authorship

group dimensions of leadership behaviour and later became Director of the Developmental Research Division at the Educational Testing Service at Princeton, New Jersey. Caroll L. Shartle was Professor of Psychology and executive secretary of the Board and had previously worked as a consultant on occupational deferments for President Roosevelt in the Second World War (Shartle, n.d.). The most prominent board member, Ralph M. Stogdill, had served as a lieutenant commander in the Second World War, working in selection in the US Maritime Service. At his start at the Personnel Research Board in 1946, he was Associate Director of the Board, later became Professor of Management Science and Psychology, and led the Board also after retirement until his death. Stogdill became a leader in leadership research with the publication of his first and very influential article 'Personal Factors Associated with Leadership: A Survey of the Literature' in 1948 (Hakel, 1980). Among many others, further prominent researchers in the team of the Personnel Research Board were economist Alvin E. Coons (former member of Iowa State College, a major in the Second World War responsible for briefing crews who flew missions; Ames History Museum, n.d.), psychologist Donald T. Campbell (known for his research on stereotypes and listed among the 100 most eminent psychologists of the twentieth century; Haggbloom et al., 2002) and sociologist Melvin Seeman (former teacher who after his PhD became an Associate Professor at Ohio State University known for his research on alienation; Kiecolt, 1997).

The board decided to study leadership in business, governmental and educational organisations. Shartle (1979, p. 131) describes the initial work of the Personnel Research Board as follows:

> Our initial planning group was from psychology, sociology, and economics with various sessions over the first two-year period ... Finally, a model was developed that we called a paradigm. Leader behavior variables were the core, with lines showing relationships to other variables such as group behavior and structure, organizational characteristics, and environmental situations (economic, social, and political). It was really an approach to the study of leadership. There was no significant theory. I soon learned that theory was an individual affair that could be expressed best in individual studies within the framework. If we had required ourselves to agree on a theory, we would never have had a program. The Ohio State leadership studies were often criticized for a lack of theory.

After this planning phase, Morris and Seeman published the paradigm of the Ohio State leadership studies in the *American Journal of Sociology* in 1950 (see Figure 10.1), which was revised seven years later in a monograph by Stogdill & Coons (1957). Shartle began to personally research the paradigm in an insurance company using job and organisational analysis, and later collected further data in other business, governmental and educational organisations. This first mass of objective data was then studied by the Personnel Research Board (Shartle, 1979), which will be described below. The Personnel Research Board kept working until 1968, when the university reorganised its research programme of behavioural science (Shartle, 1979).

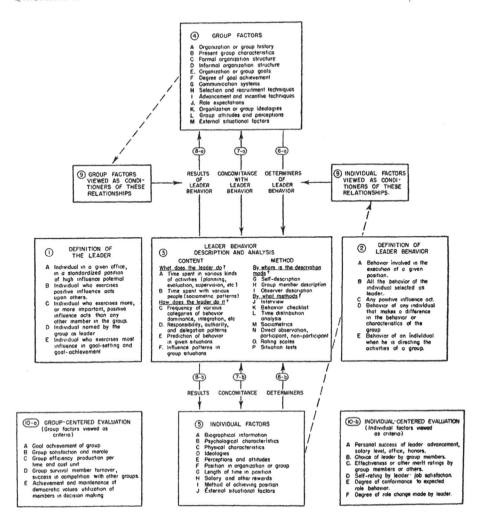

Figure 10.1 Paradigm of the Ohio State studies on leadership

(Morris & Seeman, 1950, p. 151).

DETAILED DESCRIPTION:

STOGDILL AND COONS' OHIO STATE LEADERSHIP STUDIES

The Ohio State leadership studies refer to the body of leadership studies conducted by the Personnel Research Board. In the Board's central monograph edited by Ralph M. Stogdill and Alvin E. Coons (1957), (former) board members such as John K. Hemphill, Andrew W. Halpin, Caroll L. Shartle and Ben J. Winer (former graduate student at the Personnel Research Board) described the research process that led to the core achievement of the Ohio State leadership studies:

namely, describing leadership behaviour by developing and measuring a structure through the LBDQ.

THE LEADER BEHAVIOR DESCRIPTION QUESTIONNAIRE (LBDQ)

The Personnel Research Board defined leadership as individual behaviour observable to subordinates and as 'directing the activities of the group towards a shared goal' (Hemphill & Coons, 1957, p. 7). As a first step in classifying this leadership behaviour, the researchers discussed nine dimensions: Integration, Communication, Production Emphasis, Representation, Fraternisation, Organisation, Evaluation, Initiation and Domination. With these dimensions serving as a framework, the researchers specified the respective items for their initial questionnaire (Hemphill & Coons, 1957). All staff members of the Personnel Research Board suggested items for the questionnaire, and further items were added to the pool based on responses from two classes of university students. Altogether, the researchers collected 1,790 descriptions of leadership behaviours in professional settings; from these, they derived 150 items that best represented these dimensions (Hemphill & Coons, 1957). Afterward, they presented the questionnaire to several thousand subordinates of administrative and military organisations, asking respondents to rate the extent to which the respondents' leader showed these behaviours. The data were analysed with regard to item consistency, differences between self- and subordinate ratings and factoral structure. Three factors were identified: maintenance of membership character, objective attainment behaviour and group interaction facilitation behaviour. Halpin & Winer then took this pool of 130 items (deleting 20 unsuitable ones) to administer it in the military sector. Notably, the results were based on a study of 300 crew members representing 52 air crews flying B-50 bombers[1] (Halpin & Winer, 1957). Factor analysis produced four factors: consideration, initiating structure, production emphasis and sensitivity (social awareness). As consideration and initiating structure accounted for most of the common-factor variance, new items were formulated to directly measure both constructs and then empirically examined.

> *Consideration* was defined as 'behavior indicative of friendship, mutual trust, respect, and warmth in relationships between the leader and members of the group' (Halpin, 1957, p. 1). Consideration is a class of leadership behaviour that encompasses personal orientation toward and interest in the well-being of subordinates. In this regard, leaders focus on building working relationships characterised by consideration for their subordinates' feelings. A considerate leader helps subordinates with personal problems, is friendly and accessible, treats all subordinates equally and expresses appreciation and support.

---

[1] In those days, B-50 bombers were the most innovative strategic bombers as they could be refuelled in flight, giving them the range to reach the Soviet Union. Although the researchers do not address this, this sample reflects how during and after the Second World War, the issue of effective leadership was given high priority in the military.

Initiating structure was defined as 'leader's behavior in delineating the relationship between himself and the members of his group, and in endeavoring to establish well-defined patterns of organization, channels of communication, and ways of getting the job done' (Halpin, 1957, p. 1). Initiating structure encompasses leadership behaviours oriented around tasks and performance for the purpose of ensuring that a team achieves its goals. The focus here is on setting and monitoring clear performance standards and structuring work processes. A structuring leader organises work, working relationships and goals by assigning certain tasks to group members, as well as emphasising and monitoring people's adherence to performance standards and deadlines.

Based on the results, the Personnel Research Board reduced the scale to 30 items, which became known as the Leader Behavior Description Questionnaire (LBDQ). The LBDQ captured the two independent dimensions of consideration and initiating structure (Hemphill & Coons, 1957) through 15 items. More broadly, the questionnaire (Halpin, 1957) represents subordinates' views by asking them whether and how often their leaders behave in a certain way. Respondents can choose from one of five categories: always, often, occasionally, seldom or never. Afterward, their individual responses are collected and summarised into an average per item (if one leader is rated by multiple subordinates). The item scores are then summed to form a general score for each of the two dimensions of leader behaviour (Halpin, 1957). Some comparative values (means and quartiles) were provided by the original authors for aircraft commanders and for education administrators for public schools. Altogether, this set of studies ultimately identified consideration and initiating structure as effective leadership, which essentially marked the turning point in the scholarly discussion from exploring leader traits to exploring leader behaviour.

Across several studies, the research team found that groups of subordinates tended to describe the same leader in a similar way (i.e. a small amount of within-group variance) and different leaders in different ways (i.e. a higher amount of between-group variance) (Halpin, 1957). Correlations between consideration and initiating structure varied between 0.34 and 0.50 (Halpin, 1957), which means that both dimensions are distinct but still represent the same, general quality (i.e. effective leadership). Thus one leader's score on consideration is somewhat independent of the same person's score on initiating structure. Split-half reliabilities[2] for the original LBDQ measure were 0.83 for initiating structure and 0.92 for consideration (Halpin, 1957). All these measures indicate that the Personnel Research Board constructed a useful research instrument. Moreover, both dimensions correlated differently with measures of leadership effectiveness (i.e. technical competence, effectiveness of working with other crew members, conformity to standard operating procedures, performance under stress, attitude and motivation to be effective, overall effectiveness as a combat crew member and crew's satisfaction index):

---

[2]Correlation of one-half of the items of the LBDQ with the other half to measure consistency of the test scores.

consideration correlated positively with crew satisfaction, initiating structure correlated positively (albeit non-significantly) with all effectiveness measures. Those results suggest that leader consideration mostly addresses subordinates' morale, whereas initiating structure tends to address subordinate performance. However, these results do not necessarily reflect those of other populations, which we will discuss in the section below, 'Key replications and generalisations'.

Items of the Consideration Scale (Halpin, 1957):
He[3] does personal favors for group members.

He does little things to make it pleasant to be a member of the group.

He is easy to understand.

He finds time to listen to group members.

He keeps to himself.*

He looks out for the personal welfare of individual group members.

He refuses to explain his actions.*

He acts without consulting the group.*

He backs up the members in their actions.

He treats all group members as his equals.

He is willing to make changes.

He is friendly and approachable.

He makes group members feel at ease when talking with them.

He puts suggestions made by the group into operation.

He gets group approval on important matters before going ahead.

Items of the Initiating Structure Scale (Halpin, 1957):
He makes his attitudes clear to the group.

He tries out his new ideas with the group.

He rules with an iron hand.

He criticizes poor work.

He speaks in a manner not to be questioned.

---

[3]It is striking that the typical leader in these days seemed to have no other gender than being male. Already in the construction phase of the very first items, Hemphill and Coons (1957, p. 9) described that the study participants were instructed to start the formulation of items with 'he'. Besides all the innovative spirit that must have dominated the Personnel Research Board and despite all the women who were part of the Board (Shartle, 1979), the researchers were biased by a zeitgeist rooted in the 'think manager – think male' stereotype. Of course, female leadership existed at that time, although it was not as widespread as male leadership.

He assigns group members to particular tasks.

He schedules the work to be done.

He maintains definite standards of performance.

He emphasizes the meeting of deadlines

He encourages the use of uniform procedures.

He makes sure that his part in the organization is understood by all group members.

He asks that group members follow standard rules and regulations.

He lets group members know what is expected of them.

He sees to it that group members are working up to capacity.

He sees to it that the work of group members is coordinated.

_____

(* indicates reverse-scored items)

FURTHER MEASURES OF LBDQ AND VALIDITY ISSUES

While the LBDQ is versatile enough to be applied to various industries (see Stogdill, 1963, for an overview), the Ohio State research team apparently felt a need to find additional ways of examining leadership behaviours to underline the validity of their measures (Judge et al., 2004). Shartle, for example, complained (1979, p. 132):

'There were also many criterion studies in which indices ranged from a study of bombing accuracy of air force crews to departmental ratings at Wayne State University. The criterion always involved a troublesome time dimension. New situational variables might make a leader or an organization that was rated at the top in a study at the bottom six months later when we returned on a follow-up visit.'

Shartle's comment implies a weak re-test reliability. In fact, re-test reliability information for the LBDQ has – as far as we know – never been examined (Schriesheim & Kerr, 1974). For these and further reasons, various authors developed other measures to examine consideration and initiating structure – the most widely used being the LBDQ Form XII, the SBDQ and the LOQ (Judge et al., 2004). The LBDQ-XII (Stogdill, 1963) arose from the argument that 'it has not seemed reasonable to believe that two factors are sufficient to account for all the observable variance in leader behavior' (Stogdill, 1963, p. 2). Indeed, leaders often carry out different social roles in different groups. In accordance with a new theory on leadership (Stogdill, 1959), which considers multiple personality constructs as input variables to leadership behaviour and group constructs as output variables, the LBDQ-XII proposes 12 dimensions of leader behaviour that encompass consideration and initiating structure.

Parallel to the research on the LBDQ, a former graduate student of the Personnel Research Board, Edwin A. Fleishman (1953a), noted that the measurement of leadership effectiveness varied with situational variables. Thus, he aimed to design a measure that is applicable to various situations – effectively criticising the LBDQ for a lack of independence between the consideration and initiation subscale. To suggest an alternative, he set up the 48-item Supervisory Behavior Description Questionnaire (SBDQ) (Fleishman, 1989b). The SBDQ indeed showed little intercorrelation between consideration and initiating structure (Fleishman, 1953a). However, this tool has been criticised for containing 'extraneous items measuring punitive, arbitrary, and production-oriented leader behaviors' (Schriesheim & Stogdill, 1975, p. 190). Items like 'He "rides" the foreman who made a mistake' and 'He "needles" the foreman under him for greater effort' might stem from the production emphasis scale of the first draft version of the SBDQ (Fleishman, 1953a). Still, it is hard to imagine that such items should be associated with higher leadership effectiveness, especially in the long term.

At about the same time, Fleishman (1953b) noted the urgency to develop 'dependable research instruments which can be utilized to describe adequately the various complex socio-psychological aspects of a wide variety of leader-group situations' (p. 153). Motivated by this need, he developed the 40-item Leader Opinion Questionnaire (LOQ) (Fleishman, 1989a) to measure leadership attitudes in terms of how often leaders think they should behave considerately or initiate structure when leading subordinates. Example items are 'How often schould I help people in the work group with their personal problems?' (consideration) and 'How often should I assign people in the work group to particular tasks?' (initiating structure).

Granted, the theorising and findings of the Ohio studies also received some criticism. House and Aditya (1997), for example, argued that the various measures for initiating structure and consideration correlate differently with outcomes, which naturally runs counter to their composers' reasoning: if they were designed to measure the same, they should also show similar patterns when correlated with measures of leadership success. Otherwise, their validity (the question of whether they actually measure the construct they intend to measure) would be suspect. Years later, Judge and collegues (2004) addressed this criticism in their comprehensive meta-analysis by concluding that 'whereas the validities of Consideration and Initiating Structure (in correlating with the criteria) do not vary strongly across measures (as a rule), the intercorrelation between the two behaviors does vary considerably across measures' (p. 44). This finding might be partly due to who is doing the rating. People who encounter the leader every day (i.e. subordinates) are likely able to present a much finer-grained picture than those who only encounter the leader in limited, meaningful encounters (i.e. superiors). After all, as raters get closer to and have interactions with the rated object, they become less susceptible to generalisation biases such as the halo effect (Nisbett & Wilson, 1977).

IMPACT OF THE OHIO STATE STUDIES

PROCESS, METHODOLOGICAL AND PRACTICAL CONTRIBUTIONS OF THE OHIO STUDIES

The Ohio State studies comprise one of the most important and comprehensive research programs in the fields of management and organizational behavior', praised Schriesheim and Bird in 1979 (p. 135). Indeed, the Ohio State University research on leadership, and especially the distinction between consideration and initiating structure, dominated research and views on leadership until the 1970s (Judge et al., 2004).

Focusing on the research's *theoretical contributions*, the Ohio State studies changed the concept of leadership from a trait to a behavioural approach – and thus from the rather static realm of leader personality into dynamic leader activities. With this shift of paradigm all at once, leadership (in terms of initiating structure and showing consideration) became changeable and thus trainable. At the same time, this research led to the development of certain situational theories of leadership (e.g. Morris & Seeman, 1950) where the effectiveness of certain behaviours was considered against the specific situations in which they were enacted.

Moreover, the studies' *methodological contributions* were remarkable at the time: concepts were carefully defined and thus could be operationalised into better key variables and respective measures. Indeed, the authors laid the foundation for construct validation in leadership research (i.e. the notion that related constructs should yield similar results, such as similar relationships with a key variable, as the original construct). Moreover, the published papers are mostly based on multi-sample studies, examining a subject within more than one group of respondents, often across industries, which in turn tends to generate reliable research results that are generalisable to various fields. Granted, the majority of these research publications are detailed technical research reports, which were probably mainly addressed to the research contractors from the military and industry and are thus not easily accessible.

Regarding the Ohio studies' *practical contributions*, the development and revisions of measurements (LBDQ, LBDQ-XII, SBDQ, LOQ) equipped the field of leadership research with standardised measures of assessing leadership behaviour (Schriesheim & Bird, 1979). Furthermore, as interdisciplinary teamwork was extraordinary at that time, thanks to the Personnel Research Board's innovative collaboration the researchers greatly benefitted from other disciplines' inputs and views (Schriesheim & Bird, 1979).

RELATED RESEARCH BY THE MICHIGAN GROUP AND THE HARVARD GROUP

Concurrently with the Ohio researchers' work, two other research groups – the University of Michigan's Survey Research Center[4] and the Laboratory of Social Relations at Harvard University – began a similar undertaking in 1946.

The Michigan research group was led by Rensis Likert, after whom the Likert scale is named (the questionnaire method where an item is rated by approving one of five or seven answer categories) and Albert Angus Campbell (a pioneer in public opinion research and voting behaviour). The Michigan group defined

---

[4]Find a historical outline here: https://isr.umich.edu/about/history/timeline/

successful leadership outcomes in terms of high performance and high job satisfaction among subordinates (Kahn & Katz, 1952; Katz et al., 1951). During a series of studies, they categorised successful leadership behaviour into four dimensions: support, interaction facilitation, work facilitation and goal emphasis (Bowers & Seashore, 1966). These four categories could also be mapped onto two broader dimensions: first, *subordinate-oriented leadership*, which emphasises leadership behaviour that considers subordinates' human needs; and second, *production-oriented leadership*, which allocates resources to technically support subordinates in doing their jobs. Because both dimensions appear to be rather similar to those proposed by the Ohio group, these terms are often used synonymously in leadership research (Robbins & Judge, 2013). Altogether, research indicates that both styles identified by the Michigan group lead to higher rates of subordinate performance. Job satisfaction decreased, however, when the leader's production orientation took the form of close supervision (Day & Hamblin, 1964; Kahn & Katz, 1952).

In 1946, Harvard University set up an interdisciplinary Department of Social Relations and announced plans to establish a Laboratory of Social Relations to conduct research (Allport & Boring, 1946). The laboratory, led by social psychologist Robert F. Bales, was a 'well-lighted room for the group under study and an adjoining room for observers' (Bales, 1955, p. 31). It also included one-way mirrors and a complete sound recording that was perfectly designed to study small group interactions. As part of these studies, the researchers identified group interactions that they labelled person- and task-centred leadership.

The Harvard group's work followed the same premises as the Michigan studies – that a leader could be either person-centred (socio-emotional) or task-centred (instrumental). Because these were treated as two opposite ends of one dimension, the Harvard studies implied that leaders cannot adopt both styles at the same time. In this vein, task-centred leaders address the team as a whole and make decisions to enhance group performance while person-centred leaders spend more time addressing individual subordinates to motivate them and maintain group harmony (Slater, 1955). Notably, this view was inspired by the traditional family metaphor of directive fathers and socio-emotionally caring mothers (Parsons & Bales, 1956). Consequently, guaranteeing effective leadership among a group of subordinates would require two (or in the Michigan model four) different formal and informal leaders in the team. However, researchers have since found that dual leadership (i.e. high/high) is possible and that leaders do not universally abide by exclusive leadership roles (e.g. Rees & Segal, 1984). This finding supports the idea underlying the Ohio studies: namely, that groups require both types of leadership and these can be provided by a single person – as rare as that may be. That said, the leadership approach proposed by the Michigan group did not clearly state whether a certain leadership style was rather a cause or an effect. On one hand, it did seem like a leadership style caused high performance or high job satisfaction among subordinates. On the other hand, a well-performing team may also give rise to a more subordinate-centred leadership style – an idea that later resurfaced in leader-member exchange theory (Graen & Uhl-Bien, 1995).

Perhaps because of these limitations, later scholars based much more research on the Ohio studies (Judge et al., 2004).

Surprisingly, none of the authors in the Ohio, Michigan and Harvard studies quoted each other in their publications – suggesting that they were unaware of their peers' parallel efforts since the Internet, email and scientific search engines did not exist at the time. At the time, it was uncommon to even travel to big conferences to learn about new developments in a given research area.

KEY REPLICATIONS AND GENERALISATIONS

Fifty years after the initial Ohio State studies, Timothy A. Judge, Ronald F. Piccolo & Remus Ilies (2004) conducted a comprehensive meta-analysis comprising 200 studies with a total of 300 samples. Their paper, 'The Forgotten Ones? The Validity of Consideration and Initiating Structure in Leadership Research', sought to exhaustively review the literature on the Ohio State study dimensions (consideration and initiating structure) with regard to their validity and measurement. They concluded that both concepts are still meaningful and useful in leadership research. In fact, the results of their analysis showed that leadership behaviour is clearly, albeit moderately, related to measures of leadership success: both dimensions were equally correlated with the performance of the group or organisation ($r = .23$). However, initiating structure was less strongly associated with subordinates' motivation ($r = .27$), subordinates' job satisfaction ($r = .19$) and the effectiveness of the leader ($r = .28$) compared to consideration (correspondingly $r = .68$; $r = .40$; $r = .39$). Initiating structure also demonstrated a greater variety of results, which suggests that that dimension is affected by a wider array of situational factors than consideration. By validating the basic assumptions and findings of the Ohio Group, the meta-analysis by Judge et al. (2004) provides an important contribution to leadership research and practice: namely, that relationship orientation (by whatever route) is especially crucial to leader success (Gottfredson & Aguinis, 2017).

BEYOND THE OHIO STATE STUDIES: THEORETICAL DEVELOPMENTS

THE MANAGERIAL GRID

Drawing from the findings of the Ohio State and Michigan studies, University of Texas researchers Robert R. Blake and Jane S. Mouton (1964) viewed the distinction of initiating structure ('concern for production') and consideration ('concern for people') in terms of a matrix called the 'managerial grid', which they developed while working as organisational consultants at Standard Oil (Cai et al., 2019). Accordingly, they defined five leadership styles depending on how a leader scored on both dimensions (see Figure 10.2).

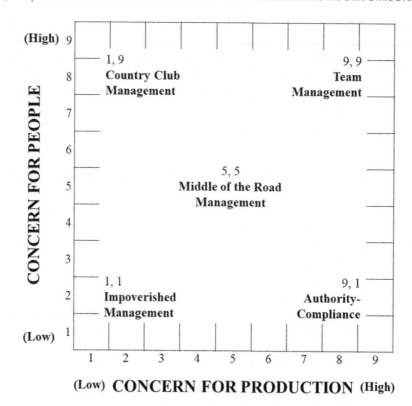

Figure 10.2 *Blake and Mouton's (1964) Managerial Grid.*

Scores could vary between 1 and 9. 'Impoverished management' is the leadership style of leaders scoring 1,1, which is the minimum concern for production and people. 'Task management' is the leadership style of leaders scoring 9,1, which is the maximum concern for production and minimum concern for people. 'Country club management' is the leadership style of leaders scoring 1,9, which is the minimum concern for production and maximum concern for people. 'Middle-of-the-road management is the leadership style of leaders scoring 5,5, which is the medium concern for production and people. 'Team management' is the leadership style of leaders scoring 9,9, which is the maximum concern for production and people. Team management is considered the ideal leadership style.

Practical validations of the model have shown that great career accomplishments are associated with both team management and task management (Blake & Mouton, 1964; Hall, 1976). Leaders usually seem to prefer one dominant style, although they may switch to a 'back-up' style in stressful situations (Blake & Mouton, 1964). In contrast to the Ohio State studies, where leadership was viewed in terms of certain behaviours, the axes of the managerial grid represent leader attitudes.

The managerial grid has been widely applied in consultancy and trainings to help participants reach the level of 9,9 (e.g. Kreinik & Colarelli, 1971). Over the years, Blake & Mouton (1979, 1982; Blake et al., 1964) supplemented the model with two more styles (paternalism/maternalism and opportunism), as well as a third dimension (thickness/depth of leadership). However, the complexity of this model encountered criticism in the following years, as did the fact that the grid disregards particular cirumstances like emergencies (Heery & Noon, 2008).

THE INCLUSION OF SITUATIONAL FACTORS

The behavioural approach was popular until the beginning of the 1970s (Robbins & Judge, 2013). During this time, studies discovered that consideration consistently motivated work teams, but initiating structure inconsistently contributed to team performance. Schriesheim (1982), for example, claimed that the need for both high consideration and high initiating structure was a 'myth'. His research instead found that high consideration alone explains most of the variance in subordinate satisfaction. Researchers concluded that other factors, like the work situation, may influence team performance (Kerr et al., 1974) – and may even be stronger drivers of team performance than leadership (e.g. Fiedler, 1971) or have the potential to substitute for leadership (Kerr & Jermier, 1978). Updated theories have thus hypothesised that the outcomes of consideration and initiating structure are moderated by situational factors. However, the literature has not consistently supported such theories, such as the situational leadership theory (i.e. where the application of consideration and initiating structure depends on the subordinate's job maturity) (Hersey & Blanchard, 1977) or House's (1971) path-goal theory (Graeff, 1983; Judge et al., 2004).

One of the better-known contingency models is that of Fiedler. Developed by Fred E. Fiedler, the model emphasised three different situational variables: the relationship between the leader and the subordinate, the structure of the tasks (highly structured vs. unstructured) and the leader's positional power. Based on his research, he concluded that leaders' consideration is most effective in medium-favourable situations (i.e. moderate situational control), while initiating structure is most effective in highly favourable or unfavourable situations (Fiedler, 1971, 1972). He examined leaders' behaviours through his instrument 'Least Preferred Coworker' (LPC), where leaders are asked to think about their least preferred coworker and rate them on a list with bipolar adjectives (e.g. friendly – unfriendly). High scores on positive adjectives were interpreted as consideration or relationship-orientedness, whereas high scores on negative adjectives were interpreted as initiating structure or task-orientedness. Although meta-analytic testing by Strube & Garcia (1981) supported the model's ability to robustly predict group performance, this result was called into question by Vecchio (1983). The latter author identified several conceptual shortcomings like unrealistic estimates of 'file-drawer' studies, biased data, and unsystematic inclusion of studies into analysis. Furthermore, the model was criticised for several weaknesses, including the basic theoretical proposition of a contingent relationship of leadership style and effectiveness, and a lack of direct measurement of situational favourableness, validity and process measurement (Rice & Kastenbaum, 1983).

CONCLUSION

The Ohio State studies of leader behaviour introduced a new perspective on leadership into the field of management – namely, that leaders are actively crafting leadership outcomes via their behaviour. Because this behavioural approach concentrates on just two main behaviours – focusing on people or on tasks – it is broadly applicable and relatively trainable. Moreover, the notion that leader behaviour shapes leadership success has been validated by many studies at various types of workplaces and leadership settings. Interestingly, the distinction between a warmth/communion orientation and a competence/agency-orientation in people's perceptions is fundamentally supported by social-psychological research on social judgements. That line of research has recently been extended with a third factor, morality (Leach et al., 2007) – and accordingly, leadership research has also begun to focus on ethical or moral issues (Lemoine et al., 2019), whether in the form of behaviours or embodied cues (Reh et al., 2017).

Not surprisingly, the Ohio State studies inspired new streams of research, such as considering the quality of leader–subordinate relationships. Over the past 50 years, academics have increasingly focused on relationship-oriented leadership approaches, such as transformational leadership (Bass, 1997), leader-member-exchange theory (Graen & Uhl-Bien, 1995), relational leadership theory (Uhl-Bien, 2006) and respectful leadership (Van Quaquebeke & Eckloff, 2010). At the same time, practitioners have applied and validated these approaches in their daily work. Google, for example, regularly surveys subordinates to evaluate whether their managers treat them with respect (Bryant, 2013) and former German Chancellor Angela Merkel has been characterised as working quietly on consensus among all involved parties while simultaneously being a whole-day problem-solver (Pazzanese, 2019).

To summarise, the Ohio State leadership studies outlined two main behavioural leadership styles: those directed at people and those directed at tasks. Although this approach has sometimes been criticised for conceptual and methodological reasons, it is still relevant and should not be considered a historical footnote in the evolution of leadership studies (Judge et al., 2004). In fact, these two dimensions indeed seem to form the two most basic tenets of leadership behaviour – as anyone who has done their own factor analaysis on a multitude of leadership scales will confirm.

IMPLICATIONS FOR PRACTITIONERS

The Ohio leadership studies show that there are at least two major roads to achieving leadership success – by being considerate to subordinates and by initiating structure. Accordingly, leadership is about cohesion (making people work together in a team) and locomotion (moving the group toward a goal). There is no general recipe regarding what works best in what situation. However, being considerate appears to be a more consistently effective strategy for leadership success – a point too quickly forgotten by leaders and those who want to become leaders. People want to work for respectful and appreciative leaders (e.g., Vogt et al., 2021). In that sense, a considerate work climate is the basis of successful leadership and not simply a perk. Imagine the work of firefighters: they have to perform as a team in order to put out fires quickly and efficiently. Each situation will be different and they need their leader to tell them where to go first and what to do, which often takes the form of military-style commands. However, firefighters can only perform well as a team and obey such commands when their leaders take the time to build a sturdy relationship. The notion that leadership is merely about giving structure is a holdover from industrialisation, when the 'man as machine' metaphor was prevalent. As society has changed, so, too, should our understanding of leadership.

DISCUSSION QUESTIONS

1. How would you explain the finding by Judge and colleagues (2004) that leaders' initiating structure is less predictive for leadership success than consideration?

2. In which situations should a leader gravitate toward either consideration or initiating structure?

3. Are consideration and initiating structure only conveyed through leader behaviour?

FURTHER READINGS

Hemphill, J. K. & Coons, A. E. (1957). Development of the Leader Behavior Description Questionnaire. In R. M. Stogdill & A. E. Coons (eds), *Leader Behavior. Its Description and Measurement*, Research Monograph (Vol. 88), pp. 6–8. Ohio State University.

This chapter provides a detailed description of the development of the LBDQ and how the Ohio State research team worked together in this regard.

Halpin, A. W. (1957). *Manual for the Leader Behavior Description Questionnaire*. Fisher College of Business, Ohio State University.

This manual describes how the LBDQ should be administered and provides the items for both subscales.

Schriesheim, C. A. & Bird, B. J. (1979). Contributions of the Ohio state studies to the field of leadership. *Journal of Management*, 5, 135–45.

This paper summarises the contributions of the Ohio State studies for leadership research.

Judge, T. A., Piccolo, R. F. & Ilies, R. (2004). The forgotten ones? The validity of consideration and initiating structure in leadership research. *Journal of Applied Psychology*, 89, 36–51.

This meta-analysis examines the effects of consideration and initiating structure on leadership outcomes. It comprises the findings of 130 studies.

DeRue, D. S., Nahrgang, J. D., Wellman, N. E. D. & Humphrey, S. E. (2011). Trait and behavioral theories of leadership: An integration and meta-analytic test of their relative validity. *Personnel Psychology*, 64, 7–52.

In this review and meta-analysis trait and behavioural approaches of leadership are integrated into one model to explain leadership effectiveness.

REFERENCES

Allport, G. W. & Boring, E. G. (1946). Psychology and social relations at Harvard University. *American Psychologist*, 1(4), 119–122. https://doi.org/10.1037/h0061868

Ames History Museum (n.d.). *Alvin E. Coons. July 26, 1945.* https://ameshistory.org/veteran/alvin-e-coons

Bales, R. F. (1955). How people interact in conferences. *Scientific American*, 192(3), 31–5. https://doi.org/10.1038/scientificamerican

Bass, B. M. (1990). *Bass and Stogdill's Handbook of Leadership*, 3rd edn. Free Press.

Bass, B. M. (1997). Does the transactional–transformational leadership paradigm transcend organizational and national boundaries? *American Psychologist*, 52(2), 130–9.

Blake, R. R. & Mouton, J. S. (1964). *The Managerial Grid: Key Orientations for Achieving Production through People*. Gulf.

Blake, R. R. & Mouton, J. S. (1979). What's new with the grid®? *Asia Pacific Journal of Human Resources*, 16(4), 41–6. https://doi.org/10.1177/103841117901600412

Blake, R. R. & Mouton, J. S. (1982). Theory and research for developing a science of leadership. *Journal of Applied Behavioral Science*, 18, 275–91. https://doi.org/10.1177/002188638201800304

Blake, R. R., Mouton, J. S., Barnes, L. B. & Greiner, L. E. (1964). Breakthrough in organization development. *Harvard Business Review*, 42, 133–55.

Bowers, D. G. & Seashore, S. E. (1966). Predicting organizational effectiveness with a four factor theory of leadership. *Administrative Science Quarterly*, 11, 238–63. https://doi.org/10.2307/2391247

Brown, M. E., Treviño, L. K. & Harrison, D. A. (2005). Ethical leadership: A social learning theory perspective for construct development. *Organizational Behavior and Human Decision Processes*, 97, 117–34. https://doi.org/10.1016/j.obhdp.2005.03.002

Bryant, A. (2013). In head-hunting, big data may not be such a big deal. *New York Times.* http://www.nytimes.com/2013/06/20/business/in-head-hunting-big-data-may-not-besuch-a-big-deal.html

Cai, D. A., Fink, E. L. & Walker, C. B. (2019). Robert R. Blake, with recognition of Jane S. Mouton. *Negotiation and Conflict Management Research.* https://doi.org/10.1111/ncmr.12151

Day, R. C. & Hamblin, R. L. (1964). Some effects of close and punitive styles of supervision. *American Journal of Sociology*, 69, 499–510. https://www.jstor.org/stable/2774276

Fiedler, F. E. (1971). *Personality and Situational Determinants of Leader Behavior*, Technical Report (TR-71-18). Department of Psychology, University of Washington. https://apps.dtic.mil/sti/citations/AD0727129

Fiedler, F. E. (1972). Personality motivational systems, and behavior of high and low LPC persons. *Human Relations*, 25, 391–412. https://journals.sagepub.com/doi/pdf/1 0.1177/001872677202500502?casa_token=gKbs578-AS8AAAAA:gbFdq0OhrT3dJKyY W0TtLZUo7sNb1zj5rCNiYe9nL5kTP8chztoljpXbPOUARX5U4cuGeuxZ8a8f

Fiske, S. T., Cuddy, A. J. C. & Glick, P. (2007). Universal dimensions of social cognition: Warmth and competence. *Trends in Cognitive Sciences*, 11, 77–83. https://doi. org/10.1016/j.tics.2006.11.005

Fleishman E. A. (1973). Twenty years of consideration and structure. In E. A. Fleishman & J. G. Hunt (eds), *Current Developments in the Study of Leadership*. Southern Illinois University Press.

Fleishman, E. A. (1953a). The description of supervisory behavior. *Journal of Applied Psychology*, 37, 1–6. https//doi.org/10.1037/h0056314

Fleishman, E. A. (1953b). The measurement of leadership attitudes in industry. *Journal of Applied Psychology*, 37, 153–8. https//doi.org/10.1037/h0063436

Fleishman, E. A. (1989a). *Leadership Opinion Questionnaire (LOQ) Examiner's Manual*. Science Research Associates.

Fleishman, E. A. (1989b). *Supervisory Behavior Description Questionnaire (SBD) Examiner's Manual*. Science Research Associates.

Gottfredson, R. K. & Aguinis, H. (2017). Leadership behaviors and follower performance: Deductive and inductive examination of theoretical rationales and underlying mechanisms. *Journal of Organizational Behavior*, 38, 558–91. https://doi. org/10.1002/job.2152

Graeff, C. L. (1983). The situational leadership theory: A critical view. *Academy of Management Review*, 8, 285–91. https://doi.org/10.5465/amr.1983.4284738

Graen, G. B. & Uhl-Bien, M. (1995). Relationship-based approach to leadership: Development of a leader-member-exchange (LMX) theory over 25 years: Applying a multi-level multi-domain perspective. *Leadership Quarterly*, 6, 219–47. https://doi. org/10.1016/1048-9843(95)90036-5

Haggbloom, S. J., Warnick, R., Warnick, J. E., Jones, V. K., Yarbrough, G. L., Russell, T. M., ... & Monte, E. (2002). The 100 most eminent psychologists of the 20th century. *Review of General Psychology*, 6, 139–52. https://doi.org/10.1037/1089-2680.6.2.139

Hakel, M. D. (1980). Obituary: Ralph M. Stogdill (1904–1978). *American Psychologist*, 35(1), 101. https://doi.org/10.1037/h0078317

Hall, J. (1976). To achieve or not: The manager's choice. *California Management Review*, 18, 5–18. https://doi.org/10.2307/41164664

Halpin, A. W. (1957). *Manual for the Leader Behavior Description Questionnaire*. Fisher College of Business, Ohio State University.

Halpin, A. W. & Winer, B. J. (1957). A factorial study of the Leader Behavior Descriptions. In R. M. Stogdill & A. E. Coons (eds), *Leader Behavior. Its Description and Measurement*. Research Monograph, Vol. 88. Ohio State University, pp. 39–51.

Heery, E. & Noon, M. (2008). *A Dictionary of Human Resource Management*, 3rd edn. Oxford University Press. https://doi.org/10.1093/acref/9780199298761.001.0001

Hemphill, J. K. & Coons, A. E. (1957). Development of the Leader Behavior Description Questionnaire. In R. M. Stogdill & A. E. Coons (eds), *Leader Behavior. Its Description and Measurement*, Research Monograph, Vol. 88. Ohio State University, pp. 6–38.

Hemphill, J. K. (1949). *Situational Factors in Leadership*. Bureau of Educational Research Monograph, Ohio State University.

Hersey, P. & Blanchard, K. H. (1977). *Management of Organization Behavior: Utilizing Human Resources*, 3rd edn. Prentice-Hall. https://doi.org/10.1177/105960117700200419

House, R. J. (1971). A path goal theory of leader effectiveness. *Administrative Science Quarterly*, 16, 321–39. https://doi.org/10.2307/2391905

House, R. J. & Aditya, R. N. (1997). The social scientific study of leadership: Quo vadis? *Journal of Management*, 23, 409–473. https://doi.org/10.1016/S0149-2063(97)90037-4

Judge, T. A., Piccolo, R. F. & Ilies, R. (2004). The forgotten ones? The validity of consideration and initiating structure in leadership research. *Journal of Applied Psychology*, 89, 36–51. https://doi.org/10.1037/0021-9010.89.1.36

Kahn, R. L. & Katz, D. (1952). *Leadership Practices in Relation to Productivity and Morale*. Survey Research Center, Institute for Social Research, University of Michigan. https://isr.umich.edu/wp-content/uploads/historicPublications/Leadership_701_.PDF

Katz, D., Maccoby, N., Gurin, G. & Floor, L. G. (1951). *Productivity, Supervision and Morale among Railroad Workers*. Survey Research Center, Institute for Social Research, University of Michigan. https://psycnet.apa.org/record/1953-00711-000

Kerr, S. & Jermier, J. M. (1978). Substitutes for leadership: Their meaning and measurement. *Organizational Behavior and Human Performance*, 22, 375–403. https://doi.org/10.1016/0030-5073(78)90023-5

Kerr, S., Schriesheim, C. A., Murphy, C. J. & Stogdill, R. M. (1974). Toward a contingency theory of leadership based upon the consideration and initiating structure literature. *Organizational Behavior and Human Performance*, 12, 62–82. https://doi.org/10.1016/0030-5073(74)90037-3

Kiecolt, K. J. (1997). Introduction of Melvin Seeman for the Cooley-Mead Award. *Social Psychology Quarterly*, 60, 1–3. https://www.jstor.org/stable/2787007

Kreinik, P. S. & Colarelli, N. J. (1971). Managerial Grid human relations training for mental hospital personnel. *Human Relations*, 24, 91–104. https://doi.org/10.1177/001872677102400105

Leach, C. W., Ellemers, N. & Barreto, M. (2007). Group virtue: The importance of morality (vs. competence and sociability) in the positive evaluation of in-groups. *Journal of Personality and Social Psychology*, 93, 234–49. https://doi.org/10.1037/0022-3514.93.2.234

Lemoine, G. J., Hartnell, C. A. & Leroy, H. (2019). Taking stock of moral approaches to leadership: An integrative review of ethical, authentic, and servant leadership. *Academy of Management Annals*, 13, 148–87. https://doi.org/10.5465/annals.2016.0121

Morris, R. T. & Seeman, M. (1950). The problem of leadership: An interdisciplinary approach. *American Journal of Sociology*, 56, 149–55. https://www.jstor.org/stable/2772163

Nisbett, R. E. & Wilson, T. D. (1977). The halo effect: Evidence for unconscious alteration of judgments. *Journal of Personality and Social Psychology*, 35, 250–6. https://doi.org/10.1037/0022-3514.35.4.250

Northouse, P. G. (2007). *Leadership: Theory and Practice*, 4th edn. Sage. https://psycnet.apa.org/record/2006-21567-000

Parsons, T. & Bales, R. F. (eds) (1956). *Family, Socialization and Interaction Process*. Routledge.

Pazzanese, C. (2019). Angela Merkel, the scientist who became a world leader. *Harvard Gazette*. https://news.harvard.edu/gazette/story/2019/05/those-who-have-known-angela-merkel-describe-her-rise-to-prominence/

Rees, C. R. & Segal, M. W. (1984). Role differentiation in groups: The relationship between instrumental and expressive leadership. *Small Group Behavior*, 15, 109–23. https://doi.org/10.1177%2F104649648401500106

Reh, S., Van Quaquebeke, N. & Giessner, S. R. (2017). The aura of charisma: A review on the embodiment perspective as signaling. *Leadership Quarterly*, 28, 486–507. https://doi.org/10.1016/j.leaqua.2017.01.001

Rice, R. W. & Kastenbaum, D. R. (1983). The contingency model of leadership: Some current issues. *Basic and Applied Social Psychology*, 4, 373–92. https://doi.org/10.1207/s15324834basp0404_6

Robbins, S. P. & Judge, T. A. (2013). *Organizational Behavior*, 15th edn. Pearson. https://www.pearson.com/us/higher-education/product/Robbins-Organizational-Behavior-15th-Edition/9780132834872.html

Schriesheim, C. A. (1982). The great high consideration – high initiating structure leadership myth: Evidence on its generalizability. *Journal of Social Psychology*, 116, 221–8. https://doi.org/10.1080/00224545.1982.9922774

Schriesheim, C. A. & Bird, B. J. (1979). Contributions of the Ohio State studies to the field of leadership. *Journal of Management*, 5, 135–45. https://doi.org/10.1177/014920637900500204

Schriesheim, C. A. & Kerr, S. (1974). Psychometric properties of the Ohio State leadership scales. *Psychological Bulletin*, 81, 756–65. https://doi.org/10.1037/h0037277

Schriesheim, C. A. & Stogdill, R. M. (1975). Differences in factor structure across three versions of the Ohio State Leadership Scales. *Personnel Psychology*, 18, 189–206. https://doi.org/10.1111/j.1744-6570.1975.tb01380.x

Shartle, C. L. (1979). Early years of the Ohio State University leadership studies. *Journal of Management*, 5, 127–34. https://doi.org/10.1177/014920637900500203

Shartle, C. L. (n.d.). *Autobiography*. Society for Industrial and Organizational Psychology. http://old.siop.org/Presidents/Shartle.aspx

Slater, P. E. (1955). Role differentiation in small groups. *American Sociological Review*, 20, 300–10. https://doi.org/10.2307/2087389

Smith, E. R. & Mackie, D. M. (1995). *Social Psychology.* Worth Publishers. https://psycnet.apa.org/record/1994-98163-000

Stogdill, R. M. (1948). Personal factors associated with leadership: A survey of the literature. *Journal of Psychology*, 25, 35–71. https://doi.org/10.1080/00223980.1948.9917362

Stogdill, R. M. (1959). *Individual Behavior and Group Achievement: A Theory: The Experimental Evidence.* Oxford University Press. https://psycnet.apa.org/record/1959-08110-000

Stogdill, R. M. (1963). *Manual for the Leader Behavior Description Questionnaire – Form XII. An Experimental Revision.* Fisher College of Business, Ohio State University. https://cyfar.org/sites/default/files/LBDQ_1962_MANUAL_SCORING.pdf

Stogdill, R. M. & Coons, A. E. (eds) (1957). *Leader Behavior. Its Description and Measurement, Research Monograph*, Vol. 88. Ohio State University.

Strube, M. J. & Garcia, J. E. (1981). A meta-analytic investigation of Fiedler's contingency model of leadership effectiveness. *Psychological Bulletin*, 90, 307–21. https://doi.org/10.1037/0033-2909.90.2.307

Tracy, L. (1987). Consideration and initiating structure: Are they basic dimensions of leader behavior? *Social Behavior and Personality: An International Journal*, 15, 21–34. https://doi.org/10.2224/sbp.1987.15.1.21

Uhl-Bien, M. (2006). Relational leadership theory: Exploring the social processes of leadership and organizing. *Leadership Quarterly*, 17, 654–76. https://doi.org/10.1016/j. leaqua.2006.10.007

van Dierendonck, D. (2011). Servant leadership: A review and synthesis. *Journal of Management*, 37, 1228–61. https://doi.org/10.1177/0149206310380462

Van Quaquebeke, N. & Eckloff, T. (2010). Defining respectful leadership: What it is, how it can be measured, and another glimpse at what it is related to. *Journal of Business Ethics*, 91, 343–58. https://doi.org/10.1007/s10551-009-0087-z

Van Quaquebeke, N., Zenker, S. & Eckloff, T. (2009). Find out how much it means to me! The importance of interpersonal respect in work values compared to perceived organizational practices. *Journal of Business Ethics*, 89, 423–431. https://doi. org/10.1007/s10551-008-0008-6

Vecchio, R. P. (1983). Assessing the validity of Fiedler's contingency model of leadership effectiveness: A closer look at Strube and Garcia. *Psychological Bulletin*, 93, 404–8. https://doi.org/10.1037/0033-2909.93.2.404

Vogt, C., van Gils, S., Van Quaquebeke, N., Grover, S., & Eckloff, T. (2021). Proactivity at work: The roles of respectful leadership and leader group prototypicality. Journal of Personnel Psychology, 20, 114-123. https://doi.org/10.1027/1866-5888/a000275

11

Followership: Revisiting Hollander & Webb's Leadership, Followership and Friendship Study

Mary Uhl-Bien & Melissa Carsten

BACKGROUND

Consider that you are about to go to war. You have to build a special unit to go with you. Who will you pick? Will it be your friends? Will it be people who are good leaders? Good followers? Are those groups made of different people?

These are the kinds of questions asked by Edwin Hollander and Wilse Webb in the 1950s in their classic study, 'Leadership, Followership, and Friendship: An analysis of peer nominations'. At the time of the study America was less than a decade out from a Second World War. Research in academia was in its infancy, and we knew little about what leadership involved, what leaders did and who emerged as leaders. We knew much less about followership. And that is what makes Hollander & Webb's study so interesting – it was one of the first analyses not only to recognise and define followership, but to place it on an equal footing with leadership. As Hollander & Webb saw it, leadership and followership are two sides of the same coin.

While this might sound obvious, it has not been the case in leadership research or practice. In the period after Hollander & Webb's (1955) article was published, an overpowering shift occurred as people became enamoured with the 'romance of leadership' (Meindl et al., 1985) to the detriment of followership (Uhl-Bien & Pillai, 2007). The impact of that can still be felt today, with leadership scholars struggling to understand or even grasp what followership means and how they can study it. The romance of leadership was made worse by the fact that followership was (and often still is) largely denigrated by leadership scholars. For example, when we started our followership work in the mid-2000s, one of the present authors (Melissa) was told by a senior scholar to not pursue this area, that it was a career dead-end because 'who would ever want to say they are a follower?'

It wasn't just academics who struggled with followership. It was also embedded in the larger cultural system. If you typed 'followership' into Microsoft Word it was flagged as a spelling error – it might still be that way for some of you today. If you tried to do a Google search on followership around 2007, which we did at the time, it generated about 2–3 results compared to hundreds of thousands of results for the word leadership. That's hard to believe now, as followership currently generates robust search results (we wish we had taken a screenshot of our Google search in 2007!).

In reading Hollander & Webb (1955) today, we can see that the quest to recognise followership has been enduring. Hollander & Webb were among the first to attempt it in their study of peer nominations of leaders and followers.

DETAILED DESCRIPTION

HOLLANDER & WEBB'S LEADERSHIP, FOLLOWERSHIP AND FRIENDSHIP NOMINATIONS STUDY

Hollander & Webb's research was positioned as a follow-up to work on sociometry that had been investigating peer nominations of leadership. The focus of the study was on the kind of people would choose to be in leadership and followership roles if they were assigned to a special military unit. This very much fitted the zeitgeist of the time, which was to better understand how leadership affects military performance and what methods were best suited for exploring leadership questions.

In the autumn of 1953, when the study was conducted, the tools available for research were rudimentary. There were no computers to process data or run analyses. Articles were handwritten and then passed off to secretaries to print up on manual typewriters. Calculations were done by hand, and papers were shared with others through the mail. As far as theory, there were few, while ideas of what constitutes sound models and theories in the social and behavioural sciences more broadly were still developing. Research questions were simple and basic, and focused on primary and practical relationships – hence Hollander & Webb's framing of their research in sociometric methods rather than in theory development and testing as is common today.

The motive for the study was straightforward: to elaborate previous findings that showed that leadership peer nominations were able to predict performance over extended periods of time. Hollander & Webb questioned what these findings meant. Were they indicative of something else going on here that may explain these findings? Could it be that those not nominated as leaders or those who were seen favourably in leadership nominations reflected a followership group?

They explored these questions by challenging the predominant idea at the time that leadership and followership are mutually exclusive, that is a person is either a leader or a follower but not both. Countering this position, they suggested that leadership and followership are in an *interdependent* relationship – that leadership and followership go together, and that a given individual can be effective at both. To test this, they examined whether individuals nominated as leaders would also be nominated as followers (and vice versa). They also investigated the 'non-leader' (not nominated) group to see how that group was viewed compared to the nominated followership group.

In addition to examining the nominations themselves, Hollander and Webb (1955) investigated the presumption that peer nominations were 'mere' popularity contests, that is 'a choice of friends for common roles' (p. 164). According to Hollander & Webb, 'It is worth recalling that the question of the relationship of popularity to leadership is fundamental to much sociometric research and has been given considerable attention' (p. 163). Referring to findings from the Signal Corps Officer Candidate School by Wherry & Fryer (1949), they suggested that peer ratings of leadership may not be reflecting popularity but instead capturing superior performance. Taken together, the two research questions they asked were (Hollander & Webb, 1955, p. 164):

- In what way, and to what degree, is followership related to leadership?
- In what way, and to what degree, is friendship related to leadership, and how does this compare with the relationship, if any, between friendship and followership?

To answer these questions, they studied a sample of 187 Naval Aviation Cadets from the Pensacola pre-flight training course. These cadets (all men) worked together in teams through a variety of conditions. Each respondent completed three forms: one on leadership, one on followership and one on friendship. For the leadership and followership forms, respondents were told that they were assigned to 'a special military unit with an undisclosed mission'. They should nominate from highest to lowest the three cadets they considered to be the *most* qualified to lead the special unit and the three (ranking them from highest to lowest) who were *least* qualified to lead. A similar question was asked for followership. If you were the leader of the special unit, who would you identify as the three cadets you would most want (from highest to lowest) to report to you and the three you would least want (from highest to lowest). Instructions stressed that they should select cadets in terms of abilities that they, the rater, considered to be the most important for the role. Finally, the friendship form asked them to identify the three cadets they considered to be their best friends within the section. All nomination forms were collected during the last week of training.

To analyse the data, leadership and followership nominations that each participant received from all respondents were algebraically summed using assigned weights (+3 to –3) divided by the potential number of nominators (N – 1). Similarly, friendship scores were a simple summation of nominations divided by N – 1. The findings showed that leadership and followership nominations were nearly perfectly positively correlated ($r = .92$), and that leadership and friendship ($r = .47$) and followership and friendship ($r = .55$) were moderately positively correlated. The partial correlation between leadership and followership holding friendship constant was .90, indicating that friendship did not significantly affect the relationship.

A series of tests showed that when rating leadership, friendship was less important than followership. Specifically, slightly more than one out of three (1.33/3) high leadership nominees were also nominated as high on followership. For friendship, slightly less than one out of three friends (0.83/3) were nominated as high on leadership. A mean of 1.33 friends were also nominated as high on followership and 1.63 were disregarded in nominations as leaders or followers, that is an average of two out of three friends were *not mentioned at all* in any of the nominations. No relationship was found between friendship and followership.

Based on the high positive correlation between leadership and followership nominations ($r =.92$), Hollander & Webb (1955) concluded that 'the more desired followers tend to be at the upper extremes of the leadership distribution', and more importantly, 'those who are low or disregarded on leadership nominations are not viewed as desirable followers' (p. 166). Moreover, leadership and followership nominations were independent of friendship. In other words, friendship was not found to be a factor in leadership or followership nominations, and leadership and friendship were correlated at a significantly lower level than friendship and followership.

The leadership status of the nominators themselves was also unrelated to followership nominations: 'the leadership status factor made little difference in the selection of followers; the correlation between the followership scores obtained independently from these two nominator groups was .82.' (p. 166). Once again, peer nominations of leadership were not a function of friendship – 'friendship appears to play only a minor role in the emergence of leadership nominations' (p. 167). Moreover, followership status and non-leader status were not the same thing – 'followership status is not necessarily implied by nonleader status on peer nominations' (p. 167). From Hollander and Webb's (1955) discussion of these findings, we can see why this is a classic study. In their words: 'It appears evident that the popular dichotomy between leadership and followership is in need of reappraisal' (p. 167). Rather than opposite ends of a continuum, characteristics of followership are instead '*one functional component of good leadership*' (p. 167 [emphasis added]). '[T]he crux of the matter lies in our definition of followership' (p. 166).

Recognising that 'followers may be evaluated on their capacity as followers or their willingness to be followers' (p. 166), they continue: 'We have chosen to view followership as it is judged from the leadership standpoint' (p. 166). 'As it emerges here, then, our definition of followership is the extent to which an individual is desired by potential leaders of a group functioning within a circumscribed institutional context' and, from this perspective, 'good leaders are also judged as good followers' (p. 166). In one of the more fascinating passages, we see observations strikingly familiar to much later criticisms of leader-centric 'hero leadership' (Meindl et al., 1985; Shamir, 2007) and even those continuing today: 'With the increasing complexity of our society, the role of the institutional leader demands something more than leaping on a white charger to gallop off in a solely self-determined direction' (p. 166). Consistent with newly emerging work on the 'connecting leader' (Jaser, 2020), Hollander and Webb's insights into hierarchy serve as foundational to the connecting leader premise: the nature of hierarchy demands that '[t]he leader must himself be a good follower' (p. 166).

IMPACT OF THE CLASSIC STUDY

Revisiting Hollander & Webb's (1955) classic study feels like a strange step through time in which both everything and nothing has changed. The issues Hollander & Webb (1955) address are, sadly, still the critical questions of the day. Rather than building on Hollander & Webb's (1955) early ideas and developing them into a more integrated and full understanding of leadership and followership, the field took a deep dive into leadership and leaders (i.e. the romance of leadership), obstructing the ability to see followership for what it is: a necessary and important complement to leadership.

It wasn't just the field of leadership that ignored earlier findings. The field of management too disregarded classic findings on the importance of 'informal' organisation and the strong impact of socio-emotional relations and interpersonal ties among workers (Follett, 1987; Trist & Bamforth, 1951) for investigation of the formal organisation as desired by managers who wanted to be able to 'command and control' workers (Barnard, 1938; Selznick, 1948, 1957), only to rediscover the importance of the informal organisation many years later (Gronn, 2002; Uhl-Bien et al., 2007).

To see where things stand currently, and to understand the impact of Hollander & Webb (1955) in the bigger picture, we need to go back to the primary insight the classic study provided: the challenge of long-standing definitions of leadership and followership. The questions Hollander & Webb (1955) asked, and the insights they demonstrated, were early precursors to issues that leadership researchers have taken much longer to return to and more fully explore, that of defining followership and its relationship to leadership (Shamir, 2007; Uhl-Bien et al., 2014).

DEFINING FOLLOWERSHIP

Prior to the classic study, leaders and followers were defined as maintaining opposing qualities and characteristics such that if someone did not have the competency to lead, they would be relegated to following. Hollander & Webb (1955) showed that this was not the case. As they say, 'one cannot make the simple assumption that those individuals not chosen as leaders may be integrated within the group as effective followers' (p. 166). Instead, characteristics of followership are highly related to characteristics of leadership, 'the leader must himself be a good follower or his group might find itself destroyed or performing inefficiently in a total organizational mission' (p. 166). According to Hollander and Webb (1955), followership is as important as leadership, and the qualities that make one a good leader and/or follower are related.

This is actually quite profound when one considers what happened to followership after this time period. Followership as a formal field of study in leadership was never fully considered again until the 2000s (Baker, 2007; Bjugstad et al., 2006; Carsten et al., 2010). Some will argue that this is not true and that leadership researchers always considered followership. But the reality is that they did not – what they considered was follow*ers*. Worse, when they spoke of followers, they largely viewed them as passive recipients of the leader's influence (Shamir, 2007). There were exceptions, of course. Hollander continued to attempt to inter- ject and remind scholars that followership is an important relation in leadership (Hollander, 1992, 2006; Hollander & Offermann, 1990), and follower-centric views brought attention to the perceptions and attributions of followers (Meindl et al., 1985). But these studies always maintained their emphasis on leaders and leadership – a focus on followers and followership never took hold.

What is the difference? What do we mean when we say a focus on follower*ship*? We can see glimmers of an answer in Hollander and Webb's (1955) definition of followership as 'the extent to which an individual is desired by potential leaders' (p. 166). This means that the difference is in *how the leader sees the follower* and the follower's value to the leader in accomplishing objectives and outcomes. This gives us the start of the definition of followership as *the contribution and value followers offer to leaders in supporting their role and attaining their (the leader's) goals.*

ESTABLISHING FOLLOWERSHIP AND LEADERSHIP AS AN INTERDEPENDENT RELATIONSHIP

To further understand the definition of followership we need to consider Hol- lander and Webb's (1955) other major insight, the interdependent relationship between leadership and followership. According to Hollander & Webb, 'leadership and followership qualities are interdependent' (p. 163). What this means is that we cannot fully understand leadership without considering its interdependent rela- tionship with followership. Doing so would be *leaving out half the equation.*

Again, scholars will argue here that they have considered both together, that followers are included in practically every study of leadership. But to reiterate, including followers does not equate to including follower*ship*. The interdependent relation means fully recognising the 'characteristics of followership as one func- tional component of good leadership' (Hollander & Webb, 1955, p. 167). Through this lens, leadership and followership are an interconnected *process* (Hollander, 1992a, 1992b), that is the way in which leadership and followership work together in relation to achieve goals (Hollander & Julian, 1969). How this interconnected process works was described in follow-up research conducted by Hollander and colleagues.

KEY REPLICATIONS AND GENERALISATIONS

The classic study in its original form has never, to our knowledge, been repli- cated, but elements of the findings have. Perhaps the closest replication was research conducted by Nelson (1964). Participants were asked to rate the attitudes and behaviours of leaders and followers they 'liked' and those they 'did not like.' The findings demonstrated that liked leaders and liked followers were more simi- lar in their attitudinal and behaviour profiles than any other group. Specifically, liked leaders and followers scored similarly on emotional control, acceptance of authority, and motivation. The author concluded that although leaders and followers are not necessarily the same people, they are highly similar in their characteristics. In this way, Nelson (1964) supports Hollander & Webb's (1955) original premise that leader and follower characteristics are overlapping and describes followership as an active and engaged element required for effective leadership (see also Peters & Haslam, 2018).

Hollander himself also conducted extensive follow-up work (Hollander, 1958, 1964, 2004). For example, his work investigating follower perceptions of leaders showed that followers seek leaders who are competent with the task and loyal to the norms of the group. Hollander then elaborated this discovery into his theory of idiosyncrasy credits (Hollander, 1958). According to Hollander (1958), leaders who display these characteristics are granted 'idiosyncrasy credits' by followers. Idiosyncrasy credits are defined as an accumulation of followers' positive impressions of the leader's group contributions that allow the leader to be perceived as having greater status, legitimacy and latitude for influence (Hollander, 2006, 2013). Once accumulated, idiosyncrasy credits can be used by the leader to garner support for innovative initiatives or courses of action. Based on this model, it is the followers, rather than the leader, that allow themselves to be influenced depending on how much trust they have in their leader.

Research conducted on idiosyncrasy credits challenged the dominant view of the time by recognising that leadership largely exists in the perceptions of followers. Rather than studying leader characteristics or behaviours, Hollander and colleagues studied follower perceptions of leaders and what constituted 'good' or 'bad' leadership in the eyes of followers (Hollander, 1993, 1995; Hollander & Kelly, 1992; Hollander et al., 1996). They recognised that follower perceptions play a significant role in leadership attributions and, by extension, leadership relations.

Building from the notion of leadership as an interdependent process, Hollander (2006) introduced the theory of inclusive leadership. According to the theory, leadership is more likely to be achieved by a process involving persuasion and the sharing of power between leaders and followers. Instead of being based on top-down directives, leadership is created when leaders and followers share power, collaborate on problem-solving, and interact through mutual influence. As Hollander (2006, p. 293) describes, inclusive leadership 'emphasizes doing things with people, rather than to people.' This emphasis on shared power implies that the autocratic use of power leads to dysfunction and harmful relations.

Hollander and Offermann (1990) also addressed the notion of interdependence and shared power in their discussion of 'power over' versus 'power to'. Power over denotes the traditional views of leaders dictating followers' actions by dominating decision-making and charting a course for the future. Power to involves allowing individuals to freely determine their own action through a power-sharing arrangement between leaders and followers. For leaders and followers to collaborate and contribute to leadership outcomes, in alignment with inclusive leadership, Hollander & Offermann (1990) argue that power-sharing is essential to promoting ethical and humane leadership.

BEYOND HOLLANDER & WEBB'S STUDY: THEORETICAL DEVELOPMENTS

The extension of the original research by Hollander and colleagues had major implications for how scholars understood the role of the follower, and introduced the idea that leadership, at least to some extent, is imbued by followers as opposed to embodied by a 'heroic' person appointed as the leader. As a result, a long line of follower-centric research ensued to identify what followers desire from a leader, and how followers perceive leadership (Meindl, 1990, 1995).

FOLLOWER-CENTRIC APPROACHES

Follower-centric approaches provide a framework for theoretical and empirical advances regarding the inputs, mechanisms and outcomes of follower constructions of leadership (Shamir et al., 2007). Within this framework, researchers consider follower perceptions of leader prominence, as well as how follower traits and beliefs create expectations for leader behaviour and outcomes (Ehrhart & Klein, 2001; Kark et al., 2003; also see Bligh & Schyns, 2007, for a review).

Perhaps the first of this genre, romance of leadership (Meindl et al., 1985), suggests that followers socially construct leadership through social information processing, and that it is these social constructions that influence follower assessments of and reactions to the leader more than the leader's actual behaviour (Meindl, 1990, 1995). This work recognises that followers imbue meaning to leaders and leadership. Similar to when Hollander & Webb (1955) questioned the meaning of findings of peer nominations of leadership, with the romance of leadership Meindl et al. (1985) questioned the meaning of variations in measures of 'organisational performance'. Meindl and colleagues posited and later found that perceptions of organisational performance were overly attributed to leadership, and that non-leadership factors related to organisational performance were regularly disregarded by observers (Meindl & Ehrlich, 1987).

A large body of literature has amassed to substantiate this claim. The findings of Pastor et al. (2007) show that ratings of charismatic leadership are affected by the emotional arousal of followers (Kohles, 2007) found that negative follower attitudes have a deleterious impact on perceptions of leadership effectiveness. Other work showed that certain follower characteristics such as extraversion, self-efficacy and motivation affect how followers perceive leaders (Dvir & Shamir, 2003; Phillips & Bedeian, 1994; Schyns & Felfe, 2006).

Another stream of follower-centric research is implicit leadership and followership theory (Lord et al., 1984; Sy, 2010). The first, implicit leadership theory (ILT), emerged from the observation that ratings of leadership were more representative of followers' assumptions and expectations than of actual leadership competencies (Eden & Leviatan, 1975). ILTs are the cognitive structures, or schemas, that hold information about the traits and behaviours they associate with leaders. Followers use these schemas to categorise individuals as leaders (Lord et al., 1984) and form expectations for how leaders will interact with followers (Epitropaki &

Martin, 2004; Engle & Lord, 1997; Offermann et al., 1994). For example, whether a follower holds a prototypic (i.e. positive) or anti-prototypic (i.e. negative) implicit theory of leadership affects the relationship quality between leaders and followers, follower liking of the leader (Engle & Lord, 1997), as well as follower job satisfaction, well-being and intention to quit (Martin & Epitropaki, 2001).

The second, implicit followership theory (IFT), represents cognitive schema that leaders hold about followers' traits and behaviour. Like ILTs, people's IFTs can consist of prototypical (i.e. positive) or anti-prototypical (i.e. negative) characteristics, and help leaders form expectations for follower behaviour and performance. In the past several years, a number of studies have found that leader's IFTs (called LIFTs) have important impacts on followers. For example, positive LIFTs are associated with greater liking and relationship quality reported by leaders (Gao & Wu, 2019; Goswami et al., 2020; Sy, 2010). Conversely, negative LIFTs are associated with reduced trust in and satisfaction with followers (Sy, 2010). Moreover, these positive and negative leader perceptions affect follower effort and performance in important ways (Leung & Sy, 2018; Sy, 2010).

Taken together, research on ILTs and IFTs provides evidence for the importance of perceptions and expectations between leaders and followers. It builds directly from the work of Hollander & Webb (1955) by placing emphasis on the ways that both leaders and followers perceive the effectiveness of their dyad partner. Moreover, the similarities between prototypical characteristics of leaders and prototypical characteristics of followers (i.e. regarding them as hard-working, intelligent) also suggests that, similar to the findings of Hollander & Webb (1955), leaders and followers may be more alike than different in their characteristics.

FOLLOWERSHIP THEORY

Building from relational leadership theory (Uhl-Bien, 2006) and extending the work of Hollander (1992a, 1992b), Uhl-Bien et al. (2014) introduced followership theory as a foundation to understand 'the nature and impact of followers and following in the leadership process' (p. 89). Rather than studying how leaders influence followers (i.e. traditional leader-centric approaches), or how followers construct leadership (i.e. follower-centric approaches), followership theory is consistent with Hollander & Webb's premise that followers bring unique attitudes, beliefs, characteristics and behaviours into the leadership process and have the potential to impact both leaders and leadership outcomes. In their review of followership research, Uhl-Bien et al. (2014) discuss two theoretical approaches to the study of followership: role-based approaches and constructionist approaches.

Role-based approaches investigate followers in a hierarchical (i.e. manager–subordinate) structure and consider the effects that lower-level employees have on managers' attitudes and behaviours. The role-based approach places followers in a more central position of affecting leaders and leadership through their unique role beliefs and behaviours, and suggests that followers can significantly impact the outcomes of work groups in organisations. This line of theorising builds on Hollander & Webb's (1955) conclusion that leadership requires effective followership.

Constructionist approaches stem from the relational nature of leadership and followership and suggest that individuals might assume the identity of leader or follower depending on the context and the task at hand. This approach suggests that leaders and followers do not entail innate characteristics, nor are they mutually exclusive roles, but rather that identities are claimed and granted by individuals working together to accomplish a shared objective (DeRue & Ashford, 2010).

Uhl-Bien (2021a, 2021b) also introduces a more generalised approach to followership grounded in the definition of leadership as a co-creation, that is a 'relational dynamic of leaders/leading and followers/following as it occurs in particular time and space' (Uhl-Bien 2021a, p. 1403). Directly related to Hollander & Webb's (1955) notion of leadership-followership interdependence, Uhl-Bien (2021a, 2021b) argues that there is no leadership without followership. For leadership to sustain, it requires the power of the follower: 'leaders can only exist and stay in power if followers are willing to follow them' (Uhl-Bien, 2021b p. 157). Thus, in examining issues like failed leadership, we must recognise that failed leadership is also often failed followership. Using the example of COVID-19, she describes how 'toxic illusio' (Mergen & Ozbilgin, 2021), i.e. 'the tendency of followers to engage in leaders' toxic game and believe in its significance' (p. 157), contributed as much to the failed outcomes as failed leadership did.

CONCLUSION

Hollander & Webb's classic study was the first to place leadership and followership on an equal footing in leadership research. It showed that leadership and followership are interdependent and overlapping, that is aspects of what makes a person an effective leader are also those that contribute to an effective follower. As a result of subsequent interrogation of these ideas, we now know much more about what this means. Effective leadership and followership involve being willing to work together in combined acts of leading and following to accomplish mutually beneficial outcomes (Uhl-Bien et al., 2014).

In this dynamic, leading involves influencing and following involves being willing to be influenced. For leadership to occur, acts of influencing must be met with agreement to be influenced (e.g. deferring), and vice versa (Uhl-Bien & Carsten, 2018). These acts do not have to be tied uniquely to only one party (leader leading, follower following) and most often they are not. Effective leadership typically involves mutual 'influencing' and 'deferring' as parties take turns leading and following depending on what they can best offer the relationship.

The leadership-followership interdependence implies that when great leadership happens it isn't because of just great leaders, it is also the work of great followers. Hollander and Webb's initial study (1955) lays the foundation for this possibility. Then Hollander spent the rest of his career trying to demonstrate it and to get others to listen. Hollander's inclusion of followers goes beyond the 'romance of leadership' (Meindl et al., 1985). He wasn't describing follower attributions (of what they think makes a great leader), he was describing followers' actions. And this is where the extension of his work into followership theory has so much to offer. Followership theory helps bring us back full circle to where Hollander & Webb (1955) started: by considering followers as full and powerful players in the leadership process.

To capitalise on this, and to complete the journey, we must build on Hollander and Webb's (1955) definition and flesh out the characteristics and actions that are associated with followership. According to Hollander & Webb (1955), 'followership is the extent to which an individual is desired by potential leaders of a group functioning within a circumscribed institutional context' (p. 166). Extending this, we can define followership from the leader's perspective as: *the value leaders receive from followers in supporting the leader's role and attaining the leader's goals.*

The relentless efforts of Ed Hollander to advocate for followership and the recognition of leadership and followership as an interdependent leadership process (Hollander & Julian, 1969; Hollander, 1986) demonstrate the challenge of being a lone wolf in a field. Hollander's message was clear all along. Followership *does* matter, and the study of leadership is not complete without fully integrating followership into it. It just took leadership scholars a half century to want to hear it.

IMPLICATIONS FOR PRACTITIONERS

Interestingly, while leadership scholars have trouble grasping followership and even actively resist using the term altogether (Miller, 1998; Raelin, 2003, 2011; Rost, 1993, 2008), practitioners have no problem with it when it is defined appropriately and explained: *followership is working in relation to a leader to co-create leadership and its outcomes.* What they have less awareness of is the idea that followers should recognise the individual differences and needs of their leaders and work to actively support them.

The most savvy, of course, have known this all along. They are the ones found in Hollander & Webb's (1955) classic study – the peers identified as effective leaders but also desirable followers. These individuals are traditionally identified as 'high potentials' and supported for advancement in organisations (Carsten et al., 2010). What organisations really need is for this to become the broader norm: *all* members of organisations should understand what followership is and what their responsibility is in performing it. Leadership development has for too long been preoccupied with leaders. As a result, the importance of followership has been missed altogether. This is easily corrected by focusing on followership training and development. Such a focus would teach organisational members to be followers who are more effective partners to leaders and place full responsibility on followers to do so.

In today's world the decision to include followership as a part of leadership is no longer a nice to have, it is a must have. If we are to advance organisational practice, we have no choice – problems and challenges facing organisations are too complex for leaders to be able to face or handle them on their own. We need full leadership force, meaning leaders *and* followers together accepting responsibility for their roles and actions in co-creating leadership and its outcomes.

DISCUSSION QUESTIONS

1. Why do you think it took so long for leadership scholars to come around to recognising followership as a fundamental part of leadership? How would you feel if you were Ed Hollander and knew you were 'right' but other people in the field were not ready to listen?

2. What is your perspective on followership? Do you also subscribe to the 'romance of leadership' and 'subordination of followership'? Did this article change your mind on that? If so, in what way? If not, why not?

3. If you had to design a study on followership right now, what would it be? How would you measure followership? What key questions do you think need to be addressed, and what are the most important implications for practitioners?

FURTHER READINGS

Carsten, M. K., Uhl-Bien, M., West, B. J., Patera, J. L. & McGregor, R. (2010). Exploring social constructs of followership: A qualitative study. *The Leadership Quarterly*, 21, 543–62.

In this qualitative interview study, the authors build from the work of Shamir (2007) to uncover how followers socially construct their role relative to leaders in organisations.

Meindl, J. R., Ehrlich, S. B. & Dukerich, J. M. (1985). The romance of leadership. *Administrative Science Quarterly*, 30, 78–102.

In a series of archival and experimental studies, the authors explore attributions to leadership and demonstrate that leadership has extraordinary power in the eyes of observers as an explanatory concept for organisational performance.

Shamir, B. (2007). From passive recipients to active co-producers: Followers' roles in the leadership process. In B. Shamir, R. Pillai, M. Bligh & M. Uhl-Bien (eds), *Follower-Centered Perspectives on Leadership: A Tribute to the Memory of James R. Meindl.* Information Age, pp. ix–xxxix.

This chapter reviews how followers have been treated in leadership theory and research and argues for a reconceptualisation of leadership as a process that is co-constructed by leaders and followers.

Uhl-Bien, M. & Pillai, R. (2007). The romance of leadership and the social construction of *followership*. In B. Shamir, R. Pillai, M. Bligh & M. Uhl-Bien (eds), *Follower-Centered Perspectives on Leadership: A Tribute to the Memory of James R. Meindl.* Information Age, pp.187–209.

This chapter points out that just as leadership has been romanticised in theory and practice, followership has been subordinated and treated as a construct that offers little value to leadership research. It then reviews the many different ways in which followership may be socially constructed and argues for a more direct investigation into followership as a process.

Uhl-Bien, M., Riggio, R. E., Lowe, K. B. & Carsten, M. K. (2014). Followership theory: A review and research agenda. *The Leadership Quarterly*, 25, 83–104.

This is the seminal piece in modern followership theory. The article includes a detailed review of how followers have been treated in leadership research, and then lays a theoretical foundation for the formal study of followership.

REFERENCES

Baker, S. D. (2007). Followership: The theoretical foundation of a contemporary construct. *Journal of Leadership & Organizational Studies*, 14, 50–60.

Barnard, C. I. (1938). *The Functions of the Executive*. Harvard University Press.

Bjugstad, K., Thach, E. C., Thompson, K. J. & Morris, A. (2006). A fresh look at followership: A model for matching followership and leadership styles. *Journal of Behavioral and Applied Management*, 7, 304–19.

Bligh, M. C. & Schyns, B. (2007). Leading question: The romance lives on: Contemporary issues surrounding the romance of leadership. *Leadership*, 3, 343–60.

Bligh, M. C., Kohles, J. C., Pearce, C. L., Justin, J. E. & Stovall, J. F. (2007). When the romance is over: Follower perspectives of aversive leadership. *Applied Psychology*, 56, 528–57.

Carsten, M. K., Uhl-Bien, M., West, B. J., Patera, J. L. & McGregor, R. (2010). Exploring social constructs of followership: A qualitative study. *The Leadership Quarterly*, 21, 543–62.

DeRue, S. & Ashford, S. (2010). Who will lead and who will follow? A social process of leadership identity construction in organizations. *Academy of Management Review*, 35, 627–47.

Dvir, T. & Shamir, B. (2003). Follower developmental characteristics as predicting transformational leadership: A longitudinal field study. *The Leadership Quarterly*, 14, 327–44.

Eden, D. & Leviatan, U. (1975). Implicit leadership theory as a determinant of the factor structure underlying supervisory behavior scales. *Journal of Applied Psychology*, 60, 736–41.

Ehrhart, M. G. & Klein, K. J. (2001). Predicting followers' preferences for charismatic leadership: The influence of follower values and personality. *The Leadership Quarterly*, 12, 153–79.

Engle, E. M. & Lord, R. G. (1997). Implicit theories, self-schemas, and leader-member exchange. *Academy of Management Journal*, 40, 988–1010.

Epitropaki, O. & Martin, R. (2004). Implicit leadership theories in applied settings: Factor structure, generalizability, and stability over time. *Journal of Applied Psychology*, 89, 293–310.

Follett, M. P. (1987). *Freedoom and Co-ordination: Lectures in Business Organization*. Garland.

Gao, P. & Wu, W. (2019). Effect of leaders' implicit followership theory on subordinates' career success. *Social Behavior and Personality: An International Journal*, 47, 1–14.

Goswami, A., Park, H. I. & Beehr, T. A. (2020). Does the congruence between leaders' implicit followership theories and their perceptions of actual followers matter? *Journal of Business and Psychology*, 35, 519–38.

Gronn, P. (2002). Distributed leadership as a unit of analysis. *The Leadership Quarterly*, 13, 423–51.

Hollander, E. P. (1958). Conformity, status, and idiosyncrasy credit. *Psychological Review*, 65, 117–27.

Hollander, E. P. (1986). On the central role of leadership processes. *Applied Psychology*, 35, 39–52.

Hollander, E. P. (1992a). The essential interdependence of leadership and followership. *Current Directions in Psychological Science*, 1, 71–75.

Hollander, E. P. (1992b). Leadership, followership, self, and others. *The Leadership Quarterly*, 3, 43–54.

Hollander, E. P. (1993). Legitimacy, power, and influence: A perspective on relational features of leadership. In M. Chemers & R. Ayman (eds), *Leadership Theory and Research: Perspectives and Directions*. Academic Press, pp. 29–47.

Hollander, E. P. (1995). Ethical challenges in the leader–follower relationship. *Business Ethics Quarterly*, 55–65.

Hollander, E. P. (2006). Influence processes in leadership-followership: Inclusion and the idiosyncrasy credit model. In D. A. Hantula (ed.), *Advances in Social & Organizational Psychology: A Tribute to Ralph Rosnow*. Lawrence Erlbaum & Associates, pp. 293–312.

Hollander, E. P. (2013). Inclusive leadership and idiosyncrasy credit in leader–follower relations. In M. G. Rumsey (ed.), *The Oxford Handbook of Leadership*. Oxford University Press, pp. 12–43.

Hollander, E. P. & Julian, J. W. (1969). Contemporary trends in the analysis of leadership processes. *Psychological Bulletin*, 71, 387–97.

Hollander, E. P. & Kelly, D. R. (1992). Appraising relational qualities of leadership and followership. *International Journal of Psychology*, 27, 289–90.

Hollander, E. P. & Offermann, L. R. (1990). Power and leadership in organizations: Relationships in transition. *American Psychologist*, 45, 179–89.

Hollander, E. P. & Webb, W. B. (1955). Leadership, followership, and friendship: An analysis of peer nominations. *Journal of Abnormal and Social Psychology*, 50, 163–67. https://doi.org/10.1037/h0044322

Hollander, E. P., Schwager, E., Russeva, K. & Nassauer, F. (1996). Intangible rewards of contributing to leader-follower relations. *International Journal of Psychology*, 31, 1435–50.

Jaser, Z. (ed.). (2020). *The Connecting Leader: Serving Concurrently as a Leader and a Follower*. IAP.

Kark, R., Shamir, B. & Chen, G. (2003). The two faces of transformational leadership: Empowerment and dependency. *Journal of Applied Psychology*, 88, 246–55.

Leung, A. & Sy, T. (2018). I am as incompetent as the prototypical group member: An investigation of naturally occurring golem effects in work groups. *Frontiers in Psychology*, 9, 1581.

Lord, R. G., Foti, R. J. & De Vader, C. L. (1984). A test of leadership categorization theory: Internal structure, information processing, and leadership perceptions. *Organizational Behavior and Human Performance*, 34, 343–78.

Martin, R. & Epitropaki, O. (2001). Role of organizational identification on implicit leadership theories (ILTs), transformational leadership and work attitudes. *Group Processes & Intergroup Relations*, 4, 247–62.

Meindl, J. R. (1990). On leadership: An alternative to the conventional wisdom. *Research in Organizational Behavior*, 12, 159–203.

Meindl, J. R. (1995). The romance of leadership as a follower-centric theory: A social constructionist approach. *The Leadership Quarterly*, 6, 329–41.

Meindl, J. R. & Ehrlich, S. B. (1987). The romance of leadership and the evaluation of organizational performance. *Academy of Management Journal*, 30, 91–109.

Meindl, J. R., Ehrlich, S. B. & Dukerich, J. M. (1985). The romance of leadership. *Administrative Science Quarterly*, 30, 78–102.

Mergen, A. & Ozbilgin, M. F. (2021). Understanding the followers of toxic leaders: Toxic illusio and personal uncertainty. *International Journal of Management Reviews*, 23, 45–63. https://doi.org/10.1111/ijmr.12240

Miller, E. J. (1998). The leader with vision: Is time running out? In E. B. Klein, F. Gabelnick & P. Herr (eds), *The Psychodynamics of Leadership*. Psychosocial Press, pp. 3–25.

Nelson, P. D. (1964). Similarities and differences among leaders and followers. *Journal of Social Psychology*, 63, 161–7.

Offermann, L. R., Kennedy Jr, J. K. & Wirtz, P. W. (1994). Implicit leadership theories: Content, structure, and generalizability. *The Leadership Quarterly*, 5, 43–58.

Pastor, J. C., Mayo, M. & Shamir, B. (2007). Adding fuel to fire: The impact of followers' arousal on ratings of charisma. *Journal of Applied Psychology*, 92, 1584.

Peters, K. & Haslam, S. A. (2018). I follow, therefore I lead: A longitudinal study of leader and follower identity and leadership in the marines. *British Journal of Psychology*, 109(4), 708–23.

Phillips, A. S. & Bedeian, A. G. (1994). Leader-follower exchange quality: The role of personal and interpersonal attributes. *Academy of Management Journal*, 37, 990–1001.

Raelin, J. A. (2003). *Creating Leaderful Organizations: How to Bring out Leadership in Everyone*. Berrett-Koehler.

Raelin, J. (2011). From leadership-as-practice to leaderful practice. *Leadership*, 7, 195–211.

Rost, J. C. (1993). *Leadership for the Twenty-First Century*. Praeger.

Rost, J. C. (2008). Followership: An outmoded concept. In R. Riggio, I. Chaleff & J. Lipman-Blumen (eds), *The Art of Followership: How Great Followers Create Great Leaders and Organizations*. Jossey-Bass, pp. 53–64.

Schyns, B. & Felfe, J. (2006). The personality of followers and its effect on the perception of leadership: An overview, a study, and a research agenda. *Small Group Research*, 37, 522–39.

Selznick, P. (1948). Foundations of the theory of organizations. *American Sociological Review*, 13, 25–35.

Selznick, P. (1957). *Leadership in Administration*. Harper & Row.

Shamir, B. (2007). From passive recipients to active co-producers: Followers' roles in the leadership process. In B. Shamir, R. Pillai, M. Bligh & M. Uhl-Bien (eds), *Follower-Centered Perspectives on Leadership: A Tribute to the Memory of James R. Meindl*. Information Age, pp. ix–xxxix.

Shamir, B., Pillai, R., Bligh, M. & Uhl-Bien, M. (eds) (2007). *Follower-Centered Perspectives on Leadership: A Tribute to the Memory of James R. Meindl*. Information Age.

Sy, T. (2010). What do you think of followers? Examining the content, structure and consequences of implicit followership theories. *Organizational Behavior & Human Decision Processes*, 113, 73–84. doi: 10.1016/j.obhdp.2010.06.001

Trist, E. L. & Bamforth, K. W. (1951). Some social and psychological consequences of the Longwall method of coal-getting. *Human Relations*, 4, 3–38.

Uhl-Bien, M. (2006). Relational leadership theory: Exploring the social processes of leadership and organizing. *The Leadership Quarterly*, 17, 654–76.

Uhl-Bien, M. (2021a). Complexity and COVID-19: Leadership and followership in a complex world. *Journal of Management Studies*, 58, 1400–4. doi: 10.1111/joms.12696

Uhl-Bien, M. (2021b). Complexity leadership and followership: Changed leadership in a changed world. *Journal of Change Management*, 21, 144–62. doi: 10.1080/14697017.2021.1917490

Uhl-Bien, M. & Carsten, M. (2018). Reversing the lens in leadership: Positioning followership in the leadership construct. In Y. Berson, I. Katz, G. Eilam-Shamir & R. Kark (eds), *Leadership Now: Reflections on the Legacy of Boas Shamir*. Emerald Publishing, pp. 95–222.

Uhl-Bien, M. & Pillai, R. (2007). The romance of leadership and the social construction of *followership*. In B. Shamir, R. Pillai, M. Bligh & M. Uhl-Bien (eds), *Follower-Centered Perspectives on Leadership: A Tribute to the Memory of James R. Meindl*. Information Age, pp. 187–209.

Uhl-Bien, M., Marion, R. & McKelvey, B. (2007). Complexity Leadership Theory: Shifting leadership from the industrial age to the knowledge era. *The Leadership Quarterly*, 18, 298–318.

Uhl-Bien, M., Riggio, R. E., Lowe, K. B. & Carsten, M. K. (2014). Followership theory: A review and research agenda. *The Leadership Quarterly*, 25, 83–104.

Wherry, R. J. & Fryer, D. H. (1949). Buddy ratings: Popularity contest or leadership criterion? *Personnel Psychology*, 2, 147–59.

Part IV | Justice, Equality and Diversity

12 Organisational Justice: Revisiting Greenberg's Pay Inequity Study

Russell S. Cropanzano, Nicole Strah, Deborah E. Rupp & Jessie A. Cannon

BACKGROUND

Jerald (Jerry) Greenberg was known for both being passionate about doing research that had real, actionable implications for organisations, and for occasionally incorporating song lyrics into his paper titles. He once noted to Cropanzano that organisational justice research should not be 'thick as a brick' (in tribute to Jethro Tull). As we will see in this chapter, Greenberg's dedication to impactful work was on full display in the early 1990s. 'Employee Theft as a Reaction to Underpayment Inequity: The hidden costs of pay cuts' has become a classic. Looking back from the 2020s, it is difficult to convey the ferment of the late 1980s and early 1990s. But Greenberg (1990a) should be viewed as a sort of intellectual watershed, a place where a cacophony of ideas – about employment-related outcomes, processes and interpersonal treatment – were captured together, providing the field with structure and direction. To capture these events, we review the state of the justice literature in the last part of the twentieth century, with a historical emphasis on these foundational concepts.

Greenberg's (1990a) classic study was published during a time of tumult and excitement, when a well-worked idea, equity theory, was being confronted with an amorphous new one, procedural justice, and the latter was only beginning to be understood. The article was among the first to consider the interplay of these concepts. At this time Greenberg (1990a) conceptualised procedural justice in two ways: in terms of formal processes, and in terms of informal processes bestowed via 'interpersonal treatment' (p. 562; see also Bies et al., 1993; Folger & Bies, 1989; Greenberg, 1990b; Tyler & Bies, 1990). The informal process would eventually evolve into a separate construct, which was called interactional justice. We will address this history later in the chapter (Bies, 2005, 2015). However, at this point in history, all of these ideas were collapsed into procedural justice, and this was central to the Greenberg (1990a) study.

EQUITY THEORY

Modern thinking about equity in the workplace began in the 1950s. Early in that decade, Homans (1953) examined the attitudes of workers as they were rotated among higher- and lower-status jobs. He found that 'when arrangements must be made ... for workers to fill in on jobs other than their "own", there will be less dissatisfaction where holders of lower-status jobs fill in on higher-status ones than where ... the opposite takes place' (p. 10). Equity involved interpersonal comparisons of both contributions and rewards. Building on this work, Homans (1961, p. 249) formulated an early theory of distributive justice. It is worth considering his equation, as it will become important later:

$$\frac{Person1}{Person2} = \frac{Rewards1}{Rewards2} \tag{1}$$

Homans (1961) maintained that even outcomes that are unequal can still be fair (i.e. equitable) to the extent that one individual contributed more than another. That is, what workers get out should be proportional to what they put in, and this is decided relative to the inputs and outcomes of referent others. In his formulation of equity theory, Adams (1963, p. 422) acknowledged his 'indebtedness ... to George C. Homans for his ideas on distributive justice, which stimulated much of the present essay.' Adams (1963) discussed both Homans (1953) and Homans (1961) at length. Two years later (1965) he went even further, rearranging the terms in Homans' (1961) equation, formally launching equity theory, which can be summarised by the equation that may be familiar to many:

$$\frac{Outcomes1}{Inputs1} = \frac{Outcomes2}{Inputs2} \tag{2}$$

For many years, the study of distributive justice, as well as organisational justice more generally, was largely the study of equity theory. Employees were said to ascertain the ratio of their work inputs (e.g. time, effort) to the outcomes they received from the organisation (e.g. pay, promotions). They then compared their ratio to the input-to-outcome ratio of a referent other (e.g. a similar co-worker). If this comparison leads to a perception of imbalance in either direction, equity theory suggests that employees will attempt to rectify it. For example, in a field experiment, Greenberg (1988) examined employees who were temporarily moved to new offices. Some of these offices were higher status, others lower and some were the same. Greenberg found that employees who were moved to the higher-status office showed improved performance (an over-reward effect), those moved to the lower-status office showed reduced performance (an under-reward effect) and those in the same-status office did not change their performance. As can be seen, Greenberg was already an expert on equity theory, aware of the theory's strengths and limitations (Greenberg, 1982, 1987a, 1987b, 1990b), well before he published his 1990a article. In fact, his master's thesis had been a two-study examination of over-reward effects on employee motivation, which was conducted under the supervision of Gerald Leventhal (Greenberg & Leventhal, 1976).[1]

PROCEDURE

From whom did Greenberg (1990a) derive the notion of procedure? Of explanations? Again, we need to return to the 1960s. It was in that decade that the term 'organisational justice' was used by Wendell French (1964a). It first appears in his textbook titled *The Personnel Management Process: Human Resources Administration*. French (1964b) elaborated his ideas later that same year in a talk given to the Academy of Management. French referred to the dichotomy between distributive justice, the equitable allocation of outcomes and what French (1964b, pp. 102–3) called 'corrective justice'. For distributive justice, French worked with the ideas of Homans (1958, 1961) and Adams (1963) described above, which had only been recently formulated.

However, his 'corrective justice', or what he called 'organisational due process' (French, 1964b, p. 108), was the more original idea. In his view, corrective justice 'consists of established procedures for handling complaints and grievances, protection against punitive action for using such established procedures, and careful, systematic, and thorough review of the substance of the complaints and grievance' (French, 1964b, p. 107). In other words, corrective justice is what we now call procedural justice, though with a strong emphasis on conflict resolution. But French was not done. On the same page, only two paragraphs later, he adds that 'informal mechanisms should not be overlooked relative to corrective justice. The degree to which managers are approachable and interested in remedying injustices is undoubtedly a major factor in the degree of corrective justice within any enterprise.' This paved the way for further inquiry on the formal and informal components of procedural justice.

During the 1970s, John Thibaut was a social psychologist in the University of North Carolina – Chapel Hill. Laurens Walker was a law professor at the University of Virginia. Together, Thibaut & Walker (1975) introduced (or re-introduced, if we think of French, 1964a), the concept of procedural justice. They further argued that procedural justice moderates the ill-effects of unfair outcomes (Thibaut & Walker, 1978, but for a more contemporary review, see Brockner, 2010). That is, if a procedure is fair, then individuals can perceive just treatment, even if the outcome is unfavourable. A series of published articles successfully tested these ideas (e.g. Walker et al., 1974; Walker et al., 1979). A few years afterwards, Greenberg's mentor Gerald Leventhal (1980) would build on them directly, proposing his now

---

[1]During the mid-1990s, Greenberg related an interesting story to the first author. According to Greenberg, Dr Leventhal eventually became disenchanted with the academic life. He gave up being a professor and retrained as a clinical psychologist, working in that capacity for many years. This departure, of course, was well before procedural justice became a major research topic. Greenberg eventually contacted Leventhal. The latter was shocked to discover that he had become a pioneering thinker in organisational behaviour!

well-known procedural justice criteria. A fair process was said to be one that is applied consistently, free of bias, based on accurate information, ethical and open to appeal (Leventhal et al., 1980).

While Greenberg worked on his master's thesis under Leventhal, Robert Folger was working on his (1977) doctoral dissertation under Adams.[2] This work considered how a procedural element, voice, could improve reactions to a distributive inequity. Drawing on these experiences, Folger proposed *referent cognitions theory* (RCT) (Folger, 1986a, 1986b). As RCT has long been supplanted by later theoretical models (Folger & Cropanzano, 1998), its historical importance is not always appreciated. RCT was originally formulated as an extension of equity theory. In fact, the main title of Folger's (1986b) chapter was 'Rethinking Equity Theory'. RCT retained the importance of referent others as a point of comparison, as well as the distinction between distributive and procedural justice. However, RCT added the ideas of 'justification' (e.g. Folger, 1986b, p. 15; Folger & Bies, 1989) and 'procedural effects', both of which could moderate the impact of distributive (in)justices (Folger, 1986b, p. 152). These effects were demonstrated by Cropanzano & Folger (1989), Folger et al. (1983), Folger & Martin (1986), Folger & Konovsky (1989) and Greenberg (1987b). Together, Folger & Greenberg (1985) applied these concepts to organisational behaviour.

As we have seen, the concept of 'informal' procedures, such as justifications, had been around for some time. French (1964a, 1964b) floated the idea, while Folger (1986a, 1986b) incorporated it into RCT. However, it was Bies & Moag (1986) who articulated the concept, clearly and explicitly separating it from formal processes. Bies and Moag later demonstrated that 'interactional justice,' the dignity and respect with which a person is treated, is an important determinant of workplace fairness (Bies, 2005). This informal and interpersonal form of justice contributes to individual reactions beyond the effect of outcomes and formal processes (Bies, 2015). Bies (1987) argued that social accounts (i.e. explanations for events) can restore a sense of fairness even when something negative occurs (Folger & Bies, 1989). Bies and his colleagues demonstrated these effects in a series of studies (e.g. Bies & Shapiro, 1987, 1988; Bies et al., 1988). Greenberg (1990a, 1990b) was clearly familiar with this work, and he and Bies would go on to publish together (Greenbeg & Bies, 1992).

It was within this maelstrom of ideas that Greenberg's (1990a) study appeared. Greenberg was analysing a potential inequity, a temporary pay cut, and examining whether its ill-effects on theft could be mitigated by a fair procedure. However, he and the rest of the field had not yet fully absorbed the impact of Bies's (1987) observations. That is, what Greenberg (1990a) saw as a process would be thought of today as interactional justice.

---

[2]Readers who enjoy academic history and genealogy might enjoy knowing that one of us (Cropanzano) wrote his master's thesis under Folger, one of us (Rupp) wrote her doctoral dissertation under Cropanzano and one of us (Strah) is writing her dissertation under Rupp. These works focused/focus on extensions of many of the concepts reviewed herein.

DETAILED DESCRIPTION

Greenberg (1990a) conducted a quasi-experimental examination of a tempo-rary pay cut. Research participants worked at three manufacturing plants in the American Midwest, all of which belonged to the same company. Workers at two of the facilities, Plants A and B, received a ten-week temporary 15 per cent pay cut. Employees at the third facility, Plant C, received no pay cut. They therefore acted as the control group. Workers at Plant A received what Greenberg (1990a) referred to as an 'adequate explanation' (p. 563). Specifically, in the adequate explanation condition, employees were provided a more detailed explanation of the reasons and context for the pay cut. For example, they were told that the company felt badly about the pay cut, but that it was necessary to prevent layoffs. Though Greenberg (1990a) did not mention this explicitly, his adequate explanation was strongly empathic:

> Let me just add that it really hurts me to do this, and the decision didn't come easily. We considered all possible avenues, but nothing was feasible. I think of you all as family, and it hurts me to take away what you've worked so hard for. (p. 563)

Workers at Plant B lacked any of this. They received an 'inadequate explanation' and were only told their pay would be cut by 15 per cent.

Greenberg (1990a, p. 563) tells the reader: 'On the basis of recent research (Folger & Bies, 1989; Tyler & Bies, 1990), I hypothesized that these explanations would mitigate reactions to the pay cut.' This is a wonderfully telling statement. First, notice the central influence of Bies's work on interactional justice, which was beginning to re-shape thinking about workplace fairness. Surprisingly, Greenberg (1990a) did not cite Bies and Shapiro's empirical work (Bies & Shapiro, 1987, 1988; Bies et al., 1988), which would have provided a clear justification for his predictions. However, Greenberg did cite, on p. 567, a contemporary study by Weiner and his colleagues (1987) which had very similar findings. Second, the two papers that were referenced, Folger & Bies (1989) and Tyler & Bies (1990), still considered interpersonal treatment to be a component of procedural justice. Consequently, Greenberg (1990a) understood himself to be studying an aspect of procedural justice, which might be called justification or explanation. Modern readers would conceptualise matters differently. We would now see Greenberg (1990a) as studying an aspect of interactional justice which would be called social accounts.

Greenberg (1990a) was wed to history in another respect as well. His self-report dependent measure was 'pay equity' (p. 564). It is worth reproducing the four items, as they help us to understand Greenberg's thinking.

- 'To what extent do you believe your current pay reflects your actual contributions to the job?'

- 'How fairly paid do you feel you currently are on your job?'

- 'How satisfied are you with your current overall pay level?'

- 'Relative to what you feel you should be paid, do you believe your current pay is: ___ much too low, ___ a little too low, about right, ___ a little too high, ___ much too high?'

Notice that the first two items, and probably all but the third, assess the distributive justice of pay, likely understood as equity (i.e. 'pay reflects your ... contributions'). Thus Greenberg (1990a) is measuring outcome fairness or distributive justice. He is not assessing the process by which pay is allocated (procedural justice) or the interpersonal treatment received (interactional justice). Using this measure of pay equity, of course, underscores Greenberg's (1990a) intellectual roots in equity theory, as was common at the time.

Also, on p. 564, Greenberg (1990a) describes 'The "pay basis" measure [that] was designed to provide a manipulation check.' The four items were as follows:

- 'How adequate was your employer's explanation regarding the basis of your current pay?'

- 'How familiar are you with the way your employer determines your pay?'

- 'How thoroughly did your employer communicate the basis for your current pay to you?'

- 'How much concern did your employer show about your feelings when communicating your pay?'

Apart from the second item, which assesses familiarity, the other three items refer directly to the explanation. Was it adequate? Was it thorough? Did it show concern? In modern language, we would see these items as reflecting interactional justice (Bies, 2005, 2015). In any event, the manipulation check was successful.

Data were collected over 30 weeks with 15 bi-weekly assessments. The first ten weeks occurred before the pay cut to provide a baseline. The second ten weeks occurred during the pay cut, the critical period for Greenberg's hypotheses tests. The third ten weeks after the pay cut allowed for a return to baseline. The two dependent measures, pay equity and theft rates, were aggregated for each ten-week period. Predictions followed mostly from equity theory. Following the pay cut at the beginning of the second ten-week period, employees were expected to report lower pay equity and exhibit more theft from the company. This was expected to continue until their original pay was restored, which would occur during the final ten weeks of the study. However, following from research on justifications, this effect was expected to be mitigated when an adequate explanation was provided.

The findings were clear and illuminating. In both the control group and the adequate explanation group, perceptions of pay equity did not significantly differ across the three time points. However, for employees in the inadequate explanation condition, perceptions of distributive justice significantly decreased when pay was reduced, returning to pre-cut levels once the normal pay was reinstated. Notably, for employees assigned to the inadequate explanation condition, theft rates increased significantly once pay was cut, and returned to normal after the normal pay-rate resumed. While theft rates also increased within the adequate explanation group (and were significantly higher than the control group during this time), theft rates for employees in this condition were significantly less than the inadequate explanation group. But there was more. Serendipitously, Greenberg (1990a) observed considerable turnover during his 30-week study. Post hoc analyses found that Plant B, the group that had a pay cut coupled with an inadequate explanation, showed the highest turnover.

IMPACT OF THE CLASSIC STUDY

In some respects, Greenberg (1990a) was a replication. The core conceptual ideas had been examined in earlier publications and the article was not intended as a piece of original theory. Greenberg (1990a, p. 567) observed this:

> In this case, several lines of analogous research converge with my claim that adequate explanations enhanced the acceptance of undesired outcomes. For example, Folger and his associates (e.g. Folger & Martin, 1986; Folger, Rosenfield, & Robinson, 1983) measured laboratory subjects' feelings of discontent in reaction to procedural changes that created unfavorable conditions for them. Consistent with referent cognitions theory (Folger, 1986[a]), Folger and his colleagues found that these feelings of discontent were reduced only when the need to make procedural changes was adequately explained.

Around the same time, Brockner and colleagues (1990) demonstrated similar effects among layoff survivors. However, Greenberg (1990a) presented a clear and compelling empirical demonstration of some important ideas, and the paper had a greater impact than other articles that had been published previously. According to Google Scholar, the article has been cited more than 2,700 times (or about 850 on Web of Science). By comparison, Bies and Shapiro (1987) has been cited about 1,300 times, Bies & Shapiro (1988) has about 980 citations, Cropanzano & Folger (1989) about 590, and Folger & Martin (1986) a little over 410 times. Greenberg (1990a) was an important article because it helped to move justice research from a small area, studied by a few dozen devotees, into the mainstream of organisational psychology. It is worth considering why this was so.

Most obviously, Greenberg (1990a) offered support for an extended version of the popular and well-known equity theory. The Discussion section begins by addressing this issue (p. 656): 'The data support the hypothesis derived from equity theory (Adams, 1965) that workers experiencing underpayment inequity would attempt to redress that inequity by raising their inputs – in the present case, by pilfering from their employer' (and, implicitly, by *not* pilfering once the pay cuts went away). However, the hold that equity theory had on our field was beginning to slip away. Greenberg (1990a) was thinking in equity terms, with an informal procedural variable – explanations or justifications – as a moderator. Even so, he also recognised that the field was changing its priorities. On p. 566, Greenberg adds: 'The present data also reveal a critical moderator of the tendency to pilfer to restore equity with one's employer – namely, the use of an adequate explanation for the pay cut.'

Greenberg (1990a) also benefitted from a strong quasi-experimental design, which strengthened causal inferences and did so in a real-world setting that boosted external validity. By taking a quasi-experimental approach, Greenberg was able to simultaneously minimise alternative explanations for the theft outcomes while observing the behaviour and attitudes of employees in the real world. This study design allowed a high level of confidence in the field's understanding of employee theft as a response to injustice and added to the accumulating evidence that organisational justice is an important driver of a wide range of employee attitudes and behaviours. Indeed, most of Greenberg's (1990a) findings have been replicated numerous times, and the results can be found in several large-scale meta-analyses. Distributive, procedural and interactional justice all serve as strong predictors of organisational outcomes (Cohen-Charash & Spector, 2001; Colquitt et al., 2001; Colquitt et al., 2013; Rupp et al., 2014).

KEY REPLICATIONS AND GENERALISATIONS

Even though his eye was mostly on equity, Greenberg (1990a) helped to establish that there were at least two kinds of justice, distributive and procedural, and both are important. The process by outcome interaction had been of interest to scholars in the years just prior to the publication of Greenberg (1990a). In fact, it had been explicitly predicted and tested by referent cognitions theory (Folger, 1986a, 1986b). In describing this phenomenon, we begin with the obvious fact that people do not like receiving unfavourable outcomes. Somewhat counterintuitively, at least to researchers at the time, fair procedures mitigate these ill-effects. Poor outcomes may become more acceptable when allocated through an appropriate process. For example, an experiment by Folger & Martin (1986, p. 531) discovered that 'high-justification procedures are those sufficiently appropriate to inhibit resentment regardless of the outcomes they produce.' In a sidenote from history, Cropanzano & Folger (1989) also replicated this interaction. This study was Cropanzano's master's thesis, conducted under the direction of Robert Folger. Thinking about the process by outcome interaction would be developed at greater length by Brockner (2010) and Brockner & Wiesenfeld (1996). It was (and is) viewed as a topic of practical importance. Poor outcomes are somewhat inevitable in work life. However, fair procedures may be able to blunt the negative reactions that might otherwise occur (Cropanzano & Konovsky, 1995).

This study also provided important evidence for interactional justice, though Greenberg (1990a) might not have been aware of it. Greenberg (1990a) found that the provision of adequate (i.e. honest and thorough) explanations can mitigate the effect of other unjust experiences. However, it is not clear that he fully recognised this contribution. Nowhere does Greenberg (1990a) avail himself of the term 'interactional'. Rather, this word only appears in the reference list when he is citing the work of others. Nor does he use the words 'account', which was associated with Bies (1987) or 'justification', from Folger et al. (1983). He does mention 'procedural justice' (p. 561), but mostly contents himself to refer to the moderator as an 'explanation' (e.g. on p. 563). This theoretical parsimony would seem to be a case of outdated terminology. In its operational specifics, Greenberg's (1990a) manipulation shares much in common with those of Bies and Shapiro (1987, 1988), who observed the same basic effects. Indeed, the use of explanations to mitigate negative reactions had already been described as inter-actional justice by Bies (1987).

When we concede that Greenberg's 'explanations' and 'social accounts' are a type of interactional justice, then we can clearly see an additional contribution. If Greenberg (1990a) examined interactional justice and interactions moderated the effect of equity, then interactional justice not only exists, but it also exhibits the same 2 × 2 interaction with distributive justice as procedural justice does. As alluded to above, these effects had already been found by Bies and Shapiro (1987, 1988) and a bit later were replicated by Brockner et al. (1990). In other words, both formal procedural justice and also interactional justice can moderate the negative emotions that come from unfortunate outcomes (Brockner & Wiesenfeld, 1996). In this way, the process-by-outcome interaction also remains important (Brockner, 2010). Beyond this, the addition of interactional justice, separated as it was from procedural, allowed the idea to grow. Later, Skarlicki & Folger (1997) would look at the three types of justice together. They observed that a three-way interaction – including distributive, procedural and interactional justice – predicted a compilation of retaliatory workplace behaviours. That is, the relationship between distributive and retaliatory behaviour was mitigated by high levels of both procedural justice and also interactional justice. This three-way interaction was subsequently replicated by Cropanzano and colleagues (2005).

BEYOND GREENBERG (1990a): THEORETICAL DEVELOPMENTS

Greenberg (1990a) can best be seen as a historical artifact; it was the product of a bygone time. Justice research proceeded, using Greenberg (1990a) as a stepping-stone. As we mentioned above, Greenberg (1990a) helped advance organisational justice theory by demonstrating the importance of interpersonal interactions in forming employees' perceptions of justice. In this regard, research on explanations continued, though researchers returned to Bies's (1987) earlier language, referring to these as social accounts (e.g. Konovsky & Folger, 1991), which were viewed as components of interactional justice (Sitkin & Bies, 1993). Interactional justice was then viewed as separate from procedural justice (Bies, 2005, 2015).

While Greenberg might have been hesitant to embrace the multiple types of justice, he soon moved in the direction of other scholars. A few years after Green-berg (1990a), Greenberg (1993a)[3] returned for a closer look at the structure of

---

[3]As another historical note, the Greenberg (1993a) chapter was published in a book edited by the first author.

fairness. He suggested that interactional justice should not only be distinguished from procedural, but it should also be further subdivided into two still smaller parts. The first of these, interpersonal justice, most closely resembled Bies & Moag (1986). By this reckoning, interpersonal justice concerns treating people with dignity and respect. The second, informational justice, was closest to Bies (1987). Informational justice emphasises open and honest communication, especially sharing information when things go awry. These messages should be timely and honest. Individuals should understand why things occurred, what sort of process was used, and the like. From this vantage point, the explanation provided to Greenberg's (1990a) research participants would now be viewed as a type of informational justice. This might be taken as an oblique reference to the staying power of that study, as his 'critical moderator' (p. 566) has now been placed into three conceptual categories – procedural, interactional and informational justice. The resulting four-factor model – distributive, procedural, interpersonal and informational justice – was later tested by Greenberg (1993b) and, more famously, by Colquitt (2001). Colquitt et al. (2001) would also use this model to organise his meta-analytic review of the literature (Colquitt et al., 2001). The four-factor model remains popular, though the earlier three dimensions are also still employed (Colquitt & Rodell, 2015).

Greenberg (2002) continued to study employee theft. He examined 270 underpaid workers. They were given the opportunity to steal from a jar of pennies. If this money was alleged to have come from individual managers, then participants tended not to steal. If payment came from the organisation as a whole, then they were more likely to take extra pennies. However, even this theft was mitigated if employees had high moral development and worked at a firm with an ethics programme. While it is generally agreed that injustice leads to theft (Greenberg & Scott, 1996), research suggests that other considerations are also important. For example, Shapiro et al. (1995) report that, in addition to procedural justice, some employees do not view stealing as wrong. These individuals, who do not see theft as especially deviant, are also more likely to steal.

Beyond these specific contributions, Greenberg (1990a) has aided in advancing general theoretical perspectives within the organisational justice literature. Prior to Greenberg (1990a), explanations of organisational justice tended to be 'cold', emphasising cognition rather than emotion. While not discounting this view, Greenberg (1990a, pp. 565–6) suggested that his findings could be interpreted in either 'hot', affective or 'cold' calculative terms. In this way, he helped organisational justice research join the affective revolution (Barsade et al., 2003). In subsequent years, Greenberg (2006) and others (e.g. Tepper, 2001; Weiss et al., 1999) continued to develop these ideas. Justice researchers have emphasised the importance of both cognition and emotion, and now study the circumstances under which each predominates (Cropanzano et al., 2020). For example, Scott et al. (2014) studied the reasons why managers behave fairly toward others. They found that 'cold' or cognitive motives were especially important for predicting distributive justice whereas 'hot' or affective motives were especially important for predicting interpersonal (or interactional) justice.

Greenberg (1990a) would have regretted one implication of his work. Some years after its publication, Folger (1998) began formulating his deontic model of justice. 'Deonance' refers to moral duty. Justice, in other words, is a good thing for its own sake and people have a motive to uphold it. Folger's (2001) deontic perspective asserts that employees care about justice because it constitutes an ethical norm that individuals believe should not be violated. For Folger, people care about fairness because being just is a moral good. In what would become an irony, Folger and his colleagues used Greenberg's (2002) theft research, as well as work on revenge (Bies & Tripp, 1996, 2001, 2002; Bies et al., 1997), to buttress their new theory (see Folger et al., 2005). Deontic justice has since obtained substantial research support (e.g. Rupp & Bell, 2010; Folger & Skarlicki, 2005; Turillo et al., 2002), but it was originally quite controversial. As it happens, Greenberg was sharply critical of deontic justice, believing that justice perceptions reduced to a type of enlightened self-interest, whereby employees wanted fairness because that would maximise the value of their outcomes over the long run (Colquitt & Greenberg, 2001; Gillespie & Greenberg, 2005). In a strange twist of fate, Greenberg may have neglected the most important implication of his own research, the idea that justice matters for its own sake. This demonstrates the Pandora-like quality of great scholarship. Once the box is open and the findings are free, we can never anticipate where they will lead.

CONCLUSION

Overall, Greenberg (1990a) constituted an important contribution to the field of organisational justice. It pushed us to re-think the structure of justice, adding the dimensions of procedural and, eventually, interactional justice. Greenberg (1990a) further recognised that these different types of justice interact, impacting employee behaviours and work attitudes. Beyond these findings, which contributed enough in their own right, Greenberg (1990a) also encouraged interest in workplace emotion and deontic justice and highlighted a number of important practical implications.

IMPLICATIONS FOR PRACTITIONERS

In the very early 1990s, one of us (Cropanzano), then an assistant professor, received a phone call from Jerry Greenberg. Greenberg was interested in discussing a then-recent publication, Konovsky & Cropanzano (1991), that had considered procedural justice effects in the context of employee drug testing. During that call, Greenberg compellingly articulated his vision for organisational justice research. In his view, justice research should inform real-world business needs. In his wonderfully titled article – 'Everybody Talks About Organizational Justice, But Nobody Does Anything About It' – Greenberg (2009, pp. 181–2) – challenged scholars to put organisational justice to work: 'Currently, we focus almost exclusively on generating knowledge about justice in organizations but do little in the way of applying it.'

He went on to add that: 'This is unfortunate because our understanding of organizational justice has advanced to the point where it now is possible to identify specific ways in which justice can be promoted.' Greenberg (1990a) was a case in point. The study had two measures, theft and turnover, that directly pertained to business success. Likewise, Greenberg (1993b) produced experimental evidence that fair interpersonal treatment could mitigate the effect of distributive injustice and theft.

These are important findings for business leaders. Their principal implication is that adequately explaining to employees why these steps had to be taken could prevent negative outcomes. Everyone recognises that bad things will sometimes happen, despite care and good intentions. Greenberg (1990a) found that his adequate explanation necessitated a non-trivial amount of time, it took about one hour, in contrast to the roughly 15-minute inadequate explanation (p. 563). However, taking the time paid dividends in terms of reduced theft and turnover. Practically speaking, these results demonstrate that justice can be relatively easy to implement and is even trainable.

Fortunately, research has supported the efficacy of training. In two studies, Skarlicki & Latham (1996, 1997) found that a short supervisory training on the tenets of procedural and interactional justice boosted employee fairness perceptions, and these gains persisted for some weeks. Moreover, the heightened fairness, in turn, increased employee citizenship behaviours toward the organisation. Rupp and colleagues (2006) discussed how simulation exercises like those used in assessment centres can be used as a component of supervisory distributive, procedural and interactional justice training. Since the dimensions of justice are typically defined as the adherence to specific rules or criteria (e.g. providing voice, consistent treatment, etc.), they can easily be treated as behavioural competencies within a developmental assessment programme. Rupp and colleagues provided a step-by-step guide for developing and validating such a programme, which includes training on the justice dimensions, simulation exercises allowing managers to engage in fair treatment, followed by detailed feedback and development planning.

The findings of Greenberg (1990a), along with the literature that has amassed since, can be leveraged to persuade upper management of the utility of training and other initiatives aimed at fostering perceptions of organisational justice. Not only can 'bottom-line' arguments be made about the cost of perceived injustice in terms of individual-level outcomes like theft, sabotage, counterproductive behaviours, turnover and the like (see Colquitt et al., 2013; Rupp et al., 2014), but a business case can be made for the importance of justice climate (e.g. collective perceptions of justice) in impacting organisationally relevant outcomes as well. For example, organisations with a strong justice climate have more effective teams, higher performance and more helpful organisational citizenship behaviours (see Li et al., 2015 for a review).

Finally, it is worth mentioning one last implication of Greenberg's (1990a) work, one that is widely recognised but has languished without extensive follow-up. In an article published at about the same time as his quasi-experiment, Greenberg (1990c) distinguished between taking steps that appear to be fair, on the one hand, and actually behaving fairly, on the other. While Greenberg (1990c) hoped that managerial leaders would behave ethically, he recognised that individuals could and do engage in self-serving impression management. That might provide, for example, insincere explanations to cover their misconduct. This dark side to justice, or at least to a sort of pseudo-justice, follows from his work. Here again, Greenberg was ahead of his time, as he understood the difference between being just and misleading stakeholders into believing that they were treated fairly when they were not. Later research found that organisations engage in socially responsible behaviour in order to cultivate a more favourable image (Hooghiemstra, 2000). Ethics statements sometimes serve similar impression management goals (Bazerman & Tenbrunsel, 2011).

Practitioners and scholars should be mindful of these unintended outcomes. Greenberg (1990c) suspected that dishonesty about justice would eventually be discovered, but this leaves open the question as to how this unveiling might take place. In this regard, we might learn one final lesson from Greenberg (1990a). In this study and throughout his career, Greenberg focused his research efforts on concrete situations when a demonstrable workplace event, such as a pay cut or an exculpatory explanation, was related to an objectively measured employee behaviour, such as theft. His emphasis on real-world events encourages us to look at what organisations actually do, not only what they say they do. Furthermore, it inspires us to concretely understand the economic and social costs of unjust behaviour. This may prove to be Dr Greenberg's most lasting legacy, an understanding of how to be fair and a recognition of the shared costs when organisations are not.

DISCUSSION QUESTIONS

1. What are the implications of Greenberg (1990a) for the nature of different types of organisational justice?

2. What research questions has Greenberg (1990a) answered and what research questions does it inspire for you?

3. What is the 'dark side' to Greenberg's (1990a) findings? How could justice be misused?

4. How can organisations promote more fairness? What are the advantages if they do so?

5. How was Greenberg 'a man of his time'? How did the post-war research milieu influence his thinking?

6. Do you think that it all comes down to self-interest? Or is justice important for its own sake?

FURTHER READINGS

Brockner, J. (2010). *A Contemporary Look at Organizational Justice: Multiplying Insult Times Injury*. Routledge.

Colquitt, J. A. & Rodell, J. B. (2015). Measuring justice and fairness. In R. S. Cropanzano & M. L. Ambrose (eds), *The Oxford Handbook of Justice in the Workplace*. Oxford University Press, pp. 187–202. https://doi.org/10.1093/oxfordhb/978019998 1410.013.8

Colquitt, J. A., Scott, B. A., Rodell, J. B., Long, D. M., Zapata, C. P., Conlon, D. E. & Wesson, M. J. (2013). Justice at the millennium, a decade later: A meta-analytic test of social exchange and affect-based perspectives. *Journal of Applied Psychology*, 98, 199–236. https://doi.org/10.1037/a0031757

Cropanzano, R. & Ambrose, M. A. (2015) (eds). *The Oxford Handbook of Justice in the Workplace*. Oxford University Press.

Cropanzano, R., Byrne, Z. S., Bobocel, D. R. & Rupp, D. R. (2001). Moral virtues, fairness heuristics, social entities, and other denizens of organizational justice. *Journal of Vocational Behavior*, 58, 164–209. https://doi.org/10.1006/jvbe.2001.1791

Cropanzano, R., Rupp, D. E., Mohler, C. J. & Schminke, M. (2001). Three roads to organizational justice. In J. Ferris (ed.), *Research in Personnel and Human Resources Management*, Vol. 20. JAI Press, pp. 1–113.

Folger, R. & Cropanzano, R. (1998). *Organizational Justice and Human Resource Management*. Sage.

Folger, R. & Salvador, R. (2008). Is management theory too 'self-ish'? *Journal of Management*, 34, 1127–51. https://doi.org/10.1177/0149206308324321

Rupp, D. E., Shao, R., Jones, K. S. & Liao, H. (2014). The utility of a multifoci approach to the study of organizational justice: A meta-analytic investigation into the consideration of normative rules, moral accountability, bandwidth-fidelity, and social exchange. *Organizational Behavior and Human Decision Processes*, 123, 159–85. https://doi.org/10.1016/j.obhdp.2013.10.011

Rupp, D. E., Shapiro, D. L., Folger, R., Skarlicki, D. S. & Shao, R. (2017). A critical analysis of the conceptualization and measurement of organizational justice: Is it time for reassessment? *Academy of Management Annals*, 11, 915–59. https://doi.org/10.5465/annals.2014.0051

REFERENCES

Adams, J. S. (1963). Toward an understanding of inequity. *Journal of Abnormal and Social Psychology*, 67, 422–36. https://doi.org/10.1037/h0040968

Adams, J. S. (1965). Inequity in social exchange. In L. Berkowitz (ed.), *Advances in Experimental Social Psychology*, Vol. 2. Academic Press, pp. 267–99. https://doi.org/10.1016/S0065-2601(08)60108-2

Barsade, S., Brief, A. P. & Spataro, S. E. (2003). The affective revolution in organizational behavior: The emergence of a paradigm. In J. Greenberg (ed.), *Organizational Behavior: The State of the Science*. Laurence Erlbaum Associates, pp. 3–50.

Bazerman, M. & Tenbrunsel, A. (2011). *Blind Spots: Why We Fail to Do What's Right and What to Do About It*. Princeton University Press.

Bies, R. J. (2005). Are procedural justice and interactional justice conceptually distinct? In J. Greenberg & J. A. Colquitt (eds), *Handbook of Organizational Justice*. Lawrence Erlbaum Associates, pp. 85–112.

Bies, R. J. (2015). Interactional justice: Looking backward, looking forward. In R. S. Cropanzano & M. L. Ambrose (eds), *Oxford Handbook of Justice in the Workplace*. Oxford University Press, pp. 89–107. https://doi.org/10.1093/oxfordhb/978019998 1410.013.4

Bies, R. J. & Moag, J. S. (1986). Interactional justice: Communication criteria of fairness. In R. J. Lewicki, B. H. Sheppard & M. H. Bazerman (eds), *Research on Negotiations in Organizations*, Vol. 1. JAI Press, pp. 43–55.

Bies, R. J. & Shapiro, D. L. (1987). Interactional fairness judgements: The influence of causal accounts. *Social Justice Research*, 1, 199–218. https://doi.org/10.1007/BF01048016

Bies, R. J. & Shapiro, D. L. (1988). Voice and justification: Their influence on procedural fairness judgments. *Academy of Management Journal*, 31, 676–85. https://doi.org/10.5465/256465

Bies, R. J. & Tripp, T. M. (1996). Beyond distrust: 'Getting even' and the need for revenge. In R. M. Kramer & T. Tyler (eds), *Trust in Organizations*. Sage, pp. 246–60.

Bies, R. J. & Tripp, T. M. (2001). A passion for justice: The rationality and morality of revenge. In R. Cropanzano (ed.), *Justice in the Workplace*. Lawrence Erlbaum, pp. 197–208.

Bies, R. J. & Tripp, T. M. (2002). 'Hot flashes, open wounds': Injustice and the tyranny of its emotions. In S. W. Gilliland, D. D. Steiner & D. P. Skarlicki (eds), *Emerging Perspectives on Managing Organizational Justice*. Information Age, pp. 203–21.

Bies, R. J., Martin, C. L. & Brockner, J. (1993). Just laid off, but still a 'good citizen?' Only if the process is fair. *Employee Responsibilities and Rights Journal*, 6, 227–38. https://doi.org/10.1007/BF01419446

Bies, R. J., Shapiro, D. & Cummings, L. L. (1988). Causal accounts and managing organizational conflict: Is it enough to say it's not my fault? *Communication Research*, 15, 381–99. https://doi.org/10.1177/009365088015004003

Bies, R. J., Tripp, T. M. & Kramer, R. M. (1997). At the breaking point: Cognitive and social dynamics of revenge in organizations. In R. A. Giacalone & J. Greenberg (eds), *Antisocial Behavior in Organizations*. Sage, pp. 18–36.

Brockner, J. (2010). *A Contemporary Look at Organizational Justice: Multiplying Insult Times Injury*. Routledge.

Brockner, J. & Wiesenfeld, B. M. (1996). An integrative framework for explaining reactions to decisions: Interactive effects of outcomes and procedures. *Psychological Bulletin*, 120, 189–208. https://doi.org/10.1037/0033-2909.120.2.189

Brockner, J., DeWitt, R., Grover, S. & Reed, T. (1990). When it is especially important to explain why: Factors affecting the relationship between managers' explanations of a layoff and survivors' reactions to the layoff. *Journal of Experimental Social Psychology*, 26, 389–407. https://doi.org/10.1016/0022-1031(90)90065-T

Cohen-Charash, Y. & Spector, P. E. (2001). The role of justice in organizations: A meta-analysis. *Organizational Behavior and Human Decision Processes*, 86, 278–321. https://doi.org/10.1006/obhd.2001.2958

Colquitt, J. A. (2001). On the dimensionality of organizational justice: A construct validation of a measure. *Journal of Applied Psychology*, 86, 386–400. https://doi.org/10.1037/0021-9010.86.3.386

Colquitt, J. A. & Greenberg, J. (2001). Doing justice to organizational justice: Forming and applying fairness judgments. In S. Gilliland, D. Steiner & D. Skarlicki (eds), *Theoretical and Cultural Perspectives on Organizational Justice*. JAI Press, pp. 217–42.

Colquitt, J. A. & Rodell, J. B. (2015). Measuring justice and fairness. In R. S. Cropanzano & M. L. Ambrose (eds), *Oxford Handbook of Justice in the Workplace*. Oxford University Press, pp. 187–202. https://doi.org/10.1093/oxfordhb/9780199981410.013.8

Colquitt, J. A., Conlon, D. E., Wesson, M. J., Porter, C. O. L. H. & Ng, K. Y. (2001). Justice at the millennium: A meta-analytic review of 25 years of organizational justice research. *Journal of Applied Psychology*, 86, 425–45. https://doi.org/10.1037/0021-9010.86.3.425

Colquitt, J. A., Scott, B. A., Rodell, J. B., Long, D. M., Zapata, C. P., Conlon, D. E. & Wesson, M. J. (2013). Justice at the millennium, a decade later: A meta-analytic test of social exchange and affect-based perspectives. *Journal of Applied Psychology*, 98, 199–236. https://doi.org/10.1037/a0031757

Cropanzano, R. & Folger, R. (1989). Referent cognitions and task decision autonomy: Beyond equity theory. *Journal of Applied Psychology*, 74, 293–99. https://doi.org/10.1037/0021-9010.74.2.293

Cropanzano, R. & Konovsky, M. A. (1995). Resolving the justice dilemma by improving the outcomes: The case of employee drug screening. *Journal of Business and Psychology*, 10, 221–44.

Cropanzano, R., Ambrose, M. A. & Van Waggoner, H. P. (2020). Organizational justice and workplace emotion. In E. A. Lind (ed.), *Social Psychology and Justice*. Routledge, pp. 243–83.

Cropanzano, R., Slaughter, J. E. & Bachiochi, P. D. (2005). Organizational justice and Black applicants' reactions to affirmative action. *Journal of Applied Psychology*, 90, 1168–84. https://doi.org/10.1037/0021-9010.90.6.1168

Folger, R. (1977). Distributive and procedural justice: Combined impact of 'voice' and improvement on experienced inequity. *Journal of Personality and Social Psychology*, 35, 108–19. https://doi.org/10.1037/0022-3514.35.2.108

Folger, R. (1986a). A referent cognitions theory of relative deprivation. In J. M. Olson, C. P. Herman & M. P. Zanna (eds), *Relative Deprivation and Social Comparisons: The Ontario Symposium*, Vol. 4. Erlbaum, pp. 33–55.

Folger, R. (1986b). Rethinking equity theory: A referent cognitions model. In H. W. Bierhoff, R. L. Cohen & J. Greenberg (eds), *Justice in Social Relations*. Plenum, pp. 145–64.

Folger, R. (1998). Fairness as a moral virtue. In M. Schminke (ed.), *Managerial Ethics: Morally Managing People and Processes*. Lawrence Erlbaum Associates, pp. 13–14.

Folger, R. (2001). Fairness as deonance. In S. W. Gilliland, D. D. Steiner & D. P. Skarlicki (eds), *Research in Social Issues in Management*. Information Age, pp. 3–31.

Folger, R. & Bies, R. J. (1989). Managerial responsibilities and procedural justice. *Employee Responsibilities and Rights Journal*, 2, 79–90. https://doi.org/10.1007/BF01384939

Folger, R. & Cropanzano, R. (1998). *Organizational Justice and Human Resource Management*. Sage.

Folger, R. & Greenberg, J. (1985). Procedural justice: An interpretive analysis of personnel systems. In K. M. Rowland & G. R. Ferris (eds), *Research in Personnel and Human Resource Management*, Vol. 3. JAI Press, pp. 141–83.

Folger, R. & Konovsky, M. A. (1989). Effects of procedural and distributive justice of reactions to pay raise decisions. *Academy of Management Journal*, 32, 115–30. https://doi.org/10.5465/256422

Folger, R. & Martin, C. (1986). Relative deprivation and referent cognitions: Distributive and procedural justice effects. *Journal Experimental Social Psychology*, 22(6), 531–46. https://doi.org/10.1016/0022-1031(86)90049-1

Folger, R. & Skarlicki, D. P. (2005). Beyond counterproductive work behavior: Moral emotions and deontic retaliation versus reconciliation. In S. Fox & P. E. Spector (eds), *Counterproductive Work Behavior: Investigations of Actors and Targets*. American Psychological Association, pp. 83–105. https://doi.org/10.1037/10893-004

Folger, R., Cropanzano, R. & Goldman, B. (2005). Justice, accountability, and moral sentiment: The deontic response to 'foul play' at work. In J. Greenberg & J. Colquitt (eds), *Handbook of Organizational Justice*. Lawrence Erlbaum Associates, pp. 215–45.

Folger, R., Rosenfield, D. D. & Robinson, T. (1983). Relative deprivation and procedural justifications. *Journal of Personality and Social Psychology*, 45(2), 268–73. https://doi.org/10.1037/0022-3514.45.2.268

French, W. (1964a). *The Personnel Management Process: Human Resources Administration*. Houghton Mifflin.

French, W. (December, 1964b). *The nature and problems of organizational justice*. Speech delivered at the 24th Annual Meetings of the Academy of Management. Chicago, IL. https://doi.org/10.5465/ambpp.1964.5067832

Gillespie, J. Z. & Greenberg, J. (2005). Are the goals of organizational justice self-interested? In J. Greenberg & J. A. Colquitt (eds), *Handbook of Organizational Justice*. Lawrence Erlbaum, pp. 179–213.

Greenberg, J. (1982). Approaching equity and avoiding inequity in groups and organizations. In J. Greenberg & R. L. Cohen (eds), *Equity and Justice in Social Behavior*. Academic Press, pp. 389–435.

Greenberg, J. (1987a). A taxonomy of organizational justice theories. *Academy of Management Review*, 12, 9–22. https://doi.org/10.5465/amr.1987.4306437

Greenberg, J. (1987b). Reactions to procedural injustice in payment distributions: Do the means justify the ends? *Journal of Applied Psychology*, 72, 55–61. https://doi.org/10.1037/0021-9010.72.1.55

Greenberg, J. (1988). Equity and workplace status: A field experiment. *Journal of Applied Psychology*, 73, 606–13. https://doi.org/10.1037/0021-9010.73.4.606

Greenberg, J. (1990a). Employee theft as a reaction to underpayment inequity: The hidden costs of pay cuts. *Journal of Applied Psychology*, 75, 561–8. https://doi.org/10.1037/0021-9010.75.5.561

Greenberg, J. (1990b). Organizational justice: Yesterday, today, and tomorrow. *Journal of Management*, 16, 399–432. https://doi.org/10.1177/014920639001600208

Greenberg, J. (1990c). Looking fair vs. being fair: Managing impressions of organizational justice. In B. M. Staw & L. L. Cummings (eds), *Research in Organizational Behavior*, Vol. 12. JAI Press, pp. 111–157.

Greenberg, J. (1993a). The social side of fairness: Interpersonal and informational classes of organizational justice. In R. Cropanzano (ed.), *Justice in the Workplace: Approaching Fairness in Human Resource Management*. Lawrence Erlbaum Associates, pp. 79–103.

Greenberg, J. (1993b). Stealing in the name of justice: Informational and interpersonal moderators of theft reactions to underpayment inequity. *Organizational Behavior and Human Decision Processes*, 54, 81–103. https://doi.org/10.1006/obhd.1993.1004

Greenberg, J. (2002). Who stole the money, and when? Individual and situational determinants of employee theft? *Organizational Behavior and Human Decision Processes*, 89, 985–1003. https://doi.org/10.1016/S0749-5978(02)00039-0

Greenberg, J. (2006). Losing sleep over organizational injustice: Attenuating insomniac reactions to underpayment inequity with supervisory training in interactional justice. *Journal of Applied Psychology*, 91, 58–69. https://doi.org/10.1037/0021-9010.91.1.58

Greenberg, J. (2009). Everybody talks about organizational justice, but nobody does anything about it. *Industrial and Organizational Psychology*, 2(2), 181–95. doi:10.1111/j.1754-9434.2009.01131.x

Greenberg, J. & Bies, R. J. (1992). Establishing the role of empirical studies of organizational justice in philosophical inquiries into business ethics. *Journal of Business Ethics*, 11, 433–44. https://www.jstor.org/stable/25072292

Greenberg, J. & Leventhal, G. S. (1976). Equity and the use of overreward to motivate performance. *Journal of Personality and Social Psychology*, 34, 179–90. doi:10.1037/0022-3514.34.2.179

Greenberg, J. & Scott, K. S. (1996). Why do workers bite the hands that feed them? Employee theft as a social exchange process. In B. M. Staw & L. L. Cummings (eds), *Research in Organizational Behavior: An Annual Series of Analytical Essays and Critical Review*, Vol. 18. Elsevier Science/JAI Press, pp. 111–56.

Homans, G. C. (1953). Status among clerical workers. *Human Organization*, 12, 5–10. https://www.jstor.org/stable/44124007

Homans, G. C. (1958). Social behavior as exchange. *American Journal of Sociology*, 63, 579–606. https://doi.org/10.1086/222355

Homans, G. C. (1961). *Social Behavior: Its Elementary Forms*. Harcourt Brace Jovanovich.

Hooghiemstra, R. (2000). Corporate communication and impression management – New perspectives why companies engage in corporate social reporting. *Journal of Business Ethics*, 27, 55–68. https://doi.org/10.1023/A:1006400707757

Konovsky, M. A. & Cropanzano, R. (1991). The perceived fairness of employee drug testing as a predictor of employee attitudes and job performance. *Journal of Applied Psychology*, 76, 698–707. doi: 0021-9010/91

Konovsky, M. A. & Folger, R. (1991). The effects of procedures, social accounts, and benefits level on victims' layoff reactions. *Journal of Applied Social Psychology*, 21(8), 630–50. https://doi.org/10.1111/j.1559-1816.1991.tb00540.x

Leventhal, G. S. (1980). What should be done with equity theory? New approaches to the study of fairness in social relationships. In K. S. Gergen, M. S. Greenberg & R. H. Willis (eds), *Social Exchange: Advances in Theory and Research*. Plenum Press, pp. 27–55.

Leventhal, G. S., Karuza, J. & Fry, W. R. (1980). Beyond fairness: A theory of allocation preferences. In G. Mikula (ed.), *Justice and Social Interaction*. Springer-Verlag, 167–218.

Li, A., Cropanzano, R. & Molina, A. (2015). Fairness at the unit level: Justice climate, justice climate strength, and peer justice. *Oxford Handbook of Justice in the Workplace*. Oxford University Press, pp. 137–64.

Rupp, D. E. & Bell, C. M. (2010). Extending the deontic model of justice: Moral self-regulation in third-party responses to injustice. *Business Ethics Quarterly*, 20, 89–102. doi:10.5840/beq20102017

Rupp, D. E., Baldwin, A. M. & Bashshur, M. R. (2006). Using developmental assessment centers to foster workplace fairness. *Psychologist-Manager Journal*, 9, 145–70. https://doi.org/10.1207/s15503461tpmj0902_6

Rupp, D. E., Shao, R., Jones, K. S. & Liao, H. (2014). The utility of a multifoci approach to the study of organizational justice: A meta-analytic investigation into the consideration of normative rules, moral accountability, bandwidth-fidelity, and social exchange. *Organizational Behavior and Human Decision Processes*, 123, 159–85. https://doi.org/10.1016/j.obhdp.2013.10.011

Scott, B. A., Garza, A. S., Conlon, D. E. & Kim, Y. J. (2014). Why do managers act fairly in the first place? A daily investigation of 'hot' and 'cold' motives and discretion. *Academy of Management Journal*, 57, 1571–91. https://doi.org/10.5465/amj.2012.0644

Shapiro, D. L., Trevino, L. K. & Victor, B. (1995). Correlates of employee theft: A multi-dimensional justice perspective. *International Journal of Conflict Management*, 6, 404–14. https://doi.org/10.1108/eb022772

Sitkin, S. B. & Bies, R. J. (1993). Social accounts in conflict situations: Using explanations to manage conflict. *Human Relations*, 46, 349–70. https://doi.org/10.1177/001872679304600303

Skarlicki, D. P. & Folger, R. (1997). Retaliation in the workplace: The roles of distributive, procedural, and interactional justice. *Journal of Applied Psychology*, 82, 434–43. https://doi.org/10.1037/0021-9010.82.3.434

Skarlicki, D. P. & Latham, G. P. (1996). Increasing citizenship behavior within a labor union: A test of organizational justice theory. *Journal of Applied Psychology*, 81, 161–9. https://doi.org/10.1037/0021-9010.81.2.161

Skarlicki, D. P. & Latham, G. P. (1997). Leadership training in organizational justice to increase citizenship behavior within a labor union. *Personnel Psychology*, 50, 617–33. https://doi.org/10.1111/j.1744-6570.1997.tb00707.x

Tepper, B. J. (2001). Health consequences of organizational injustice: Test of main and interactive effects. *Organizational Behavior and Human Decision Processes*, 86, 197–215. https://doi.org/10.1006/obhd.2001.2951

Thibaut, J. & Walker, L. (1975). *Procedural Justice: Psychological Analysis*. Lawrence Erlbaum.

Thibaut, J. & Walker, L. (1978). A theory of procedure. *California Law Review*, 66, 541–66.

Turillo, C. J., Folger, R., Lavelle, J. J., Umphress, E. E. & Gee, J. O. (2002). Is virtue its own reward? Self-sacrificial decisions for the sake of fairness. *Organizational Behavior and Human Decision Processes*, 89, 839–65. https://doi.org/10.1016/S0749-5978(02)00032-8

Tyler, T. R. & Bies, R. J. (1990). Beyond formal procedures: The interpersonal context of procedural justice. In J. S. Carroll (ed.), *Applied Social Psychology in Organizational Settings*. Lawrence Erlbaum Associates, pp. 77–98.

Walker, L., Lind, E. A. & Thibaut, J. (1979). The relation between procedural and distributive justice. *Virginia Law Review*, 65, 1401–20.

Walker, L., LaTour, S., Lind, E. A. & Thibaut, J. (1974). Reactions of participants and observers to modes of adjudication. *Journal of Applied Social Psychology*, 4, 295–310. https://doi.org/10.1111/j.1559-1816.1974.tb02601.x

Weiner, B., Amirkhan, J., Folkes, V. S. & Varette, J. A. (1987). An attributional analysis of excuse giving: Studies of a naive theory of emotion. *Journal of Personality and Social Psychology*, 52, 316–24. https://doi.org/10.1037/0022-3514.52.2.316

Weiss, H. M., Suckow, K. & Cropanzano, R. (1999). Effects of justice conditions on discrete emotions. *Journal of Applied Psychology*, 84, 786–94. https://doi.org/10.1037/0021-9010.84.5.786

13

Gender at Work: Revisiting Schein's Think Manager – Think Male Study

Madeline Heilman & Francesca Manzi

BACKGROUND

In 1973, Virginia Schein, a recent graduate of the prestigious New York University doctoral programme in industrial/organisational psychology, was employed at the Personnel Research group at the Metropolitan Life Insurance Company. She had been the first female graduate of the NYU programme – an educational breakthrough that occurred simultaneously with a crucial turning point for women in the United States. The venerable all-male Ivy League schools were opening their doors to women undergraduates, and at the same time, the passage of the Title IX amendment to the Higher Education Act provided women with protection from discrimination based on sex in any federally funded educational programme or activity.

It was not only in educational spheres that there were gains for women. The 92nd Congress, in session from 1971 to 1972, passed more women's rights bills than all previous legislative sessions combined. The 1972 Supreme Court case *Eisenstadt v. Baird* gave unmarried women legal access to birth control, and in 1973, *Roe v. Wade* made abortion legal across the country, assuring women the right to choose whether to terminate their pregnancies. There is little question that the women's movement was flourishing. Even the openly anti-feminist President Nixon supported a 1972 Republican Party platform that included feminist goals, and the Equal Rights Amendment (ERA), the goal of which was to provide women and men with equality in all aspects of life, passed both houses of the United States Congress with overwhelming support (although it later failed to meet the criterion to become law).

Social and cultural change also was afoot in the United States. By the 1970s, dual-earner couples were at an all-time high, continuing a trend underway since the end of the Second World War (Pew Research Center, 2015). The divorce rate increased, and single, working mothers became more commonplace. An increasing number of women pursued careers in historically male-dominated fields, such as law, medicine and business. The constraints of traditional women's roles as home-makers were openly challenged as women attempted to break through barriers that had historically barred them from full participation in the workforce. Life was rapidly changing for American women, and opportunities to redefine their societal roles were burgeoning and being enthusiastically embraced.

This was the backdrop against which Schein's 1973 study entitled, 'The Relationship Between Sex Role Stereotypes and Requisite Management Characteristics' was published in the *Journal of Applied Psychology*. As Schein indicates in the opening paragraphs of her paper, despite the undeniable progress women had made, they still were not fully integrated into the workforce – only 5 per cent of middle- and upper-level managers were women. Her study, which was designed to address the question of why the number of women in managerial and executive positions was so limited, has become a classic.

Schein posited that the scarcity of women in managerial and executive roles results from men's unfavourable attitudes toward women in management and went on to propose that stereotypes designating what women and men are like were a key factor. That is, she suggested that the way in which women were viewed (as less aggressive and independent, and more tactful, gentle and quiet than men) can be a problem for their career advancement. This was not where Schein stopped. Drawing upon the notion of occupational sex-typing, she contended that management is construed as a masculine occupation, requiring personal attributes more characteristic of men than women. And that was exactly what she found: Schein's study provided strong empirical evidence that successful managers are indeed thought to possess attributes more commonly ascribed to men than to women. It was the first demonstration of the 'think manager – think male' association.

Schein's findings may not seem particularly surprising today, but their implications were ground-breaking at the time. They suggested that women were not actually unfit to be managers but rather were *perceived* to be unfit due to shared beliefs about what most women are like (i.e. female stereotypes). If managers believed that men, but not women, have 'the right stuff' to be successful managers, women would have a lesser chance of gaining access to management positions. Moreover, if women, too, 'think manager – think male', they might be discouraged from pursuing these positions.

DETAILED DESCRIPTION

Schein began by examining her hypotheses in a study using only male managers as participants. The focus on male managers was understandable. Given that men represented 95 per cent of middle and upper managers, an all-male sample would have been highly representative of management in 1973. Moreover, if male managers held most of the decision-making power, their perceptions would be particularly important in determining women's chances of success in management. With this in mind, Schein contacted representatives of nine insurance companies in the United States. She asked them to distribute questionnaires among male managers who were told that the research was concerned with 'the establishment of a Descriptive Index to be used for management development'. Of the 462 questionnaires distributed, 354 (or 76.6 per cent) were returned. After excluding female participants and managers who did not include information about gender and age, the final sample consisted of 300 male managers.

The design for the study was simple and straightforward. Participants were asked to describe a target according to a series of characteristics, attitudes and temperaments included in the 'Descriptive Index' (now called the 'Schein Descriptive Index'). For each of the 92 items, participants were to select how characteristic it was of the target on a 5-point scale where '1' was labelled as 'not characteristic', '3' was labelled as 'neutral', and '5' was labelled as 'characteristic'. Although the list of items was always the same, the target of evaluation was not. That is, participants were randomly assigned to describe either women in general, men in general or successful middle managers in terms of the same 92 items. Participants received the following instructions:

> On the following pages you will find a series of descriptive terms commonly used to characterize people in general. Some of these terms are positive in connotation, others are negative, and some are neither very positive nor very negative.

> We would like you to use this list to tell us what you think [women in general, men in general, successful middle managers] are like. In making your judgments, it may be helpful to imagine that you are about to meet a person for the first time and the only thing you know in advance is that the person is [an adult female, an adult male, a successful middle manager]. Please rate each word or phrase in terms of how characteristic it is of [women in general, men in general, successful middle managers].

All items had been pre-tested to represent perceptions of women and men at the time. The goal was to include those characteristics, attitudes and temperaments that described one gender more than the other. Out of an initial pool of 131 items (taken from previous research by Basil, in Epstein, 1970; Bennett & Cohen, 1959; Brim, 1958; and Rosenkrantz et al., 1968), 92 items were shown to differentially describe women and men. The 92 items included in the final Descriptive Index are presented in Appendix 1 (see the end of the chapter).

To test the hypothesis that descriptions of successful middle managers would be more similar to descriptions of men than to descriptions of women, Schein performed two main analyses. The first involved computing intraclass correlation coefficients between two groups: men and managers, and women and managers. In line with Schein's predictions, there was a large and statistically significant resemblance between the ratings of men and successful managers, $r' = .62$, while the similarity between women and successful managers was close to zero, $r' = .06$. The second set of analyses, involving the computation of linear correlations, showed the same pattern of results ($r = .81$ and $r = .10$, respectively).

These findings provided the first empirical evidence that when people think of managers, they think of men, not women. Not only did the results demonstrate that managers' ideas about what it takes to succeed in management strongly overlapped with their own stereotypes about men, but they also showed that stereotypes about women did not include the characteristics, attitudes and temperaments ascribed to successful managers.

Other aspects of Schein's seminal study have received less attention, and the moderating effect of age is often overlooked. Older managers (those over 48 years of age) not only indicated a strong resemblance between men and managers but also indicated a small, but statistically significant resemblance between the attributes of successful managers and women – an effect that was not apparent in younger age groups and not reflected in the overall results. To Schein, this finding, small as it was, suggested that experience and increased exposure to female managers may help reduce anti-female bias.

In addition to testing the overall resemblance between men, women and managers, Schein examined the items of the Index individually. She found that ratings of successful managers were more similar to ratings of men on 60 of the 92 items presented to participants. Examples of these items are emotionally stable, aggressive, leadership ability, self-reliant, (not) uncertain, vigorous, desires responsibility, (not) frivolous, objective, well-informed and direct. Interestingly, a small number of items (eight of the 92) showed a greater resemblance between successful managers and women. These items were understanding, helpful, sophisticated, aware of feelings of others, intuitive, neat, (not) vulgar and humanitarian values.

Schein drew several important conclusions from her results. The first was to highlight the need to examine the downstream consequences of her findings on organisational decision-making and women's actual on-the-job performance. She argued that the perceived similarity between successful middle managers and men – and the perceived dissimilarity between successful middle managers and women – was likely to lead to a pro-male bias in the selection and upward mobility of managers.

Schein also suggested that these perceptions could have important effects on women. To the extent that women shared these beliefs, they may be less likely to seek out managerial roles. Moreover, because women may actively avoid acting in ways that are inconsistent with their feminine self-image, they may inhibit their display of the masculine attributes ascribed to successful managers, thereby limiting their career opportunities. However, despite the negative implications of her study's results for women, Schein also saw some positives. In particular, she speculated that there may be managerial areas for which women are considered to be particularly acceptable – areas in which being considerate and supportive are thought to be advantageous for performance outcomes and facilitative of managerial success.

IMPACT OF THE CLASSIC STUDY

Women now comprise half of the paid workforce worldwide. However, nearly 50 years after Schein's classic study was conducted, women remain dramatically under-represented in positions of power (UN Women, 2019). Female representation has increased most noticeably in middle management, but high-level leadership continues to be male-dominated, with women occupying less than a third of corporate boards and only 6 per cent of CEO positions worldwide (Catalyst, 2020a, 2020b). Although there is some evidence to suggest that think manager – think male beliefs are decreasing, especially among women (see Koenig et al., 2011), the idea that women lack what it takes to be a good leader continues to affect women's upward mobility across the globe. Take, for instance, the United Nation's most recent human development report on gender equality: nearly half of the world's men and women continue to think that men make better political leaders, and more than 40 per cent believe that men make better business executives (United Nations Development Programme, 2020).

It is not surprising, then, that Schein's ground-breaking ideas continue to resonate among gender researchers. The original study has been cited over 2,000 times, shaping the way researchers and practitioners think about discrimination against women not only in management, but in leadership realms more generally. As the very first to test the relationship between gender stereotypes and the perceived requirements for managerial success, Schein paved the way for researchers to examine, discuss and theorise about the role of sociocultural beliefs on the social standing of women. Her work has had a direct impact on many theories accounting for the processes underlying gender discrimination in the workplace. Perhaps the most recognised extensions and elaborations of Schein's work have been Heilman's 'lack of fit model' (1983), and Eagly & Karau's 'role congruity theory' (2002). Taking a slightly different approach, each of these theoretical models has built upon the idea that discrimination against women stems from a perceived mismatch between women and traditionally male-dominated occupations. Connections also could be made between Schein's work and other theoretical perspectives (see, for example, Lord et al., 1984; Ridgeway, 2001; Rudman et al., 2012).

In addition to its theoretical contribution, the think manager – think male association has become an exceptionally valuable explanatory tool. Until this day, practitioners and journalists alike use Schein's simple and straightforward demonstration to illustrate how gender bias against female leaders plays out in the real world. For example, in a 2015 news article, the writer asks readers to think about the best leader they have ever worked with. 'If you are like most people,' she goes on to write, 'the person you have brought to mind is male' (Brands, 2015). Recruiters and job consultants also draw from the think manger – think male studies to warn organisations about the ease with which gender bias can affect decision-making.

KEY REPLICATIONS AND GENERALISATIONS

REPLICATIONS OVER TIME

Over the years, research has provided concurring evidence that both managers and non-managers perceive a strong resemblance between men and successful managers, and a weak to non-existent resemblance between women and successful managers (e.g. Brenner et al., 1989; Dodge et al., 1995; Powell et al., 2002). Moreover, the perception that women are more different from successful managers than are men has been shown to be tenacious – it prevails even when people are asked not about 'women in general', which might conjure up the view of women as homemakers, but about 'women managers'. The think manager – think male association only appears to recede when women are presented as unequivocally successful managers (Heilman et al., 1989).

There also is evidence for think manager – think male beliefs across cultures and geographic boundaries. The basic finding – that the perceived resemblance between men and managers is greater than that between women and managers – has been replicated in the UK and Germany (Schein & Mueller, 1992) as well as Japan and China (Schein et al., 1996). In 2001, Schein published an article in which she concluded that the think manager – think male association was a global phenomenon.

Recent research suggests, however, that the association of leadership *solely* with masculinity is less pronounced than it once was. A meta-analysis of 40 studies conducted between 1973 and 2010 revealed that, although successful leaders continue to be seen as possessing characteristics that align more with men than with women, there has been an increase in the perceived resemblance between women and leadership success (Koenig et al., 2011). Contrary to Schein's initial predictions (see Schein, 1975), the data suggest that this shift is not driven by changes in perceptions of women in general or female stereotypes, but rather by the incorporation of feminine traits to perceptions of successful leadership.

REPLICATIONS ACROSS GENDER

In the decades following Schein's first study using an all-male sample, much attention has been given to whether there are gender differences in think manager – think male beliefs. In 1975, Schein replicated her findings among female managers, confirming that both men and women shared stereotype-based beliefs about what it takes to succeed in management. Like male managers, female managers showed stronger associations between men and successful managers than between women and successful managers. To Schein, these results suggested that women managers accepted and emulated a masculine model for leadership success.

The replication of the think manager – think male association among women was revolutionary. At the time, most studies of its kind used all-male samples, and Schein's 1975 study was among the first to use a sample of women in management. Perhaps more importantly, it was one of the first to provide evidence that women, too, endorse negative views about women's managerial aptitude. To Schein, these findings indicated that men were not the only perpetrators of gender discrimination in management, an interpretation that has received much support. The idea that women, like men, adhere to gender stereotypes about women has been widely corroborated, and evidence that women can be biased against female leaders has been repeatedly demonstrated (e.g. Heilman, 2001; Rudman, 1998). There even is evidence that under some conditions female leaders behave in ways that hinder rather than help the advancement of other women (see Derks et al., 2016).

Although there is evidence to support the idea that women as well as men hold perceptions of successful leaders that resemble men more than women (Powell & Butterfield, 1979, 1989; Powell et al., 2002; Vial & Napier, 2018), there also is evidence that the shift away from the exclusive association of leadership with masculinity is particularly notable for women. Fifteen years after the initial research, Schein and her colleagues conducted a number of studies that showed the think manager – think male association to persist among male managers, but not among female managers (Brenner et al., 1989; Schein et al., 1989). Specifically, female managers in these studies were found to view both men *and* women to strongly resemble successful managers.

Subsequent research has provided further support for the idea that think manager – think male beliefs are stronger among men than women, and that the source of this gender difference is a greater change in women's than men's conceptions of the requirements for leadership success. Koenig and colleagues' 2011 meta-analysis confirmed this trend, showing that both men and women strongly associated masculine stereotypes and leadership, but women also strongly associated feminine stereotypes and leadership – something that was less true of men.

It is important to note that gender differences in think manager – think male beliefs are not necessarily universal. These differences have not been found in some research conducted in the UK, Germany, Japan and China (see Schein, 2001), where people, whether male or female, tend to view leadership in traditionally male terms (see also Koenig et al., 2010). Whether gender differences in the think manager – think male association will become more generalised or dissipate with time as views of the managerial role continue to evolve, remains to be seen.

BEYOND THE CLASSIC STUDY: THEORETICAL DEVELOPMENTS

CONGRUITY MODELS OF GENDER DISCRIMINATION

Since 1973, many scholars have re-examined and elaborated the ideas that motivated the original Schein studies. Inspired by Schein's findings, subsequent work has provided depth and nuance to our understanding of the think manager – think male association. Some of these theoretical developments have become the most important models of gender discrimination in the social sciences today.

In 1983, Heilman built on Schein's ideas to propose the 'lack of fit model'. Heilman shifted the focus from the perceived congruence between men and successful managers to the perceived disparity between women and managers. For Heilman, the most important implication of Schein's findings was not the think manager – think male association per se, but rather the dramatic mismatch between managers' perceptions of women and successful leaders. Not only did managers 'think manager, think male', they also 'think manager, think not-female'. Heilman contended that discrimination against women stemmed from this perceived mismatch and expanded the scope of Schein's research to include areas that, like management, are highly male gender-typed (e.g. engineering, the military, athletics, etc.). She proposed that the lack of fit between the *communal* way in which women are viewed (e.g. kind, caring, helpful) and the *agentic* attributes required for success in roles and positions that have been historically dominated by men (e.g. confident, decisive, competitive) create the expectation that women are not well-equipped to perform successfully in these domains. According to Heilman, it is these negative expectations and the cognitive distortions they produce that create an anti-female bias in male gender-typed roles and occupations. Further expanding Schein's ideas, Heilman posited that lack of fit perceptions affected not only the selection of women into traditionally male domains, but also their recruitment, performance evaluation, promotion, compensation and career opportunities (Heilman & Caleo, 2017).

In 2002, Eagly & Karau's role congruity theory also re-examined Schein's ideas. Role congruity theory, too, focuses on stereotypes about women and men, which Eagly and her colleagues propose to be rooted in societal roles. She argued that beliefs about what women and men are like (gender stereotypes) are inferred from the different activities in which they have typically engaged. Women's historical over-representation in domestic roles has led to stereotypes about women being more communal than men, and men's historical over-representation in the workforce has led to stereotypes about men being more agentic than women. Like 'think manager – think male' and 'lack of fit', role congruity theory proposes that the discrepancy between female stereotypes and the masculine requirements of positions of authority lead to prejudice and discrimination. However, the issue is not 'think manager – think male', but rather 'think manager – think agency' – the associations attached to women and men are thought not to be due to their biological sex, but to the personality traits associated with them due to their social roles. To the extent that stereotypes follow from our ordinary experiences with women and men, role congruity theory predicts that with societal changes, gender stereotypes also will change (see, for example, Eagly et al., 2020).

Interestingly, Schein's findings regarding weaker think manager – think male beliefs among more experienced managers (later supported by Koenig et al., 2010) foreshadowed some of the predictions made by role congruity theory. Schein believed that one of the reasons older managers showed greater overlap in their perceptions of women and managers was that they had had more interaction with working women and more exposure to female managers – in other words, more exposure to women in agentic roles. The idea that this increased exposure might have modified to some extent older managers' stereotypical perceptions of women is consistent with role congruity theory.

BEYOND CONGRUITY MODELS

In her initial work Schein speculated that the think manager – think male association might lead to the under-representation of women in management not only by affecting how women were evaluated by others but also by affecting women's own behaviour. She suggested that if women believe that being an effective manager requires traditionally masculine characteristics, they might hold back from seeking managerial positions, an idea that found support in subsequent research (Powell & Butterfield, 1979; Ryan et al., 2007). Schein also suggested that this belief could cause women to regulate and limit the agentic behaviour that is so critical for success in managerial positions, for fear of being perceived as overly masculine. Not only has subsequent work supported this idea (e.g. women's reluctance to promote themselves, communicate authoritatively, negotiate on their own behalf, etc.), but the concerns that Schein thought might underlie this type of self-limiting behaviour also have been born out (e.g. Amanatullah & Morris, 2010; Carli, 2001; Moss-Racussin & Rudman, 2010). Indeed, the finding that women incur penalties for behaving in traditionally masculine ways has been at the centre of research on backlash against agentic women (e.g. Heilman et al., 2004, Rudman & Glick, 2001).

Backlash research is based on the idea that in addition to designating how women and men are (i.e. descriptive gender stereotypes), gender stereotypes also designate how they should be (i.e. prescriptive gender stereotypes) (Heilman, 2001). These prescriptions function as norms and, like all norms, provoke disapproval when violated. Therefore, much as Schein had anticipated, behaving in traditionally masculine ways has been shown to hurt female managers. When female leaders behave like men to fit beliefs about what it takes to be a successful leader, they are viewed as unpleasant and hostile, and are disliked (Heilman & Okimoto, 2007; Rudman & Glick, 1999). These negative reactions to women who deviate from gender norms can be costly, leading to fewer promotions and decreased hireability (Loughlin et al., 2012). Thus women are caught: they are penalised for not being agentic enough because agency is seen as essential to managerial success, but they also are penalised if they are too agentic because it violates gender norms. To succeed, they must navigate carefully, a process that has been illustrated by Eagly and Carli in their book, *Through the Labyrinth* (2007).

CONCLUSION

A great number of studies inspired by Schein's original work – and the theories that grew out of her ideas – do not focus on whether the think manager – think male association occurs, but rather on the reasons behind its emergence and the consequences of these beliefs for women. All are grounded in the idea that it is the perceived, not the actual, qualities of women that so heavily impacts their experiences. This research has not only tested theoretical tenets, but has also helped to identify when, where and for whom the perceived mismatch between gender stereotypes and job requirements is most potent, to determine its many potential outcomes and to examine the conditions that might avert its negative consequences for women.

Issues such as how stereotype-based bias among supervisors affects training, mentoring and opportunity for advancement of female employees, whether women and men are differentially assigned credit or blame for the same work products, how pregnancy, motherhood and physical attractiveness affect women's work evaluations, whether the presence of female role models promotes feelings of belongingness and self-efficacy among junior women, how women can escape the backlash for behaving in traditionally masculine ways, how organisational structures and policies shape reactions to female workers, how the gender-typing of the work context and the status of the particular position affects bias and discrimination, and how political attitudes and personality characteristics amplify or attenuate reactions to women managers, are just some of the questions that have been explored, all becoming part of a literature that has its genesis in Schein's 1973 study.

But the implications of Schein's work are not limited to women in management. Building on the role of perceived incongruity between stereotypes and job requirements in discrimination, research has explored whether the processes behind the think manager – think male association can be used to explain bias against members of other groups in different occupations. Recent research has suggested, for example, that people might not merely 'think manager – think male', but might 'think manager – think White, heterosexual, male', leading not only to bias against women, but against Black and gay men (Barrantes & Eaton, 2018; Rosette et al., 2008). Incongruity perceptions may also be to blame, in part, for discrimination against Blacks and Latinos in STEM professions, against men in early childhood education and against women in sports. Much in line with Schein's basic idea, this work strongly suggests that *whenever* people sense a mismatch between the stereotypes associated with a person's group and the perceived requirements for success in an occupation, stereotype-based discrimination ensues.

IMPLICATIONS FOR PRACTITIONERS

The support and validation of the think manager – think male association through years of research, together with the demonstration of its discriminatory consequences, is suggestive of strategies for interventions.

Tackling gender stereotypes. Changing stereotypes is neither easy nor straightforward. Despite decades of concerted efforts by organisations to eliminate stereotypes, most evident in training and other types of educational programmes, the results are not encouraging (Kulik & Roberson, 2008). Gender stereotypes depicting women as less agentic than men have not changed appreciably (e.g. Haines et al., 2016), and the incidence of bias against women has not decidedly decreased (Jones et al., 2016; Koch et al., 2015). However, even if stereotypic beliefs remain intact, reducing the salience of gender can inhibit their use. Actions such as including more than one 'token' woman in work groups, designing outreach programmes to realise goals of diversity and inclusion rather than focusing solely on female-exclusive affirmative action or quotas, and initiating organisational programmes that benefit 'parents' and not just 'moms', can minimise the salience of gender and the consequent activation of female stereotypes in characterisations of women (for a review, see Caleo & Heilman, 2019).

Tackling beliefs about the position. Although there is some evidence of a shift away from the exclusively masculine gender-typing of leadership, organisations can work to further this process by monitoring the practices of human resource departments and the images perpetuated by corporate strategies and institutional contexts. The use of exclusively male-gendered language should be avoided in job descriptions, as this can deter women from applying for these positions (Gaucher et al., 2011) and negatively affect their likelihood of being selected (Horvath & Sczesny, 2016). Moreover, physical symbols, rituals and stories that convey the masculinity of a particular organisational role can signal to women that they 'do not belong' (Cheryan et al., 2009). Attending to practices and behaviours that perpetuate the 'men-only' aura can mitigate the image of masculinity as the defining feature of managerial roles.

Creating motivation for accuracy. The motivation to make the right choice can stop decision-makers from 'going on automatic' and not thinking too hard about what they are doing (Fiske & Taylor, 2013). It forces them to consider the available information more systematically and to be more deliberative. When this occurs, phenomena such as think manager – think male are less likely. Motivation to be accurate often is prompted by concerns about being a good person. People typically want to 'do the right thing' and for many, being anything less than evenhanded in the treatment of others is not acceptable. These motivations are also fostered by people's concerns about impression management and the desire to demonstrate to others that they are rigorous and fair. Organisations can appeal to these motivations by introducing more transparency in evaluative decision-making processes, making them visible to all. Even better is to require accountability. Having to explain and justify evaluations and decisions fuels the motivation to appear fair-minded and competent, whether to oneself or others, and has been found to lessen gender bias (Koch et al., 2015).

DISCUSSION QUESTIONS

1. Do we all have a 'think manager – think male' bias? Where do you think it comes from? Why do you think the 'think manager – think male' association might be a problem?

2. What would you do if you observe someone endorsing 'think manager – think male' beliefs in their attitudes or actions?

3. How would you advise women who are facing 'think manager – think male' beliefs in their careers?

APPENDIX 1

SCHEIN'S DESCRIPTIVE INDEX ITEMS (IN ALPHABETICAL ORDER)

1. Able to separate feelings from ideas

2. Adventurous

3. Aggressive

4. Ambitious

5. Analytical ability

6. Assertive

7. Authoritative

8. Aware of feelings of others

9. Bitter

10. Cheerful

11. Competent

12. Competitive

13. Consistent

14. Courteous

15. Creative

16. Curious

17. Dawdler and procrastinator

18. Deceitful

19. Decisive

20. Demure

21. Desire for friendship

22. Desire to avoid controversy

23. Desires responsibility

24. Devious

25. Direct

26. Dominant

27. Easily influenced

28. Emotionally stable

29. Exhibitionist

30. Fearful

31. Feelings not easily hurt

32. Firm

33. Forceful

34. Frank

35. Frivolous

36. Generous

37. Grateful

38. Hasty

39. Helpful

40. Hides emotion

41. High need for autonomy

42. High need for power

43. High self-regard

44. Humanitarian values

45. Independent

46. Industrious

47. Intelligent

48. Interested in own appearance

49. Intuitive

50. Kind

51. Knows the way of the world

52. Leadership ability

53. Logical

54. Modest

55. Neat

56. Nervous

57. Not conceited about appearance

58. Not uncomfortable about being aggressive

59. Obedient

60. Objective

61. Passive

62. Persistent

63. Prompt

64. Quarrelsome

65. Reserved

66. Self-confident

67. Self-controlled

68. Selfish

69. Self-reliant

70. Sentimental

71. Shy

72. Skilled in business matters

73. Sociable

74. Sophisticated

75. Speedy recovery from emotional disturbance

76. Steady

77. Strong need for achievement

78. Strong need for monetary rewards

79. Strong need for security

80. Strong need for social acceptance

81. Submissive

82. Sympathetic

83. Tactful

84. Talkative

85. Timid

86. Uncertain

87. Understanding

88. Values pleasant surroundings

89. Vigorous

90. Vulgar

91. Wavering in decision

92. Well informed

FURTHER READINGS

Schein, V. E. (1973). The relationship between sex role stereotypes and requisite management characteristics. *Journal of Applied Psychology*, 57, 95–100.

The very first conceptualisation and empirical test of the 'think manager – think male' phenomenon. Here, Schein lays out her initial hypotheses and describes her findings. She also speculates about the origins and downstream consequences of the association between men and successful managers.

Schein, V. E. (2001). A global look at psychological barriers to women's progress in management. *Journal of Social Issues*, 57, 675–88.

More than 25 years after her original study was published, Schein examines the role of 'think manager – think male' beliefs in an increasingly globalised world. She reviews research from the United States, the United Kingdom, Germany, China and Japan, concluding that 'think manager – think male' may very well be a global phenomenon, particularly among men.

Heilman, M. E. (2012). Gender stereotypes and workplace bias. *Research in Organizational Behavior*, 32, 113–35.

This article describes an influential model of gender discrimination to emerge as a result of Schein's studies: the lack of fit model. Here, Heilman explains the main tenets of her model and illustrates how gender stereotypes remain a barrier to women's advancement in traditionally masculine roles and occupations by fostering negative expectations about women's competence.

Eagly, A. H. & Karau, S. J. (2002). Role congruity theory of prejudice toward female leaders. *Psychological Review*, 109, 573.

Role congruity theory is undoubtedly one of the most prominent models to explain women's continued underrepresentation in leadership. The authors expand and enrich Schein's original ideas by proposing a model that integrates perspectives from social-cognitive psychology (e.g. stereotyping and prejudice) as well as insights from industrial-organisational psychology (e.g. leadership).

Koenig, A. M., Eagly, A. H., Mitchell, A. A. & Ristikari, T. (2011). Are leader stereotypes masculine? A meta-analysis of three research paradigms. *Psychological Bulletin*, 137, 616.

This meta-analysis synthesises over three decades of research on gender stereotypes and leadership. Koenig and colleagues examine past findings in light of three paradigms: think manager – think male (Schein, 1973), agency–communion (Powell & Butterfield, 1979) and masculinity–femininity (Shinar, 1975). While 'think manager – think male' associations remain, the findings underscore the differential effects of participant gender and type of organisation in the strength of the association between male stereotypes and leadership.

REFERENCES

Amanatullah, E. T. & Morris, M. W. (2010). Negotiating gender roles: Gender differences in assertive negotiating are mediated by women's fear of backlash and attenuated when negotiating on behalf of others. *Journal of Personality and Social Psychology*, 98, 256. https://doi.org/10.1037/a0017094

Barrantes, R. J. & Eaton, A. A. (2018). Sexual orientation and leadership suitability: How being a gay man affects perceptions of fit in gender-stereotyped positions. *Sex Roles*, 79, 549–64. https://doi.org/10.1007/s11199-018-0894-8

Bennett, E. M. & Cohen, L. R. (1959). Men and women: Personality patterns and contrasts. *Genetic Psychology Monographs*, 59, 101–55.

Brands, R. (2015). 'Think manager, think man' stops us seeing woman as leaders. *The Guardian*. Retrieved from https://www.theguardian.com/women-in-leadership/2015/jul/15/think-manager-think-man-women-leaders-biase-workplace#:~:text=If%20you%20are%20like%20most,are%20stereotypically%20associated%20with%20men

Brenner, O. C., Tomkiewicz, J. & Schein, V. E. (1989). The relationship between sex role stereotypes and requisite management characteristics revisited. *Academy of Management Journal*, 32, 662–9. https://doi.org/10.5465/256439

Brim, O. G. (1958). Family structure and sex-role learning by children: A further analysis of Helen Koch's data. *Sociometry*, 21, 1–16. https://doi.org/10.2307/2786054

Broverman, I. K., Broverman, D. M., Clarkson, F. E., Rosenkrantz, P. S. & Vogel, S. R. (1970). Sex-role stereotypes and clinical judgments of mental health. *Journal of Consulting and Clinical Psychology*, 34, 1–7. https://doi.org/10.1037/h0028797

Caleo, S. & Heilman, M. E. (2019). What could go wrong? Some unintended consequences of gender bias interventions. *Archives of Scientific Psychology*, 7, 71. http://dx.doi.org/10.1037/arc0000063

Carli, L. L. (2001). Gender and social influence. *Journal of Social Issues*, 57, 725–41. https://doi.org/10.1111/0022-4537.00238

Catalyst (2020a). *Quick Take: Women on Corporate Boards*. Retrieved from https://www.catalyst.org/research/women-on-corporate-boards/

Catalyst (2020b). *Women CEOs of the S&P 500*. Retrieved from https://www.catalyst.org/research/women-ceos-of-the-sp-500/

Cheryan, S., Plaut, V. C., Davies, P. G. & Steele, C. M. (2009). Ambient belonging: How stereotypical cues impact gender participation in computer science. *Journal of Personality and Social Psychology*, 97, 1045. https://doi.org/10.1037/a0016239

Derks, B., Van Laar, C. & Ellemers, N. (2016). The queen bee phenomenon: Why women leaders distance themselves from junior women. *Leadership Quarterly*, 27, 456–69. https://doi.org/10.1016/j.leaqua.2015.12.007

Dodge, K. A., Gilroy, F. D. & Fenzel, L. M. (1995). Requisite management characteristics revisited: Two decades later. *Journal of Social Behavior & Personality*, 10, 253–64.

Eagly, A. H. & Carli, L. L. (2007). *Through the Labyrinth: The Truth about how Women Become Leaders*. Harvard Business Press.

Eagly, A. H. & Karau, S. J. (2002). Role congruity theory of prejudice toward female leaders. *Psychological Review*, 109, 573. https://doi.org/10.1037/0033-295x.109.3.573

Eagly, A. H., Nater, C., Miller, D. I., Kaufmann, M. & Sczesny, S. (2020). Gender stereotypes have changed: A cross-temporal meta-analysis of US public opinion polls from 1946 to 2018. *American Psychologist*, 75, 301. https://doi.org/10.1037/amp0000494

Epstein, C. F. (1970). *Woman's Place*. University of California Press.

Fiske, S. T. & Taylor, S. E. (2013). *Social Cognition: From Brains to Culture*. Sage.

Gaucher, D., Friesen, J. & Kay, A. C. (2011). Evidence that gendered wording in job advertisements exists and sustains gender inequality. *Journal of Personality and Social Psychology*, 101, 109. https://doi.org/10.1037/a0022530

Haines, E. L., Deaux, K. & Lofaro, N. (2016). The times they are a-changing ... or are they not? A comparison of gender stereotypes, 1983–2014. *Psychology of Women Quarterly*, 40, 353–63. https://doi.org/10.1177/0361684316634081

Heilman, M. E. (1983). Sex bias in work settings: The lack of fit model. *Research in Organizational Behavior*, 5, 269–98.

Heilman, M. E. (2001). Description and prescription: How gender stereotypes prevent women's ascent up the organizational ladder. *Journal of Social Issues*, 57, 657–74. https://doi.org/10.1111/0022-4537.00234

Heilman, M. E. (2012). Gender stereotypes and workplace bias. *Research in Organizational Behavior*, 32, 113–35. https://doi.org/10.1016/j.riob.2012.11.003

Heilman, M. E. & Caleo, S. (2017). Gender discrimination in the workplace. In A. Collela & E. King (eds), *Oxford Handbook of Discrimination at Work*. https://doi.org/10.1093/oxfordhb/9780199363643.013.7

Heilman, M. E. & Okimoto, T. G. (2007). Why are women penalized for success at male tasks? The implied communality deficit. *Journal of Applied Psychology*, 92, 81. https://doi.org/10.1037/0021-9010.92.1.81

Heilman, M. E., Block, C. J., Martell, R. F. & Simon, M. C. (1989). Has anything changed? Current characterizations of men, women, and managers. *Journal of Applied Psychology*, 74, 935. https://doi.org/10.1037/0021-9010.74.6.935

Heilman, M. E., Wallen, A. S., Fuchs, D. & Tamkins, M. M. (2004). Penalties for success: Reactions to women who succeed at male gender-typed tasks. *Journal of Applied Psychology*, 89, 416. https://doi.org/10.1037/0021-9010.89.3.416

Horvath, L. K. & Sczesny, S. (2016). Reducing women's lack of fit with leadership positions? Effects of the wording of job advertisements. *European Journal of Work and Organizational Psychology*, 25, 316–28. https://doi.org/10.1080/1359432x.2015.1067611

Jones, K. P., Peddie, C. I., Gilrane, V. L., King, E. B. & Gray, A. L. (2016). Not so subtle: A meta-analytic investigation of the correlates of subtle and overt discrimination. *Journal of Management*, 42, 1588–1613. https://doi.org/10.1177/01492063 13506466

Koch, A. J., D'Mello, S. D. & Sackett, P. R. (2015). A meta-analysis of gender stereotypes and bias in experimental simulations of employment decision making. *Journal of Applied Psychology*, 100, 128. https://doi.org/10.1037/a0036734

Koenig, A. M., Eagly, A. H., Mitchell, A. A. & Ristikari, T. (2011). Are leader stereotypes masculine? A meta-analysis of three research paradigms. *Psychological Bulletin*, 137, 616. https://doi.org/10.1037/e617292010-001

Kulik, C. T. & Roberson, L. (2008). Common goals and golden opportunities: Evaluations of diversity education in academic and organizational settings. *Academy of Management Learning & Education*, 7, 309–31. https://doi.org/10.5465/amle.2008.34251670

Lord, R. G., Foti, R. J. & De Vader, C. L. (1984). A test of leadership categorization theory: Internal structure, information processing, and leadership perceptions. *Organizational Behavior and Human Performance*, 34, 343–78. https://doi.org/10.1016/0030-5073(84)90043-6

Loughlin, C., Arnold, K. A. & Bell Crawford, J. (2012). Lost opportunity: Is transformational leadership accurately recognized and rewarded in all managers? *Equality, Diversity and Inclusion: An International Journal*, 31(1), 43–64.

Moss-Racusin, C. A. & Rudman, L. A. (2010). Disruptions in women's self-promotion: The backlash avoidance model. *Psychology of Women Quarterly*, 34, 186–202. https://doi.org/10.1111/j.1471-6402.2010.01561.x

Pew Research Center. (2015). *Raising Kids and Running a Household: How Working Parents Share the Load*. Retrieved from https://www.pewresearch.org/social-trends/wp-content/uploads/sites/3/2015/11/2015-11-04_working-parents_FINAL.pdf

Powell, G. N. & Butterfield, D. A. (1979). The 'good manager': Masculine or androgynous? *Academy of Management Journal*, 22, 395–403.

Powell, G. N. & Butterfield, D. A. (1989). The 'good manager': Did androgyny fare better in the 1980s? *Group & Organization Studies*, 14, 216–33.

Powell, G. N., Butterfield, D. A. & Parent, J. D. (2002). Gender and managerial stereotypes: Have the times changed? *Journal of Management*, 28, 177–93. https://doi.org/10.1177/014920630202800203

Prentice, D. A. & Carranza, E. (2002). What women and men should be, shouldn't be, are allowed to be, and don't have to be: The contents of prescriptive gender stereotypes. *Psychology of Women Quarterly*, 26, 269–81. https://doi.org/10.1111/1471-6402.t01-1-00066

Ridgeway, C. L. (2001). Gender, status, and leadership. *Journal of Social Issues*, 57, 637–55. https://doi.org/10.1111/0022-4537.00233

Rosenkrantz, P., Vogel, S., Bee, H., Broverman, I. & Broverman, D. M. (1968). Sex-role stereotypes and self-concepts in college students. *Journal of Consulting and Clinical Psychology*, 32, 287–95. https://doi.org/10.1037/h0025909

Rosette, A. S., Leonardelli, G. J. & Phillips, K. W. (2008). The White standard: Racial bias in leader categorization. *Journal of Applied Psychology*, 93, 758. https://doi.org/10.1037/0021-9010.93.4.758

Rudman, L. A. (1998). Self-promotion as a risk factor for women: The costs and benefits of counterstereotypical impression management. *Journal of Personality and Social Psychology*, 74, 629. https://doi.org/10.1037/0022-3514.74.3.629

Rudman, L. A. & Glick, P. (1999). Feminized management and backlash toward agentic women: The hidden costs to women of a kinder, gentler image of middle managers. *Journal of Personality and Social Psychology*, 77, 1004. https://doi.org/10.1037/0022-3514.77.5.1004

Rudman, L. A. & Glick, P. (2001). Prescriptive gender stereotypes and backlash toward agentic women. *Journal of Social Issues*, 57, 743–62. https://doi.org/10.1111/0022-4537.00239

Rudman, L. A., Moss-Racusin, C. A., Phelan, J. E. & Nauts, S. (2012). Status incongruity and backlash effects: Defending the gender hierarchy motivates prejudice against female leaders. *Journal of Experimental Social Psychology*, 48, 165–79. https://doi.org/10.1016/j.jesp.2011.10.008

Ryan, M. K., Haslam, S. A., Hersby, M. D., Kulich, C. & Atkins, C. (2007). Opting out or pushed off the edge? The glass cliff and the precariousness of women's leadership positions. *Social and Personality Psychology Compass*, 1, 266–79. https://doi.org/10.1111/j.1751-9004.2007.00007.x

Schein, V. E. (1973). The relationship between sex role stereotypes and requisite management characteristics. *Journal of Applied Psychology*, 57, 95–100. https://doi.org/10.1037/h0037128

Schein, V. E. (1975). The relationship between sex role stereotypes and requisite management characteristics among female managers. *Journal of Applied Psychology*, 60, 340–4. https://doi.org/10.1037/h0076637

Schein, V. E. (2001). A global look at psychological barriers to women's progress in management. *Journal of Social Issues*, 57, 675–88. https://doi.org/10.1111/0022-4537.00235

Schein, V. E. & Mueller, R. (1992). Sex role stereotyping and requisite management characteristics: A cross cultural look. *Journal of Organizational Behavior*, 13, 439–47. https://doi.org/10.1002/job.4030130502

Schein, V. E., Mueller, R. & Jacobson, C. (1989). The relationship between sex role stereotypes and requisite management characteristics among college students. *Sex Roles*, 20, 103–10. https://doi.org/10.1007/BF00288030

Schein, V. E., Mueller, R., Lituchy, T. & Liu, J. (1996). Think manager–think male: A global phenomenon? *Journal of Organizational Behavior*, 17, 33–41. https://doi.org/10.1002/(sici)1099-1379(199601)17:1<33::aid-job778>3.0.co;2-f

Shinar, E. H. (1975). Sexual stereotypes of occupations. *Journal of Vocational Behavior*, 7, 99–111. https://doi.org/10.1016/0001-8791(75)90037-8

United Nations Development Programme (2020). *2020 Human Development Perspectives: Tackling Social Norms.* Retrieved from http://hdr.undp.org/en/GSNI

United Nations Women (2019). *Facts and Figures: Leadership and Political Participation.* Retrieved from http://www.unwomen.org/en/what-we-do/leadership-and-political-participation/facts-and-figures

Vial, A. C. & Napier, J. L. (2018). Unnecessary frills: Communality as a nice (but expendable) trait in leaders. *Frontiers in Psychology*, 9, 1866. https://doi.org/10.3389/fpsyg.2018.01866

14

Diversity: Revisiting Ancona & Caldwell's 'Demography and Design' Study

C. Y. Edwina Wong, Floor Rink & Michelle K. Ryan

BACKGROUND

After the American civil rights movements, research into organisational diversity in the 1970s and 1980s was heavily shaped by anti-discrimination and equal opportunity policies in the workplace (Nkomo et al., 2019). Such research focused on differences in treatment on the basis of race and gender, women in management, and the experiences of other individuals who were targets of discrimination (e.g. Bartol, 1978; Bartol et al., 1978; Bell, 1990; Brief et al., 1979; Brown & Ford, 1977; Cox & Nkomo, 1986; Dipboye, 1985; Kanter, 1977; Nieva & Gutek, 1980; Powell, 1987; Thomas & Alderfer, 1989). Accordingly, this work primarily investigated and underscored the inequity faced by discriminated individuals and advocated for reasserting civil rights for oppressed groups.

These developments were in stark contrast to a view put forward by an influential projection of the future of the workforce published in the 1980s by a conservative think tank: The *Workforce 2000: Work and Workers for the Twenty-First-Century Report* (Johnston & Packer, 1987). This publication shifted the focus of organisational diversity and inclusion research to diversity issues as a management affair rather than an issue of social (in)equity. It also predicted that by the year 2000, most new participants in the US labour market would be women and ethnic minorities (Nkomo et al., 2019). In conjunction with these predictions, the macro socio-political environment became a source of backlash against affirmative action policies. More conservative political ideology reigned under the Reagan administration, and contributed to increased perceptions that affirmative action and equal-opportunity initiatives were offences to individual rights, freedoms and agency (Devins, 1989; Nkomo et al., 2019). The growing political and economic conservatism made it increasingly difficult for organisations to (continue to) work on diversity from an egalitarian perspective.

To ensure that diversity and inclusion remained on the agenda, practitioners and academics started to reframe their approach to diversity by disentangling it from issues of marginalisation and social inequality (Lorbiecki & Jack, 2000; Nkomo et al., 2019; Nkomo & Cox, 1996; Roberson et al., 2017; Zanoni et al., 2010). They did this in the hope that it would be a more palatable way of encouraging organisations to commit voluntarily to establishing a diverse workforce (Edelman et al., 2001; Kelly & Dobbin, 1998).

Separating diversity from issues of marginalisation moved the academic agenda towards the successful management of a wider range of differences that may exist between employees. In line with this, consultants broadened the term 'diversity', by not only including minoritised and marginalised characteristics (i.e. surface-level diversity) (e.g. Thomas, 1992), but also by expanding it to include job or task-related characteristics that were more directly associated with organisational performance (i.e. deep-level diversity, e.g. tenure, education, functional diversity[1]). Hence, because diversity initiatives were generally discouraged by conservative forces, practitioners and researchers started to analyse demographics of marginalisation as task-related diversity. In doing so, this often led to the presumption that one substituted the other; for example, findings that pointed to the 'benefits' of deep-level diversity characteristics, may also be used to argue for introducing greater surface-level diversity in an organisation.

Further distancing the motivation of conducting research in diversity from investigating and working towards social equity, researchers and consultants alike growingly emphasised the need for *management* of diversity as a means to gain a competitive advantage for organisations (Cox & Blake, 1991). The focus on deep-level diversities and more cognitive characteristics was viewed as a way to reduce intra-team conflict, and promote creativity and innovation (Jehn et al., 1999; Williams & O'Reilly, 1998). Ultimately, a more 'business case of diversity' precipitated and overshadowed the more 'moral cases of diversity', such that diversity in organisations became seen as reflecting inherent strategic value.

DETAILED DESCRIPTION:

ANCONA & CALDWELL'S 'DEMOGRAPHY AND DESIGN' STUDY

In light of this broadened definition of demographic diversity, Ancona & Caldwell's (1992) study was one of the first in an academic wave to focus solely on task-related demographics. Specifically, they examined the impact of functional and organisational tenure diversity in product development. They argued that demographic diversity had so far only contributed to a myriad of societally relevant

---

[1]Although there are differences in how the terms are used in the literature, for the purposes of this paper surface-level diversity and demographics typically based on marginalised characteristics are used interchangeably. In a similar fashion, deep-level diversity and task-related demographics are used interchangeably throughout the paper, at times to maintain brevity throughout.

and organisational outcomes (e.g. marriage practices (Guttentag & Secord, 1983); turnover among top managers (Reed, 1978; Wagner et al., 1984)). On this basis, and as a reflection of the larger macro trends described earlier, Ancona and Caldwell argued that research needed to consider how demographic and task-related differences may affect teams as the working unit of an organisation.

Ancona & Caldwell (1992) suggested that functional and tenure diversity were especially relevant to product development teams because of how these affect interactions between team members. They anticipated a positive relationship between team performance and both functional diversity and tenure diversity. In their study, Ancona & Caldwell measured team performance using both team evaluations (i.e. efficiency, quality, technical innovation, adherence to schedules, adherence to budgets and work excellence) and manager evaluations (i.e. ratings of adherence to budgets and schedules, efficiency in product development).

Due to its established theoretical and practical relevance, tenure diversity seemed to primarily serve as a baseline variable when accounting for diversity effects. Ancona and Caldwell argued that tenure diversity (using a coefficient of variation of tenure as a measure of dispersion) reflected the different viewpoints held by different cohorts of people within an organisation (Zenger & Lawrence, 1989). Moreover, they anticipated that greater tenure diversity would provide greater resources to a team through providing access to a broader range of experiences, biases and contacts.

Functional diversity (e.g. the different job roles and accompanying educational backgrounds team members possess), however, was a newer concept. Ancona & Caldwell (1992) suggested that functional diversity was particularly important because it was more indicative of the underlying expertise that team members have to offer. Ancona & Caldwell predicted that functional diversity facilitated product transfer from one department to another (e.g. from product development to marketing); they reasoned that within a very functionally diverse team, the lack of similar others within the group would encourage group members to seek communication with outsiders that would therefore facilitate cross-departmental product transfers. They also expected that greater functional diversity would offer the team greater access to cognitive resources and ideas that would otherwise be unavailable to the group.

Ancona & Caldwell made two major contributions to the field of organisational psychology. The first was examining the diversity or disentangling task-related attributes from demographic ones in a team, rather than using a single indicator of both diversity features (through a mean or proportion measure). The second was examining how diversity affected *team* functioning and performance, rather than observing their impact on organisations (e.g. firm performance) or individuals (e.g. perceived inclusion or discrimination, or work-related outcomes such as task effort, task performance or job satisfaction).

In examining how functional and tenure diversity affect team performance, they looked at the mediating influence of group process variables. Until this point, group processes were frequently examined using group members' perceptions and experiences (e.g. social integration, cohesiveness) (Williams &

O'Reilly, 1998), which, the authors argued, had little impact on group performance (Goodman et al., 1987). Hence, Ancona & Caldwell studied the influence of two task-focused group processes: (1) communication of the product development teams with external networks (i.e. communication to the marketing and manufacturing team, which is pivotal for product transfer to other departments); and (2) internal team processes (i.e. ability to define goals, develop workable plans and prioritise work to ensure the effective functioning and smooth operation of the team).

Both communication with external networks and internal team processes were argued to reflect how team members functioned or worked together as a team unit. Ancona & Caldwell (1992) suggested that these processes were more closely associated with the cognitive diversity brought about by task-related demographics (i.e. functional and tenure diversity) than with social demographics (e.g. age, sex, gender, race). They reasoned that task-related demographics had a pronounced potential to increase strain within a group by merging different cognitive styles, values and attitudes (Bettenhausen & Murnighan, 1985; Shaw, 1971). Therefore they theorised that task-related diversity was likely to lead to slower decision-making, hampering task performance and preventing team members from concentrating on their task.

To examine these questions, Ancona & Caldwell (1992) distributed a questionnaire eliciting responses from 47 product teams in five technology companies. Teams were instructed to develop a prototype product and to transfer this product to the manufacturing and marketing department. Thus the teams were responsible for the design, manufacturing and marketing of their prototype. They found that functional diversity was positively, but indirectly, associated with team performance via increased external communication. However, this was only a small effect which was outweighed by an unexpected larger negative effect between functional diversity and team performance. Thus functional diversity had an overall negative effect on team performance. Ancona & Caldwell also found that increasing functional diversity in teams was associated with less adherence to teams' budgets and lower team efficiency.

At the same time, Ancona & Caldwell expected greater tenure diversity to be associated with better team performance because of better external communications and improved internal group processes. In this case, too, they found a pronounced negative direct effect between tenure diversity and team performance, with no indirect effects.

From these results, Ancona & Caldwell concluded that while diverse groups may have greater resources related to the actual task at hand (particularly in innovation and design), these groups may fall short in capitalising on their cognitive resources. From their findings, they theorised that diverse groups may experience a greater conflict of different perspectives, and reduced social integration, that prevents them from effectively using the diversity of resources that the team holds. They then advised that diverse teams should be given incentives for team outcomes that enhance the entitativity or 'groupiness' of the team (Campbell, 2007; Lickel et al., 2000), rather than for material outcomes.

IMPACT OF 'DEMOGRAPHY AND DESIGN'

Since its publication, Ancona & Caldwell's (1992) study has been cited 2,837 times (according to Google Scholar), and is still highly referenced in team diversity research. This study helped pique interest in the black box of group diversity at work, conflict and performance (e.g. Pelled et al., 1999) and pioneered a response to *The Workforce 2000* report. In the last 20 years, new ways of thinking about groups and group processes have emerged in the team performance literature. One of Ancona & Caldwell's lasting contributions was the focus on diversity and performance at a team-level. Further, while some researchers at the time already conducted studies that examined the multi-level impact of team measures, Ancona & Caldwell's work really stimulated more work that examined the effects of teams at multiple levels, including that of the individual level (e.g. cognitive team diversity and individual team member creativity; Shin et al., 2012), and the organisational level (e.g. team longevity and firm performance (Boerner et al., 2011).

KEY REPLICATIONS AND GENERALISATIONS

Since Ancona & Caldwell's (1992) study, many scholars have attempted to replicate or extend their findings and revealed substantial variability in the effects of organisational and functional diversity. Notably, Bell and colleagues (2011) conducted a meta-analysis looking back on more than a decade of research on demographic diversity in team performance. Based on 92 sources (e.g. journal articles, dissertations), they included 275 independent correlations. Across the body of studies, their meta-analytic findings did not align with those of Ancona & Caldwell's (1992) – at least, not at first glance. Taken together, the studies showed no relationship between tenure diversity and team performance. Moreover, rather than observing a direct negative relationship between functional diversity and team performance, they found a small positive relationship, particularly in design teams.

Further consideration of the included studies showed that these inconsistencies might have been due to a lack of agreement in the literature regarding how key variables were operationalised (e.g. performance, diversity). Both Ancona & Caldwell (1992) and Bell and colleagues (2011) argued that models of diversity must be clear on which kind of demographic and task-related diversity is under consideration. Bell and colleagues distinguished team performance by efficiency, general performance (i.e. the extent the team met its objectives), and creativity or innovation (i.e. capturing the relative uniqueness of an output). They found the strongest positive relationship in studies that investigated the relationship between functional diversity and the team producing innovative or creative outputs.

Meanwhile, Ancona & Caldwell (1992) found a negative relationship between diversity of functional background and team performance, but this was measured in terms of manager-rated adherence to budgets and schedules, and efficiency in developing technological innovations. In light of Bell and colleagues' (2011) distinction, the measures of team performance in the Ancona & Caldwell study primarily consisted of efficiency-related performance, but not general performance or creativity.

Moreover, in discussing their findings, Ancona & Caldwell contended that greater team diversity may promote greater access to resources and a greater likelihood of using this diverse information in performing a task (i.e. indicative of general performance or creativity) (Cummings, 2004; Phelps et al., 2012). Yet, they further theorised that the expanded knowledge base is likely to come at the expense of team efficiency. They suggested that handling more varied sources of information resulted in more complex and strained team communication and coordination that bring about greater difficulty in implementing the increased knowledge.

Consistent with this relationship between team diversity and efficiency, Pelled and colleagues (Pelled et al., 1999) demonstrated that greater functional diversity was positively associated with task conflict. Task conflict has been shown to have mixed results in relation to efficiency and other aspects of team performance, dependent on the climate of the team (Bradley et al., 2012) and the complexity of the task (De Dreu & Weingart, 2003). Therefore, Ancona & Caldwell (1992) may have demonstrated only one way in which functional and tenure diversity affect team performance. Specifically, they found that efficiency was compromised, but they may not have accounted for additional team processes that might have contributed to their unexpected findings (e.g. conflict).

Moreover, considering the teams examined in these studies, it is also apparent that the researchers varied in how they accounted for the different properties of a team or team processes. For instance, the longevity of a team – that is, the length of time a team has existed (Schippers et al., 2003) – may affect the relationship between diversity in certain demographics and performance. More explicit considerations of these kinds of team descriptives may also shine light on various boundary conditions that Ancona & Caldwell's (1992) study did not account for, but may have a role in explaining inconsistent findings in team diversity research.

Indeed, in their review, Williams & O'Reilly (1998) included studies with long-term functioning groups and showed that there were positive outcomes of functional diversity, even if the effect of functional diversity on implementation was limited. Contrastingly, Ancona & Caldwell (1992) used newly formed teams, and their findings indicated a negative relationship between functional diversity and performance. Therefore, when interpreting studies conducted after Ancona and Caldwell's work, it is important to consider the operationalisations, definitions and group properties that are at hand and how they may have influenced their findings. Accordingly, considering how these definitions and conditions greatly impact the direction and interpretations of findings, researchers must be observant and transparent in their own decision-making when designing and disseminating their research for clear posterior insight into how these works build upon each other.

BEYOND 'DEMOGRAPHY AND DESIGN': THEORETICAL DEVELOPMENTS

ADVANCE 1: DISTINGUISHING DEEP-LEVEL AND SURFACE-LEVEL DIVERSITY

We discussed earlier that the way diversity and inclusion work was framed to include task-related or deep-level demographics and led to an assumption that these characteristics could act as a stand-in for demographic diversity relating to marginalisation (and vice versa). However, this is not always the case. The literature on diversity in teams now actively considers issues that may affect performance through directly examining the sources of knowledge pools that are present in a team – rather than using race/ethnicity, gender or other social categories as proxies (Ellemers & Rink, 2016). Ancona & Caldwell's (1992) study helped distinguish diversity in cognitive resources from diversity in terms of distributive (in)justice and (in)equity.

The differentiation between 'deep-level' and 'surface-level' diversity also led to deep-level differences being seen as more 'relevant, influential and generalisable' to organisational performance than more surface-level experiences of marginalisation (Nkomo et al., 2019). Distinguishing between task-related demographics opened up a new line of research and theory development in relation to a resource-based view of organisational diversity. This added momentum to diversity being viewed as an important aspect of organisational life and potential competitive advantage. It also became the dominant theoretical lens through which to explain the relationship between diversity and performance (Nkomo et al., 2019). Furthermore, it opened up a field of research largely focusing on team composition and performance, rather than one associated with group dynamics brought up by stigmatised differences. In the meantime, theoretical attention to such stigmatised differences has lagged behind (Bell et al., 2010; Colella et al., 2017; Ruggs et al., 2013; Stone & Colella, 1996).

This has led research on organisational diversity to more cautiously determine whether social groups necessarily map onto cognitive differences to affect task performance (Ellemers & Rink, 2016). To this end, the notion that 'highly job related' diversity attributes are more relevant to assess team performance very quickly brought functional diversity and tenure diversity to the foreground of team research (Williams & O'Reilly, 1998). To this day, functional diversity and organisational tenure continue to be some of the most commonly studied variables in team performance literature (Harrison & Klein, 2007).

Going beyond these differentiations of diversity, the effects of any given type of diversity characteristic (i.e. deep or surface-level) have also been increasingly researched to be affected by the surrounding social understanding of 'diversity and inclusion'. The way in which demographics or other diversity characteristics are evaluated can affect how these diversities affect team and even organisational outcomes (van Knippenberg et al., 2007; Van Knippenberg et al., 2004). Therefore any effects of deep or surface level diversity have been found to be not solely due to the characteristic in itself, but also by the way in which these diversities are thought of to be (un)important.

ADVANCE 2: DEFINING DIVERSITY

Now that researchers have developed a greater taste for the nuance of the context in which we expect demographic diversity to affect team performance (Bell et al., 2011; Harrison & Klein, 2007), scholars are progressively refining their theories and analyses. A growing consideration is directed at possible mediators and moderators of connections between team diversity and team outcomes (e.g. Bloom & Michel, 2002; Carpenter, 2002; Chatman & Flynn, 2001; Simons et al., 1999; Williams & O'Reilly, 1998). Despite such refinement, studies continued to reveal mixed findings. As we discussed previously, this may be due to the need to carefully define concepts such as group longevity and performance. At the same time, a larger discussion has emerged around the very idea of 'diversity' and the extent to which this is a construct that deserves further examination and specification.

Many scholars have suggested the need for a more honed understanding of diversity. In Bunderson & Sutcliffe's (2002) study, we can again see how different definitions of diversity may impact upon findings. The researchers demonstrated that the way in which functional diversity was conceptualised was associated with various team and performance effects. When functional diversity was defined by *dominant function diversity* (i.e. describing the diversity of functional experts in a team), it was negatively related to performance, in line with Ancona & Caldwell's (1992) findings. Bunderson & Sutcliffe reasoned that this is because the diversity of expertise makes it more likely that team members come from different backgrounds and have different experiences, leading to difficulties in communication and interpersonal relationships. This reasoning parallels that of Ancona & Caldwell in highlighting possible issues in coordinating multiple perspectives and inputs due to increased diversity.

However, when Bunderson & Sutcliffe (2002) also looked at *intrapersonal functional diversity* (i.e. the degree to which broad generalists whose work experiences span a range of functional domains are present) they found that it strongly and positively related to performance. Bunderson & Sutcliffe theorised that this may be because these teams are made up of individuals who are functionally broad and show greater motivation to exchange information while being less susceptible to stereotypes and group biases that may hinder information sharing. Such differences in conceptualising diversity in diversity research may thus help explain the mixed results.

Due to these inconsistencies and the lack of specification of what is meant by diversity, scholars have been exploring various conceptualisations of diversity, in a broader sense, and a spectrum of specific diversity-related variables. Harrison & Klein (2007) offer a general typology of what is meant by 'diversity', which may offer a sliver of the fuller picture when pondering diversity effects. They suggest that researchers often use terms such as diversity, heterogeneity, dissimilarity and dispersion interchangeably. Yet their precise meanings and operationalisations are distinct.

Harrison & Klein (2007) describe three ways in which diversity attributes can be viewed by researchers to more accurately convey and interpret their findings. First, they describe instances where diversity may be indicative of *separation*, where differences reflect disagreement or lack of support. They describe these differences as sitting horizontally on a single continuum reflecting similarity and dissimilarity (e.g. to what extent do you endorse qualitative research?). Second, they describe diversity in terms of *variety*, where differences are categorical and reflect variation in the knowledge, expertise or experience present in a group (e.g. Ancona & Caldwell's, 1992, functional background diversity). The greater multiplicity in the group, the more *variety*. Third, they describe diversity defined as *disparity*, where differences are reflected in the concentration of social assets or resources and illustrated by vertical differences. Diversity by *variety* is most aptly illustrated by pay or status disparities.

While these typologies may seem clearly distinguishable, oftentimes it may not always be so clear-cut, depending on the type of diversity under examination. One example is tenure diversity in Ancona & Caldwell's (1992) study. They anticipated that greater tenure diversity would reflect greater availability and accessibility to different experiences and insights, consistent with a *variety* view of diversity. However, they used a distribution measure that coincides with a *separation* view of diversity; Ancona & Caldwell's measure of tenure assumed that when participants reported greater similarity in tenures this indicated more agreement in attitudes, beliefs and values (Harrison & Klein, 2007), and not as they theorised, more different experiences and insights. This disconnect between how diversity is conceptualised and measured may be a major reason why, like in the Ancona & Caldwell study, findings in the team diversity literature are not neatly aligned in anticipated directions.

As it may be increasingly clear, the typology of diversity at hand may influence emerging patterns. Ancona & Caldwell (1992) found a negative relationship between tenure diversity and performance, which they explained in terms of reduced social cohesion and 'groupiness'. If another measure of organisational tenure had been used, say one that truly reflected a *variety* type of diversity (e.g. constellation of people with different backgrounds), a different relationship might have been found.

In fact, mixed findings for tenure have been shown in Bell and colleagues' (2011) meta-analysis, which they suggest may be due to the different conceptualisations of diversity. Bell and colleagues contend that clarifying what is meant by 'diversity' was rarely done when their reviewed studies related task-related demographics to group performance, both conceptually and methodologically. Therefore, we suggest future research should specify more clearly how they define diversity and use matching operationalisations in examining resultant outcomes.

CONCLUSION

Ancona & Caldwell (1992) lay the groundwork for demonstrating how task-related demographics affect team processes and ultimately team outcomes. We've seen in this chapter, however, that subsequent research points to mixed findings and the need for a wider definitional and conceptual conversation on what is meant when posing questions about the nature and effects of team diversity.

In this chapter we briefly discussed the history of diversity and inclusion research that provided the basis for Ancona & Caldwell's (1992) study. Turning to task-related demographics, their study contributed to new ways of discerning theoretical differences between experiences of marginalisation and differences in knowledge, skills or values. From then onwards, meta-analyses and related studies have provided a more refined understanding of the conditions and theoretical nuances necessary to comprehensively investigate team diversity. While it has always been important to examine diversity in terms of difference, only more recently have researchers started to develop a shared framework to define different types of difference. Therefore, while we may know much about the effects of a certain demographic operationalised in one way, we still may not know enough about that same demographic operationalised in another. Moving forward, the field may benefit from employing such typologies to articulate the nuanced effects of diversities on team performance.

We also discussed how the shift to the more management aspect of diversity in team research has resulted in a proliferation of the number of task-related demographics that are now studied. Concurrently, moving away from considerations of how social groups relate to team processes and team outcomes has resulted in a relative lag in research on the team and the multi-level effects of stigma in teams. As Ancona & Caldwell (1992) emphasised that greater group entitativity is likely to be important when reaping the benefits of functional and tenure diversity, further studies into social group diversity through a *disparity* perspective may be the way to additionally provide these very insights into social and power dynamics within teams.

IMPLICATIONS FOR PRACTITIONERS

Regardless of any instrumental benefit, understanding questions of diversity is pivotal in designing and developing an inclusive and equitable workplace. As such, it is especially relevant to consider how to minimise any potential negative consequences of friction within teams and examine how to best facilitate team functioning in, and across, teams. Enhancing task-related diversity characteristics may place teams in a more resourceful position. All the same, practitioners should be mindful of the hurdles regarding the implementation and integration of these resources. While a design team can benefit from having one team member experienced in marketing and another experienced in product design, can they effectively join forces to benefit from those expertise? As Ancona & Caldwell (1992) suggest, encouraging teams to fulfil team outcomes that promote the cohesion and 'groupiness' of a team may help, rather than placing the onus on task outcomes.

Moreover, we have discussed advances in research where diversity associated with aspects of marginalisation are distinguished from task-related diversity. While the business cases for diversity tend to conflate these demographics, marginalised demographics – particularly those that reflect visual differences – do not map wholly onto task-related differences. Thus expecting that marginalised individuals will necessarily bring about cognitive diversity by the sole basis of their marginalisation is very likely erroneous, and errs on the side of pigeonholing or tokenising individuals based on their marginalised demographics.

At the same time, there is value in appreciating that these demographics are interrelated. In a team, would a Black woman in the tech industry be able to have the same influence and level of command as a White man with the same background? In the face of various social structures and forces of socialisation, marginalised groups may be disproportionately represented or under-represented in some task-related demographics but not in others. Such aspects of social hierarchies and status should be taken into account when evaluating individual team members and overall team functioning.

DISCUSSION QUESTIONS

1. How can academic research contend with distinguishing 'surface-level' demographics from 'deep-level' demographics, when the two are interlinked and interrelated (e.g. some marginalised groups are disproportionately represented in some areas of expertise and occupations, compared to advantaged groups)?

2. The study of team diversity has often been studied independently from the phenomenon of hierarchisation within teams, yet we can see how they can mutually influence one another (e.g. compare the influence of an old-timer versus a newcomer to a team, or an individual with a STEM background versus an individual with an Arts background). How can these processes be studied in conjunction such that diversity is linked to the power dynamics that feed into hierarchisation within teams?

3. Contrary to focusing on single team units as Ancona & Caldwell (1992) did, organisations increasingly rely on multi-team projects where team members often possess membership in multiple teams. How would team diversity play out in multi-team membership settings with increased complexity in how the teams relate to each other? And how would individual team members flex these membership positions?

FURTHER READINGS

Nkomo, S. M., Bell, M. P., Roberts, L. M., Joshi, A. & Thatcher, S. M. B. (2019). Diversity at a critical juncture: New theories for a complex phenomenon. *Academy of Management Review*, 44(3), 498–517. https://doi.org/10.5465/amr.2019.0103

This paper follows the trajectory of diversity theorising over the past five decades, and takes a critical look at future research directions in diversity while highlighting the complexity and importance of studying diversity to understand team and organisational functioning.

Pelled, L. H., Eisenhardt, K. M. & Xin, K. R. (1999). Exploring the black box: An analysis of work group diversity, conflict, and performance. *Administrative Science Quarterly*, 44(1), 1. https://doi.org/10.2307/2667029

The authors bring attention to the mechanisms behind diversity's effect on team performance, with specific emphasis on how relationship and task conflict are involved.

Ellemers, N. & Rink, F. (2016). Diversity in work groups. *Current Opinion in Psychology*, 11, 49–53. https://doi.org/10.1016/j.copsyc.2016.06.001

This paper makes the case that visual differences do not necessarily indicate different skills, ideas or abilities. Moreover, the authors elaborate how workplace diversity can both have beneficial and detrimental effects.

Harrison, D. A. & Klein, K. J. (2007). What's the difference? Diversity constructs as separation, variety, or disparity in organizations. *Academy of Management Review*, 32(4), 1199–228. https://doi.org/10.5465/amr.2007.26586096

The authors offer a typology of diversity outlining three different conceptualisations of diversity, associated theories and operationalisations.

Bell, S. T., Villado, A. J., Lukasik, M. A., Belau, L. & Briggs, A. L. (2011). Getting specific about demographic diversity variables and team performance relationships: A meta-analysis. *Journal of Management*, 37(3), 709–43. https://doi.org/10.1177/01492063 10365001

A more recent meta-analysis examining the relationship between various surface and deep-level demographics and team performance. The authors also situate their findings using Harrison & Klein's (2007) typology of diversity.

REFERENCES

Ancona, D. & Caldwell, D. (1992). Demography and design: Predictors of new product team performance. *Organization Science*, 3(3), 321–41. https://doi.org/10.1287/orsc.3.3.321

Bartol, K. M. (1978). The sex structuring of organizations: A search for possible causes. *Academy of Management Review*, 3(4), 805–15. https://doi.org/10.5465/amr.1978.4289287

Bartol, K. M., Evans, C. L. & Stith, M. T. (1978). Black versus White leaders: A comparative review of the literature. *Academy of Management Review*, 3(2), 293–304. https://doi.org/10.5465/amr.1978.4294890

Bell, E. L. (1990). The bicultural life experience of career-oriented black women. *Journal of Organizational Behavior*, 11(6), 459–77. https://doi.org/10.1002/job.4030110607

Bell, M., Kwesiga, E. N. & Berry, D. (2010). Immigrants. *Journal of Managerial Psychology*, 25(2), 177–88. https://doi.org/10.1108/02683941011019375

Bell, S., Villado, A., Lukasik, M., Belau, L. & Briggs, A. (2011). Getting specific about demographic diversity variable and team performance relationships: A meta-analysis. *Journal of Management*, 37(3), 709–43. https://doi.org/10.1177/01492063 10365001

Bettenhausen, K. & Murnighan, J. K. (1985). The emergence of norms in competitive decision-making groups. *Administrative Science Quarterly*, 30(3), 350. https://doi.org/10.2307/2392667

Bloom, M. & Michel, J. G. (2002). The relationships among organizational context, pay dispersion, and among managerial turnover. *Academy of Management Journal*, 45(1), 33–42. https://doi.org/10.5465/3069283

Boerner, S., Linkohr, M. & Kiefer, S. (2011). Top management team diversity: Positive in the short run, but negative in the long run? *Team Performance Management: An International Journal*, 17(7/8), 328–53. https://doi.org/10.1108/13527591111182616

Bradley, B. H., Postlethwaite, B. E., Klotz, A. C., Hamdani, M. R. & Brown, K. G. (2012). Reaping the benefits of task conflict in teams: The critical role of team psychological safety climate. *Journal of Applied Psychology*, 97(1), 151–58. https://doi.org/10.1037/a0024200

Brief, A. P., Van Sell, M. & Aldag, R. J. (1979). Vocational decision making among women: Implications for organizational behavior. *Academy of Management Review*, 4(4), 521–30. https://doi.org/10.5465/amr.1979.4498329

Brown, H. A. & Ford, D. L. (1977). An exploratory analysis of discrimination in the employment of Black MBA graduates. *Journal of Applied Psychology*, 62(1), 50–56. https://doi.org/10.1037/0021-9010.62.1.50

Bunderson, J. S. & Sutcliffe, K. M. (2002). Comparing alternative conceptualizations of functional diversity in management teams: Process and performance effects. *Academy of Management Journal*, 45(5), 875–93. https://doi.org/10.5465/3069319

Campbell, D. T. (2007). Common fate, similarity, and other indices of the status of aggregates of persons as social entities. *Behavioral Science*, 3(1), 14–25. https://doi.org/10.1002/bs.3830030103

Carpenter, M. A. (2002). The implications of strategy and social context for the relationship between top management team heterogeneity and firm performance. *Strategic Management Journal*, 23(3), 275–84. https://doi.org/10.1002/smj.226

Chatman, J. A. & Flynn, F. J. (2001). The influence of demographic heterogeneity on the emergence and consequences of cooperative norms in work teams. *Academy of Management Journal*, 44(5), 956–74. https://doi.org/10.5465/3069440

Colella, A., Hebl, M. & King, E. (2017). One hundred years of discrimination research in the Journal of Applied Psychology: A sobering synopsis. *Journal of Applied Psychology*, 102(3), 500–13. https://doi.org/10.1037/apl0000084

Cox, T. & Blake, S. (1991). Managing cultural diversity: Implications for organizational competitiveness. *Academy of Management Perspectives*, 5(3), 45–56. https://doi.org/10.5465/ame.1991.4274465

Cox, T. & Nkomo, S. M. (1986). Differential performance appraisal criteria: A field study of Black and White managers. *Group & Organization Studies*, 11(1–2), 101–19. https://doi.org/10.1177/105960118601100109

Cummings, J. N. (2004). Work groups, structural diversity, and knowledge sharing in a global organization. *Management Science*, 50(3), 352–64. https://doi.org/10.1287/mnsc.1030.0134

De Dreu, C. K. W. & Weingart, L. R. (2003). Task versus relationship conflict, team performance, and team member satisfaction: A meta-analysis. *Journal of Applied Psychology*, 88(4), 741–49. https://doi.org/10.1037/0021-9010.88.4.741

Devins, N. (1989). Affirmative actions after Reagan. *Texas Law Review*, 68, 353.

Dipboye, R. L. (1985). Some neglected variables in research on discrimination in appraisals. *Academy of Management Review*, 10(1), 116–27. https://doi.org/10.5465/amr.1985.4277365

Edelman, L. B., Fuller, S. R. & Mara-Drita, I. (2001). Diversity rhetoric and the managerialization of Law. *American Journal of Sociology*, 106(6), 1589–641. https://doi.org/10.1086/321303

Ellemers, N. & Rink, F. (2016). Diversity in work groups. *Current Opinion in Psychology*, 11, 49–53. https://doi.org/10.1016/j.copsyc.2016.06.001

Goodman, P. S., Ravlion, E. & Schminke, M. (1987). Understanding groups in organizations. *Research in Organizational Behavior*, 9, 121–73.

Guttentag, M. & Secord, P. F. (1983). *Too Many Women? The Sex Ratio Question*. Sage.

Harrison, D. A. & Klein, K. J. (2007). What's the difference? Diversity constructs as separation, variety, or disparity in organizations. *Academy of Management Review*, 32(4), 1199–228. https://doi.org/10.5465/AMR.2007.26586096

Jehn, K. A., Northcraft, G. B. & Neale, M. A. (1999). Why differences make a difference: A field study of diversity, conflict, and performance in workgroups. *Administrative Science Quarterly*, 44(4), 741–63. https://doi.org/10.2307/2667054

Johnston, W. B. & Packer, A. E. (1987). *Workforce 2000: Work and Workers for the Twenty-first Century*. (p. 143). Publisher: Hudson Institute, Inc.

Kanter, R. M. (1977). Some effects of proportions on group life. In P. P. Rieker & E. (Hilberman) Carmen (eds), *The Gender Gap in Psychotherapy*. Springer, pp. 53–78. https://doi.org/10.1007/978-1-4684-4754-5_5

Kelly, E. & Dobbin, F. (1998). How affirmative action became diversity management. *American Behavioral Scientist*, 41(7), 960–84. https://doi.org/10.1177/000276 4298041007008

Lickel, B., Hamilton, D. L., Wieczorkowska, G., Lewis, A., Sherman, S. J. & Uhles, A. N. (2000). Varieties of groups and the perception of group entitativity. *Journal of Personality and Social Psychology*, 78(2), 223–46. https://doi.org/10.1037/0022-3514.78.2.223

Lorbiecki, A. & Jack, G. (2000). Critical turns in the evolution of diversity management. *British Journal of Management*, 11(1), 17–31. https://doi.org/10.1111/1467-8551.11.s1.3

Nieva, V. F. & Gutek, B. A. (1980). Sex effects on evaluation. *Academy of Management Review*, 5(2), 267–76. https://doi.org/10.5465/amr.1980.4288749

Nkomo, S. M. & Cox, T. (1996). Diversity identities in organizations. In S. R. Clegg, C. Hardy & W. R. Nord (eds), *Handbook of Organization Studies*. Sage, pp. 338–56.

Nkomo, S., Bell, M., Roberts, L., Joshi, A. & Thatcher, S. (2019). Diversity at a critical juncture: New theories for a complex phenomenon. *Academy of Management Review*, 44(3), 498–517. https://doi.org/10.5465/amr.2019.0103

Pelled, L. H., Eisenhardt, K. M. & Xin, K. R. (1999). Exploring the black box: An analysis of work group diversity, conflict, and performance. *Administrative Science Quarterly*, 44(1), 1–28. https://doi.org/10.2307/2667029

Phelps, C., Heidl, R. & Wadhwa, A. (2012). Knowledge, networks, and knowledge networks: A review and research agenda. *Journal of Management*, 38(4). https://doi.org/10.1177/0149206311432640

Powell, G. N. (1987). The effects of sex and gender on recruitment. *Academy of Management Review*, 12(4), 731–43. https://doi.org/10.5465/amr.1987.4306737

Reed, T. L. (1978). Organizational change in the American foreign service, 1925–1965: The utility of cohort analysis. *American Sociological Review*, 43(3), 404. https://doi.org/10.2307/2094498

Roberson, Q., Ryan, A. M. & Ragins, B. R. (2017). The evolution and future of diversity at work. *Journal of Applied Psychology*, 102(3), 483–99. https://doi.org/10.1037/apl0000161

Ruggs, E. N., Hebl, M. R., Law, C., Cox, C. B., Roehling, M. V. & Wiener, R. L. (2013). Gone fishing: I–O psychologists' missed opportunities to understand marginalized employees' experiences with discrimination. *Industrial and Organizational Psychology*, 6(1), 39–60. https://doi.org/10.1111/iops.12007

Schippers, M. C., Den Hartog, D. N., Koopman, P. L. & Wienk, J. A. (2003). Diversity and team outcomes: The moderating effects of outcome interdependence and group longevity and the mediating effect of reflexivity. *Journal of Organizational Behavior*, 24(6), 779–802. https://doi.org/10.1002/job.220

Shaw, M. E. (1971). *Group Dynamics: The Psychology of Small Group Behavior*. McGraw-Hill.

Shin, S. J., Kim, T.-Y., Lee, J.-Y. & Bian, L. (2012). Cognitive team diversity and individual team member creativity: A cross-level interaction. *Academy of Management Journal*, 55(1), 197–212. https://doi.org/10.5465/amj.2010.0270

Simons, T., Pelled, L. H. & Smith, K. A. (1999). Making use of difference: Diversity, debate, and decision comprehensiveness in top management teams. *Academy of Management Journal*, 42(6), 662–73. https://doi.org/10.5465/256987

Stone, D. L. & Colella, A. (1996). A model of factors affecting the treatment of disabled individuals in organizations. *Academy of Management Review*, 21(2), 352–401. https://doi.org/10.5465/amr.1996.9605060216

Thomas, D. A. & Alderfer, C. P. (1989). The influence of race on career dynamics: Theory and research on minority career experiences. In M. B Arthur, D. T. Hall & B. S. Lawrence (eds), *Handbook of Career Theory*. Cambridge University Press, pp. 133–58. https://doi.org/10.1017/CBO9780511625459.009

Thomas, R. (1992). *Beyond Race and Gender: Unleashing the Power of Your Total Workforce by Managing Diversity*. Amazcom.

Van Knippenberg, D., De Dreu, C. K. W. & Homan, A. C. (2004). Work group diversity and group performance: An integrative model and research agenda. *Journal of Applied Psychology*, 89(6), 1008–22. https://doi.org/10.1037/0021-9010.89.6.1008

van Knippenberg, D., Haslam, S. A. & Platow, M. J. (2007). Unity through diversity: Value-in-diversity beliefs, work group diversity, and group identification. *Group Dynamics: Theory, Research, and Practice*, 11(3), 207–22. https://doi.org/10.1037/1089-2699.11.3.207

Wagner, W. G., Pfeffer, J. & O'Reilly, C. A. (1984). Organizational demography and turnover in top-management groups. *Administrative Science Quarterly*, 29(1), 74. https://doi.org/10.2307/2393081

Williams, K. & O'Reilly, C. (1998). Demography and diversity in organizations: A review of 40 years of research. *Research in Organizational Behavior*, 20(July), 77. https://doi.org/10.1177/104649640003100505

Zanoni, P., Janssens, M., Benschop, Y. & Nkomo, S. (2010). Unpacking diversity, grasping inequality: Rethinking difference through critical perspectives. *Organization*, 17(1), 9–29. https://doi.org/10.1177/1350508409350344

Zenger, T. R. & Lawrence, B. S. (1989). Organizational demography: The differential effects of age and tenure distributions on technical communication. *Academy of Management Journal*, 32(2), 353–76. https://doi.org/10.5465/256366

Index

Made in the USA
Columbia, SC
05 December 2023

27809672R00154